D0208870

ROUNDING
THE
HORN

ROUNDING

 THE

HORN

Being the Story of Williwaws and
Windjammers, Drake, Darwin, Murdered
Missionaries and Naked Natives —
A Deck's-Eye View of Cape Horn

DALLAS MURPHY

BASIC
B
BOOKS
A Member of the Perseus Books Group
New York

Copyright © 2004 by Dallas Murphy

Maps by Hank Buchanan

Published by Basic Books,

A Member of the Perseus Books Group

All rights reserved. Printed in the United States of America.
No part of this book may be reproduced in any manner whatsoever
without written permission except in the case of brief quotations embodied
in critical articles and reviews. For information, address Basic Books,
387 Park Avenue South, New York, NY 10016-8810.

Basic Books are available at special discounts for bulk purchases in the
United States by corporations, institutions, and other organizations. For more
information, please contact the Special Markets Department at the Perseus Books
Group, 11 Cambridge Center, Cambridge, MA 02142; or call (617) 252-5298 or
(800) 255-1514; or e-mail special.markets@perseusbooks.com.

Designed by Reginald R. Thompson

The Library of Congress has cataloged the hardcover edition as follows:
Murphy, Dallas.
    Rounding the Horn : being a story of williwaws and windjammers,
Drake, Darwin, murdered missionaries and naked natives—a deck's-eye
view of Cape Horn / Dallas Murphy.—1st ed.
    p. cm.
    ISBN 0-465-04759-9 (hardcover)
    1. Cape Horn (Chile)—Description and travel.   2. Murphy, Dallas.
I. Title.
F3186.M87   2004
918.3'6—dc22
                                                              2004000848

ISBN 0-465-04760-2 (paperback)

05 06 07 / 10 9 8 7 6 5 4 3 2 1

For my Mother

Contents

Maps

Introduction

COASTAL NEW ENGLANDERS HAD A TERM for a kid who hung around the docks pestering people to take him along. He was said to be "sea struck." He would soon be gone; everybody knew the signs. But for sea-struck kids too young or too landlocked to go to sea, there was only literature to relieve the longing. So it was often in a vulnerable, dreamy state that many of us first encountered those two magical words: *Cape Horn.* An adolescent fetched up temporarily in Ohio, I read everything in the lubberly library to feed the ocean fantasy. Hurricane winds and towering breakers—only the real sailors rounded the Horn. I understood. I was the saltiest kid in seventh grade, with a library card to prove it. However, my classmates out on the alluvial plain didn't even know where Cape Horn was.

"Now that's Africa, right? Or is it the other one?"

"It's the *other* one."

But I could see the question in their eyes: *So?* What's so special about this Cape Horn?

What's so special about Cape Horn is the subject of this book.

Literally, Cape Horn is a pyramid of naked rock standing 425 meters above the sea in 55 degrees 59 minutes South latitude by 67 degrees 16 minutes West longitude—at the foot of South America, not the other one. There is no land to the west, none to the east, all the way around the world. Antarctica is the nearest continental landmass, 600 miles south. The water between Cape Horn and the tip of the Antarctic Peninsula is called the Drake Passage, and to put it succinctly for now, no strip of ocean behaves more violently more often than the Drake. In the cool language of the mariner's Baedeker,

Sailing Directions, "In the historically stormy region about and to the south of Cape Horn, there is a sharp rise in gale occurrence." The myth and legend of Cape Horn—the sea stories—are rooted in the *conditions.* Extreme weather is the antagonist. However, if it were limited to that, to man-against-nature stories, Cape Horn would have remained an alluring geographical curiosity, thrilling to the sea-struck, but useless. Rounding the Horn had historical significance because of this geographical accident: From the Arctic Circle all the way to the sub-Antarctic, there was no natural break in the continental coastlines of North and South America (the Panama Canal was both unnatural and recent) through which you could sail big ships—except the Drake Passage.

This wouldn't have mattered to human history if every nation had been willing to stick to its home ocean. The nautically advanced Chinese quit the sea forever about 1420 for fear of cultural pollution by sailors, burning their great ships and declaring it a capital offense to sail out of sight of land. The competent Arabs remained content with their profitable seasonal shuttles across the Indian Ocean. And once the brilliant Polynesian voyagers peopled the central Pacific, they did not sail on to discover California. But Europeans weren't content to stay in the Atlantic. They *wanted* things, and by the rise of the Renaissance they had ships that almost matched their will to acquire them. First it was pepper, nutmeg, cloves, and cinnamon from the Spice Islands of the East, and then it was Spanish plunder in the Pacific. The promise of the big profits from either (or both in one voyage) induced Europeans to explore the world. There was also sandalwood from Hawaii, bêche-de-mer and mother-of-pearl from Oceania; there were whales enough for the killing to turn sleepy Yankee backwaters like New Bedford and Nantucket into seats of wealth and power; and the hot market in China for otter and seal pelts from the Pacific Northwest funded a new American aristocracy. The products changed over time, but there were always products and always the will to sail across oceans to get them. And there was of course the dark side to their hot will to sail. Nations with North Atlantic shorelines poured through the Drake Passage aboard floating fragments of Western culture to dominate or destroy most cultures in the Pacific and the New World.

But not everyone sought only to round Cape Horn and head north as soon as possible. For some this was the destination. Cape Horn is the southernmost point on the southernmost island in a string of islands that stretches northward seventy-five miles to the south shore of Tierra del Fuego. This—the Fuegian Archipelago—was a range of high alpine mountains before the ice sheet moved in to decapitate them. Then when the ice melted some seven to ten thousand years ago, the resulting rise in sea level inundated the mountains, turning them into islands. And humans arrived soon after the ice retreated. They came in canoes about 7,500 years ago, but no one knows who they were, where they came from, or why they came here. They found enough prey—seals, finfish, sea birds, and shellfish—to keep them alive if they were willing to live as marine nomads in this harsh, demanding environment. It allowed no other means of survival, and it produced one of the simplest cultures ever to live on earth. These, the southernmost people in the world, who came to be called the Yahgan, had no permanent structures, no leaders, no central location, no art, no religion, and no clothes. This is a place where blizzards can blow on the summer solstice and surprise no one. Sixty-knot storms can linger for weeks, but even the "typical" weather is cold, windy, and wet. The Yahgan went naked down by the Horn, and Europeans were astounded. Their nakedness was a conscious adaptation, and, naked, they survived for eons, but they couldn't survive a century of contact with whites. The story of that contact, a tragicomedy so extravagant and absurd that one wouldn't dare make up such a thing, is an integral chapter in the Cape Horn story. There were two bright lights amid all the religious foolishness. Missionary Thomas Bridges, arriving in Fuegia in 1871, immediately recognized that the Yahgan needed protection, not conversion. He was the first to learn their language and the first to fully recognize the true genius of their adaptations. His son Lucas, who grew up among the Yahgan, wrote a sensitive anthropological masterpiece that contains almost everything we know to be true about the natives, *Uttermost Part of the Earth*.

Often passing time and experience erode childhood fantasies, but sometimes they expand and mature and cross wakes with reality. It took a while, but in the austral autumn of 2000 I sailed to Cape Horn from Ushuaia, Argentina, aboard a fifty-three-foot steel sloop called *Pelagic*. We did not *round* the Horn. That had a very specific meaning in traditional terms, a passage to windward of about 1,200 miles. We *visited* Cape Horn, and we were scrupulous about our usage of the word so as not to offend the drowned. We didn't lose the boat or any crew member, no scurvy or privation, no call whatever for cannibalism. At times we were even warm and comfortable. We attempted no "firsts," nor did we seek to duplicate a famous voyage, and our trip is not the subject of this book. We sailed to and landed on Cape Horn Island solely to experience firsthand the ocean and island wilderness, observe the birds and the animals, and witness that cold-steel wind we'd heard so much about. We sailed there as a means to understand the myth in the light of reality.

This place that abused, terrified, and drowned our predecessors is staggeringly beautiful. You don't hear much about that in the literature, because it can be a forlorn and foreboding beauty, not the sort that cold, tired, and frightened men tend to extol. Cape Horn has become an attraction for a certain kind of sea-struck visitor. It's still hard to get to, and foul weather often blows out any chance to land on Isla Hornos, but in the way of wilderness places when they grow scarce, the meaning of Cape Horn has changed. The Drake Passage is empty of ships of any kind. No one rounds Cape Horn on business anymore; none have since square-rigged sailing ships vanished from the sea. Ocean-racing yachts pass this way, and the research vessel bound for Antarctica, but only occasionally, because there is no longer any practical reason to come here. At times when gray-black clouds drop to masthead height and the sleet flies, one glimpses bark canoes on the move, a paddle lifting and dipping, but it's probably just a trick of the light or kelp flapping in the breeze. The Indians are gone, just like the square-riggers.

Today there is a little wooden house near the Horn where a Chilean navy family of four and their dog live. The kids offer you handmade banners and painted rocks depicting the lighthouse and the little log chapel out on the point when their parents have you in for refreshments. On the top of an elegant tussock-grass slope nearby, there is a monument in the form of a wandering albatross in flight, and on a plaque at the foot of the hill, this poem by Sara Vial is printed in Spanish:

> I am the albatross that waits for you
> at the end of the world.
> I am the forgotten soul of the
> dead sailors lost rounding the Horn
> from all the seas in the world.
> But they did not die in the wild seas.
> Today they fly on my wings towards eternity
> in the high cry of the Antarctic winds.

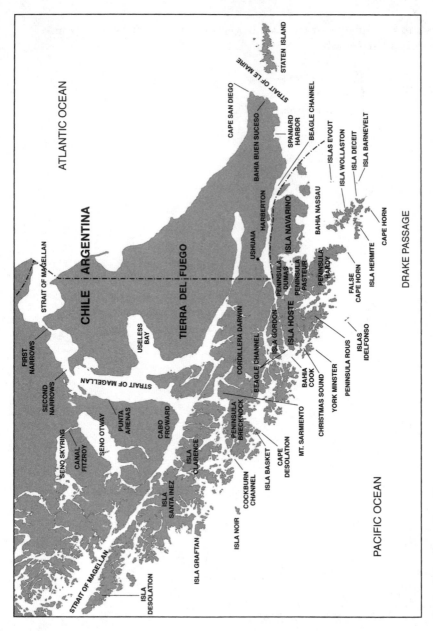

Strait of Magellan to Cape Horn

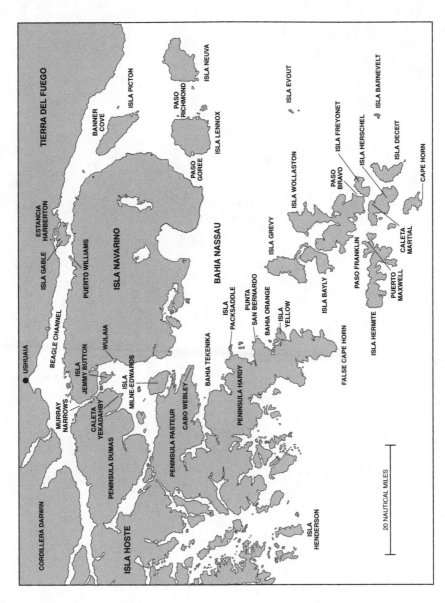

Beagle Channel to Cape Horn

I

From Ushuaia
to Puerto Williams

Now when I was a little chap I had a passion for maps. I would look for hours at South America, or Africa, or Australia, and lose myself in all the glories of exploration. At that time there were many blank spaces, and when I saw one that looked particularly inviting on a map, I would put my finger on it and say, "When I grow up I will go there."

—Joseph Conrad, *Heart of Darkness*

I am hartily sick of this palgy durty good-for-nothing weather—I would advise no one to come round Cape Horn for Pleasure.

—**Nathan Appleton, mate on the sealer *Concord*, 1800**

ON A SPARKLING, WARM, ATYPICAL DAY IN MARCH, we shouldered up our gear and headed down the hill to the harbor at Ushuaia, Argentina. It's deep enough to accommodate oceangoing freighters at wharves fronting Avenue Mupai. But the west end, where the sailboats live, is mud-bank shallow at low tide when the moon is new or full. This morning's low had left the concrete wharf high and dry except for a shallow pool at the outer end, where *Pelagic* and three of her colleagues were rafted beam-to-beam, barely afloat. *Pelagic* was the outermost boat in the raft.

We were here in Argentina to go sailing in Chile. To a boat in the business of exploring Southern Hemisphere wilderness, a civilized base of operations is essential. Ushuaia, isolated on the Beagle Channel at the far south shore of Tierra del Fuego, is the only practical option. It has a real airport, hotels, grocery stores, telephones, mail service, and a population of 32,000. Ushuaia is the southernmost city in the world. That Ushuaia is in Argentina, while Cape Horn and the entire Fuegian Archipelago are part of Chile, wouldn't matter if the two nations didn't distrust and despise each other with abiding passion. They've carved utterly arbitrary borders on Tierra del Fuego, an enormous island of 25,754 square miles, the size of Scotland. Chile owns the western portion out to the Pacific Ocean. Argentina owns the eastern section along the Atlantic coast out around the toe at Cape San Diego and back along the south shore as far as Ushuaia. The rest of the island west of Ushuaia's suburbs and all the islands to the south belong to Chile. And since there are no border crossings on Tierra del Fuego and no interisland transport, Ushuaia is isolated by politics as well as nature.

I was vaguely aware of their mutual animosity, but I didn't see what that could have to do with us aboard *Pelagic*. None of us was a citizen of either nation, and she was registered in England. But then I heard that Chile was prohibiting us from huge tracts of their wilderness waters and islands. It must be a formality or something, and once they understood our purpose, which was merely to observe this piece of their beautiful country, they would suspend their prohibitions. Then I heard about the gunboats. Painted flat black for maximum menace and bristling with guided missile pods, they patrol at flank speed back and forth in the Beagle Channel, Argentines on their side of the border (it runs down the middle of the channel), Chileans on theirs.

Chile has closed off sections of the archipelago for reasons of national security, for fear of invasion by Argentina. It's happened before, Chileans say, look how Argentina stole Patagonia. And then I heard about the land mines. Chile has planted *antipersonnel mines* on Cape Horn. . . . No one was laughing. As we walked down the dock to meet *Pelagic,* a gunboat rounded Punta Escarpados and carved a dead-slow turn through the harbor while lookouts with binoculars on the bridge wings searched for Chileans.

Pelagic's particulars:
 Length: 53 feet
 Beam: 14.6 feet
 Draft: Keel up — 3 feet
    Keel down — 9.7 feet (3m)
 Sail area: 470 sq. ft. (145 sq. m)
 Weight: 30 tons
 Range, motoring: 2,000 miles at 7 knots
 Power: 115-hp diesel engine
 Water: 1,000 liters (42 days' worth for six people)
 Food: four months' worth for six to eight people

"Pelagic": *relating to the open seas and especially those portions beyond the outer border of the littoral zone.*

Pelagic was ready to go, said her captain, Hamish Laird, a man with a posh British accent, a quick wit, and fifteen years' experience in these waters. Kate Ford, his mate in both the nautical and domestic sense, was downtown buying a lamb, she'd be right back. As for the customs man, well, you couldn't always tell about him, but he'd promised dispatch. We couldn't go anywhere until he'd cleared us out of Argentina's waters. After that we would be required to proceed directly to the little settlement at Puerto Williams on Isla Navarino to clear into Chile's waters and to receive our cruising permit. In Spanish the permit is called *el zarpe,* from the verb *zarpar,* "to set sail." No one sets sail from Puerto Williams without *el zarpe*, but we were hoping for a special *zarpe*. While we waited, Hamish suggested we might want to stow our gear below and pick a berth, and then he'd give us a safety tour. I lingered awhile to look her over.

This is a rugged, go-anywhere boat, whose reputation precedes her. Her hull is built of steel. All the deck hardware is beefed up a size or two and doubly reinforced. She's rigged as a sloop, which is to say she has one mast, and it's as stout as a bridge abutment. She carries two sails forward of the mast, a big one and small one, both set on roller-furling devices for easy handling. I liked her already, and of course I respected the hard miles she'd logged. She'd crossed the Drake Passage to the Antarctic Peninsula numerous times as well as to South Georgia Island, the Falkland Islands, and of course Cape Horn. She had stood up to weather that we, her weakest link, hoped to avoid.

Pelagic is not a handsome vessel. Her deckline is dead flat, her profile frankly trapezoidal, and her doghouse is boxy. She has no elegant overhangs at bow and stern, no varnished wood or other cosmetic niceties. This environment doesn't respect brightwork. Nor is she particularly nimble or slippery through the water. Speed is a direct function of weight, but the need for self-sufficiency precludes lightness, and besides, fast boats tend to break. Her owner, Skip Novak, professional ocean racer and high-latitude mountaineer, believes that strength and simplicity should trump every other design consideration for the sake of dependability. The combination of deepwater sailing and wilderness mountaineering is *Pelagic*'s purpose, a concept pioneered in the sixties by one Bill Tilman, whose name is spoken with reverence aboard *Pelagic*. Novak may have learned his priorities, the commitment to simplicity, from Tilman, and maybe a little of the Skipper's disrespect for dudish comforts. We had no refrigeration or water makers, because those things are both unnecessary and liable to breakdown. If you want a cold beer, stick a case up in the unheated forepeak next to the metal hull. And if you run short of fresh water, stop and borrow a tankful from a mountain stream or a melting ice floe. That's Skip's view, and we'd known it long before we came here. We weren't expecting hot showers or piña coladas served at sunset, nor did we crave them.

Her deck layout is smart and simple, with all the sail-control lines conveniently to hand. She'd be an easy boat to handle. On deck, all sailboats are similar, and once an experienced sailor learns the ropes, he or she can sail any boat. But there was one substantial difference between this deck and others we'd known in the lower latitudes. Mounted around the mast are three keg-sized spools of heavy rope, 150 meters on each spool. Because the weather often turns vicious without notice, one cannot merely drop an anchor and expect the boat to stay put. In addition to the big plow-style anchor, we would need to take the lines ashore and tie them off to trees or boulders. I loved that the spooled decklines were coated with molted penguin feathers.

Below the waterline—at the keel—there is a remarkable nautical adaptation. Keels are crucial because they provide stability by counterbalancing the press of wind against the sails, without which the boat would flop over on its side. But keels are literally a drag. Not only must this multiton protuberance from the bottom be hauled through the water, but to be efficient the keel needs to go deep; seven feet would do, but nine would be better for a sea boat, which she certainly is. But for an expedition boat meant to approach poorly charted rocky shores, which she also is, deep draft is an impediment to her objectives and a threat to her safety.

Novak and her designer addressed the paradox aggressively. Her keel can be retracted up into her belly (with aid from an electric winch) as if it were a centerboard on a racing dinghy. This reduces her draft from over nine feet to three. She can't sail with the keel retracted, but she can tuck her nose into the tiniest cove, offering intimacy with the environment. But in sailboats, everything compromises something else; nothing is without cost. The retracting keel has nowhere to go but up inside the body of the boat, residing in a floor-to-ceiling box, twelve feet long, three feet wide, running down the middle of her living space. There's a row of berths in double tiers along the port side of the box. Kate and the captain have a tiny cabin on the other side, next to the head.

My friends had finished stowing their gear in the small allotted spaces, and they'd left me a nice berth on the starboard side above the settees and dining table, which looked like a pleasing place to spend an evening with friends. This brings up the selection of people to sail with when one has a choice. Tim, David, and Jonathan are old friends from other boats. Dick, from England via Australia, was a new friend, but you could tell from his sailing résumé and his manner that he'd be a boon on any trip. Plus, he'd taught meteorology at the University of Papua, New Guinea! We had plenty of sailing skill, but for that matter, Kate and Hamish can handle *Pelagic* by themselves, and often do.

We'd need sailors with inner resources to amuse themselves quietly, people who could converse, but not *have* to; we'd need those
who subscribed to the expedition ethic, holding that shipmates should
be of good cheer even if they're not.

Hamish gave us a tour of the boat's innards, pulling up the floorboards to show us where all the seacocks were located. These are
valves that let in water for plumbing and other purposes, which
means that the seacocks are located below the waterline, where you
don't like to have holes. If you find yourself hopping out of bed into
ankle-deep water, seacocks are the first places to look for the leak. In
the event of failure, Hamish had placed a wooden bung beside each
and a hammer to drive it home. Topside he showed us where the
safety gear was stowed, flares and strobes and safety harnesses, and
how to deploy the self-inflating life raft. But he said if the worst happened, we would take to the hard-bottom inflatable dinghy, which
was stowed upside down on the foredeck. "Much more comfortable.
With a motor."

"Oh, look," said Hamish, interrupting his man-overboard proce-
dures. "Here comes Kate with the lamb. I hope you guys like lamb.
This is Argentina, after all."

Kate was climbing over lifelines and working her way around the
rigging on the neighboring French and German boats, declining offers
of assistance.

"What else?" said Hamish, wrapping it up. "Oh, yes. See that
chimney?" It was poking through the cabin top just forward of the
doghouse. "Don't stand downwind of it. The back draft puts out the
cabin stove. You'll like that stove. This is a heat wave."

Wait a minute, *that* was the lamb? Kate was cradling a black plastic body bag from which hoofless hindquarters protruded.

"The butcher asked if I wanted it all cut up in chops and shanks
and such," said Kate. "But I told him, no, all in one piece. He was so
pleased."

Hamish took the corpse off her hands. He withdrew the skinned,
decapitated lamb, blue veins visible beneath the translucent fat, and
lashed it spread-eagled to the split backstay with the long belly slit
gaping. It was then we noticed that the three other boats in the raft all
had lambs lashed to their backstays like sacrifices to the wind gods.

"Well, do we have any mint?" Jonathan wondered.

There was a story going around the docks. I heard it first from Skip Novak, subsequently from Hamish, then someone else. This family from Ushuaia sailed their little boat across the Beagle Channel for a barbecue on the north shore of Isla Navarino. That's only four miles away, but it lies in Chilean territory. While the family roasted their lamb, a Chilean gunboat arrived, slipped the sailboat's anchor, and without a word, towed the boat to Puerto Williams, leaving the family stranded. As the story had it, the gunboat towed the sailboat *backward*. That was egregious. I pictured the little fiberglass boat bucking and slewing behind the warship, the rudder cracking off, floating up in the churning wake. Even if the story is apocryphal, and it might be, its general acceptance as fact reflected the local mood. Like the antipersonnel mines on Cape Horn.

Back home, ignorant of the geopolitical friction in Fuegia, I'd planned a sailboat route through the archipelago using a British Admiralty chart with the enthralling title "South-Eastern Part of Tierra del Fuego." Navigation charts might be the most poetical of practical documents ever conceived, truth and beauty on a single stiff sheet. I love the planning stage when all things seem possible. I'd sailed every high-latitude wilderness from the Sverdrup Islands to the South Shetlands using charts to lend verisimilitude to fantasy voyages, but this one down to the Horn would soon become real. I wanted to be prepared. I pored over the chart until I could call up from memory the complex configuration of islands and channels so that the most harmonious route might reveal itself. I knew that weather can turn concrete plans into vague abstractions, but that's no reason to forgo the pleasure of laying them.

After clearing customs in Puerto Williams, we'd continue on around the east side of Isla Navarino and then south across the open water of Bahía Nassau. It was clear from the chart and several disappointed sailors I'd spoken with that Isla Hornos lacked a secure anchorage. It made sense, therefore, to position ourselves for a quick dash to the Horn, taking advantage of fair weather if it came our way.

Cape Horn was, of course, the objective of the trip, but there were several other important places I meant to visit. On the west side of Bahía Nassau there are three mountainous peninsulas, Hardy, Pasteur, and Dumas, which are part of an enormous island called Hoste that stretches all the way to the Pacific. Between Peninsula Hardy and Peninsula Pasteur, I found a narrow fjord twenty miles long twisting deep into the wilderness. It had no name. The funnel-shaped bay at its mouth had one, Bahía Tekenika, but the fjord had none. The mountains and glaciers that flanked it had no names. And most alluring, there were no soundings on the chart. No one had ever measured the depths because there was no reason to bother. It might not be navigable, but it probably was, since fjords tend to be deep. That's what we'd find out, the old-fashioned way, without foreknowledge, nothing between us and the environment. I shouldn't get giddy. We'd probably have an electric depth indicator. But still we'd be exploring in the sense that the piloting, the boat handling, the decision making, would need to be done by eye and instinct.

After exploring our fjord, we'd nip around the corner of Bahía Tekenika, twenty miles north to that cove on the west side of Isla Navarino called Wulaia. There, more than anywhere else except Ushuaia, whites and natives interacted most extensively and unfortunately. Robert FitzRoy, captain of the *Beagle* (with a young Charles Darwin aboard), tried to establish a Christian mission at Wulaia in the 1830s. In 1859 (the year Darwin published *On the Origin of Species*), the topsail schooner *Allen Gardiner* brought seven hopeful, feckless missionaries to pick up where FitzRoy had left off. The party built a little church on the meadow while the natives watched the proceedings, pilfering whatever wasn't nailed down. Not a one of the missionaries spoke a syllable of Yahgan, but they felt confident that the Word of God would cross the language barrier to protect them. It didn't.

A few miles north of Wulaia, there is this remarkable geographic feature, the Murray Narrows. It's a jigsaw crack between the west side of Isla Navarino and Peninsula Dumas. We would use the Murray Narrows to return to the Beagle Channel, then sail eastward back to Puerto Williams to clear out of Chilean water before we returned to Ushuaia. The Murray would lend a pleasing circularity with little backtracking. I was happy with my route. Though still untried on the lee shores of reality, it made solid nautical sense. I sent it off to Skip Novak for his suggestions.

"Forget it," he suggested. "Peninsula Hardy, Wulaia, and especially the Murray are closed up tight by the Chilean navy. Off limits, *prohibido*." It wasn't that these places had been closed recently, but that they'd never been open. "I've never been to the fjords on Hardy, and I've never been through the Murray."

"Wulaia?"

"Never. I've been trying to get permission every season for fifteen years. I agree those places look fabulous, but it's a no-go. I'm sorry." That's when he told me about the land mines on Cape Horn.

Argentina and Chile have been at each other's throats ever since the Spanish empire fell apart in the 1820s. In the 1960s, they'd squabbled over the precise location of the Andean watershed that defined their long border. That got settled somehow, but tension and acrimony resurfaced 1,200 miles south—in Fuegia. In 1978, they shoved each other to within twenty-four hours of their own commence-fire deadline. While gunboats cleared their decks for battle, the pope stepped in to cool hot blood—look, we're all Catholics here, can't we just get along? Apparently, they were willing to go to war over three little islands lying off the eastern flank of Navarino near the mouth of the Beagle Channel.

Lennox, Picton, and Nuevo, always mentioned together, like a doo-wop group, someone said, are uninhabited, beautiful, and useless. Were they just rough places where the aggrieved nations could rub open old wounds? And if so, what did that have to do with sailors passing through? Why prohibit North Americans in small boats? Learning little from history, I turned again to Skip Novak.

Suppose, I said, I contacted someone with clout in Chile and explained in rational language that I just wanted to *visit*, that I'd take nothing except a small souvenir rock from the foot of Cape Horn, leave nothing except anchor furrows in the bottom and a chunk of cash. Might someone be moved by my sincere interest in the region to relax the (absurd) prohibitions?

"No," he said patiently. "It's all been tried before. Somebody even called Pinochet. I don't know if they got through or not. No, I wouldn't spend much time in that area. Locked up tight."

I didn't know any Chileans with clout, anyway. I didn't know any Chileans at all. So I started asking unlikely acquaintances if they happened to know anyone in the U.S. Navy who might know someone in the Chilean navy. Most giggled. One said, "Cape Horn? Now that's Africa, right?"

I happened to have dinner in New York with Vladislav Murnikov, a Russian émigré yacht designer. While the Soviet Union was falling apart around him, he'd managed to design and build—with hand tools and borrowed aluminum—an eighty-three-foot ocean racer named *Fazisi*, which he meant to enter in the 1994 Whitbread Round the World Race. She was elegant and fast but brutal, lacking all amenities—including standing headroom. Most of her Russian crew had never even seen a body of water bigger than the Black Sea, let alone raced around Cape Horn. Vlad recognized that she needed an experienced (Western) captain who'd done the 33,000-mile race before. He knew from the outset, when *Fazisi* was still a rough sketch, who he wanted: a brilliant sailor/navigator known for his eccentric career choices, Skip Novak. *Fazisi* turned into a wonderful story of underdog determination and individual effort in the face of impossible odds, flipping the Cold War ethos on its head. Here were Russians with no money but a keen work ethic doing battle with rich corporate-sponsored yachts from the Free World. Though they didn't stand a chance of winning, they got the boat around the world in respectable time, and they attracted a lot of attention. She made Vlad's reputation. I met him after the Whitbread race, when I navigated *Fazisi* in a 220-mile race in New England waters, a debacle as it turned out, but not, I swear, because of the navigation.

"Well," said Vlad, "my sponsor for citizenship was navy man. A career officer from Naval Academy, retired now. He might know what to do."

There was symmetry here. I phoned this officer and gentleman, Fred Hallett by name, at his home in Annapolis. He said, "Why don't I drive over to D.C. and talk to their naval attaché? It'd be fun. Can't guarantee anything."

Wow, the Chilean Naval Attaché. I phoned Novak with the news. The coincidence about Vladislav amused him, but he said, "We've already done the attaché thing. Three times, I think. But the port captain in Puerto Williams just says no, you can't go."

Meanwhile, Fred Hallett had met with the attaché, and they'd hit it off, talked for hours, sipping coffee in front of the fireplace, as I imagined it, discussing Nelson's tactics at the Battle of the Nile. The next day the attaché called me. A soft-spoken man with impeccable English, Captain Sergio Robinson saw no reason why I shouldn't be allowed into the Hardy Peninsula and Wulaia, and the Murray Narrows seemed no problem as long as I obeyed the usual rules of deportment and navigation. He said, in fact, that he'd phone the port captain in Puerto Williams right away to set things up for me.

A couple of hours later Fred phoned me. Something had happened between the attaché and the port captain. Naval feathers had gotten ruffled. The attaché was really pissed, Fred said. "He told me to tell you that he's *ordering* the port captain to let you go anywhere you want."

I called Novak, who was growing bored with the matter. What I still didn't grasp, Skip said, was the extreme remoteness of Puerto Williams. Power down there was vested singularly in the port captain. It was his own isolated dukedom, and he decided what was open and what was closed. He decided *everything,* and naval attachés in North America cut no ice with him. . . . Had I managed only to anger the duke of Navarino? A vindictive duke?

The next day I received a fax from the attaché stating that I could go anywhere I wanted. There it was, in black and white, but neither Skip nor Hamish thought it worth the paper it was printed on. And politically speaking, that's how things stood when Hamish deftly extricated us from the mud suction at the bottom of Ushuaia harbor. We motored east in the Beagle Channel toward Puerto Williams, Chile, on a dazzlingly beautiful but utterly windless afternoon.

The Beagle Channel is a 700-foot-deep glacial gouge that runs east to west linking the Atlantic with the Pacific. It's straight and narrow in the eastern section where we were heading. But before it opens into the Pacific, the Beagle splinters into blind fjords, ragged channels, coves, and bays as irregular as broken glass in the alley, deviant geography. The seaward edges of the islands aren't even charted precisely, but drawn on Admiralty charts with dotted lines, which means "Position Approximate." This coast, which will figure in the story of the *Beagle* expeditions, absorbs the full brunt of the westerly storms; Dar-

win watched in awe as waves broke onto 200-foot cliffs. The Pacific
side is a giant lee-shore death trap, and since no one in his right mind
approaches it, there's no reason to chart its jaws.

The weather in the Beagle's eastern stretch is not quite so vile, because it's farther east. The alpine mountains between Ushuaia and the
Pacific tend to eviscerate the heavy hurricane-style storms before they
reach Ushuaia. When weather is the subject, it's risky to talk in ab-
solutes, but this one comes very close: Storms blow in from the west,
from the Pacific side. There's a windward side and a leeward side to
everything. Life for animals, plants, and humans isn't gentle on the
leeward sides, but it's possible. White people settled this eastern piece
of the Beagle because it was the only place where the climate would
accommodate their kind of civilization. They founded sheep *estancias*
with lilting names, Río Olivia, Punta Segunda, Río Remolino, Al-
manza, on the sloping apron of land along the Tierra del Fuego side,
and they established the mission that would grow into the city of
Ushuaia.

But this is not to say it doesn't blow like hell over here. Because of
its high sides and east-west axis, the Beagle is a natural wind tunnel,
which by squeezing the volume of wind increases its velocity. Hamish
says that gusts up around 100 knots aren't particularly rare. Wind is
etched on the landscape. The beech trees crouch in the lees of ravines
and ridgelines, and those few that have exposed themselves to the
west are permanently bent to leeward—like topiaries.

The sky was cobalt blue and cloudless, the water pure silver, our
languid wake the only disturbance. This was not as it should be. It
caused a quality of disorientation and vague bewilderment among the
greenhorns aboard *Pelagic,* even though we were not surprised. Before we left Ushuaia, we knew there would be no wind. On Hamish's
computer, we'd seen weather maps showing a high-pressure system
the size of Western Europe parked over the Horn. Cold, heavy wind
from the west, the antagonist in every Cape Horn sea story, is the
essence of the place. You read about calms only as fleeting intervals
between big blows. You never hear about giant high-pressure calms as
if they were a natural part of the climate. And you never hear about
the old salts passing around a tube of high-powered-SPF sunscreen. It
just wasn't right.

"I think," said Dick, slathering his nose, "we'll need to reassess our assumptions about the weather patterns. They may be a bit more finely granulated than we'd anticipated." Dick loves weather.

And then there was this light. We'd heard about the qualities of sub-Antarctic light, its dazzling transparency, but that didn't prepare us for the effect on the brain when nothing but the curvature of the earth limits vision. This light was an intoxicant. By sharpening the edges of things, by casting them in vibrant relief one from the next, the light warped our sense of scale and distance. (It took me three days to adjust, by which time the weather had reduced visibility to a boat length.)

"See that farthest point on the starboard side of the channel?" Hamish asked. "Puerto Williams is just around the corner."

Not only could we see the point (Gusano by name), we could see the off-lying rocks, the entrance buoy, and the serrated treetops along the ridgeline.

"Uh, how far away would you say that is?" I asked.

"About twenty miles."

Where we come from, you can seldom see a thing the size of Martha's Vineyard from twenty miles off. I'd been trying to follow our course on the chart, but I gave up when I recognized that I couldn't judge distance at all.

Hamish wanted to go below and work on his database. He was referencing the best anchorages in the archipelago and ranking them according to ease of entrance, holding ground, exposure, and aesthetics. But you could tell he was reluctant to leave his boat with the likes of us, too distracted by the weather, the landscape, and the light to attend to her heading.

Dick stepped to the wheel with a vigilant air.

"Keep an eye out for kelp," Hamish said. "It marks rocks. . . . What else?"

"Don't stand in front of the chimney?" said David.

"Oh, yes."

An hour or so later I went below to shed a layer of clothing in the heat wave, and I found him peering at the Admiralty chart instead of his computer. "Do you have your fax from the attaché handy?" he asked.

I dug it out of my bag and placed it in front of him on the nav desk. "It would be smashing to see that fjord on the Hardy. The Murray Narrows. And Wulaia. Not even Skip Novak's been allowed in there."

"So do you think we have a chance?"

"No."

Isla Navarino forms the south shore of the Beagle, Chilean territory. Navarino is shaped remarkably like a walrus, tusks and all, facing west, twenty-five miles from nose to tail, twenty miles tall. The boggy interior of the island remains quite literally unexplored. A wildly theatrical range of mountains that look like a row of rotting fangs, named in fact, Los Dientes de Navarino, the Teeth, dominates the shoreline. The tree line runs dead flat like a carefully landscaped hedge. Above it, naked, crumbling shale and sandstone soar straight up to snow-dusted points, and ribbons of melt water free-fall down their flanks into the forest. Visually, the coast of Navarino seems utterly unlikely, as if designed for an extravagant melodrama about Christians and cannibals.

On the spine of Navarino, a two-pronged notch has been carved in the coastline by a pair of rivers draining a tier of mountains named Cordon Diente del Perro, or the Dog Jaw Range. This is Seno ("sound") Lauta, the site of Puerto Williams. The minute settlement climbs three stubby mesas and ends abruptly at the forest. In 1953, the Chilean navy took over the site, a sawmill originally owned by one of the first European families, the Lawrences, who'd called it Puerto Louisa for their daughter. The navy renamed it for John Williams, an expatriate Englishman, captain of the *Ancud,* who in 1843 claimed the Strait of Magellan for Chile. With its low-slung buildings of desiccated wood and corrugated metal, Puerto Williams looks like some forlorn Conrad setting, its incongruous presence emphasizing the dominance of the wilderness more emphatically than if the trees had never been cleared.

Hamish took a local-knowledge shortcut through a minefield of rocks off-lying Punta Gusano and turned into the sound in the late af-

ternoon, while we lined the rail like cruise-ship passengers until he reminded us, bloody yachties, that there were things to do. "Quit faffing
around," he said with a grin, "and run some dock lines. Fenders,
too."

"Which side?"

"Starboard, probably." When we passed two of those black gunboats tied against a spiffy new wharf, he advised we stow the cam-
eras.

There was no dock for visiting sailboats at Puerto Williams. We
were to proceed to the bottom of the sound, where the tannin-dark
rivers spilled out of the forest, and there raft up against the rusting
side of a once-stately little ship squatting on a mud bank. She is the
Micalvi, a Chilean supply ship much loved by everyone in the region
for her bravery and humanitarian services. In 1962, after thirty-four
years on the job, she was retired to this mud bank. The state of the
tide (low) was clearly delineated up her side, green algae at the bottom, brown mud above, as if she were a rock. There's talk of restoring
her as a naval museum, which, considering the climate and her condition, would require unswerving devotion and a shipload of pesos.
Three boats had already rafted beam to beam against *Micalvi*'s side
toward her bow, and another raft of three was making up toward her
stern. We were to join that group, but there wasn't much water.

"Raise the keel all the way, please, Kate. We're on the ground."

Between the three-boat rafts, a canary-yellow British sloop had
edged in at an angle, her wizened captain, alone apparently, wearing
ancient yellow rubber foulies, was weaving his dock lines into the spi-
derweb of lines tied to the *Micalvi.* "It gets a little shallow in there,
Captain," he pointed out to Hamish, who thanked him politely.

Keel up, *Pelagic* was afloat again, and we passed our lines to helpful Frenchmen aboard *Damian II,* another high-latitude trailblazer. I
didn't see her captain, Jérôme Poncet, but two of his children were
playing tag on the foredeck. Dion, the eldest, about four, was born
aboard *Damian* at the abandoned whaling station of Grytviken on
South Georgia Island without medical assistance to his mother, a stunning Tasmanian named Sally, except from Captain Poncet. Distracted
by the company, by the snowy Dog Jaw Range and the weird incon-
gruity of the town, it took us a long time to get the lines adjusted; af-

terward Hamish went around and changed them all. With *Pelagic* snugly set for the night, people on the other boats who'd come topside to help and to greet Hamish and Kate repaired below.

After the customs man had come and gone, Kate and the others went into town to see the monument featuring the severed bows of the *Yelcho*, the Chilean ship that rescued Shackleton's crew from Elephant Island in 1916. Hamish and I went to see the duke of Navarino, about whom we'd been saying hard words. We made our way uphill from the *Micalvi* along a weaving footpath through tufts of tussock grass.

On the second mesa, we passed a white-frame, two-story building with bleached whale vertebrae lying around, a bowhead's jaw arching over the front walk, and in the yard, an authentic-looking replica of a Yahgan wigwam made out of beech boughs and saplings. This was the Museo Martin Gusinde, named for a Silesian missionary/ethnographer who observed Yahgan culture between 1919 and 1924 and wrote a voluminous tome about them in German (*Die Feuerland-Indianer*, 1931). His words are quoted in Spanish on a plaque over the museum entrance: "Only the waves of Cape Horn in their constant motion are whispering reply to the vanished Indians."

From the topmost mesa, we could see the ice-white points of the Cordillera Darwin, seventy miles west, backlit by the setting sun. The footpath merged with a gravel track to become Main Street, neatly bordered by rows of whitewashed rocks, overlooking the gunboat wharf. The track led to a row of single-story cubes of wood and corrugated tin, officialdom, El Gobernación Maritima de Puerto Williams. Ornamental artillery pieces in front pointed across the water at Argentina; at least we assumed they were ornamental. Hamish led the way into the duke's domain. The temperature outside was about forty degrees. Inside, it was eighty-five. The young ratings behind the counter all wore black woolen sweaters with turtlenecks.

A darkly serious young officer looked up from an ancient, misfiring fax machine, and his face brightened. "Ah, Captain Hamish Laird of *Pelagic*. Welcome to Puerto Williams." He offered his hand.

Hamish blinked before shaking it. This greeting, I gathered, was warmer than usual.

The officer turned to his desk, picked up a solitary file with my name marked in two-inch letters, and spread it open on the counter.

The front page was a copy of my fax from the naval attaché. "*No problema*," he said.

"Pardon me?" said Hamish.

"It is okay. Okay."

"*Para Peninsula Hardy y Canal Murray?* Okay?"

"*Sí, sí.*"

"Wulaia?"

"*No problema.*"

"Bahía Tekenika?"

"Wherever you wish. You may go anywhere."

A Chilean chart of the Beagle Channel south to the Horn in much bigger scale (more detail) than my Admiralty chart was framed and mounted on the opposite wall. Hamish stepped over to it, pointed one by one, just to be sure, at the places in question, and after each the officer nodded, *sí, sí.* He spoke several sentences in Spanish, but I missed the drift, then excused himself and left through a door on his side of the counter.

"Incredible," Hamish said softly.

"*What?*"

"The duke wants to meet you."

The door on our side of the counter snapped open, and there stood the duke himself. He was a fit fifty, short and sturdy with a seaman's low center of gravity. He shook our hands, lightly clicking his heels. He held the door and with a broad gesture invited us into his private office overlooking his gunboats. He said something in Spanish, excused himself, and left through another door.

I looked to Hamish—

He shook his head, astonished. "He wants us to meet his wife."

She was an elegant woman with the features of a Spanish aristocrat. We all smiled and nodded and said gracious things. I asked how she liked living in Puerto Williams.

"Boring." She rolled her eyes. The port captain—whose real name was Christian Cid Monroy—and his family of four were serving the closing two months of a three-year stint. Señora Monroy was happy to see it ending.

Then Teniente Monroy (no more sarcastic appellations) began to look around his room for things to give us, a cruising guide to the

Chilean channels, helpful safety literature, and his card. I wished I'd brought something for him. I'd come only wanting.

We thanked him profusely. He was allowing us to go exploring, and I found myself bowing as I left like a grandee in *Zorro* to the señora and the *teniente*. He hoped that we would stop to visit on our return, and that we'd have a happy and safe trip in Chilean waters. Before Hamish and I backed out into the cool air smiling and bowing, I bought a copy of the chart on the wall from the serious young officer. He calculated that it cost $15 American. I gave him a twenty, keep the change, thank you very much.

"Congratulations," said Hamish, as we headed downhill to the boat. "And thanks."

"Thank you, Captain." I felt like whooping.

"Señor Moorphy, Señor Moorphy—" A rating in black uniform was jogging after us. "Change," he said, waving three ones and several hundred pesos.

"Please keep it," I said.

"Oh, no, no."

We'd just finished after-dinner cleanup when a visitor knocked on the doghouse. "It is Armand. Hello."

"Armand. Welcome. Everybody, this is Armand, captain of *Hasta Siempre*," said Hamish. She was the inside boat in our raft, a yachty sixty-foot pilothouse ketch owned by a Santiago businessman. Armand was a very tightly wound young man. His face was round, hair shorter than a four-day beard, and his smoldering black eyes darted around the cabin, fixing things and people with a withering gaze. A heat field emanated from Armand. He had the general aspect of a man defusing a land mine. Hamish told him that I had just gotten permission to visit the *prohibido* places. Armand was surprised to hear that, and apparently he disapproved.

"When's the last time anybody was allowed back there?" Hamish asked.

"I think never," Armand said, looking me up and down.

"Have you ever been back there?" I asked, since I had his attention.

"No."

"But you could if you wished?" asked Hamish.

"*Sí*, I am Chilean." He straightened as if about to salute. "I was in the navy. I see their view."

"Well, what is it?" Hamish wanted to know.

"Take Canal Murray. You can see on the chart." He stabbed it with a thick finger. "If you control the Murray, you control everything to the south. What is word? Strategy?"

"Strategic."

"*Sí*. It is strategic place."

"But where's the war?"

"Yes, but if we let you in, then what about the French, the German? If we let them in also, soon an Argentine boat will want to come. What then?"

"All right," Hamish pressed, "what about these islands?" He tapped Lennox, Picton, and Nuevo, over which the war nearly started. "What was that squabble all about?"

"Oh. Well. That. That is about Antarctica."

"Antarctica?"

Only Chile and Argentina have claimed territory in Antarctica. Russia, the U.K. and U.S., Australia, Norway, and others keep permanent scientific stations, but no nation has actually planted its flag in the ice and said, "This is *mine*." Except Argentina and Chile. On this, they agree. Chile calls their slice of the continent Región de Magallanes y de la Antartida Chileños, with its capital right here in Puerto Williams. Chile established a six-family settlement and built a hospital on the ice in 1984 so that citizens could be born in Antartida Chileña, and Pinochet flew down for opening ceremonies to affirm sovereignty. Argentina, in an equally absurd production, took a pregnant woman down to the ice, so they too could say that nationals were born in Antarctica.

Naturally, their territorial claims overlap.

"That's why we must defend Picton, Nuevo, Lennox."

"*Why?*" Hamish insisted. He was sick and tired of the prohibitions.

Armand's eyes flashed, his brow furrowed and twitched. His English could not contain the greatness of the issue nor his emotion. He and Hamish switched to Spanish. . . . Both countries claim a thin isosceles triangle of territory with the South Pole at its apex. But where are the sides? How long is the base? If, as international arbitration determined in 1977, Chile owns Isla Nueva, the easternmost of the islands, then the side of their triangle moves east, thereby increasing their share, as they see it, of Antarctica. . . .

I excused myself and went topside to breathe some cool, moist air. I was thoroughly ready to drop all mooring lines to civilization.

However, finding oneself of an evening in Puerto Williams, Chile, one *must* visit the yacht club headquartered aboard the *Micalvi*, which lists a good ten degrees to port. In the old mess room, there is a bar, and out in front, ashore, a billboard welcomes everyone to "The Southest Yacht Club in the World."

Inside, the temperature hovered around eighty degrees, and a pall of cigarette smoke hung at eye level. Laughter and talk in four languages ricocheted around the room. Buddy Holly was singing, "but it's raining, raining in my heart." People from the French and German boats in Ushuaia were there, so was the grizzled old salt from the yellow boat, and about a dozen others.

Hamish and Kate went to chat with Jérôme and Sally Poncet, who'd just returned from a 15,000-mile trip up over the Arctic Circle to northernmost Greenland. I could see that Hamish was telling Captain Poncet about my coup. Word got around the bar. People looked at me. Why'd they let him in and not me? their eyes asked. I appeared self-contained and mysterious, a shadowy figure who knew people you didn't want to ask any questions about.

As the evening wore on and we consumed reckless quantities of a Chilean hallucinogen called pisco, we seemed to gravitate down-list, congregating in a clot on the port side. I chatted with Eric, the studious Swiss captain of *Philos*, who wondered if I'd read Edmund Burke's *A Philosophical Enquiry into the Origin of Our Ideas of the Sublime and Beautiful*, not a work that comes up very often in other yacht club bars I know.

"You are going to Cape Horn, yes? Then you will see everything that is sublime."

The sublime in nature, Burke wrote, "fills the mind with grand ideas, and turns the soul in upon itself."

"Cape Horn. . . . It is the most sublime place I've ever seen," said Eric, while Joan Baez sang, "I saw you leaning out the window of that crummy hotel over Washington Square—"

I told Eric that Philos was the nickname given Charles Darwin by the crew of the *Beagle,* and he was glad to know that.

Tim and Kate joined us, but when the conversation switched to French, I went to see what was shaking at the bar, where a ring of Germans had congregated.

In the center, our old bud Armand was holding forth, his eyes flashing from German to German. "Look at this," he insisted. Holding it up beside his cheek, he presented a tourist postcard depicting a pretty boat sailing a calm blue sea at sunset beneath the pitch of the Horn. "Cape Horn. Beautiful, wonderful. What true sailor would not want to see this thing? None would not. But look here, this at the bottom. What does it say? *Ushuaia, Argentina.*" His eyes flickered. "But Cape Horn is not in Argentina. Cape Horn is in Chile."

"So why do you not have cards?" asked a well-piscoed German.

"Yes. This is a good question. My country is . . . backward in this. It is a failure of, how do you say—market?"

"Marketing?"

"*Sí,* marketing. We do not understand what a magnificent thing it is to have Cape Horn. So of course Argentina takes it away from us."

"Why don't you just give it to them?" the German asked with a frivolous giggle, and the others giggled along.

But Armand shot them a ferocious glance. Levity lodged in German throats, and Armand's acetylene gaze rocked them back on their heels. There was silence as he rose slowly from his stool, gathered himself, touched the top of his fist to his heart and slowly, softly said: "I would die first."

2

Sea-Struck

Cape Horn is the place where the devil made the biggest mess
he could.

—Robert Mieth, Captain, *Pitlochry*

In the winter of 1905, a sailing ship called *British Isles* tried
for seventy-one days to round Cape Horn. She made it, finally, into
the Pacific to her destination on the coast of Chile, but she'd been savaged and broken, her crew shattered, several killed. It was an excruciating passage, one of the worst. William Jones was an apprentice on
that voyage, his first, a sea-struck fifteen-year-old.

After his retirement, he wrote of that voyage in the chilling classic
memoir *The Cape Horn Breed*, "I have never seen anything to equal
this in ferocity, in fifty years of sea experience since, and hope that I
never shall again on land or sea."

In 1905, the square-rigged deepwater sailing ship, the only kind
there had ever been, was about to vanish from the seas. And when
the last square-rigger went to the breaker's yard, the history of Cape
Horn commercial seafaring came to an end. Steamships never ventured down here; the Horn was too far from water and coaling stations, and soon the Panama Canal would make the trip moot. The
canal was of no use to sailing ships, not because they couldn't get
through it, but because on the Pacific side lurks the largest patch of
windlessness on the planet. Though their end was inevitable, sailing

ships did not go quietly. In the final years, say between 1890 and 1930, something ambitious and spectacular made a living at sea. It was a huge square-rigger, 300 to 400 feet long with three, four, even five masts carrying acres of sail, and it came to be called a windjammer. The difference between the windjammer and every sailing ship that came before was steel. Every bit of her except the decks and the wainscoting in the captain's cabin was made of steel. The hull, masts, yardarms, and even the standing rigging were steel. Steel made it possible to build big ships when size was a necessity for economic survival.

In 1905, sailing ships could still do only one thing better than steamers. Since they were entirely self-sufficient and their motive power was free, sailing ships could haul heavy bulk cargo such as coal, case oil, and grain halfway around the world nonstop. However, steamships were also improving and enlarging. When the clumsy side-paddlewheel gave way to the propeller, the steamer began to cut into the heavy-cargo trades. Then the Suez Canal opened the Indian Ocean and the East Indies to the European steamship. One trade after another fell to the soulless machine, until only several of the toughest and the longest routes remained to the sailing ship. And all of them required a Cape Horn rounding. Some, like the "west coast trade"—outbound from Northern Europe with coal to dreary roadsteads such as Iquique, Antofagasta, Taltal, and Pisagua at the foot of the Andes and then back to Europe with nitrates—required two roundings of Cape Horn in a single voyage.

Even if William Jones had known the danger and hardships to which he was about to subject himself, he probably would have gone anyway. Young Jones, from a solid middle-class family, didn't *have* to go to sea. He could have taken up yachting, but no, he was obsessed with deepwater sailing ships. His case was hopeless, and recognizing that, his parents reluctantly signed the apprenticeship papers, with Thomas Shute & Co., hoping that one voyage would clear this bug from his system. His father took him to a London tailor for a uniform fitting: a pair of stovepipe-stiff twill pants, jaunty cloth cap, and the blue coat called a monkey jacket. Because the jacket sported twin files of bright yellow buttons, apprentices were known as brassbounders.

A letter soon arrived from the Shute offices assigning him to a big three-masted windjammer, *British Isles,* James P. Barker, captain, berthed at the venerable East India Docks. When the day came, apprentice Jones begged his parents not to accompany him to the ship. He imagined a row of grizzled salts leaning on the dockside rail waiting to ridicule brassbounders whose mothers wept for them. William's mother told him to change immediately out of his wet clothes and to be sure "to maintain bodily cleanliness at all times." Then, like thousands before him, Jones pulled the collar of his monkey jacket up around his ears, shouldered his sea chest, and walked on spongy knees down those famous docks alone, a boy trying to seem a man, to join his first ship.

The *British Isles* was one of the two largest three-masted ships ever built. Her main deck stretched 309 feet from the point of her elegant clipper bow to her stern rail, and if you counted the bowsprit, she'd go another thirty feet overall. She was forty-five feet wide and, loaded to her lines, she rode twenty-five feet deep in the water. To drive such a vessel required an enormous sail plan: eighteen square sails, about an acre's worth in area, set from six yardarms on each mast, as well as a dozen triangular jibs and staysails set fore and aft between the masts. Because she was rigged as a three-master, instead of four, each sail needed to be relatively bigger. The biggest, the main course, as it was called, hung from a yardarm spanning 105 feet from tip to tip. Six feet thick at the deck, the mainmast (the one in the middle) soared 180 feet above the deck.

Looking up through the raw, shiny drizzle, Jones admits in his book that he was frightened of the ship. She was so big and black with a terrible kind of beauty, like a war machine. . . . It wasn't too late to bolt.

"Are you the new apprentice?" a friendly voice called from the high rail. "I'm Paul Nelson, the senior apprentice. Welcome."

Jones shouldered up his sea chest and took that first step in all voyages great and small by going aboard.

The mate's welcome was not so warm. Middle-aged, older than the captain, Mr. Rand was a powerful, capable, scowling man who'd been at sea since he was Jones's age, but he'd never had a command of his own. It was the mate's work to stay aboard while the ship was discharging cargo, keep an eye on the land pirates or they'd steal her blind. That done, Rand was now busy making her ready for sea again, and Jones's arrival meant nothing to him. "Nelson, show—what's your name again?"

"Jones, sir."

"Show Jones the half-deck, get his gear stowed."

Traditionally but not arbitrarily, the common sailor lived in the forward part of the ship, in the forecastle (or "fo'c'sle"). This kept the mutinous scum separate from the officers, but there was also a nautical reason for berthing the common herd forward. It was the wettest, liveliest, least comfortable place aboard any kind of vessel. By the *British Isles*'s time, the fo'c'sle had become a deckhouse, but it was still in the forward part of the ship. The crew's galley was attached, and the men ate and slept in the same room. The captain, two mates, specialists like the sailmaker, carpenter, and steward lived in the stern of the ship beneath the raised quarter deck, where she was drier and her motion gentler. Barker's quarters, known as "the cabin," were the size of a middle-class London flat. He had a sitting room and a bedroom with mahogany paneling, and he had a stove. The officers' mess was adjacent to the cabin.

But apprentices—training to be officers—couldn't berth forward with the common sailors. Yet for the same reason, they didn't deserve officers' privileges. Apprentices (four on this voyage) lived separate from officers and men alike in a space called the "half deck" under the forward edge of the raised afterdeck on the starboard side. It was nothing but a twelve-by-twelve steel-walled room containing four bunks in two tiers and a folding table without chairs. Sea chests were used for seating. There was no natural light or ventilation, no stowage space other than sea chests, and no stove. When conditions turned severe down by the Horn, two feet of water would slosh back and forth in the half deck for weeks at a time.

The next day, Captain Barker summoned Jones to the cabin, looked the boy up and down with a steely gaze, then in a softer voice said, "Are you sure you want to be a sailor? It's a hard life, m'son. Do you want to back out before it's too late?"

"Oh, no, sir," Jones squeaked. "I don't want to back out."

"Very well then, if you've made up your mind, I'll expect you to apply yourself to your duties cheerfully at all times, and I'll keep an eye on you." Burly, with a weathered, hard-bitten face and authoritarian gaze, this Captain Barker, at sea since he was Jones's age, had become one of the youngest masters in sail when, at twenty-six, he'd assumed command of another Thomas Shute–owned ship, the *Dovenby Hall*. Barker had made a good voyage of it, around the Horn in some foul weather to Chile and back, impressing Old Man Shute, who then gave him command of the bigger, tougher *British Isles*.

He had, however, besmirched his reputation among his colleagues when he made a speed claim for the *British Isles* no one believed. At dawn, running south before a fresh breeze in the Bay of Biscay, Barker said he'd sighted the German vessel *Pruessen* hull-down over the horizon, also heading south. By noon, he said, he'd overtaken her, and by four o'clock, he'd left the *Pruessen* hull-down astern. Didn't happen. It *couldn't* have happened. The *Pruessen* was the largest and most powerful sailing ship ever built. She set vast acres of sail on *five* masts. She was 400 feet long at the waterline. Speed is a direct function of waterline length; the longer it is, the faster the ship (or boat). The *Pruessen*'s waterline was a good 100 feet longer than the *British Isles*'s. The two ships simply weren't in the same league in any wind conditions, and Barker's claim was preposterous. But why did he make it? If a flat lie, it was one nobody would believe, and he would have known that. An honest mistake? No pro, no sea-struck kid, for that matter, would have mistaken the *Pruessen* for anything else afloat, because there was simply nothing else like her. Barker's ego would have mortal impact on everyone aboard the *British Isles*.

Three days later, a steam tug towed the big ship down the English Channel, around Land's End, then north to Port Talbot, Wales, where she was to load her outbound cargo of coal and take on her crew. She didn't sail around to Wales on her own because such inshore work was way too risky for an engineless square-rigger meant for the open ocean. She discharged the "stiffening" ballast and began loading 3,600 tons of coal under the mate's suspicious eye. This was serious business. When improperly stowed, cargo shifted in heavy weather, causing the ship to list and potentially capsize. But something else was worrying Rand. It was raining as the coal was loading. Wet coal stowed in the airless hull of a steel ship sailing for weeks in the tropics was like a science project on spontaneous combustion. Everyone knew that, but they did it anyway. The *British Isles,* lucky to have a cargo at all, couldn't afford to wait around for the rain to stop before loading it.

Meanwhile, Barker had gone to Cardiff to sign on crew, equally serious business. And in something of a reversal, Jones and his fellow apprentices leaned on the rail to watch the new crew come aboard unaccompanied by their mothers. They were a hard-looking lot from various nations, and they were older than Jones had expected, some well into their fifties. They'd all been to sea before in sail, and Barker was lucky to find them. Most had nothing to show for a life at sea except their straw-filled, bug-ridden mattresses ("donkey break-fasts"), a sheath knife, maybe oilskins and boots, tin plates and spoons—the ship supplied nothing but water and, loosely speaking, food. Those who came with nothing but the clothes on their backs would have to buy basic gear from the "Captain's slop chest" on credit against their wages, and they'd probably end the voyage ow-ing the ship money, compelling reason to desert should the opportu-nity arise. Some British owners operating on slim margins considered their crews pure overhead to be cut at every corner. Living condi-tions as a result were execrable.

Though Barker had signed up twenty-seven, only twenty crewmen actually went aboard. Seven deserted en masse after taking one look at the *British Isles.* It seems they saw something they didn't like, turned on their heels and walked off without even setting foot on deck. Instead of waiting to replace the deserters, Barker decided to sail with twenty crewmen. The coal was loaded, hatches battened for sea, a tug contracted, and wharfage was costing his owners money. Barker reasoned that he could fill out the scanty ten-man watches, plus a mate, with apprentices, and he could call the cook, carpenter, and sail-maker on deck when things turned nasty. Shorthanded voyaging had become more the rule than the exception in those days, but with only ten to a watch, Barker was pressing everyone's luck. The *British Isles* was bound nonstop for Pisagua, Chile, 10,000 miles from the English Channel, and she'd be rounding the Horn in the dead of winter. And Barker was taking an additional, a personal chance. He was bringing his wife and two children along, one barely out of infancy, the other a toddler. That they were allowed to bring their families in sailing ships, but not in steamships, kept some qualified captains sailing when life in steam would have been much easier.

On a sparkling summer morning, June 11, 1905, a tug called *Sarah Jolliffe* towed the big black ship down the Bristol Channel toward the open Atlantic. All hands assembled astern, like thousands of crews before them, to choose up watches. It happened just like a schoolyard baseball game, the mate and second mate taking turns picking men, the best and ablest first. Jones was chosen last, by the second mate, Mr. Atkinson, who happened to be Barker's wife's brother, for all the good that did him. ("Being a relative of mine by marriage," Barker would write thirty years on, "I felt compelled to keep at an even greater distance, and very rarely did I address him save to issue crisp orders. . . . I had forbidden him to approach my wife and children other than as a stranger.") Once the watches were fixed, Barker ordered the full crew to make all sail, and then cast off the towline. The *Sarah Jolliffe* wished her farewell with a string of whistles, while her crew hauled the yardarms forward on the starboard side to catch the west wind. The helmsman, under Barker's critical gaze, pointed her head south southwest, toward Cape Horn a half a world away. The voyage had begun.

The *British Isles* made short work of the temperate-zone run in the prevailing westerlies. She bowled down the Bay of Biscay past Gibraltar, romped past Madeira, then the Canaries, heading for the trade winds. Barker showed himself to be a "hard driver," which meant that he carried a lot of sail in big wind, and the crew respected him for that. During those weeks of plain sailing, Jones learned the ropes from a tough Irishman called Paddy Furlong, the unofficial crew leader. He took Jones under his wing, taught him sailor's techniques, and told him stories of Cape Horn, which Paddy had rounded man and boy, some thirty times. Jones was falling in love with the life.

The belt of westerlies in the Northern Hemisphere ends in a transition zone of light and variable winds near the Tropic of Cancer, but Barker found a fast lane into the northeast trades. Trade winds gird the global oceans in two irregular belts on either side of the equator—blowing northeast in the Northern Hemisphere, southeast in the Southern. No weather phenomenon anywhere is more constant or reliable. Henry the Navigator's explorers discovered the trade winds, and Columbus made creative use of them. I'll bet even grim old Vasco da Gama felt a twinge of poetry in the trades. It remains a magical experience no sailor ever forgets, clicking off hundreds of free miles a day without ever touching a line or a sail one exquisite day and sparkling night after another. In that perpetual wind, twenty to thirty knots hardly varying in direction, nothing seemed to make more sense than this romantic, archaic machine, the sailing vessel.

Harmonica and concertina music wafted aft from the fo'c'sle in the evenings, chanties, folk songs, and an occasional dirty ditty. Life was sweet and easy, no work aloft, no heavy hauling. The mates could relax, because in fair wind everyone, even Captain Barker, relaxed. Stepping buoyantly on the quarterdeck, he made occasional casual observations to the helmsman, almost like conversation. Mrs. Barker strolled the deck cooing and singing to her baby while her daughter skipped along behind, inventing games. One day the sailmaker presented the girl with a doll he had made out of light-air canvas scraps stuffed with oakum, little daubs of red paint for a face. She treasured it, and the tarry oakum stank up the cabin.

The only trouble with trade-wind sailing is that it ends, often abruptly. Along the equator, wavering north and south, there lies a belt of windlessness between the trade winds known technically as the Inter Tropical Convergence Zone and popularly as the doldrums. If brisk, fair winds inflate sailors' spirits, calms make them crazy. Without wind, sails slat and bang as the ship rolls helplessly, and everything, including dispositions, chafes raw.

Barker made a poor passage through the doldrums, and a sullen mood settled over his ship. The mates, sick of his critical glower, took it out on the crew, berating them, calling them farmers. Most of the time there was no breeze at all, Coleridge's calm. Sometimes, however, inexplicable patches and columns of breeze settled on the surface, and to gain any distance ships had to be "worked." Tack right now to fetch the breeze, get the sails trimmed and drawing, then set up to tack again before you sail out of the breeze, hateful hard labor the old salts called "pully-hauly." And the *British Isles* was a brute to work. Everything was too big, heavy, and her crew was too few. She needed a week to ghost across the equator and meet the blessed southeast trades, but by then the damage was done. The coal had caught fire.

Every day Cronberg, the carpenter, sounded the hold for water and measured the internal temperature by lowering a thermometer through a little hatch. One day, he retrieved his thermometer to find the bulb popped by the heat. Rand had seen the shock wash across the old Swede's face, and he knew what it meant. They hurried aft to inform Barker while the word *fire* ricocheted through the fo'c'sle and every man appeared on deck. How bad was it? Were the boats run out and ready to lower? They watched Cronberg and the officers gather on the quarterdeck and waited for orders.

Barker had two alternatives, both ugly. He could square away and run for Rio de Janeiro 200 miles, a day's sail, downwind. There, at a proper dock, the coal could be safely unloaded, the source of the fire located and extinguished. But stopping would cost his owners more than the voyage was worth. The first rule of success for a captain in sail was "keep the sea." Stay out there in other words, and go fast. If something broke, it was to be fixed at sea with free fo'c'sle labor, not shore-side, land-pirate labor. Rand kept pushing for Rio, until Barker told him to shut the hell up. But Rand had a point, and everyone knew it. Opening the hatch could turn a smolder into an oxygen-rich inferno. Even if it didn't, opening the hatch would expose the ship's innards to the sea. If the weather turned foul, if the *British Isles* took water over the side while her hatches were open, and she always took water in heavy weather, she'd fill and sink. Barker never for a moment considered squaring away for Rio.

"Dig it out, Mister Mate," he barked. "Pile it along the deck, free of the belaying pins. Rig a gyn [a hoist] over the hatch, and get some baskets. Eight men will go below to shovel, six will tail on the gantline, four will build a heap along the deck with the hand truck, and two will draw water from overboard to souse it. Not a lump of this coal must be allowed to go overboard. Keep the men moving, Mister, this weather may not last long."

They removed the canvas cover, hammered out the heavy wooden battens, and then, gingerly, gradually, hoping not to be suddenly incinerated, they lifted the steel hatch. It came away with a great whoosh of black smoke, and everyone leapt to the windward side, shielding their faces. The smoke cleared. No flames followed.

The crew set to shoveling, hauling, trucking, and sousing. They worked in shifts to relieve the eight men who actually had to enter the hold and stand on the coal to shovel it into the baskets. They did this watch-on watch-off for four solid days. As they neared the source of the fire, fumes and dust suffocated the men, and no one could stand more than a fifteen-minute stint below. As they burrowed nearer still, the heat grew unendurable.

The *British Isles* carried a small steam engine mounted at the foot of the main mast ten feet from the open hatch. Used to handle cargo in undeveloped Chilean roadsteads, this so-called donkey engine turned a winch drum about the size of a wastebasket. The thing could have easily and quickly hoisted the coal baskets out of the hold, and it was positioned perfectly for the job. Barker, however, refused to fire it up. The crew complained loudly and aggressively to the mates, who told them to shut up and keep shoveling. The men didn't really expect the captain to run for shore; they were used to solving their own problems, but this made no sense.

Incredibly, the reason Barker refused to run the engine was because he didn't want to burn his owners' coal. Never mind his disregard for the crew's pain and fatigue. In the view of the times, that's what crews were for, and Barker wasn't the first captain to exploit them nor anywhere near the worst. Crews expected to be exploited, just as they expected weevils in their biscuits. Never mind the humanitarian argument, Barker was jeopardizing his ship, and therefore the lives of all aboard, including his family's. His was *nautical* folly. The longer the job took, the longer the hatch lay open, the greater the danger of heavy weather blowing in and literally sinking her. Shute, the owner, was a skinflint, but he was also known as a seaman and a rational man; it's hard to imagine he would have appreciated Barker's priorities.

Rand and the crew found the source of the fire and drowned it late on the fourth day. That danger was past, but not the other one. The hatch was still open, and the deck still covered with tons of coal, which the sailors began to shovel back into the hold. Again the engine would have expedited the process, but it remained silent.

The ship hadn't stopped during that five-day struggle with the fire. Holding her southerly heading, she could have covered 800 miles if she averaged a speed of only seven knots (around nine miles per hour). She sailed through the southeast trades, narrower than their counterpart in the Northern Hemisphere, carried wind through the doldrums, and now she was dipping into the notorious belt of westerlies called the Roaring Forties—with the hatch open. The barometer began to slide, and then rose skittishly—before it plummeted. A big blow, exactly what they'd feared, was heading their way. Filthy, exhausted, the crew shoveled like machines in a race against the rising wind. The ship heeled, as sailing vessels must when the wind blows hard, before the men could get all the coal restowed. No water was coming aboard yet, but with that heel on her, they couldn't level the coal, and this caused her to list severely to port. There was no time to address that now—just get the stuff below, then batten down. The carpenter barely managed it before the full brunt of a Roaring Forties gale struck the ship.

The crew leapt into the rigging to shorten sail, doing the best they could, but they were spent from their stevedore labors. Jones was high up the mizzenmast when the full force of the storm struck, lying on his belly across the topgallant yard with his mates trying to run lashings around the bundle of sail. Don't look at the sea, he told himself. That had been Paddy Furlong's advice. Concentrate on the job at hand, do one piece of it at a time, move quickly, but don't rush, and never stop thinking. And don't look down. The sight of the sea below can freeze you solid, he'd said, when it's bad. The initial blast of wind caught two crucial sails (upper topsails on the fore- and mainmast) as they were being hauled up to their yardarms. The big sails snapped full, flogged once, and disappeared into the freezing rain and flying spray to leeward. She'd lost her first sails of the voyage.

With the ship heading south, the west wind and its waves attacked from her starboard side. Windjammers, made of steel and loaded to the gills, rode low in the water, and this made them vulnerable to boarding seas. That's a dry nautical term for something lethal, the thing that sailors feared most—waves that roll over the rail and sweep the main deck six feet deep. (Technically, the main deck is the lowest one that runs the full length of the ship.) The *British Isles*'s main deck was a dangerous place to be. It was huge for one thing, but also, since she was a three-master, instead of four, there was a lot of open expanse with nothing to hold on to when heavy water washed over the side. One of those boarding seas caught an experienced sailor named

John Witney out on the open deck and dashed him into the steel bulwarks to leeward.

Fighting waist-deep water, his shipmates linked arms and made their way to him, unconscious but alive, and very lucky to have stayed aboard. His leg, however, was shattered. Gentle handling was not possible. They dragged him like a bundle of storm canvas aft to the captain's mess room, where they lashed him to the table. Cronberg fashioned splints, and then he and Barker set Witney's leg as best they could according to rudimentary instructions in the *Ship Captain's Medical Guide*.

The storm blew hard for five days with barely a lull. It would have inflicted a severe beating on any ship, but hers was exacerbated by the list. Listing ships don't bounce back between the waves, they only slowly answer their helms, they sag. The coal had to be leveled; she could not face Cape Horn like that and expect to survive. Yet down here in this zone of heavy westerlies reopening her hatches was unthinkable. There was nothing to do but send men into the hold through the lazarette hatch under the captain's cabin. They crawled forward in the tiny, cave-dark space between the cargo and the bottom of the deck (a lamp flame would have ignited the dust) to shovel, kick, and claw lumps of coal uphill from port to starboard. In a quiet anchorage with the holds open, they might have trimmed her upright, but not out there, not while her motion was so violent. Though they lessened the list, they couldn't remove it.

But the storm, its center passing to the north, left a wonderful gift in its wake—an *east* wind. God, if it would only hold, she might run around the Horn with a following breeze, and then her list and her shorthanded crew wouldn't matter. Hope brought new energy as the sky cleared, the seas settled, and the easterly held strong. The men dragged new topsails from the sail locker, singing hauling chanties as they winched the canvas bundles aloft and bent them to their yards. The new sails billowed to cheers, and the ship accelerated. She was making fourteen knots, a bit short of top speed, but that was enough to put 336 miles a day behind her.

In this easterly, Barker didn't hesitate to take the shortcut between the toe of Tierra del Fuego and Staten Island through the Strait of Le Maire, that magnificently treacherous strip of water. With wind and current in his favor, Barker blasted through the strait on a spectacular full-moon night. Jones scurried up the mainmast to watch in awe as the water seethed and black land loomed close aboard on port and starboard. He'd been dreaming of this all his life, not the coal fire, of course, or Witney's ruined leg, but this, running free and fast in the wild ocean approaches to Cape Horn while the Southern Cross flickered through the light cloud cover.

Cape Horn lay only 150 miles away to the southwest. Every stitch of canvas was up and pulling in the stiff easterly, and now she'd need only one day to sneak around the Horn. Even the hardened, skeptical veterans began to believe in their good fortune, though they didn't dare talk about it. Mrs. Barker and her children reappeared on deck, bundled against the deepening cold but happy and hopeful.

On August 8, fifty-eight days and nearly 9,000 sailing miles from Port Talbot, the *British Isles* crossed the latitude of Cape Horn. Though too far east to actually see the headland, everyone could feel its presence in the cold, crystalline air and blue-black ocean, ominous, threatening, beautiful. Barker held her southerly heading to put some sea room between the ship and the Horn, but not long for fear of sailing out of his own fair wind. After breakfast on the ninth, he gave the orders everyone wanted to hear—square the yards and head her west. The crew cheered, even Paddy and the other crusty shellbacks.

Shortly after lunch on August 9, 1905, she crossed 67 degrees and 16 minutes West, the longitude of Cape Horn. Traditionally, officers held their ship's position strictly secret as a means of keeping crews dependent, thus compliant. But now, as Cape Horn fell away to the northeast, Barker shouted out their position from the quarterdeck, and again everyone cheered. He couldn't turn her north just yet, because he needed to put plenty of open ocean between his ship and the jagged west coast of Chile, but twelve more hours would do it, maybe less. . . .

The fresh wind dropped abruptly to a light, fickle breeze. That's the way of easterlies at the Horn. The ship slowed, lost steerageway, and stopped. The temperature plunged, and soon icicles began to drip from the rigging. The barometer dropped in short, skittish increments, then plunged so fast and low that Barker imagined it was leaking. But, no, the instrument was noting the hurricane-deep hole in the atmosphere.

A long, sinister gray swell rolled out of the west. Clouds stacked up in layers over the horizon. Barker's family fled below. The veterans—Cronberg, Paddy Furlong, and the officers—knew what they were in for, and from their grim looks, the apprentices knew it would be bad. No one cheered this time when, shortly before dark, the mate stuck his head in the fo'c'sle door and shouted, "All hands on deck!"

"Clew up the royals! Look sharp there on the buntlines. Get two men on the clew lines! What's the matter with you bloody farmers! Slack away those halyards! Have you forgotten how to bloody sail!"

Buntlines and clew lines, attached to the bottom and sides of the sails, were used to spill the wind and draw the canvas up into loose bundles beneath their yards rather like venetian-blind mechanisms. That done, the crew scrambled up the masts and out on the yards to lash the sails into tight, windproof furls. In the near calm, handling frozen canvas, the full crew needed four hours to strip her down to three lower topsails, a foresail, and a jib. By midnight, after the long, oily swells had turned to running waves, she was ready.

A high white slash over the western horizon glistened in the moonlight. Some of the crew said it was an ice field, because what else could it be, so white and so high. But it wasn't ice. It was seawater, a chaos of bone-white spray and spume thrown up by the creature raging behind it, and for a moment all hands, even those hardened veterans, stood watching in stunned silence.

"Hard up the helm!" Barker bellowed. He meant to take the first assault over the starboard bow rather than against her vulnerable slab side or, worse, bow-on. If the wind caught the front of the sails ("taken aback," in the parlance), it would bring down the masts domino fashion. But in the light, fluky breeze, she was slow to answer her helm. "Lee fore brace! All hands! Lee fore brace!"

The crew hauled for their lives on the fore braces to pivot the yardarms forward on the starboard side to meet the onslaught. They managed to get her up and drawing on this new point of sail—the starboard tack—as the leading edge of the storm whined through her rigging. Minutes later, the full body of the thing struck, and knocked the big ship flat. The masts didn't touch the water, but the tips of the yards went under, and the portside rail submerged along with the crew who'd been hauling on the lee braces. She lay there trembling, cringing as if she knew she was dying. Her list had been to port, and now she lay on her port side. Maybe she was too far out of trim ever to rise again.

Miraculously, the crew had surfaced intact, clambered and swam for shrouds, ratlines, pin rails, anything solid, and hung on, awaiting the verdict. Jones's parents would read the stark words some weeks later in the *Shipping News:* "Ship *British Isles* overdue, presumed lost."

"She's rising, boys!" screamed Paddy Furlong. "Feel her, she's comin' up!"

Jones couldn't feel her coming up. He could feel nothing but the steel wind and the cold, but if Paddy said so, then there was hope. . . . Yes, he felt her now, trying. She shook herself as if to signal her decision to fight on, and then she rose, not upright—nothing could stand straight in the teeth of such wind—but she was becoming a sailing ship again. Cheers broke out as the men relinquished their death grips, climbed into the meager shelter of the quarterdeck, and huddled together, soaked, cold, exhausted, but alive.

Up on the quarterdeck, lashed by sleet and shotgun hail, Barker dragged himself to the wheel, and he bellowed for two more men to help (there were two linked steering wheels for that purpose). Four men could keep her under control, and every sentimental soul on deck loved her at that moment, because she wasn't going to pack it in, but fight for their lives.

However, her alternatives were severely limited. She couldn't make any westward distance into the wind. Even if they could have brought her bow around to the north, all but impossible in those conditions, Cape Horn and the islands lay in that direction. She was pointing southwest toward Antarctica, away from her destination, but at least there was nothing to hit down that way. But when the endless winter dark finally broke into pale, bleak light, the men could see that, though she was pointing southwest, she wasn't *going* southwest. Her wake was streaming away to windward. The wind and the wind-driven current were setting them southeast, from where they'd come with such high hopes. By noontime she crossed Cape Horn's line of longitude once again, only this time she was going backward.

3

Wind

I time the wind: Now it is calm (7:11 PM). I hear the wind coming (7:13). Now more quickly. The wind is on us (7:14), and we heel 20, 30, 40 degrees. . . . I grab the wind indicator, push back the hatch, and rush outside to measure the wind. The red disc flies to the top of the scale, 63 knots. The cold is terrible. I slam the hatch, shake the snow from my hair and run to the stove.

—**Hal Roth aboard** *Whisper*
at anchor near Cape Horn, 1973

THE WEATHER—WHICH IS TO SAY THE WIND—that has bedeviled ships down the centuries is unique to Cape Horn. Individual storms don't necessarily blow harder than anywhere else, no harder, say, than a bad autumn nor'easter in New England or a winter storm in the North Sea, and only a few twist themselves into category-four hurricanes. From the human, on-deck perspective, it makes little difference which ocean you're floating on when the atmosphere gets moving at highway speeds—you're in for a severe pummeling. However, these winds, these nor'easters, hurricanes, and North Atlantic storms, are seasonal. New England is mainly gale-free in June and July; the Caribbean gets no hurricanes for Christmas; and even the surly northern seas stretch out and relax a little in summer. Down by the Horn, however, there is no seasonal respite. Extreme violence is just as likely in high summer (November through February) as in the dark of winter—because the atmospheric machinery that causes storms never shuts down. That's what makes Cape Horn weather unique.

A kid captivated by the adventure and the language, I never thought to ask *why* Cape Horn was so stormy. Had I understood then how science could enrich fantasy, I would have pursued the matter. But there would not have been a lot of readily available information. Until fairly recently, few scientists had asked the question, because the field of study was too vast, and since no one went down there, understanding the Southern Ocean was low on everyone's to-do list. Then, in the middle of Cold War mindlessness, something truly enlightened took place. Scientists from multiple nations and disciplines joined forces to explore the relationship between Earth and outer space. What, they wondered, did solar activity in the upper atmosphere, auroras and cosmic rays, have to do with geomagnetism, and what part did the oceans play in the relationship? This cooperative spirit of discovery would soon dissolve into *Sputnik* hysteria, but during the eighteen months between July 1, 1957, and December 31, 1958— the International Geophysical Year—scientists and governments turned their concerted attention southward, to Antarctica. It was the perfect laboratory because it was unaltered by technology or human population, pure in every way. Antarctica, in its extremes, resembled interplanetary space. The Cold Warriors agreed to make no territorial or commercial claims on Antarctica, leave it forever to nature and peaceful inquiry (Argentina and Chile demurred). Cape Horn seafaring was on no one's mind during IGY, yet in Antarctica, scientists verified the cause of Cape Horn wind: It was their laboratory, Antarctica itself.

Here is a continent about the size of the United States and Mexico combined, permanently locked in ice. There is land beneath the ice, but not much, two scraggly mountain ranges and rock islands— nowhere higher than 1,500 feet, while the dome of ice that covers the land climbs to ten thousand feet. The unimaginable weight of ice has compressed the bedrock seven thousand feet. Antarctica is determined and defined by ice, it *is* ice. Some 95 percent of the earth's fresh water is locked up in Antarctic ice. This ice never melts (at least at this writing). In winter (May through September), the pack spreads outward over the surrounding ocean, adding another fifteen million square kilometers to the continent; in summer it retreats by calving tabular bergs the size of Manhattan. But it never melts.

The Arctic by contrast is generous and relatively gentle in summer. The Arctic is a frozen ocean surrounded by continents; Antarctica is a frozen continent surrounded by oceans. This is more than a geographical tidbit. Oceans moderate temperature by retaining heat far longer than land. So when, in summer, Arctic ice retreats poleward, ocean water spreads warmth over Siberia, Alaska, northern Scandinavia, and Canada, and temperatures climb well above freezing. Life explodes headlong in the sea and on land, caribou, musk oxen, bears, wolves—only the Serengeti compares for the sheer numbers of animals on the move. Eight thousand years ago, the Inuit followed them into the High Arctic, found it accommodating, if harsh, and maintained a stable, layered culture, pockets of which still exist.

The ocean likewise warms the fringes of Antarctica, but not by much because the continent is composed not of land, but of ice. The only exception, the rocky arm of the Antarctic Peninsula reaching northward from under the ice to form the bottom of the Drake Passage, has a climate more akin to that of Cape Horn than to the rest of Antarctica. It's the only place on the continent where the temperature climbs above zero. Now that hunters are prohibited, wide varieties of seals, whales, and birds flourish in the krill-rich boundary waters. But inland, on the ice, Antarctica is all but lifeless. Ancient lichens, certain bacteria survive, but the largest land animal is a flightless midge about the size of a housefly.

Antarctica is by far the highest of the continents, with an average elevation of 6,000 feet. Composed of ice, it is also the coldest and windiest of the continents. Wind is directly related to high altitude and deep cold. Cold air is heavy; it wants to fall. Because the ice never melts, the air is always cold, and because the dome of ice is two miles high, the air plunges downslope at insane velocity. Russian scientists at their station near the Pole of Relative Inaccessibility (a wonderful name for the geographic center of the continent, which is not the same as the South Pole) clocked winds at 215 mph. Typically, these falling winds, called "katabatics," blow 60 to 80 mph every day in the winter, only somewhat less in summer, but they seldom stop. Nothing can live in the teeth of a wind like that.

I talked with climatologists at the National Oceanic and Atmospheric Administration (NOAA) who are building computer models to demonstrate a causal relationship between cold, deep-welling ocean

water from Antarctica and, among other phenomena, the El Niño oc-
currences half a world away. This work is part of a beautiful new
model of global climate called, perhaps too prosaically, the Conveyor
Belt Theory. It holds that climate everywhere is stabilized by the vertical, circular exchange of deep-running cold water from the poles
with warm surface water from the tropics. When this conveyor belt is
interrupted, instability results, and when the machinery shuts down
for a prolonged period, huge-scale changes, such as ice ages, occur.
So if this frozen continent sends shivers all the way to the equator, it's
naturally going to influence Cape Horn, only 600 miles from the tip
of the Antarctic Peninsula. Antarctic cold sentences Cape Horn—the
Drake Passage—to storms in greater number than anywhere else on
earth.

Antarctic cold pressing northward butts up against warm air over
the southern reaches of the Atlantic, Pacific, and Indian oceans. Cold
confronts warm between 40 and 60 degrees South latitude all the way
around the world. (There are sixty nautical miles in each degree of latitude, and so 40 degrees South latitude lies 3,200 miles north of the
South Pole.) Inherent in the disparity between warm air and cold is a
disparity in atmospheric pressure, the thing that barometers measure.
High pressure and low never meet peaceably. They abrade and accost
each other like rival street gangs in overlapping neighborhoods.

We're talking about why Cape Horn is uniquely stormy, about the
broad patterns that produce many storms, so we can brush by
the physics of individual storm formation. Suffice it to say that something like abrasion, like friction, along the intersection of warm and
cold drags up waves of unstable air with high pressure on one side of
the wave, low on the other. When conditions are right, as they are so
often down by the Horn, the waves bend back on themselves to form
circles of low pressure, essentially craters in the atmosphere, with the
lowest pressure located in the center. In weather language, these are
called *depressions,* another word for storm.

All wind, from afternoon breezes at the seashore to Hurricane Andrew, results from the "downhill" flow of air from regions of high
pressure toward regions of low pressure as the atmosphere tries to
equalize itself. Summer-afternoon sea breezes are light because the disparity in pressure is not very great. But in the Southern Hemisphere

south of 40 degrees South, storms are ferocious because the disparity between Antarctic cold and oceanic warmth, the *gradient,* is extremely steep and deep. The deeper the gradient slope within the depression, the faster the wind rushes in to fill it, which is why a plunging barometer alarms mariners. And since the Antarctic cold presses unrelentingly northward to engage the warmer air and water, since the combatants never leave the field, there can be no peace south of 40 degrees South, at least not for long.

Because the earth is not stationary, because it rotates on its axis, two things happen to the storm. First, it begins to spin around its own axis, or the center of lowest pressure. The wind flowing downhill from high to low pressure bends as it heads toward the center, essentially spiraling in—just as water circles the drain as it flows from a bathtub, and for the very same reason, the rotation of the earth. It's called the Coriolis effect. Second, the rotation causes the storm to move over the earth in the same direction as the rotation, like a top spinning on an inclined surface. (They resemble miniature earths in that they both rotate on their own axis and orbit something much larger than themselves.) Southern Hemisphere storms rotate in a clockwise direction and circle the earth from west to east. Almost all heavy weather, therefore, approaches Cape Horn from the west out of the vast, empty reaches of the Pacific. And this is why rounding the Horn from the Atlantic to the Pacific, to windward, is a lot tougher than going the other way.

These big ("synoptic scale") storms are exclusively oceanic. They depend for fuel on ocean warmth and moisture. Deprived of it—as when they pass onto large landmasses like continents—the storms break apart, weaken, and die out. Tropical hurricanes, for instance, live only as long as it takes them to cross the Atlantic from their birthplace off the bulge of Africa to the coasts of Central or North America. Nor'easters cross the Atlantic going the other way, but when the crossing is complete and they slam into the wall of Western Europe, their lives have ended. The point is all Northern Hemisphere storms are trapped between continents, because the oceans that spawn and nurture them are all bounded by continents.

But that's not true of the Southern Hemisphere. The two halves of the earth couldn't be more different. The Northern Hemisphere is crowded

with continents—all of Europe, Asia and North America, much of
Africa and South America. Only the two smallest continents, Australia
and Antarctica, lie wholly south of the equator. Eighty-one percent of the
Southern Hemisphere is covered by ocean. In addition to the constant
presence of the steep gradient conditions that spawn depressions, this absence of land is the other aspect that makes Cape Horn waters uniquely
violent. Maybe we can best illustrate this vast oceanic system by following an idealized storm around the world. The consensus of scientific
opinion is that single storms seldom make it all the way around intact.
But the oceanographers and climatologists I pestered all agreed that it's
possible, probably happens, there being nothing to stop it.

Let's place the center of our storm on 50 degrees South latitude as if
that parallel were a rail, then send the storm around the world to see
what it hits. Fifty South slices through the stalk of South America 239
miles north of Cape Horn (at 55 degrees 59 minutes South) in the middle of the Patagonian desert. Since big storms track eastward, let's
begin on the Atlantic side of South America. The storm would cross
the South Atlantic without brushing any land except two tiny, obscure
islands, Gough and Bouvet. It would pass so far south of Africa that
the residents of Cape Town wouldn't get their shoes wet. On across the
bottom of the Indian Ocean it would go, disturbing no one unless they
happened to be anchored on Crozet or Kerguelen Island. Residents of
Adelaide and Melbourne on the far southeastern bulge of Australia,
over 600 miles from the storm center, might need their umbrellas. Only
Tasmanians and New Zealanders on the South Island would call this a
storm, rain with hard, gusty wind. Now passing east of New Zealand,
our storm would step out into the largest expanse of nothingness on
the globe, 7,000 miles across the Pacific to Cape Horn.

This world-round band of open water south of any continental influence (except from Antarctica) has a straightforward name that
evokes from the sea-struck the same mix of fear and fascination as
Cape Horn itself: the Southern Ocean. Though it takes its components from the very bottoms of the Atlantic, Indian, and Pacific
oceans, the Southern Ocean is unique in that it is unified by meteorological conditions, not the landmasses that contain it. In modern
weather parlance, the Southern Ocean is "zonally uniform," characterized by the endless march from west to east of large-scale depressions and smaller "disturbances"; or, to put it differently, by

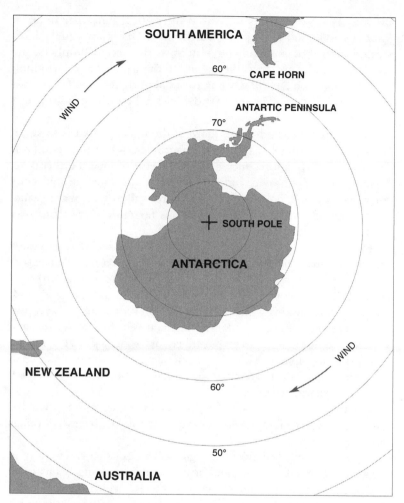

Map 3.1   Southern Ocean Circulation

dependably violent weather, if not tomorrow, then before the week is out. And the only land that sticks itself down deep in the Southern Ocean, into the flow of storms, is the narrow stalk of South America, at the bottom of which stands Cape Horn. And it had to be rounded.

As the wind's velocity increases, so does its *force*. That's a fairly obvious statement, but for sailors, there's cruelty lurking in the physics. Wind velocity is measured in nautical miles per hour, or knots (one doesn't say "knots per hour"). One knot equals 1.15-statute mph. But anemometer readings, the actual numbers, are meaningful only insofar as they relate to the wind's *force,* the blunt-trauma impact on anything trying to stand upright in the face of it—masts, sails, rigging, people. And here's where the cruel physics comes in.

Wind force is equal to the square of the velocity. That is to say, if the wind speed doubles, the force quadruples. When the velocity of the wind triples, its force increases by a factor of nine. Furthermore, because cold air is heavier and denser (containing more air molecules for equal volume), cold wind packs more wallop than warm wind. Forty knots down by the Horn contains far more force than forty knots in the Gulf Stream.

Joseph Conrad, who knew what he was talking about, suggested that in extreme conditions, the human psyche was a reliable measure of wind force. "It was off the Horn . . . ," he wrote in *The Mirror of the Sea.* "I was a youngster then, and suffering from weariness, cold, and imperfect oilskins which let water in at every seam. I craved human companionship. . . ." Conrad encountered the bo's'n, "(a man whom I did not like) in a comparatively dry spot where at worst we had water only up to our knees. . . . And just from that need of human companionship, being very close to the man, I said, or rather shouted: 'Blows very hard, boatswain.'

His answer was: 'Aye, and if it blows a little harder things will begin to go. I don't mind as long as everything holds, but when things begin to go it's bad.'"

That bo's'n would have feared gusts. Things often carry away in the gusts. No wind is steady, and heavy wind is particularly unsteady. The pitch of the noise climbs, the vessel heels, rigging creaks, shoulders hunch when the gusts come on, because in gusts the force increases with a jerk. A sail or fatigued piece of metal that might have survived a steady, gradual increase often disintegrates under the snap-load.

Wind is the prime cause of everything. Every aspect of life aboard is determined by the velocity and direction of the wind in relation to desired course. Wind can make life beautiful, evoking poetry from hearts of oak, and it can make life treacherous, narrowing it to the next handhold. But when worst comes to worst, it's not wind that sinks ships and boats, but the wind's agents—waves.

Three factors of wind combine to determine the size and shape of waves. Naturally, *velocity* matters, that's obvious. But *duration* is almost equally important. A brief blast of wind, like that in an isolated Gulf Stream squall, will not put up much of a sea, because water is heavy and takes a while to build up energy. The other factor is less obvious, that is, the distance the wind blows over open water. The technical word is *fetch*. A wind can blow hell for a long time over a small bay and still not set up large waves. People who live around the bay will say what big waves those were, and they were by bay standards, but not by ocean standards. To put it baldly, the faster, longer, and farther the wind blows, the higher the waves will be. And that's what makes the Southern Ocean and the Drake Passage unique in the world. Velocity, duration, and fetch: All three live in their most extreme form south of 45 degrees South. And south of 50 South, the fetch is literally endless—around and around the icy continent they go, wind, wind-driven current, and the waves with nothing in their way, nothing at all—except at Cape Horn.

Large waves may turn day-to-day life primitive and basic; cozy cabins become scenes of domestic violence, and fatigue comes quickly because energy must be spent just staying in one place. But ocean waves aren't normally lethal, because they just go up and down. An individual water molecule in a wave moves only a short distance forward, then falls back as the crest passes, describing a small vertical circle. Somebody compared it to a mouse running under a rug. Or as oceanographers put it, waves transfer energy but not mass—*until they break*. That's the difference between a passing wave and a catastrophe.

Many of us remember when on a day at the beach, the ocean betrayed our love by dropping a breaker on our heads, yanking us every which way at once before belching us up onto the beach in a jetsam heap. Beach waves break because the rising bottom trips their equilibrium and the crest topples over, and as every surfer knows, the shape and character of the break will be determined by the contour of the bottom. There is no bottom influence on ocean waves, but beach

waves are a fair model of what happens in the ocean when the wind
blows hard and long over distant fetch. The wave outgrows its own
stability, the face flattens, and the wind shoves it over. There are various kinds of breaks, some more malicious than others, but in any
case, breaking waves, transferring energy *and* mass, turn from
agents of fatigue, contusion, and constipation into killers. A big
breaking wave can exert a force of one ton per square foot on anything under it.

To determine whether waves in the Southern Ocean reach the
breaking point more often than in other oceans would require a level
of attention that the size and remoteness of the Southern Ocean has
thus far precluded. But all the elements of instability are there. According to the *Sailing Directions*, "South of Tierra del Fuego, in the
historically stormy region to the south of Cape Horn, there is a sharp
rise in gale occurrence. Within the area 55 degrees to 60 degrees
South, and 65 to 70 degrees West, where nearly 70 percent of the
winds are from the west, gales are recorded in 20 percent of the annual observation." In that usage, *gale* is a technical term referring to
wind speeds between 34 and 40 knots (shy of 50 mph). However,
when the *Directions* states that gales occur 20 percent of the year, it
means at least a gale, a gale and up. So that figure includes *storms* (48
to 55 knots), *violent storms* (56 to 63 knots), and a smattering of *hurricanes* (over 64 knots). And almost everywhere around the Southern
Ocean those same conditions generally obtain. The waters can never
rest. The numbers are very different in civilized oceans: In the waters
around Nantucket, gales occur 2.4 percent of the year, and winds, figured on an annual basis, exceed 41 knots only 0.7 percent of the time.
Gales and their heavier relatives circle the Southern Ocean like beads
on a string, each setting up waves and swells that fan out and overrun
slower-moving waves and swells, and then the whole system tries to
squeeze through the Drake Passage.

"Think chaos," advised Michael Carr, meteorologist, seaman, and
author of *Weather Predicting Simplified*. He cautioned that neither
Cape Horn nor the Southern Ocean was his province, but the several
great round-the-world yacht races, fully crewed and single-handed,
have drawn attention to the waters south of 50 South. Describing the
system, Carr repeated the word *dynamic*. That's what I should bear in

mind, the dynamics of the Southern Ocean circulation, everything spinning and churning and plowing eastward toward the Horn. He said he couldn't prove it due to the dearth of information, "but everything adds up to very large, breaking waves."

David Feit at the Storm Prediction Center, a branch of NOAA, said, "Remote, subject to large wind speeds over extraordinary fetch, fully developed sea states, and the odds all say you will experience dangerous breakers in the Drake Passage." Just consider the numbers, he added. Take the principle of Significant Wave Height. Let's say that 1,000 waves with an average height of 9 feet pass a fixed point in the ocean. Forecasters and wave modelers are concerned with the highest one-third of those waves, the "significant height." The average wave within that highest third will run to 14 feet (measuring from trough to crest). Ten percent of those will be 18 feet. And one wave in that 1,000 will be 24 to 31 feet high, or over three times the average. Here's the origin of the rogue wave, the anomalous giant, which the old Cape Horners called "niners." You could count on it, every ninth wave, and be ready. There's comfort in that, and sometimes science soothes anxiety by dispelling superstition and the inchoate shakes, but it doesn't seem to work that way with the science of wave growth.

William Van Dorn in his *Oceanography and Seamanship* displays a "commutative sea state diagram," a mathematical model of wave growth over time. The graph shows that in heavy conditions—60 knots of wind blowing for sixteen hours over a 500-mile fetch—the significant wave height will be 58 feet. Ten percent of those will average 72 feet. About 260 waves will pass in an hour, "the largest of which might exceed 117 feet!" Sixty knots is a hell of a lot of wind by anyone's standards, but reliable contemporary and historical eyewitnesses reported storms that blew 60 for weeks on end, and it didn't matter whether it was winter or summer. This is the place for 60 knots. Van Dorn contends that in such weather, the waves would be breaking 100 percent of the time.

Not all oceanographers would be comfortable with the Southern Ocean boundaries I've offered, from 40 South to about 60 South. They agree that this span of ocean is "zonally uniform," but they need to draw the outer rim down closer to the edges of the continent in order to focus on ocean phenomena—the Antarctic Convergence

Zone—that have little relevance to sailors trying to round the Horn. But all mariners since Magellan have recognized that when their bows crossed the Fortieth Parallel, they were entering an ocean entirely different from all the rest. Everything was exaggerated, accelerated in the "Roaring Forties" and the "Screaming Fifties." Big wind came on harder, faster, than in other oceans. Thermometers plunged along with barometers. Flying spray froze on the decks and in the rigging. Ships turned top-heavy under the clutch of ice, grew sluggish, unresponsive, and therefore vulnerable. The cold knifed through the bowels of the ships, and there could be no relief until they'd rounded the Horn and climbed back above 40 South into the other, normal ocean. Even the look of the Southern Ocean was different from the rest, gray and grim, death colors. But there were also those explosions of light when, for a time, the low murk parted and shafts of splendid brightness shone on the white crests like a hint of hope, and sometimes multiple rainbows arced across the horizon, intersecting. The fatigue, pain, and danger were all magnified, but so, too, was the magnificence of this ocean, its wildness. With each degree of south latitude, through the forties into the fifties, down to the Horn at nearly 56 South and beyond, the conditions inevitably worsened. Cape Horn sailors had a saying for it:

Below 40 South there is no law,
Below 50 South there is no God.

4

Discovering Seas

Modern exploration had to be an adventure of
the mind, a thrust of someone's imagination,
before it became a worldwide adventure of
seafaring. . . . The pioneer explorer was one
lonely man thinking.
                    —Daniel Boorstin, *The Discoverers*

And I believe that nevermore will any man
undertake to make such a voyage.
                    —Antonio Pigafetta, *Magellan's Voyage*

CHRISTOPHER COLUMBUS, WHO WAS ALWAYS in it for the gold,
must have been delirious with joy when on October 12, 1492, the
thirty-third day at sea, he heard the lookout shout, *"Tierra! Tierra!"*
For finding a new sea route to the East, he would receive, according to
his contract with their Most Catholic Majesties Ferdinand and Isabella, 10 percent of all the profit from all the trade with the East in
addition to hereditary titles, land grants, and governorship of the
places he'd discovered. Christopher Columbus stood to become the
richest man in Christendom, but of course he had not discovered
Cipangu, Cathay, or the Golden Chersonese. He had bumped into a
New World no one had imagined or wanted, and for our purposes,
Columbus discovered the problem that Cape Horn would solve. He

landed on a "low, green island," planted flags and banners in the sand, said prayers, and claimed it for God and Spain, a curious act, since he thought these islands were part of the Great Khan's empire. The locals (Tainos) stood around stark naked and watched. Since they were natives of the East Indies, even if they didn't seem to know it, Columbus named them *Indians*. Two decades after their first contact with God and Spain, the Taino were extinct.

It seems sometimes reading the literature that the discovery of the New World was the most significant single event in Western history. It's hard to imagine any suitable modern metaphor to help us empathize with the contemporary shock, once the truth of it sank in. Writers have compared it to our reaction should we discover life on Mars. Maybe, but at least we know that Mars exists. And probably the discovery of life on Mars would prove to have less far-reaching historical impact, unless the Martians, with their sense of righteous entitlement, took us over, as the West took over the New World. In that case, historians might say about Martian conquest what Frederick Turner in *Beyond Geography* said about European conquest: "A world millions of years in the making vanished into the voracious, insatiable maw of an alien Civilization."

Columbus had every reason to believe that he had reached the East. In 1492 everyone including Columbus assumed that the world was as Ptolemy drew it in the second century: a single landmass containing Europe, Asia, and North Africa. There was no North or South America on Ptolemy's map or on anyone's mind, and no Pacific Ocean. The great land-island occupied six-sevenths of the earth, people knew, because the Bible said so: "Upon the third day, thou didst command that the waters should be gathered in the seventh part of the earth; six parts hast thou dried up." (Esd. 6:42) Therefore, the Western Sea that separated Spain from Asia must be one-seventh of the earth wide, or about 3,000 miles by most reckonings.

The best source of true information about the geography (and the wealth) of the East was Marco Polo's *Travels*. Polo had lived in China for seventeen years, serving as an unofficial emissary of Kublai Kahn to the far reaches of the Mongol Empire. He returned home to Venice in 1295, and almost immediately he was captured by Genoa (Columbus's hometown) during one of the endless skirmishes between the two city-states over distribution rights to the trade goods coming from Asia over the ancient Silk Road. In prison he collaborated with an out-of-favor romance writer named Rustichello, who jazzed up *Travels* with beasts and fantasies for commercial purpose, but Polo's clear-eyed observations remain. And Polo had been clear and specific about this huge archipelago stretching far to the east (toward Europe if we think of the world as a single landmass) from Cipangu and Cathay, Polo's names for Japan and China. Therefore, to someone sailing in from the east, the first glimpse of Asia would consist of "low, green islands."

Ferdinand and Isabella had every reason to hope that their weird, redheaded Italian mariner had reached the East, because that would turn the combined crowns of Aragon and Castile into a superpower. Columbus hadn't brought them any gold or spices on his return, only some new fruits and tubers (potatoes), and two natives (Arawaks) who upon close scrutiny by experts were deemed to be Chinamen. Their Most Catholic Majesties, preoccupied with their brand-new Inquisition, hadn't taken Columbus very seriously, and the story of Isabella hocking her crown jewels to back the voyage is bunk. Figuring they'd never see those three ships again, they saw no reason to waste good ones. *Niña*, *Pinta*, and *Santa Maria* were old and sprung long before they sailed west, and they were crewed mostly by convicts, reprobates, and harbor riffraff. While he hadn't reached the rich parts of the East, he had come close, maybe only a few days' sail from the Great Khan's court. So certainly there would be another voyage, this one with seventeen of the finest ships money could buy, crewed by solid Christians, nothing but the best for their Admiral of the Ocean Sea.

Columbus made three additional voyages, during which he explored most of the Caribbean Basin. With each, evidence against his discovery accumulated. Columbus was a hard man to like, but one must feel sorry for him in his desperation and mounting panic as he pressed against the unbroken coastline of Central America. On the Third Voyage in 1498, he came upon the Orinoco River delta in present-day Venezuela, and his blood must have run cold at the sight of brown water staining the sea for miles around.

A river of that size and power could only drain an enormous landmass. Maybe a continent. That would be disastrous to Columbus, a

Map 4.1   Columbus in the Caribbean

continent blocking his way to fame and fortune. Unable to brook that possibility, and being a bit of a mystic, he wrote in his journal that the river must flow from Earthly Paradise, in which case all bets were off, geographically speaking. Despite the evidence of his eyes, Columbus never departed from the delusion that the real riches lay only a little farther west, a day's sail. By his death in 1506, he had been ridiculed for his absurd rationalizations and nearly forgotten, gone without an inkling of the fame that would follow him down the centuries.

Columbus ushered the slave trade into the Caribbean Basin less than a decade after he discovered it, and he slaughtered the natives with a kind of crazy wantonness. A few of his modern admirers have dismissed this by saying that he was a poor administrator. Now revisionist historians have demolished the myths. But Columbus will never get his due, because his true accomplishments and his genius were nautical. They had to do with wind, with sailing. Columbus wasn't the first to try to reach the East by sailing west. The Portuguese Dulmo and Estreito tried it in 1485, but they died somewhere out in the mid-Atlantic because they were mistaken about the wind. To cross the Atlantic from the Iberian Peninsula, you must first sail south halfway to the equator in order to pick up the northeast trade winds before turning west and riding the fair wind all the way across to the Caribbean. Turning west before they'd reached the trades, Dulmo and Estreito sailed straight into the prevailing westerlies, against which they could make no progress.

Through leap of mind, not trial and error, Columbus also understood how to get home again. He extrapolated sailing conditions on the unknown side of the Atlantic from those on the Old World side. In other words, he intuited that the westerlies familiar in Spain originated on the New World side of the Atlantic. Therefore, on the homebound route, he sailed north from the Caribbean until he reached the belt of westerlies (the same westerlies that killed the two Portuguese going the other way), then rode them east to Spain. These remain the best sailing routes from Europe to the Caribbean and back again. And though he didn't know it, he discovered the clockwise rotation of wind that scientists of today call the North Atlantic Gyre. However, the problem he discovered remained.

If there was some kind of New World where Asia was supposed to be, where was Asia? It could only be farther west—on the other side of the New World. The question, then, was how to get through or over or under it to reach the Indies, the *East* Indies, not these goldless, dirt-poor West Indies, while almost no one asked what the New World contained. "The unexpected continent continued to seem less a resource for new hopes than an obstacle to the old," as Daniel Boorstin put it. Maybe there were straits or passes through the obstacle, and maybe they'd be short and easy. Maybe you could see right through them. Then the waters beyond would open up, offering clear sailing to the riches beyond dreams. It couldn't be far. In Western wishful thinking, Boorstin points out, the earth was never very large, and the East was never very far away.

The search for the strait, for *el paso,* became the single unified objective of all westward exploration for the next two decades. It's called the Great Age of Discovery. But none of those explorers, Hudson, both Cabots, Cartier, Verrazano, Corte-Real, was "discovering America," except incidentally. They were probing every west-trending bay, sound, and river searching for a way past the damn thing. Davis, Frobisher, Hudson, and others looked north to the Arctic for a sea route to the East—the fabled Northwest Passage—and when it didn't turn up, they looked farther north. Meanwhile, Spanish explorers poked at the coastline of South America. By 1502, Amerigo Vespucci had sailed at least as far south as the Río de la Plata, site of present-day Buenos Aires. Every European kingdom capable of building one of the new ships, the caravel, was using it to search for Asia. This was a cultural as well as a technical explosion, and it sent ships, like shrapnel, out farther than any ship had ever been before—and to more lasting effect.

⁀

Vasco da Gama, a heartless Portuguese head-splitter, dropped anchor off Calicut, India, on May 22, 1498, after a 12,000-mile passage from Lisbon around the Cape of Good Hope to India, a voyage four times as long and far more difficult than Columbus's. A few Europeans had been to India before, Marco Polo, most notably, but none had ever gone by ship, and that made all the difference. The Portuguese had been worried about rumors of the lands in the west that Columbus had claimed for Spain. If it turned out to be some new world, fine, but if it turned out to be the East, then there would be war on the Iberian Peninsula and the high seas. Columbus had tried to sell his Enterprise of the Indies to the Portuguese in 1487, but they, like the French and the English, had turned him down. Ironically, he'd been in Lisbon making his pitch on the very day that Bartholomeu Dias sailed into the harbor with triumphant news: Africa had a bottom. A ship could indeed reach the Indian Ocean by doubling the cape—the Cape of Storms, Dias named it, storms being his experience of the place. Naturally, King John and his geographers rejected Columbus's highly speculative route now that Dias had discovered the real thing. But as for that name, Cape of Storms, that had to go, too defeatist. . . . Cape of . . . Good Hope. Without pressing competition, the Portuguese had been sanguine about Dias's discovery until they got wind of Columbus's. They immediately dispatched Vasco da Gama to round the Cape of Good Hope, then find India, known to lie somewhere to the north, which he did, landing at Calicut. (This was again a case of reaching a known place by an unknown sea route, but in this case the place was actually part of the Old World.)

Da Gama went ashore to meet the sultan, but it didn't go well, this encounter between West and East. Da Gama brought gifts, bits of red cloth, beads, little mirrors, knives, and cheap shirts, which insulted the sultan. *Trinkets?* You arrogant Christians bring trinkets meant to please naked savages to *me,* king of this splendid realm! (Curiously, Columbus did the same thing. Expecting to reach the Great Khan, richest of the rich, he brought trinkets and cloth.) The sultan was, to da Gama's surprise, a Muslim who hated Christians as utterly as da Gama hated Muslims—the Crusades were still fresh in the air. Da Gama was a bad fellow to ridicule in front of the entire court like that, as he'd soon demonstrate. But the sultan had a point and both men knew it. In matters of trade, the West was at a hopeless disadvantage. The East had everything, all the gold, pearls, perfumes, precious jewels, and spices, especially spices. Hell, the East even had the central symbol of the West's religion, the Holy Sepulchre. The West had nothing that the East wanted, except continued absence.

Da Gama, browsing the marketplace, couldn't help but notice that the price of a sack of pepper was about 1,000 percent cheaper than the same sack of pepper in Lisbon. For nutmeg, cloves, and cinnamon, he could pull down a soothing 3,000 percent. And he noticed one other thing, maybe, historically speaking, his most effectual discovery. He had the locals entirely outgunned. These snooty Muslim potentates were armed with junk left over from the last crusade. Their *cannons* were trinkets. Times had changed; the technology of strife had advanced in Europe. While these effete sultans and puffed-up pashas were lounging around enjoying life, the West had been smelting serious firepower. Da Gama ran out his guns and ordered the sultan to surrender Calicut. This was bluster, as the sultan suspected. As a type, da Gama's guns could have leveled the town, as they would in the years to come, but he didn't have enough men to hold it. Signaling just what sort of fellow they were dealing with, da Gama snatched small-boat fishermen and inshore traders, about seventy people, tied their feet together, then cut off their hands. He threw them, alive, blood gushing, into a small boat, set the boat on fire, and sent it sailing shoreward. Then he went home, where he was accorded titles, grants, and trade percentages, everything Columbus had ever wanted.

The men who followed da Gama, Albuquerque and Almeida, rounded the Cape of Good Hope and tore through the Indian Ocean, hacking up any pashas, sultans, caliphs, or potentates who complained. By 1505, the Portuguese had taken over everything west of India to the Arabian Peninsula and east to the Malay Peninsula, gateway to the Spice Islands. And in fact, as time would show, they had found the best sea route to the Indies, where the riches grew on trees. But then, the Portuguese had it easier than Columbus and the Spanish, there being no irksome *Novus Mundus* in their way.

Over on that side, certain stark truths had become clear by 1505. There was definitely no easy strait, and maybe there was no strait at all. Every likely-looking indentation—Hudson's Bay, the Gulf of St. Lawrence, the Hudson River, Chesapeake Bay—had been explored by French, English, or Dutch expeditions. Spanish explorers had probed the Orinoco and the Amazon, rounded the bulge of Brazil, and sailed into the Río de la Plata—and they'd found no *paso*. Not only was the New World coastline unbroken from the Arctic Circle to Argentina, the land itself was enormous. Huge rivers drained its interior, each dwarfing the largest rivers in Europe. Maybe the New World was actually a continent, maybe two, and maybe there was no way around or through it. If so, then Spain would remain bottled up in the Atlantic, leaving the Portuguese to pick the East clean.

Before the Spanish found Aztec riches, their empire consisted of islands and isolated outposts only nominally governed by Columbus's son Diego from Santo Domingo. The settlements in the far west, along the coast of Panama, basically lawless, tended to attract the worst sort, desperate and dangerous men with nothing to lose— there were almost no women. Psychosis, sadism, and homicidal tendencies weren't the same sort of drawbacks in the New World as they sometimes were in Spain. In fact, that was just the sort of scum needed in the New World, the crown and the Church agreed. If the sociopaths found gold, most of it would become the property of Spain and the Church anyway, and if they died searching, well, good riddance.

Vasco Núñez de Balboa arrived in 1500, part of an expedition to explore the interior of Hispaniola, and stayed on to try his hand at sugar planting. A failure as a planter, falling hopelessly in debt, he skipped, stowing away in a food barrel aboard a supply ship bound for Panama. The story has it that once at sea, he popped from his barrel—I picture the lid still on his head like a sombrero—and announced to the captain, "God has chosen me to do great deeds." (Spanish murderousness in the New World was always marbled with strains of comic bombast and absurdity that seem thoroughly modern.) Balboa found the settlement encircled by endless deadly jungle, its citizens decimated by mosquitoes and curare-laced arrows. The hopeless, malnourished look of it filled Balboa with a sense of destiny. He rustled up enough local malcontents to overthrow the standing governor, one Martín Fernandez de Enciso, and then Balboa moved the settlement out of poisoned-arrow range to the site of present-day Darién. He cemented his grip by marrying into the family of a local cacique called Comaco, who was delighted to have Balboa's blades on his side, since his numerous enemies had nothing but Stone Age clubs.

Thanks to the chronicler Peter Martyr, we have this theatrical moment recorded in history: After Balboa's hoods and their war dogs shredded Comaco's enemies, the cacique awarded them 4,000 ounces of gold. In some jungle clearing, the Spanish made a balance scale to divvy it up, and the boys crowded around to protect their interests. They began to quibble, to squabble, with "much brabbling and contention." Comaco's son, disgusted by this display of greed, kicked over the scales and cried: "What is the matter, you Christian men, that you so greatly esteeme so little portion of gold more than your owne quietnesse!" Balboa was probably not deeply stung by this, gold being the whole point. But Comaco Jr. didn't leave it at that: "If your hunger for gold be so insatiable, . . . I will shew you a region flowing with gold, where you may satisfie your ravening appetites. . . . When you are passing these mountains (poynting with his finger towarde the south mountains) . . . you shall see another sea—"

Say what? Conquistadors doing double takes. "Another *sea?*"

Balboa rallied 190 of his own men and several hundred native bearers and guides, and they set out through the sunless jungle to cross the cordillera. Balboa appeased the natives when he could, hired them as guides, but if they resisted, then he and his men went at them "like butchers cutting up beef and mutton." Martyr reported another of those scenes at once comic and horrific when Balboa encountered the Quarequas, who "were stained by the foulest vice." The cacique and some others liked to wear women's clothes. Cross-dressers so offended Balboa's pious Christian sensibilities that "he ordered forty of them to be torn to pieces by dogs." Balboa was a big proponent of the war dog, a variety of bull mastiff, apparently, and one of their most enthusiastic breeders was the "fountain of youth" psychopath Ponce de León. Both men were most impressed by the effect on the morale of naked natives when set upon by a dozen war dogs in full cry. Balboa's favorite dog, a grizzled veteran named Leoncico, always received a full share of the loot just like everybody else.

It took three weeks and hundreds of lives to cross the mountains. As the expedition slogged up the side of still another row of peaks, one of Balboa's guides told him that from the summit, right up there, he would be able to see this other ocean. Balboa ordered a halt so he could go up alone, leaving no doubt in history as to who had been first. He climbed a little tree at the top, and, moved by the way this endless sea reflected his own greatness, he dropped to his knees and gave thanks to God.

A week later, when they reached the coast, he donned his armor, drew his sword, waded into the surf, and claimed the "Mar del Sur" and all the shores it washed for God and Spain. (He called it the South Sea because the isthmus trends east-west where he was wading.) Later that afternoon he borrowed a canoe and paddled around to explore his new ocean. Among the other recurring ironies in the story, there is this: Balboa was not the first European to look upon the Pacific Ocean. Marco Polo himself had seen it in the 13th century from the shores of China, but he had assumed that it was the west side of the

Atlantic. However, Balboa might rightly be remembered as the first European to wet his testicles in the Pacific Ocean.

Balboa's discovery was significant in the larger story because it demonstrated two new facts: There was indeed water on the "other" side of the New World, and the New World, at least in this particular place, was narrow. Balboa scurried back over the isthmus to Darién with a bold plan to exploit his find. He began to prefabricate little ships, which he meant to carry in pieces across the cordillera and assemble on the other side. This, the first inkling of the Panama Canal concept, laid a policy the Spanish would follow for nearly a century of using the isthmus as a transshipment point for goods pillaged from the west side of South America. But Balboa didn't get far in this before his first great deed came back to haunt him. Another band of thugs representing the deposed Enciso arrested him on the Pacific side, dragged him back to Darién, and lopped off his head, dumping his body on the outskirts of town for the carrion eaters. (Among Enciso's band was another servant of God, one Francisco Pizarro.)

Ferdinand Magellan, the man who would find the *paso* and cross the Pacific, thus remaking the map of the world, was born about 1480, the youngest of three siblings, to minor nobility in the unfashionable north of Portugal. He was twelve when Columbus landed in the New World. That same year Magellan left home for the first time, off to Lisbon to serve as a page in the court of King John. A bumpkin, he never learned the intricacies and niceties of court life, and that he was a short, squat, homely fellow probably didn't help. He gained the peculiar, ardent enmity of the duke charged with overseeing the pages. Unfortunately, that duke became King Manuel when John died suddenly in 1495. Magellan had always been planning for a career overseas, and with no favor at home, he sailed for India in 1505 with Almeida to hack up some uncooperative Muslims. Magellan had a talent for it. Helping Albuquerque demonstrate his concept of the future for the Indian Ocean by sawing off women's noses and severing men's hands, Magellan was stabbed in the thigh by a spear and only barely survived, leaving him with a severe, jarring limp.

After five years of fighting, penniless and in pain, Magellan headed home, hoping that his record of bravery and loyalty would win him favor in the court. Magellan felt he was owed money, but what he really wanted was a promotion. He wanted to be a *cavaleiro fidalgo,* a small thing to ask, in his view, for services rendered. But the king ignored repeated requests for an audience. You were supposed to drop your suit after a cold shoulder from the king, but Magellan pressed it. Finally, Manuel agreed to an audience, and it remains unclear whether he did so planning to humiliate Magellan or whether Magellan came on too strong. In any case, the king ostentatiously turned his back on Magellan while he knelt at the royal feet. If his services were not wanted in Portugal, might he sell them to another crown? Magellan asked. The king spun on him: What you do is of absolutely no interest to Portugal. As the spurned little man walked away, the courtiers mocked his limp.

Magellan seems to have conceived the voyage during an ensuing period of seclusion (with his Malayan slave, Enrique) spent studying maps of the New World and explorers' journals, immersing himself in the search for the *paso.* He emerged with a new cosmological certainty about the location of the *paso* and the position of the Spice Islands, and then he set about selling the voyage to King Charles of Spain. Magellan wasn't proposing a speculative voyage of discovery. He said he absolutely knew that there was a strait and that he knew where to find it, no question. And he knew another thing, he insisted, the most important thing, the whole point of the voyage: He knew that the Spice Islands (the Bandas and Moluccas), the richest of the rich, rightfully belonged to Spain under the terms of the 1493 Treaty of Tordesillas, an absurd, comic-opera document that would shape geopolitics for centuries.

When word reached Lisbon that Columbus had found something out in the west that might be the East, King John howled in protest. A Portuguese—Henry the Navigator—had conceived this whole exploration business fifty years before Columbus. Portugal wasn't about to step aside. So instead of going to war, Spain and Portugal sat down to divvy up the world between them. The deal was brokered by none other than Rodrigo Borgia, who had just bought the papacy for himself, reasoning that Spain and Portugal, both Catholic countries, could each have half a world, while His Holiness would have the whole world. Negotiators finally picked a line of longitude running down the middle of the Atlantic about 300 miles west of the Azores (about 46 degrees West). Everything east of the "Demarcation Line" belonged to Portugal, and everything on the west side belonged to Spain. The bulge of Brazil protruded east of the line, and that's why Brazilians still speak Portuguese today. But the pertinent question was, Where did the demarcation cross the *other* side of the world, the side that contained the Spice Islands? Who "owned" the nutmeg? Magellan admitted that he hadn't actually been there, but he'd been to Malaya, and that was close enough to know that the Moluccas were in the Spanish zone. This was what his voyage would prove for Spain. Never mind that in his day, and for the next 250 years, no one knew how to compute longitude with anything better than guesswork.

But Charles must have been convinced, because he invested the crown's own money in the venture, instead of the usual contract in which the king gave consent to commercial interests for a cut of the proceeds. He knighted Magellan and formally appointed him Capitán-General of the "Armada de Molucca." Magellan had guaranteed success. Failure was out of the question.

He needed three months to ready his ships for sea, provision and crew them up, during which the entire Iberian Peninsula conspired against him. Anyone could see that something big was afoot in San Lugar, and that could only mean a voyage to the East. Manuel, the king who'd said he didn't care what Magellan did, tried to discredit him with lies, but they were so stupid no one believed them. Manuel then sent spies, saboteurs, and monkey wrenches. Meanwhile, elements in the Spanish marine establishment, disgruntled that a Portuguese was in command, tried to foist inferior gear and rancid provisions on him. That Magellan could trust no one meant he had to oversee everything himself.

Five ships, *San Antonio, Concepción, Victoria, Santiago,* and Magellan's flagship *Trinidad* cleared the mouth of the Guadalquivir on the morning of September 20, 1519, and stood out to sea. The magnificent nightmare of a voyage had begun.

Three of the four other captains were Spanish dons, haughty young aristocrats who didn't really know the pointy end from the

square end but resented taking orders from a Portuguese. (This unsea-
manlike system—ignorant dons in command while masters and pilots
handled the actual sailing—would help sink the Spanish Armada in
1588.) The dons were plotting mutiny, and Magellan knew it. Further,
he'd gotten word before he shoved off that a Portuguese fleet was
lurking athwart Columbus's now-traditional route to the New World.
To foil the ambush, Magellan carried on south, hugging the African
coast to Cape Verde, but he neglected to inform the dons of the Portuguese threat, or of anything else. Each night he hung a lantern in his
mizzen rigging and ordered the dons to shut up and follow the light.
In fact, Magellan, perhaps to incite the mutiny he knew was coming,
took every opportunity to tromp on their protocols and egos, but it's
hard to know his motives. Of all the Great Age explorers, Magellan
may be the most opaque, writing nothing himself, confiding in no one,
not even the hero-worshiping chronicler Antonio Pigafetta, who'd
come along as a sort of adventurer in the modern sense to learn, he
wrote, "the wondrous things of the sea." But as a nautical matter,
sail-powered vessels couldn't cross the Atlantic any old way their captains wished (they still can't), and Magellan's evasive route took his
ships straight into the fat belly of the doldrums, where they parked for
two weeks. This proved, the dons said, that the little man was incom-
petent as well as Portuguese.

Magellan wasn't bluffing when he told Charles he absolutely knew
where to find the *paso*. He had a specific place in mind, but it was the
wrong place. The funnel-shaped bay at the mouth of the Río de la
Plata, between Uruguay and Argentina, is 150 miles wide. The north
shore trends westward another 140 miles before it narrows enough to
see the south shore. Even from an airplane approaching Buenos Aires,
the Río de la Plata looks like open ocean. It's easy to understand how
an explorer rounding Punta del Este might conclude that he'd found
the blessed strait—or even the bottom of South America. Magellan
had deceived himself into believing that the Plata *was* the *paso*. He
should have known better.

In 1514, five years before Magellan sailed, one Juan Díaz de Solis
had discovered the bay, but he didn't live to explore it. Caught ashore,
he and five of his men were murdered by the natives, butchered,
roasted, and eaten in full view of his horrified crew aboard ship.

There were records of that disaster, of course, and some historians believe that Magellan interviewed the survivors. Also, an acquaintance of his, an obscure figure called John of Lisbon, had reached the Plata a couple of years after Solis was devoured, but John claimed only to have sighted, not explored it. However, in typical Magellan fashion, he fixed his steely gaze on the Plata, undistracted by doubt, even though two decades of exploration had shown repeatedly that geography in the New World was seldom what it seemed.

He rounded Punta del Este (today a beach resort near Montevideo and Buenos Aires) in early January 1520. He spent the next twenty-three days poking at the edges of the cul-de-sac, hiding his panic, one supposes, utterly alone, as the bay steadily narrowed and saltwater turned to fresh. It was the mouth of a river, the confluence of two, actually, the Uruguay and Paraná—and it led nowhere. He had been wrong, wrong from the very outset. If the dons, considering any lame excuse to overthrow him, had gotten an inkling of this, the greatest single voyage in human history would have ended right there, without warranting a footnote in esoteric texts. But Magellan, who stopped at nothing, ordered the fleet to follow him south on February 2, because south was the only the place the strait could be, and there simply had to be a strait.

He probed every indentation on the coast of Argentina. Golfo San Matías, Bahía de los Patos, Bahía de los Trabajos, all dead-end disappointments. Of course, the weather worsened with each degree of southerly latitude. Penguins and other new animals appeared. Ships, sails, and crews were showing the strain, men were beginning to freeze to death in their sleep, and scurvy was creeping aboard. But then they rounded a high headland beyond which no land was visible to the south and none to the west. Hope surging, they turned to starboard, following the land westward, but, no, it soon bent south, then back eastward—this was just another big bay, Golfo San Jorge.

No one had ever seen an ocean so malevolent as this. Every several days another gale lashed the fleet, and these storms, too, were more severe and sudden than the most experienced sailors had ever seen before. Did this granitic, silent man who seemed not to feel pain like other men mean to carry on regardless, until he'd sealed the ships into some frozen hell? They'd been five weeks exploring the fruitless coast, almost 1,500 straight-line miles from the Río de la Plata, and now winter was coming on. Not even Magellan could sail on against the sub-Antarctic winter in 16th-century ships. (The reversed seasons came as a surprise.)

The dons pressed him to winter back in the gentler lower latitudes, but Magellan wasn't about to relinquish ground gained. While the dons fumed and conspired, Magellan picked a dreary little cove protected on the seaward side by a gravel spit, Puerto San Julián, at 49 degrees South latitude, and there, he announced on March 31, they would spend the winter. Come spring, they would continue searching southward. Not only that, they would spend the winter on half rations. Most students of Magellan's voyage agree that he meant to have it out with the dons there in the depths of nowhere. It didn't take long.

After dark on April 2, 1520, a cadre of thirty men rowed silently alongside the *San Antonio*, climbed aboard, and took the ship by surprise, but in the brief scuffle, the *San Antonio*'s master was knifed to death. Magellan moved quickly to plug the mouth of the cove with two ships still loyal to him, then sat back to await the mutineers' next move. It was pathetic. Compared to Magellan, the dons were weaklings (compared to Magellan, *everyone* was a weakling), but they also had a political problem. They were servants of the king of Spain, and this was his trip, Magellan his man. To mutiny because he offended their pride would have cost them their heads. So instead of swords and cannons, the dons came at Magellan with a *letter,* a sort of petition. It made no demands, posed no ultimatums. It *asked* that, given their high stations, couldn't they be kept informed by the rightful commander of the fleet as to his intentions? The dons just wanted a little respect, and that made them no match for Magellan. They could walk over the little man at court, but not down here around 50 degrees South. If ever in his life Magellan giggled at anything, this soggy missive would have been it.

He patiently sorted out his loyalists, and almost casually overwhelmed the mutineers. Then he paused to consider the best punishments for his purpose. Apparently only about forty crewmen fleet-wide wanted to overthrow Magellan, but he couldn't execute them all even if he wanted to. He would need all the men he had, given the expected mortality rate of the time. He executed Gaspar Quesada, who had killed the master of the *San Antonio*. Magellan offered Quesada's servant clemency if he agreed to chop off his master's head, a good deal, and the servant leapt at it. Magellan decided that two quartered bodies stuck up on stakes with the gore drying in the wind was demonstration enough. (The other was Luís Mendoza, killed in the mutiny.) He "spared" the ringleader, Juan de Cartagena, keeping him prisoner until the spring, when he'd be marooned, along with a rabble-rousing priest, where of course they'd starve to death.

And then as winter tightened around his fleet, Magellan inventoried his stores to discover that he'd been cheated or sabotaged by victualers back in Spain. They'd skimmed off one-third of his provisions. And here in southern Patagonia, where nothing grew and nothing moved except the wind, there was no hope of supplementing their food supply. In the face of this emergency, other commanders might reasonably have made a run for the temperate zone. Instead, Magellan took another whack from their daily rations, and stayed put for the winter. In spring, they headed south still deeper into the cold unknown.

It was October 21, 1520, a Sunday, St. Ursula's Day, when the weary fleet drew abeam of a high, white cape with no land visible to the south or west like so many others. With instruction to return in five days, Magellan sent the *San Antonio* and *Concepción* to investigate. Watching the ships being sucked through a tight channel (called the First Narrows) on an eight-knot flood tide, he despaired of ever seeing them again. But on the afternoon of the fifth day he spotted them blasting out through the same narrows on a speeding ebb-tide current. The ships, all dressed in flags and banners, fired their cannon, and their crews lined the rails to wave and cheer. They buzzed the flagship, in one of the great scenes of the age, men screaming with joy, the cannons and colors, a sparkling blue day, the death and the conflict forgotten. They had found it.

Magellan played it straight. Oh yes, *el paso*, he knew it all along, and the dons honored his knowledge and brilliance. However, they didn't actually want to transit the strait. Who knew how long it might be? The reconnaissance ships had ventured in about 100 miles, far enough to determine from the tidal flow that it would lead eventually to another ocean, but the ocean might still be hundreds of leagues away. Their stores were running dangerously low, and most of what remained was rotten. Everything argued for retreat. Except Magellan. Pigafetta, the chronicler, famously quoted him as saying that "even if they were reduced to eating the leather [anti-chafing gear] on the ship's yards, he was determined to proceed, and keep his promises to the Emperor." And so they set out westward into the longed-for strait, which he named Canal de Todos Santos, but it would become and forever remain the Strait of Magellan.

The twisting strait, full of cul-de-sac bays, bulging in places thirty miles wide, constricting in others to the width of a tide-swept river channel, either too deep to anchor or strewn with ship-killing reefs and shallows, is 310 miles long according to the *South American Pilot,* which also remarks, "Violent and unpredictable squalls are frequent all over the strait." Magellan named the land to the south Land of Fire. He obviously saw something burning, most likely native smoke signals, and one story has it that he named it Land of Smokes, but Spanish geographers, finding that a tad soft, changed it to Tierra del Fuego. Counting the recon trips into deceptive bays and fjords and constant tacking in tight quarters against the west wind, the fleet probably covered 1,000 miles.

Finally, on November 28, 1520, they rounded a sharp point, which Magellan had already named Cape Desire, and in another grand moment from this magnificent and terrible period, the three-ship fleet stood out into open ocean. The admiral couldn't play this one straight. He broke down sobbing in front of everyone. It looked so beautiful, misty blue and serene in the crisp air and bright sun. Recovering himself, Magellan gave it a name: El Mar Pacífico. And here was a fine day to set out across his new ocean. He had no way of knowing that this Pacific Ocean dwarfed the Atlantic and every other ocean combined.

While searching for a route through the strait, the ships had separated for the sake of efficiency. Alvaro de Mesquita, captain of the *San Antonio,* with coaxing from his Portuguese pilot, Estavio Gomes, abandoned the expedition. He retraced the track back to the Atlantic and sailed to Spain, where he and Gomes were thrown into prison. The *San Antonio* had been carrying most of the fleet's food. If the voyage had been fraught, stormy, and excruciating to date, they hadn't seen anything yet.

Poignantly, Magellan held a northerly course from Cape Desire because he expected the Pacific to be narrow and Asia to be near. But of course Asia didn't turn up, and around 35 degrees South, Magellan turned northwest to cross the ocean. By sheer bad luck, he picked the only track a vessel can take across this island-rich ocean without seeing land. They sailed for eighty-nine days without once taking on water or fresh provisions. Men began to die of scurvy. Here's Pigafetta's description: "We ate only biscuit turned to powder all full of worms and stinking of urine which the rats had made on it, having eaten the good. And we drank water impure and yellow. We ate also ox hides [that chafing gear] which were very hard because of the sun, rain, and wind. And we left them four or five days in the sea, then laid them a short time on embers, and so we ate them. And of the rats, which were sold for half an ecu apiece, some of us could not get enough." According to Pigafetta, twenty-nine men died of scurvy (it was actually nineteen), and the rest were skeletons, more dead than alive. Most students of the voyage propose that Magellan and Pigafetta inadvertently survived the mysterious disease, the greatest killer of Great Age sailors, because they were ingesting enough vitamin C from quince preserves in the officers' mess.

By March 5, the food, even the barrel scrapings and the rats, was gone, and so was the water. That was it, they recognized. No one would know of their great discoveries; their privation and death would count for nothing. And the men who could still move lay down to die. Death would be a relief from the pain of starvation and thirst, but by dark on that very day salvation in the form of a high, lush island hove up over the horizon. The next day they entered the first bay they found, and because nobody was capable of handling sail, Magellan ordered the halyards cut. Magellan had crossed the endless ocean and bumped into Guam, which he named the Isle of Thieves, because the natives came aboard and carried off everything they could lift.

Now Guam is a long way from Cape Horn, but since the whole point of rounding the Horn would be to reach the Pacific, we can't leave its discoverer recuperating on Guam and skip his tragic end.

Magellan, in that frustrating way of tragic heroes, caused his own death. Refreshed and reasonably healthy after a stay ashore, the fleet sailed west from Guam in search of the Spice Islands, but they were too far north. West of Guam lay the Philippines, which Magellan claimed for Spain. By that time, Magellan had undergone some kind of psychological lurch. He'd become a fervent, obsessive evangelist.

All the Spanish expeditions during the Great Age listed the Christian conversion of the natives among their objectives, but that was largely hypocritical. The priests came along to bless whatever genocide the boys got up to, especially if it promised profit. But Magellan was suddenly serious about soul saving, and he was successful at it. He staged full-on religious-theatrical rituals with all possible pomp and grandeur to impress the converts, and as Filipinos by the hundreds embraced the Catholic Church, Magellan became possessed by what one historian called "divine madness."

He reckoned himself invincible. Only such a one could have logged his immortal deeds, overcoming antagonism from both man and nature. In the Philippines, as in Europe, religion and war were wed, and as Magellan converted the natives, he wantonly involved himself in local power struggles. Having promised the Sultan of Cebu to fight for him against the Sultan of Mactan, Magellan rowed over to Mactan with a ragtag handful of cooks, stewards, and sailors without soldiering experience—instead of his fierce marines—to face what he knew to be an army of thousands. He did this to demonstrate that to the invincible, armies weren't really necessary. Ironically, the dons who lacked the spine to confront him directly egged him on in his folly when they recognized that it would kill him. The Mactans hacked him to pieces on the beach. He died senselessly but valiantly, as befits the tragic hero, covering his men's (including Pigafetta's) retreat to the boats before he was cut down in waist-deep water. "[T]hey killed our mirror, our light and comfort, and our true guide," Pigafetta lamented.

Of the five ships that left San Lugar on September 20, 1519, one ship and eighteen skeletal, scurvy-ridden men returned on September 8, 1522, after a voyage of about 39,500 miles. It was the ship's pall of stench that alerted the town to its arrival. The *Victoria*, leaking like a basket, every seam working, was then under the command of Juan Sebastián del Cano, one of the Puerto San Julián mutineers, and it was

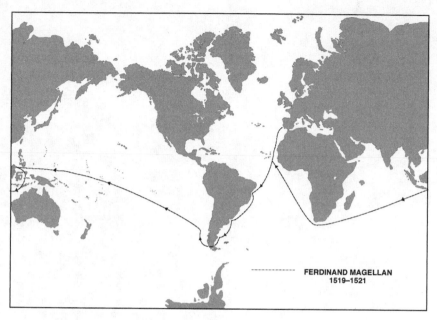

Map 4.2   Magellan: the First Circumnavigation

he—a Spaniard—who sailed her triumphantly upriver to Seville. In a final bitter piece of irony, Cano received full credit and rewards for his
captain's accomplishment. As a Portuguese (and dead), Magellan was
easily forgotten by the Spanish court, but eventually the truth came out,
thanks to the young man who'd sailed to see the "wondrous things of
the sea," Antonio Pigafetta, and his book, *Magellan's Voyage*.

Among the many new facts revealed by Magellan's voyage was
this: God's Creation was far larger than man had ever imagined. Further, He had covered a hell of a lot of it with water, thus creating
opportunities for sailors. The nation to reach the riches and spread
the word of God (but mainly reach the riches) would be the one
with the best ships and the will to sail them anywhere. The future
would be shaped by God, gold, and sailors.

5

Drake

We fell in with the uttermost part of the land towards the South
Pole, and had certainly discovered how far the same doth reach
southward from the coast of America.
—Francis Fletcher, *The World Encompassed*

Cocky, foppish, with his pointy goatee and extravagant handlebar, the bright red hair, and the dashing arrow scar on his right cheek, Francis Drake is the original Captain Blood. He's the prototypical swashbuckler with a sense of humor and fair play, friend to the common sailor and to damsels in distress, the pirate with a twinkle in his eye. Even the Spanish whom he attacked his entire career and who reviled and feared him couldn't exactly hate him. Today Drake has fan-club aficionados and serious marine historians poring over his circumnavigation and his psychology, because Drake is an amusing nautical genius. Look at him finishing his game of bowls before heading out to sail rings around the Spanish Armada. But often obscured by his flash as a pirate and an admiral, by the brilliance of the circumnavigation itself, and sometimes by landlocked biographers with a different story to tell is that Francis Drake discovered Cape Horn. Which is to say he discovered what again no one imagined was there, a wide-open ocean south of Magellan's Tierra del Fuego. The Drake Passage. This, however, was not a voyage of discovery. He was out to get the

Spanish. Drake despised the Spanish and all things Catholic, but he loved their New World plunder.

During the quarter century between Magellan's voyage and Drake's birth, the conquistadors discovered riches beyond the pope's most avaricious dreams. In 1519, while Magellan was at sea, a thug named Hernando Cortéz landed at Vera Cruz on the Gulf Coast of Mexico, burned his boats behind him to signal his resolve, struck out overland, and happened upon the Aztec capital of Tenochtitlán, site of present-day Mexico City. This was more like it, gold everywhere. Their leader Montezuma was literally festooned in the stuff. Unfortunately for the Aztecs, Cortéz and his band showed up on the very day prophesied for the return of the god Quetzalcoatl. That moment—welcoming the conquistador instead of killing him—spelled the end of the Aztecs. He destroyed their capital and then their entire culture, taking their gold for Spain, God, and Cortéz.

Aztec wealth inspired a new generation of conquistadors who went looking for more, and that's how, in a series of brutal yet brilliant expeditions, the New World got explored. Navaez explored the Gulf coast from Tampa Bay to the mouth of the Río Grande. De Soto, searching for the fabled Seven Cities of Cibola, found the Mississippi River. Coronado, who pressed north from Mexico into present-day Arizona and Colorado, actually found this Cibola, but it turned out to be a parched, penniless Indian settlement. The Coronado and de Soto expeditions remain two of the greatest overland journeys in history, but they're dark and sad, and they left a holocaust of disease behind. Others, such as Alvarada, Quesada, Valdivia, would soon strike out across the Andes into Amazonia, riding the great rivers east toward the Atlantic (it couldn't be far). Gold was all these men cared about.

And then Francisco Pizarro came upon the mother lode—the Inca Empire. The scene has been described, filmed, and dramatized time and again. We know what happened that November 15, 1532, in the town of Cajamarca (in Peru), but it still seems too extravagant to be true. Pizarro, who had followed the trail of the Inca chief Atahualpa for a thousand miles over frozen Andean passes and heartless coastal deserts, sent word ahead that he was coming to town as a friend, a brother. Atahualpa believed him, or if he didn't, he saw no reason to fear a force of 180 foreigners. Thousands of unarmed Inca, some accounts say as many as 40,000, turned out in and around the city square to meet the strange foreigners. The crowd parted as Atahualpa was borne in aboard his royal litter. A Catholic priest stepped forward to offer Atahualpa a Bible, but he didn't want a Bible, what could a Bible mean to him? He tossed it on the ground. The priest screamed, "Come out! Come out, Christians! Come at these enemy dogs who reject the things of God." But this was an ambush, nothing spontaneous about it, and the Bible nonsense was as good a cue as any. Then the slaughter began.

Four thousand Inca, it's said, were killed in the first orgy of violence, and Atahualpa was taken prisoner. Pizarro demanded a ransom—enough gold to fill a room twenty-two feet by seventeen as high as Atahualpa, a tall fellow, could reach. The Inca paid up, but Pizarro, outnumbered, was afraid to release him. So he charged Atahualpa with *treason against the Spanish crown*. The priests bestowed the rites of salvation. Atahualpa accepted the religion of his murderers after Pizarro told him that if he did his body would not be burned. Therefore, according to Inca religion, he might one day return from the dead to resume his reign. Pizarro had him strangled, then beheaded. There was a lot of mopping up still to do, there was still the capital at Cusco to loot, but the Inca Empire (accumulated by conquest, like the Spanish) that had stretched 3,000 miles from present Ecuador to Santiago, Chile, was over.

Then in 1545, conquistadors came upon the fabulous Potosí silver mines. Never mind the East. This was better than the East, riches right here in their own New World. Furthermore, they wouldn't even have to trade for it with a bunch of arrogant pashas and treacherous sultans. Now all the Spanish had to do was engineer a system to bleed the New World of its treasure and transfuse it to Seville. The Aztec treasure had been relatively easy to plunder, because the civilization was compact and near the Caribbean. But this was different; this was a veritable continental coastline-worth of riches. And it lay on the Pacific side.

One way to get the riches home was through the Strait of Magellan. But the Spanish had had some bad experiences in that water. The fleets that tried to copy Magellan's route (Loaysa, Alcazaba, Carmargo) had been savaged. This strait was a hateful thing, ten-knot currents, lee shores everywhere you turned, close quarters, and a wind like no wind anyone had ever felt before. Some of the older salts who'd been there swore the place was cursed by God. So the Spanish never really considered the strait for a homebound treasure route, and by the time they needed one, they had essentially forgotten that the strait existed. There was a shorter, far easier, and safer way.

It was Balboa's old idea. Build the ships on the Pacific side. These ships could sail down to Peru and Chile to pick up the loot and take it back to the Isthmus of Panama, a treasure shuttle. They could be built fat to carry more loot because speed wasn't really an issue, and for that matter, they didn't even need to be armed, because El Mar Pacifico, as that Portuguese fellow had named it, was incontestably Spain's private ocean. Landed at the isthmus, the treasure was packed on mules and driven by slaves over the cordillera to the Caribbean side—at a place called Nombre de Díos. There it was loaded onto the ships that would take it to Spain in convoy with armed escort via Columbus's route. Under this system, at least one flota a year, the unimaginable wealth of the New World made Spain the only superpower in the Old World. The others could only pick at her far-flung weak points.

Almost nothing is known of Drake's childhood, including his precise date of birth, somewhere between 1541 and 1545. (The Spanish found the Potosí silver mines in 1545.) He spent his earliest years in the little Devon town of Tavistock a few miles inland from Plymouth, where he would play that game of bowls. (The nautical truth, by the way, is that a stiff southerly was blowing straight into the harbor; he couldn't have sailed if he'd wanted to.) His father, Edmund, was a seaman-turned-tenant farmer who lived on Lord Russell's estate when Francis was born. But Edmund Drake was also a most enthusiastic preacher of the charismatic Christian persuasion, a "hot gospeler" in contemporary slang. This was not a safe calling during Drake's childhood, when Catholics and Protestants were persecuting each other with a level of fervor and viciousness best inspired by religion.

The Reformation had taken different form in England than on the Continent, where it had something to do with theology and doctrine. In England, it was a straight-ahead conflict between church and state. Henry VIII always saw himself as a good Catholic appalled by Luther's heresies, but he had that secular problem. He needed Rome to annul his marriage to Catherine of Aragon (daughter of Ferdinand and Isabella) because she couldn't produce a viable heir. She'd produced a daughter, Mary, but no one wanted a queen. Henry needed *male* issue. As everyone knows, the pope refused, Henry divorced Catherine, married one of her ladies in waiting, Anne Boleyn, and thereupon, the pope excommunicated Henry. The stark battle lines were drawn. Henry declared a new state religion, and made it official by bullying Parliament into passing the Act of Supremacy in 1534, establishing the Church of England with him at its head. To demur, therefore, was capital treason.

The Catholic Church had owned about one-sixth of all the land in England, which Henry now seized. Being supreme, Henry saw no reason to share the land with England. By 1540, he had dismantled the old monasteries and passed the land to his pals and supporters (including Drake's godfather Lord Russell and George Washington's family) at bargain-basement prices. This windfall for the wealthy was a hard blow for the poor, since Henry's pals turned out to be meaner landlords than the monks ever were. Not only did the monks' charitable services vanish under the new lords but many tenants were evicted entirely, replaced with more profitable sheep. Civil unrest, back-and-forth religious persecution, some of it state supported, and crazy violence shaped the backdrop of Francis Drake's youth and the course of his adulthood.

In 1549, aggrieved priests and their flocks rampaged across the West Country, and the mob drove the Drakes from their farm with little besides their lives. The family fled east toward London, settling near the navy base at Gillingham Reach, where the River Medway empties into the Thames estuary. After a period of near-poverty, Edmund got a job as a preacher to seamen. Records of the period are pretty sketchy, and the often-repeated story that the family lived aboard an old hulk bottomed out in the black Medway mud may be an attractive legend. Hulk or no hulk, Drake spent his childhood on and in saltwater, and it took hold of him forever. If anyone has ever been sea-struck, it was Francis Drake.

For the Drakes and others like them, there was still Bloody Mary's reign to get through. Mary was a fanatic, psychically damaged by her childhood and her mother's humiliation, who meant to force Catholicism on England when she came to the throne in 1553. In one infamous episode, she burned 300 "heretics" at the stake in Smithfield, near London. She also married Philip II of Spain, as if punishing England itself for Henry's sins against her mother. He humiliated and ignored her, and involved England in a stupid war with France, while prohibiting English ships from trading in his New World empire. The announcement of her death in 1558 was met with cheers in the streets.

Drake was already at sea, age ten, during the worst of Mary's persecutions, apprenticed to the captain of a small coastal trading vessel. This was blue-collar maritime commerce, but the heavy currents, fog, shifting sand banks, and gale-studded weather made English waters the best possible school of seamanship. (Captain Cook was an alumnus.) Drake flourished, a gifted sailor and natural-born navigator. Politically, those were timely skills to own. Drake was thirteen or fourteen when Queen Elizabeth came to the throne. With her own gifts, she was settling the religious issue: For now at least, England would not be a Catholic country, or exactly a Protestant country. It would be an *Elizabethan* country. Her forty-year reign would encompass and nurture literary geniuses—Jonson, Marlowe, Sidney, Spenser, Shakespeare—and an equally stellar list of nautical geniuses, many from Drake's own county. Gilbert Humphrey, John Davis, the Hawkins family, Walter Raleigh, Martin Frobisher, Richard Grenville. Elizabeth recognized that she could avail herself of all this talent, using her "gentleman adventurers" as a maritime arm of state. She meant to have a piece of the spice-trade action out East. Frobisher, Grenville, Davis, and others searched for a Northwest Passage over the top of North America, in order to circumvent Spanish and Portuguese routes to Asia. Another set of sea dogs, led by the Hawkinses, would pirate Spanish riches in the Caribbean while Elizabeth feigned ignorance. Nautical geniuses had bright futures under the Virgin Queen. As a friend and perhaps a relative of the Hawkins family

(William Hawkins's sons, John and William, called Drake cousin, but that may have been merely a term of endearment), Drake soon got himself a berth aboard a Hawkins ship bound for the New World. Drake aficionados like to trip lightly over the fact that it was a slaver.

Though disappointed by the absence of precious metals, Christopher Columbus had proposed that Cuba, Hispaniola, and most of the islands named after saints would make good sugar plantations. But the trouble with sugar as a product was that it required lots of laborers, and the only way you could make a go of it was with free labor. Apologists for Spanish savagery in the Caribbean point to the good works of the priest Bartolomé de las Casas, who decried the looming extinction of the Caribs and Arawaks caused by Spanish blades and germs. These Indians were humans, said the kindly priest, with souls just like Catholic folk, and God didn't intend them to be slaves. For that purpose, he advised, you want to import blacks, without souls, from West Africa. But this presented a paradox for the struggling plantation owners. The crown had decreed that only Spanish ships could trade in the New World, but the West African slave trade, reaching back a century to Henry the Navigator, was controlled by Portugal, against whom the decree was directed. To make a go of it under those circumstances, Spanish planters would have to trade surreptitiously with slave smugglers. Like Hawkins and Drake.

When he could dodge or bribe shore-side officials, Hawkins bought his own slaves in West African markets, but it was just as easy and cheaper to pirate homebound Portuguese slave ships. When he had a complement of slaves, Hawkins crossed the Atlantic to the Caribbean, where he traded them for gold or pearls. And one of Hawkins's most reliable backers, both in ships and money, was none other than Her Royal Majesty. Before long, however, Seville cracked down, making examples of the local port captains who'd been getting fat on English bribes, and prosecuting planters.

King Philip complained aggressively to Elizabeth, who made a fine show of outrage at the unmitigated gall of this insolent renegade, what's his name? Captain Hawkins. "I'm shocked, *shocked!*" Meanwhile, she continued slipping him ships and money for future incursions. There was serious profit in it, and she always liked money, but she was also conducting her special kind of foreign policy, taking

Map 5.1   Drake in the Caribbean

whatever she could from the Spanish at every opportunity without provoking actual war. She was masterly at it. In 1567 Elizabeth allowed him one more trip via West Africa to the Spanish Main. She knew the increased risk of war, but that didn't stop her.

This, Drake's third voyage with Hawkins, would be his first command, of the tiny *Judith,* about *Pelagic*'s size. The five-ship fleet got underway after hurricane season, plundered a load of humans from a Portuguese ship off the bulge of Africa, then laid a course for Colombia. Things had definitely changed in the Caribbean basin; the old easygoing days were done. Either true believers or simply fearful for their lives, the port captains couldn't be bribed, at least not like before. But these were still wild and remote outposts. A righteous port captain could sputter and rage and order the English out in the name of King Philip, but Philip wasn't there, and the sugar plantations, the sole purpose of the settlements' existence, still needed slaves. They tended, uncooperatively, to die in droves.

At Río de la Hacha, Colombia, Hawkins stormed ashore and drove off the stroppy port captain so he could conduct his business in peace. Drake loved the work. There wasn't all that much combat, most ships striking their colors when Hawkins ran out his guns, but when needed, Drake was talented close in with a sword and pistol. The English didn't bother to storm the next stop, Cartagena. Instead, they stood offshore and bombarded the town until the residents invited them in. This was way beyond the pale geopolitically, and Elizabeth wouldn't approve of his style, but she'd appreciate the fortune Hawkins would be bringing home.

A late-season hurricane slammed the fleet in the Yucatán Channel, however, taking down masts, shredding sails and rigging. Redhanded, helpless, they limped into the harbor at San Juan de Ulua near Vera Cruz, Mexico. This was very awkward. San Juan de Ulua was one of the main ports from which the Spanish shipped Aztec plunder back to Spain. And at that very moment, a fleet of a dozen fat, fully loaded treasure ships lay at anchor waiting for wind. Hawkins's request to use the harbor for repairs put the port captain in a tricky spot. He could plainly see that Hawkins had enough firepower and men to seize the treasure ships at will, so flatly denying his request seemed imprudent. On the other hand, by granting it the port captain put himself in direct defiance of his king. But Hawkins was also vulnerable. He wasn't supposed to be in these waters at all, let alone with all that hot property. He had no choice while his ships remained unseaworthy. They could fight, but they couldn't sail. So the two parties struck a deal: The English could use the harbor long enough to make their repairs, and the Spanish would leave them to it. In return, the English would promise not to attack the treasure ships.

The story of Elizabethan seafaring is studded with these marvelous moments of coincidence and climax, sometimes Shakespearean in scope (he was three at the time) and sometimes as melodramatic as a Saturday matinee. On the day after the uneasy truce was struck, the new viceroy of Mexico sailed into San Juan de Ulua with a fleet of thirteen ships. Don Martín Enriquez, who had been dispatched by Philip with a single task—keep those English pirates the hell out of Mexican waters—was aghast to find five of them parked in the harbor within shouting distance of the silver fleet. Enraged, Enriquez went ashore to berate the port captain, but then, when he cooled off, he began to see the opportunity before him. He sent word to Hawkins that the deal would hold.

It did, for three days. On the fourth day, Enriquez sounded the signal, and the Spanish attacked. They murdered or captured any English sailors who happened to be ashore. They captured Hawkins's flagship *Jesus of Lübeck* and two smaller vessels. Drake on the *Judith* and Hawkins on *Minion* saved their ships by beating back the Spanish boarders hand to hand. After picking up some of the survivors from the three lost ships, *Judith* and *Minion* fled out into the Gulf of Mexico. There is no record of Drake's homebound passage, but Hawkins wrote an account of his. It was a hell trip—dysentery, starvation, and thirst—on the desperately overcrowded *Minion*. There's the suggestion that Drake panicked and sailed away before he'd picked up his share of survivors. We know that Hawkins was angry with Drake after the Ulua episode, and they parted ways for a long time. Hawkins dropped his hook in Plymouth harbor by the end of January 1569. Drake arrived shortly thereafter.

A wave of righteous outrage swept England—the vile treachery of the perfidious papists, the villainy! Only Catholics would stoop this low, only Spaniards. San Juan de Ulua became the rallying cry for a faction of hawks in Elizabeth's court, and patriotic throngs in the streets called for vengeance. All this fine moral fervor seems a bit disingenuous, however, or at least theatrical. Drake aficionados tell the story in black-and-white terms: Don Martín Enriquez's treachery fixed Drake's hatred of the Spanish and launched him on his lifelong war against them. It's decidedly difficult to like the Spanish during this period, but what about English treachery? When they limped into Ulua, Drake and Hawkins were not innocent mariners in distress. They were predators. They had just shot up Río Hacha and bombarded Cartagena. Enriquez saw no obligation to treat honestly with the likes of them. One can't help wondering what would have happened if Enriquez had not shown up. Would Hawkins have kept his word after repairing his ships; would he have sailed away satisfied with the treasure he already had, leaving the helpless treasure fleet in peace—because an Englishman's word was his bond? Maybe.

However, if Elizabeth's indignation had a touch of political show-manship about it, Drake's did not. Drake declared his own private war, and he set upon the Spanish ferociously, fanatically. During this period of several years beginning in 1570, Drake became *El Draco,* the legendary scourge of the Spanish Main. Daring, dashing, re-sourceful, gallant, and lucky, always lucky, he was everywhere at once, sacking Cartagena, attacking treasure ships within sight of Santo Domingo, raiding Nombre de Díos with a gang of Maroons and French corsairs. His cunning sailing tactics, superior gunnery, and the big reputation itself made resistance futile. When his topsails hove up over the horizon, Spanish captains struck their colors. The legend of *El Draco* spread far and wide. Spanish mothers told their children they'd better be good or *El Draco* would get them. But Drake was no killer, no Pizarro or da Gama, and this is an essential aspect of the legend and of the man. He wanted their loot and he wanted to humiliate the Spanish, but he did not want to slaughter them. If they surrendered, Drake took what he wanted, then sent the ship on its way. If he wanted the ship, he put the crew and passengers ashore safely. And he never, ever took advantage of a lady.

With Drake around, Nombre de Díos had been armed to the teeth, impregnable, but back on the trail, he reasoned, the mule train would be helpless. So Drake and a band of Indians, Maroons, and French pi-rates set out into the jungle to intercept the treasure. Halfway across the cordillera, the chief of the Maroons led Drake by the hand to an ancient tree into which steps had been cut leading to a high bower. From there, the Maroon said, you will see both the Caribbean and the South Sea. It's tempting to imagine Drake, in one breathless moment, understanding that his destiny would lie in this other ocean, that out there beyond the blue horizon greatness waited, but that's pretty ro-mantic. Yet there is some evidence. The anonymous, sympathetic au-thor of *Sir Francis Drake Revisited* writes, "After our Captain had ascended to this bower, he besought Almighty God of his goodness to give him life and leave to sail once in an English ship on that sea." And perhaps at that very moment, peering out at the shimmering new ocean, he conceived the great voyage that would immortalize his name. It's not out of the question; this is Francis Drake we're talking about.

Drake was back in England in 1576, and shortly after his return, the bones of his plan for the great voyage reached Elizabeth, though no one knows exactly who carried it to her. It might have been Sir Christopher Hatton, vice-chamberlain, member of the Privy Council, and a favorite just then of the Queen. Hatton had as a personal secretary a gentleman, soldier, scholar, a bright, witty, and haughty courtier named Thomas Doughty. Hatton's family crest happened to contain a "hind trippant or"—a golden hind. The plan was bold, ambitious, devious, and yet simple. Elizabeth probably took right to it: Instead of attacking the Spanish in the Caribbean, where resistance had stiffened, Drake would slip through the Strait of Magellan and attack them from behind—in the Pacific. It would be a long, dangerous voyage, but there were obvious advantages. The Spanish would be taken completely by surprise. Drake could pick off their fat, lumbering treasure haulers almost at his leisure. All he had to do was find his way through the strait. He knew from reading Pigafetta that it was a bleak, savage place, and he'd probably heard shop talk about how it might be cursed, murdering so many sailors. But those were Spanish sailors, not English sailors, and they hadn't had Francis Drake at the helm.

Queen Elizabeth met with Drake privately for several hours in 1576, and we have only his word, but years later Drake claimed she had said that he was "the only man that might do this exploit." Also: "Her Majesty gave me special commandment that of all men my Lord Treasurer should not know of it." She was referring to Lord Burghley, a powerful and useful member of her court who did not approve of Drake and Hawkins provoking the Spanish. He had no ethical qualms; he thought England could make more money through legitimate trade with Spain. Elizabeth, playing both sides of the issue as usual, figured that all-out war wasn't in Spain's interest, since her pirates were taking but a tiny fraction of the New World riches that safely reached Seville. Besides, she enjoyed her pirates. Drake got all he needed in money, men, and material, and as for ships, Queen Elizabeth considered kicking in the royal *Swallow,* but she decided that might not look so good. Word was leaked around the Plymouth docks that Drake was bound for Alexandria, for currants. Five well-armed ships, for fruit? Francis Drake a merchant? No doubt Drake was headed for the Caribbean to continue the work that had already made him famous and fortunate. The preacher's son from the old hulk had bought himself an estate in Devon and taken a wife. He was now landed gentry, or at least landed. He didn't need to set foot on a rolling deck ever again if he didn't want to. But obviously he did. And he meant, quite consciously, to sail it into history.

There were five ships, *Pelican, Elizabeth, Marigold, Swan,* and *Christopher,* from largest to smallest. Even the largest of them, *Pelican,* was small, barely eighty feet from figurehead to taffrail. They were better ships than Magellan's, but not far different in design. They were able to carry more sail, and the extravagantly high freeboards—those absurd forecastles and stern castles—had been lowered to reduce windage and weight above the waterline, but as marine architecture they were still folly. Leeway must have been heartbreaking, and with their shallow draft and round bottoms they must have rolled something hideous. *Pelican* was the fastest, but as a fleet they could sail no faster than the slowest member, and that was seldom more than 100 miles in twenty-four hours. When we try to understand the events of a very long voyage in Drake's day and the human motivation behind them, we need to factor in a high level of fatigue, sickness from an awful diet, and prolonged discomfort with periods of downright misery. Anyone who has sailed over distance aboard small boats in rough conditions knows how physical life erodes to basic biology and, further, how even small injuries, sores, grievances, and annoyances can wear down the spirit and sometimes foster irrational behavior.

Aboard the five ships were 150 men and fourteen boys. Drake would have had no trouble raising competent crews, since they shared in the loot on a fixed scale, and Drake's success in the loot department was known in every waterfront town on both sides of the English Channel. There was a Dane (named Big Nele), two Dutchman (one named Little Nele), Spaniards, Portuguese, several blacks, a Greek, and a New World Indian, as well as the Englishmen. Captains, officers, Drake's brother among them, and sailing masters were mostly trusted comrades from the Caribbean. But then there was that other group, similar to Magellan's dons, gentlemen soldiers without shipboard duties while at sea. It was beneath their station to pull on ropes or climb ratlines like common sailors, yet, historians have remarked, Drake took more than was common on other voyages. Among them was that urbane, arrogant courtier Thomas Doughty, who had been in on the voyage from its conception, and his brother John. In fact, Drake and Thomas Doughty had gone soldiering together in Ireland. There was also a pastor aboard, a Protestant of course, named Francis Fletcher. Often called Drake's Pigafetta, Fletcher would compile from three other sources and his own journal the best firsthand account we have, *The World Encompassed by Francis Drake*.

Just before he sailed, Queen Elizabeth in private presented him with a sword and spoke, we're told, those famous words, "We do account that he which striketh at thee, Drake, striketh at us." Without fanfare or ceremony, which would have been unusual for a fruit run to the Med, the fleet sailed on November 15, 1577, straight into a savage autumn storm that drove them back to harbor—it seemed to happen a lot on great voyages. But then they enjoyed fair weather down the bulge of Africa, where they captured a Spanish and a Portuguese ship. Drake kept the latter and its pilot, a master mariner with Southern Hemisphere experience, Nunho da Silva, who would come to admire Drake and supply one of the firsthand accounts. The Atlantic crossing to the coast of Brazil was uneventful but long. By then the bewildering Thomas Doughty affair had begun. Somehow Drake came to suspect that Doughty, commander of the Portuguese prize ship *Maria,* was stealing silver from the hold, and Drake accused him of it. Doughty responded by saying no, it was Drake's own brother, Thomas, who was stealing. With that, Drake stripped Doughty of his command and turned it over to Thomas Drake.

In the mind-numbing heat and light airs of the tropics, tension festered, and things turned weird. Thomas Doughty was a supercilious aristocrat who probably made Drake, always sensitive about his low birth, feel inferior. However, there is no real evidence that he was fomenting mutiny, but that's what Drake fretted about, then obsessed on. In the increasing latitudes of the Southern Hemisphere, where the sea and sky turned ominous, Drake decided that Doughty was a necromancer, a conjurer in league not only with factions back home who wanted his voyage to fail but with the devil himself. Drake's brand of Christianity credited devils active in the world, and any adversity, foul or contrary wind, storms, even a violent encounter where he wasn't present between Drake and Patagonian Indians—he blamed on Doughty. Then Drake got word that the younger Doughty was going around saying he and his brother "could conjure as well as any man and that they could raise the devil and make him to meet any man in the likeness of a bear, a lion, or a man in harness." It was probably somewhere in the Roaring Forties that Drake decided to be rid of him.

Drake, who had kept the Doughty brothers aboard his flagship, *Pelican,* where he could keep an eye on them, decided to shunt them off on the *Elizabeth* for a while, and he made a big production of it. In a calm, he had himself rowed over to the ship to address the crew. He announced that he was sending them ". . . a conjuror, a seditious fellow, and a very bad and lewd fellow . . . and his brother, a witch, a poisoner, and such a one as the world can judge of. I cannot tell from whence he came, but from the devil, I think."

And now winter was coming on. So where did Drake decide to stop? Puerto San Julián, the bleak, despairing hole in the side of the Patagonian desert where Magellan, faced with a real mutiny, had executed and dismembered Luís de Mendoza. Drake had read his Pigafetta, and so had his officers; they knew what had happened here fifty-eight years before. The stub of Magellan's gibbet hove into sight, a pile of human bones at its base. Once his ships were set in their winter anchorage near a sandbank island at the north end of the bay, he brought charges against Doughty. Most Drake scholars concur that at this point he had convinced himself his voyage would be ruined if Doughty were allowed to live. The late Raymond Aker, president of the Drake Navigators Guild, told me that he believed Drake had decided to execute Doughty before the trial, and that Doughty, who may have been exceedingly foolish talking against Drake, was not guilty of conspiring to overthrow the voyage. Doughty had powerful friends at court to whom Drake would have to answer, particularly if his voyage failed. If it succeeded, then few at home would press for his prosecution, but he still needed to put a cloak of legality around the proceedings at San Julián.

And so there followed one of the strangest scenes in exploration history, or at least since Magellan held his trial in this same cold, barren place. On that low, sandy island, Drake pitched a colorful tent to serve as a courtroom, ran up his flags and banners, and empaneled a jury with an old friend from the Spanish Main, Captain John Winter, as foreman. Doughty's judge would be Francis Drake. When the judge asked Doughty how he pled, Doughty stood up and questioned Drake's authority to convene a court. He wanted to see Drake's commission from the Queen to do so. If Drake had any doubts about axing Doughty, they vanished when Doughty questioned him. Drake flew into a rage, berating and cursing Doughty. When that was finished, for some reason that will remain forever murky, Doughty signed his own death warrant when he said, unasked: "My Lord Treasurer has a plot of the voyage." He meant Lord Burghley, the very man Elizabeth had said should not know of the voyage, according to Drake.

"No, that he has not," Drake snapped.

"General, he has."

"How has he?"

"He had it from me," Doughty replied inexplicably. He was found guilty.

Now for the sentence: Away from Doughty and the courtroom, Drake assembled his crews and said, "And now, my masters, consider what a great voyage we are going to make, the like of which has never been made from England, for as a result the worst of you shall become a gentlemen." But, he said, the voyage will never succeed as long as Doughty lives. . . . Now let's see, we can choose this mouthy aristocrat or we can choose wealth, but not both. The verdict— death—was unanimous.

That night, as if actors in a grand Elizabethan drama, Drake and Doughty first received communion from Fletcher, and ". . . after this holy repast they dined, also at the same table, together, as cheerful in sobriety, as ever in their lives they had done aforetime: each cheering up the other, and taking their leave, by drinking each to other, as if some journey only had been in hand." And then the executioner showed up. Doughty was led to a corner of the island and beheaded. I admit I do not understand the Doughty story, but there it was, and now Drake wanted out of that depressing place, winter or not.

In perfect weather, *Pelican, Elizabeth,* and *Marigold* jogged down the Patagonian coast, sighting Cape Virgins, the entrance to Magellan's strait, on August 20. There Drake signaled his ships to gather that he might conduct a ceremony (Drake loved ceremony), part religious, part patriotic, with a dash of shrewd politics. Fletcher preached a sermon as the ships rode a long swell, banners snapping in the wind, and Drake affirmed his devotion to Her Majesty—any prizes or discoveries issuing from the voyage would belong to her. To close the ceremony, he officially renamed *Pelican* the *Golden Hind* after the image on Sir Christopher Hatton's family crest, a gesture to smooth over the fact that he had just beheaded Hatton's protégé. It would only work, of course, if Drake came home with treasure.

Then the three little ships set everything to the topsails and danced through the First Narrows at adrenaline pace, then the Second Narrows, reaching down the wide bay (Paso Ancho) past the present site of Punta Arenas, past Bahía Inútil (Useless Bay), and near Cape Froward, the last gasp of the continental mainland, the fleet anchored to take on wood and water. They also killed 3,000 (Magellanic) penguins, "a very good and wholesome victual," in one day. Penguins also suffered for the passing of European explorers. Magellan had called them sea geese—it was Fletcher who first called them "penguins," taking the Celtic word for the great auk, a flightless sea bird that would be driven to extinction in the late 19th century. The English sailors also met their first Fuegians—Alacaluf—near Cape Froward. Fletcher, noting their appearance, tools, and supposed way of life, was unique among European explorers in that he found the Canoe Indians "comely and harmless." They were "of a mean stature, but well set and compact in all their parts and limbs." And the mountains, wrote Fletcher, "arise with such tops and spires into the air, and of so rare a height, as they may be accounted among the wonders of the world."

Pigafetta's book is not a *Sailing Directions* or a cruising guide to the Strait of Magellan, and though Magellan's accomplishment in finding his way was seminal, Drake's was a brilliant piece of sailing and navigation. They reached the Pacific Ocean at Cape Desire on September 6, having transited the dreaded strait in seventeen days. Drake had big plans for a ceremony on the tip of Desolation Island, a bronze plaque already made, a speech prepared, no doubt, but it did not come off. He couldn't find safe anchorage before a heavy west wind forced him out of the strait, sailing northwest out into the Pacific. After about seventy-five miles on that heading, one of those terrible storms struck them dead in the face. Now they had no choice but to get away from land by reaching southwest under tiny scraps of sail.

Based on all available sources, Ray Aker drew a design, a "representative reconstruction," of the *Golden Hind* in 1974. He shows a vessel only eighty feet long on deck ("between perpendiculars," technically) with little "wetted surface," that part of the ship in the water, plus very high topsides and an excessively high stern castle above that. This would add up to a heartbreakingly top-heavy vessel that would have rolled hideously in a cross sea. And then there was the matter of her rig. Three-masted, she carried square sails on the forward two masts, that is, the foremast and the mainmast. On the stubby aftermost mast, the mizzen, she set a small triangular sail ("lateen-rigged," if you want to know), which would have helped steer the ship, but added little motive power. This was a common configuration, called a bark rig, but she carried only two relatively large sails on the fore- and mainmast. There's no versatility in that. When the wind got up, she had to take in her topsails, reducing her sail area by maybe 40 percent. If the wind continued to increase, she'd have to further reduce her sail area. It didn't take much wind to leave her naked and helpless. I recognize that certain people, for whom I have the utmost respect, would wince at the travesty of criticizing the *Golden Hind,* but it seems clear from basic tenets of marine architecture that Drake and others of the period made great voyages despite, not because of, their ships. Remarkably, however, these three hung together on this southwest heading, according to the captured Portuguese pilot, da Silva.

On September 15, the hard wind blew a hole in the cloud to expose the moon. Then, moments later, a total eclipse erased it from the sky. Sixteenth-century crews already chilled, fatigued, and in fear for their lives would have found a total eclipse rather unnerving. What did it mean? Was it a good omen or ill? A couple of days later the wind got up to a velocity none aboard had ever known before, "such as if the bowels of the earth had set all at liberty, or as if all the clouds under heaven had been called together to lay their force upon that one place," wrote Fletcher. "[W]e were rather looking for immediate death than hope for any delivery." Da Silva says "they took in all their sails, and lay driving till the last of September." On the twenty-eighth, within sight of the *Golden Hind*'s crew, a great wave overwhelmed little *Marigold* and drove her down with all hands. Fletcher claims to have heard the screams of drowning friends, but that seems unlikely.

It drove them all the way down to 57 South, sixty-one frigid miles below Cape Horn's latitude but far to the west, before the wind relented enough to allow the two survivors to set some sail and head back north. On October 7, they found an anchorage in a place now called Nelson Strait about sixty miles north of Magellan's strait, and there they hoped to lick their wounds, dry out, repair the storm damage, and kill a few thousand penguins. It wasn't to be. Another drastic storm tore in from the northwest and snapped Drake's anchor cable. But he managed in what must have been a consummate act of seamanship to get the *Golden Hind* sailing, when in lesser hands she would have died on the rocks to leeward. Drake would later name this place the Bay of Severing Friends.

Trusted old Captain Winter turned out not to be such a true friend, however. He had had it with this terrible place, totally lost his nerve. He sailed back into the strait, set signal fires, and waited, making no effort to reach the prearranged rendezvous point up in Peru. Then he turned tail and ran back to the Atlantic, returning to England after a slow trip. One can sympathize with his fear, less with his desertion, but then he began slandering Drake, holding up Doughty's execution as evidence that Drake was a mad tyrant. Besides, he was probably dead. It is storybook coincidence that the first circumnavigator and the second both executed members of their expeditions in the same remote bay, and that both were abandoned by captains who went home and lied about them.

For Drake, after his anchor line parted, survival must have seemed unlikely. The storm was too strong for him to shape his own destiny by running to sea. Instead, he was hurled along this extreme lee shore. "The impossibility of anchoring or spreading any sail, the most mad seas, the lee shores, the dangerous rocks, the contrary and most intolerable winds ... and the perils, all offer us such small likelihood of escaping destruction. ... For truly it was more likely that mountains should have been rent asunder from the top to the bottom, and cast headlong into the sea by these unnatural winds than any should survive," wrote Fletcher. Though he attributes survival to "special providence," it was more likely Drake and his crew's brilliance that saved the *Golden Hind*. In my opinion, Drake was at his best down here, overcoming the most difficult conditions in the entire circumnavigation and perhaps his entire career. Alone now, the *Hind* found a three-day respite when the storm abated long enough to anchor in Desolation Bay near 55 South, but the rejuvenated wind blew her out again on October 17. And again all she could do was run with the wind, apparently under bare poles, and try to keep herself off the rocks. The tension must have worn them to nubs, cold, constantly wet, no hot food—the usual Cape Horn miseries, plus scurvy, plus the constant presence of certain death close aboard on their port hand. Drake found another anchorage several days later in what Captain Cook would name Christmas Sound a little over 200 years on. They encountered friendly Alacaluf in canoes, and they traded Anjou cloth for fish. But still again the furious wind attacked from the northwest, forcing her out into the open to run southeast before it, but this would be the last time.

The land was changing. These were clearly islands, still high, bleak, and murderous—their character was the same as the others they'd scudded past, but they were not quite as high down here, nor so numerous. The land was fragmenting, no question about it, though it was impossible to understand the precise lay of it, because the wind was still howling, seas monstrous, and there was still death to leeward. Then, one likes to imagine, at the moment when the low murk parted and under shafts of that Fuegian light, endless and sharp, maybe even under rainbows, they saw what no one had imagined to exist.

"We fell in with the uttermost part of land towards the South Pole, and had certainly discovered how far the same doth reach southward from the coast of America. . . . The uttermost cape or headland of all these islands stands near in 56 degrees, without which there is no main or island to be seen to the southwards, but that the Atlantic Ocean and South Sea meet in a most large and free scope." The Yahgan knew about the "Drake Passage," had done for centuries, but that didn't matter, because they did not need ocean passages. They never projected their will across oceans in ships.

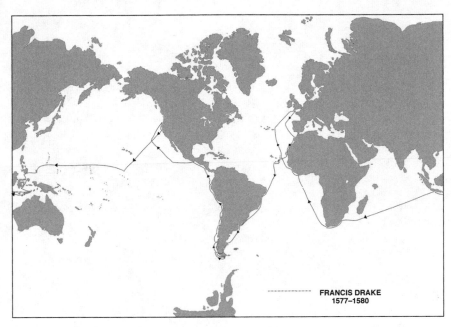

Map 5.2   Drake: the Second Circumnavigation

6

From Puerto Williams
to Caleta Martial

On that wild coast, near that dark and frowning land, during
that inky night relieved occasionally by fitful gleams of a
strange and peculiar light, with the large hail pelting upon
one like showers of bullets, I could not but feel deeply anxious.
  —**Captain Parker Snow,**
  A Two Years' Cruise in Tierra del Fuego

NEXT MORNING WE FOUND A SKEIN of ice coating *Pelagic*'s deck
and gear. Actually, the first man topside found it when he volunteered
to scout the weather, then tell the rest of us lurking in the warm,
closed cabin how to dress. His hard thud followed by a string of overhead invective suggested cold.

"Oh, I forgot to warn him," said Hamish, making toast on the
cabin heater.

The ice conspired with that dazzling light to turn simple chores
downright treacherous. We skated from handhold to handhold or
crawled around detaching the net of dock lines. It seemed abundantly
clear to me that the entire Dog Jaw Range, freshly dusted with snow,
had moved several miles closer to *Pelagic,* but I didn't mention it to
the others.

Eric, a bit bleary-eyed himself, poked his head out of his companionway to wish us bon voyage and, I suspect, to watch Hamish extricate himself from this cul-de-sac. (One of the charms of Puerto Williams as a small-boat harbor is that it's such a rotten small-boat harbor.) What I had taken for low tide yesterday was bottomless luxury. Now the *Micalvi* was high and dry and fully forlorn. The "harbor" had turned into a skinny creek with sprawling, naked mud flats on either hand and no room to turn around. We all stopped skating, stood coiling dock lines, to watch Hamish's next move.

He backed her stern away from *Philos*, but he had to stop halfway out or hit *Micalvi*. "Kate, would you lower the keel about three feet, please."

She went below to the power switch. It whirred.

"Good. Stop there."

"Oh, I see," said Dick, making up a spring line.

I didn't see.

Hamish backed the keel into the mud until she came to a gentle stop. He spun the wheel hard over, and then goosed the throttle in sharp, short spurts. *Pelagic* rotated on her keel in the only space wide enough to do so, until he had her bow pointing toward the exit.

"Kate, please raise the keel."

The electric winch whirred briefly, and we were afloat again just like that, no fuss, bother, or raised voices. It's always pleasing when the guy in charge demonstrates why he belongs there.

"Look at that—" Hamish pointed away to port.

It was the yellow boat. She was lying on her side in the mud ten yards from the nearest water. Hamish edged as close as he dared without joining her.

The salty singlehander's face popped up over the cockpit combing. He climbed up the savage list, hugging the lifelines on the high side. Wearing those same antique yellow rubber foulies, he crawled out onto the gunwale and hung his yellow boots over the side. No, thank you very much, he said, he was not in need of assistance. You could tell he'd never accepted assistance. He'd die first, like Armand. I've sailed with guys like him before, masochists or dramatists who always do things the hard way. There was no proper chart of the harbor, but there was plenty of local knowledge tied to the *Micalvi* that morning. He didn't want any. He'd rather go aground on his own.

"Keep to the starboard side of the sound," Hamish shouted at him.

He cupped his hand behind his ear and cocked his chin.

Hamish tried again, with the same response, then twice more before we left him. It was never clear if the old salt understood or not, but he'd have plenty of time on the slant—amazingly, the tide was still ebbing—to ponder the navigation.

Done with officialdom, we turned east into the Beagle Channel. The sky was cobalt blue, cloudless, endless. A light, cool breeze slid down the sides of the mountains on the Tierra del Fuego side setting up little wavelets, and the magic light glinted on their facets. The temperature was climbing into the forties. If this weather predominated, the flat places on the berm of the Beagle would be studded with resorts and holiday homes, but it doesn't. We hoisted the mainsail just for show and sheeted it amidships so it wouldn't flap as we motored along the south shore of Gable Island.

This is a strange chunk of land. About twenty miles square, Gable Island partially plugs the Beagle Channel, squeezing it down at it narrowest point to about a mile, the MacKinlay Pass. Gable gets its name from the formations on its western shore, which look like contiguous, peaked roofs in a planned community. The resemblance is uncanny, more so because each "gable" is identical in size and shape to its neighbor. But ice and erosion are responsible for the island. Some 9,000 years ago, the retreating glacier, having carved the Beagle Channel, paused perhaps for centuries before moving on, leaving a spasm of gravel and sand in a hump. Then the west wind in concert with rain and ice began its work, scouring off the softer material, leaving pointed eaves, but why they're so regular, identical, is not fully known, another mystery in a mysterious land. Gable Island is part of the Bridges family's Estancia Harberton. To the Yahgan, Gable Island was the center of the universe. A long time ago the moon fell into the sea, and its displacement caused a great flood. Only Gable Island remained afloat, and its residents and their animals were the only survivors on earth. Then when the moon rose from the sea, the water subsided, and Gable settled back to its original position. "From these, the world was peopled again." Lucas Bridges warns that you had to be careful with Yahgan myths, because the natives tended to tell the missionaries what they wanted to hear.

As we passed just shy of the island's eastern end, Hamish explained that this was the point where the Beagle Channel tides meet. On the flood tide, water flows eastward from the western stretches of the channel and simultaneously westward from the open water east of Navarino. And vice versa on the ebb. (In proper nautical usage, wind is designated by the direction from which it blows, whereas a current is designated by the direction in which it flows, which makes sense when one thinks in terms of what a sailor wants to know about both forces.) We rode a building ebb eastward toward the sloping shoulder of Navarino, where we'd turn south toward the Horn.

Just before the land began its trend southward, around the corner from a high, hook-shaped headland called Punta Eugenia, Hamish directed us through a scattering of islets, some thickly forested, others mere rock piles, that seemed to have exploded from the side of the big island. Cormorants and Magellanic penguins stood on the rocks shoulder to shoulder in their segregated flocks watching *Pelagic* pass without fear or interest.

I happened to be steering, but I could see no way through the maze, a dead end.

"Come right about twenty degrees. The channel's nearest shore."

I pointed his boat that way, and just when it looked as though we were about to run up on the rocks, the opening, about the width of a country road, revealed itself. This, said Hamish, easing back on the throttle, was a favorite site of the Yahgan, and it was easy to see why, sheltered and safe even in a serious westerly blow. I spun the wheel this way and that, dodging little islands, reefs, and sunkers at his direction, heading deeper into the side of Navarino, into the forest. Nothing of the Beagle was visible and little of the sky. Only local knowledge could get us through here. The Chilean chart I'd bought at the naval station showed these islets and skerries about the size of fat periods and commas, useless for safe piloting, but Hamish knew the way. It felt cool and soft back there, like late summer in the Adirondacks. One could stay awhile. With a single screw-up, one would stay for a long time.

Suddenly several of us saw him at once, a shirtless man edging along an old rockslide at the water's edge. Some of us might have blurted, "Yahgan!" but just then another man—wearing a Mickey Mouse T-shirt—materialized from the dark thicket and joined the first, and together they wrested a large wire-mesh crab trap from the shallows. We saw them before they saw us. Their eyes went wide for an instant, then they looked away. We waved, they didn't. Both men were dripping wet.

"Where's their boat?" David wondered.

"Probably don't have one. There's a road from Puerto Williams—well, sort of a road—but it ends about five miles back. They probably bushwhacked from there."

We watched them in silence, hard toilers, old before their time, doing what the Yahgan did except that they were Chilean, until we turned the next corner. When we emerged from the little labyrinth through another secret channel, we followed Navarino's coast south toward open water. We motored between the big island and Isla Picton, where in 1850 a zealot named Allen Gardiner tried to establish a Christian mission. The Yahgan, unmoved by the simple truths of Christianity, hounded Gardiner for his stuff and drove him east along the Fuegian coast to a desolate cove where even the Yahgan didn't go. Sprawled on the cold moonstone beach or huddled in a nearby cave, Gardiner and his followers starved to death in a state of religious ecstasy.

I turned a little south of west for Paso Goree, the *Beagle*'s favorite anchorage, between the rump of the Navarino walrus and Isla Lennox, the southernmost of the trio that had nearly caused the war.

But Hamish waved me off. "Don't do that. Let's go between Lennox and Isla Nueva."

After I'd made the turn I asked him why, it being the most direct route toward the Horn, and plenty deep.

"Paso Goree has always been prohibited."

"Don't you trust our *zarpe?*"

". . . Let's not push it so early in the trip."

The chart showed Paso Richmond between Lennox and Nuevo to be about eight miles wide, but it also showed that squiggly-line symbol for kelp claiming half that distance. The brown leathery leaves (it's a form of algae) undulated ominously in the southerly swell. The stunning beauty of this place on a clear, fine day numbs outlanders to its dangers. And of course that's one of the comfortable aspects of not being in charge, you can give in, let it take you where it will.

"Keep Lennox close aboard on starboard," said the captain.

I was still bewildered by the scale of things. I couldn't make the chart fit the visible world. The twin peaks on Isla Lennox were charted at 250 meters, but, naked above the tree line, they seemed to tower like the Alps. At the southeast corner of the island, what appeared on the chart to be merely a clump of rock turned into an island (Isla Luff) about the size of a Manhattan block with its own dense forest, and we passed between Luff and Lennox through a channel wide enough for an aircraft carrier if the helmsman took care.

We headed out into open water for the first time, Bahía Nassau, about thirty-five miles from Isla Hermite, where we planned to stop for the night within an easy shot of the Horn. Weather permitting.

"There's Staten Island," said Hamish pointing away off our port side—

What? How could we be seeing Staten Island from here? Inconceivable. Yet there it was, plain and distinct and impossible to confuse with any other place even if you've never seen it before. Anyway, there's nothing else out there in the east beyond the tip of Tierra del Fuego except Staten Island (like the borough of New York City, Staten Island was named by Dutch explorers for the national governing body, the States-General). I ducked below long enough to measure the distance from our position to the nearest point of land, Cabo San Bartolomé—forty-six nautical miles! I returned topside to gape with the others at the spires of naked rock, the slanting sun glinting on their snowcapped points like some hallucination that would vanish if we took our eyes from it.

I like Richard Walter's passionate description of Staten Island. He was chaplain and chronicler on Admiral George Anson's debacle of a voyage around the Horn in 1740 to attack the Spanish treasure ships along the Pacific coast. Thanks to widespread corruption in the Royal Navy, Anson had been lumbered with rotten, leaking ships provisioned with putrid horse and pig meat still bristling with hair, crewed by invalids, malcontents, and the insane. It may have been the worst expedition in the history of Cape Horn. About 200 of 500 men who sailed from England were dead of scurvy before they'd even reached the Horn. As they passed through the Strait of Le Maire, the clouds parted, and Walter saw what we were seeing: "I cannot but remark that though Tierra del Fuego [is] entirely barren and desolate, yet this island far surpasses it in the wildness and horror of its appearance; it is seemingly entirely composed of inaccessible rocks, without the least mixture of earth or mould between them. These rocks terminate in a vast number of ragged points . . . surrounded on every side with frightful precipices, and often overhung in an astonishing manner. Nothing can be imagined more savage and gloomy than the whole aspect of this coast."

That's what Eric, the studious captain of *Philos,* meant when he said we'd "see much that is sublime" down by the Horn. And that's the language of the sublime, *wildness, horror, frightful, astonishing,* nature seen in the light of the human emotions it evokes, as if nature were art. Yet the exaggerated, sinister appearance of the place, those dreadful rock fangs, seems to out-clamor cool-headed scientific explanations for the nature of things. A place so improbable and extreme couldn't be real. It was improbable that we could see the thing at all, fifty miles away. Yet we could see individual convolutions in the rock strata as if it were close aboard. The very air down here is improbable.

But that's part of what's wondrous about the Horn and its environs. Everything is exaggerated and extreme, not only visually, but nautically, too. Take Staten Island's geography. Trending east-to-west, thirty-four miles long, never more than nine wide, Staten Island and the eastern toe of Tierra del Fuego form the edges of the sixteen-mile-wide Strait of Le Maire. That places it directly athwart the course of all ships approaching the Horn from Europe and North America. Most of the time Staten Island, its 823-meter peaks, and the sea for miles around it were covered by cloud (ours was a rare, privileged sighting). Ships, often approaching at high speed in the strong westerlies, hadn't seen the sun or any other navigation star for weeks on end. Yet there was this lethal thing ringed with uncharted offshore reefs somewhere ahead in the dead murk. During the heyday of Cape Horn sailing, from the middle of the 19th century to, say, the Great Depression, about ten ships a year died on Staten Island, though some of these were abandoned there after incurring fatal injuries rounding the Horn.

The southbound captain had a decision to make, loop out around Staten Island to the east in the open Atlantic or duck through the Strait of Le Maire, a shortcut. In these hostile waters it was smart to take the shortcuts, decreasing exposure time—unless it was stupid. If he couldn't see the island, he had no choice but to turn left and stand out to sea. Yet even if he knew where he was, even if he could see right down the strait, it would still be suicide to enter on anything but a fair wind and a strong one at that. This was no place to be becalmed, at the mercy of the current. Four times each day the Atlantic Ocean and the Southern Ocean take turns trying to squeeze through the sixteen-mile-wide constriction. *Sailing Directions* says that the tidal current can run seven knots, but Hamish thinks that's a conservative call. He thinks ten knots is more like it; that's the speed of a rushing mountain river. When too much water tries to crowd through too small an opening, the current compresses accordion fashion, and waves stack up one behind the other. A wind blowing against that current further impedes its flow, significantly increasing the size of the waves while shortening the distance between the crests. We've all seen those distinctive short, steep, nasty waves in bays and sounds when wind blows against current, but they're minuscule compared to the monsters that get up in the Strait of Le Maire when wind and current oppose one another. That water is infamous for giant waves that just stand there (called, in fact, standing waves) in a terrible, temporary equilibrium. Nothing is safe in those conditions.

Hamish, who'd taken the wheel so the rest of us could gawk at the magic island and imagine the conditions in the strait, told us that only once in his sailing career he'd feared for his life, and it was right out there. He and Novak, returning *Pelagic* to Ushuaia after her annual winter refit in Brazil, decided to slip through the strait riding a favorable wind. But they got the tide slightly wrong. I can't remember what direction the wind was blowing or whether the tide was ebbing or flooding (it floods north and ebbs south), but they were running in opposite directions. Suddenly, he said, this boat was dropping over the faces of standing waves the size of suburban rooflines. "Bloody *falling*," he said. "Never seen anything like it. . . . Of course, there isn't anything like it." Once into that crazy cauldron, there was no way out. Laird and Novak couldn't flee because they couldn't turn the boat. Turning would have left her side-on to the waves, and they would have capsized her in an instant. The only choice was to carry on, keeping her bow into the waves, letting her plunge, hoping she'd hold together.

"You see what a tank she is," said Hamish. "She trembled like a toy. I swear, I thought we were going to lose her. We took turns at the helm—you couldn't steer in those conditions for more than a half hour at a time—but we were getting tired. Beginning to make mistakes."

They managed to edge her to starboard a boat length or two at a time between the crests, until after hours of fear and fatigue, they reached shelter on the Tierra del Fuego side near Cape San Diego. "But I'll tell you we were deeply shaken."

A place that shivers the timbers of this tank and seamen of their caliber is no place for the likes of us, yet it's alluring, too, these extremes. One wants to experience them. A little misery and some sublime marine terror is one thing, a watery grave quite another, however. A shaft of light settled on the island for a moment, a celestial pin-spot turning the peaks golden, and then it shut off abruptly as the last quadrant of the sun dipped beneath the western mountains, a flair of natural showmanship for which we felt grateful and privileged.

Hamish tapped the top of the wheel, the traditional signal for someone else to take it. Tim stepped up in his hat with the Elmer Fudd earflaps.

"Two-two-zero," Hamish said, ducking below to consider his night approach to the Wollaston Islands and to choose a harbor. I followed him down. We'd decided, given this spate of exquisite weather, to continue on across Bahía Nassau and get ourselves within a half day's shot of the Horn. If fair weather held through tomorrow, we'd be able to land. We spread out my Chilean chart on the nav desk. Hamish put the points of his dividers on a cleft in the east side of Isla Wollaston: "Bahía Scourfield. That's an easy in at night, but we could probably get closer. . . . Maybe to Caleta Martial down here on Isla Herschel. Not bad in the dark. But here's the only problem—" He pointed to the spot three-quarters of an inch north of Caleta Martial. I could see the problem. It was called Paso Bravo.

Map 6.1   From Puerto Williams to Caleta Martial

Holding our southerly course, 220 degrees, over the next thirty miles of open water (four to five hours) we'd enter Paso Bravo, an exquisite natural trap, about midnight. Bravo is a funnel-shaped strait between the east side of Wollaston and the west side of its smaller neighbor, Isla Freycinet. The mouth is just over a mile wide, but it narrows quickly, and at the spout the land closes down to a couple of hundred yards. And if that weren't enough, there's an islet called Adriana plopped right in the middle of the constriction. Of course there are no buoys, lights, or other visual aids.

"A bit dodgy," said Hamish. "But doable. I'll just make sure the radar's participating." He switched it on. "We're going to need this." It seemed to be working. "Some of the charts are wrong, you know."

"Wrong?"

"I'll show you when we get down in here around Isla Hermite. Land's in the wrong place. The charted position and the actual position, by the GPS, don't agree."

"By a lot?"

"Two miles in some places. Also, there are magnetic anomalies out near False Cape Horn. The compass goes wandering off about forty degrees. No kidding. That's another reason I use the radar almost exclusively. All high and steep-sided, the islands make dependable radar targets."

"Tea?" said Kate, offering up a tray to the guys topside, then to Hamish and me. "I'll send up some cookies in a minute," she assured us. There are advantages to fair-weather sailing. You don't get tea and cookies of an evening fighting the standing waves in the Strait of Le Maire.

I put on another thermal layer, then the heavy-duty foulies, and took my tea topside to watch the Gulf of Nassau go by. The others were sitting in a circle in the cockpit hunched against the deepening cold, holding hot teacups in both hands. Soon they'd file below one by one for more gear, but now they were enjoying the solitude and the fellowship, talking quietly about the old salts and the first explorers.

"I mean, look at this place. Imagine how tense you'd be if you didn't know where the hell you were."

"I'm tense and I know where I am."

The Gulf of Nassau lies exposed for forty miles and more in the west all the way to the Hardy Peninsula. To the east there is no land at all the whole world round. None to the southeast, either, except Antarctica. The barely sailable trickle of wind had faded to a gasp, and with Hamish's permission, we cranked up the diesel. A long, gunmetal-gray swell rolled in from that direction, and *Pelagic* yawed and rolled in a funny combination. Tim was trying to find the best throttle setting and bow angle to dampen the motion. Ahead an undeterminable distance, sea and sky faded together.

"It looks like the end of the world."

Underdressed after her stint at the stove, Kate stepped out of the companionway, shivered, and returned below in a single motion.

"The Indians came this way, right? In canoes."

"All the way to the Horn." But I wondered if they often did so, if the pickings in seals and otters warranted regular open-water crossings of Golfo Nassau. I made a note to consult Lucas Bridges. I'd brought a copy of *Uttermost Part of the Earth,* and there were a couple more in the ship's library. It's impossible to experience this place without thinking of those vanished natives and their way of life.

Kate returned topside dressed now for a dash up the Beardmore Glacier. Geared up for the same cold the Yahgan met naked, we'd become anonymous in our red foulies with hoods pulled close around our faces. We fell silent.

"Hey, who's over-revving this vessel?" Hamish called from the nav desk.

Kate shined her light on the tachometer—

"I'm right on 1400," Tim said.

"No, you aren't. You're 100 over. . . . Almost."

"Jesus, he can feel eighty rpms?"

"He can feel an insect walk across the deck when he's sound asleep," said Kate.

"Call it—" Tim said, throttling back.

"There."

"Happy, Captain?"

"Deliriously."

The haze that had materialized with full dark suddenly lifted— maybe it had never been there at all, another atmospheric trick. The taut horizon distinguished water from air, and the sky filled with stars we'd never seen before except on charts. A strange, indistinct brightness arced over our masthead light like a scattering of luminescent powder—

Dick stood up on the side deck and looked aloft. "I wondered if we'd see them."

"What? See what?"

"The Magellanic Clouds."

"What's that?"

"Well, maybe it's only one cloud. I can't tell. It's another galaxy, you know, that orbits the Milky Way. It's only visible in the Southern Hemisphere."

We all stood up, went forward for a better view.

"There are two, actually, the Large and Small Magellanic Clouds."

As we stared, they seemed to expand, smudging the entire southern sky with dusty white light.

Hamish came topside. "You're seeing the Clouds? Oh yes, wonderful." He joined us, peering up nearly vertically, losing our balance every now and then in the swells, scrabbling for handholds.

"Do you see two clouds, Hamish, or just the one?"

"I don't know. I can never tell."

They are indeed two separate galaxies, I later affirmed from a volume in the *Pelagic* public library. The Large Magellanic Cloud, which contains fifteen billion stars, is nearer to earth, 179,000 light-years against the smaller's 200,000 light-years. They were first noted by a Persian astronomer, Al Sufi, in 946, but they were largely unknown in the West until Magellan. But there's only a fleeting reference in Pigafetta's *Narrative* to "small stars clustered together." The clouds were first studied in a scientific way by the astronomer John Herschel, who had so deeply influenced Charles Darwin during his young Cambridge days before the *Beagle*. The island we were heading for on the far side of Paso Bravo was named Isla Herschel during the first *Beagle* expedition.

It dawned on us then that we were seeing the Southern Cross just below the arc of the Magellanic Clouds. Most of us had never seen either before, and again we stood staring in silence.

It was nearing midnight when land appeared ahead, first a single ragged black point rising over the horizon, then another away to starboard, the high points of the Wollaston Islands. The next time I looked, fifteen minutes later, solid black land loomed in irregular clumps against the lighter sky until land entirely blocked our way. On a heading of 195 magnetic (there's an east variation of 13 degrees), the heading we'd held all night, we seemed to be going like a freight train toward a mountain range. It's remarkable how the sensation of speed increases when a boat is approaching a featureless coast at night. The mood changes.

I slipped below to plot our position for my own edification, and when I returned topside, I listened to Kate and Dick talking about what a suicidal move it would be to attempt Paso Bravo in the dark if we couldn't know precisely where we were. But we could. We're essentially the first generation of sailors in the history of ships who have the luxury of a dead-accurate fix at the press of a button whenever we want it. Our global positioning system knows where it is on the surface of the earth within a few yards, and reports it to us in the age-old language of latitude and longitude. A machine that knows where it is from moment to moment also knows how fast it's moving—over the bottom. We are, therefore, the first generation in thousands to know where the current is setting us without visual references. Drake, FitzRoy, Cook, and the other artists would never have attempted to nail a narrow cut like Paso Bravo in the dark. And we probably wouldn't be doing it if we had to rely on the GPS alone, since, as Hamish said, the chart isn't all that accurate. In other seas, the navigator can be fairly certain that the land and other obstructions are accurately charted. But you can't bet the boat on it down here. A spot-on position fix isn't much use if the land is drawn in the wrong place. The radar would show us exactly where the land was located.

We were in the jaws now, and everyone was alert, bright-eyed, standing lookout for dangers impossible to see as the black cliffs closed in around us on port, starboard, and dead ahead. We had to crane our necks now to see the remaining sliver of lighter sky, still smudged by Magellan's galaxies. The navigator grows edgy in these circumstances, pencil tapping, now that he's committed to this hole in the wall; doubts can cloud his logic. What if this is the wrong hole? What if this turns out to be a cove, not a channel? Only known things, numbers and angles applied with practiced technique, can assuage the anxiety. In Magellan's day, sailors suspected that navigators practiced necromancy, for how else could they know their way? I was glad not to be responsible for tonight's nav.

Hamish called something from below.

David leaned into the doghouse to relay instructions from the captain. "He said slow down."

Driving, Kate pulled off several hundred rpm.

Dick nudged me and nodded toward the masthead. Above it, in the little patch of sky still visible, appeared the Southern Cross like an emblem of something if we could only read it, but almost immediately the mountains, narrowing, squeezed it off. I went below to look at reality on the radar screen, since the view on deck encouraged superstition. Night, fog, necromancy meant nothing to the microwaves. Trying not to breathe down the real navigator's neck, I reconciled the radar image with the charted shape of Paso Bravo. Microwaves can't see around corners, so the narrow southern exit to the channel was still invisible. . . . Maybe there was none after all.

"Tell them to come right ten degrees." Hamish meant to clear his angle of approach, take it right down the middle.

I relayed the order to the helm, then came back to watch the course adjustment take shape on the screen. Hamish was using dividers to measure distances right off the screen—nothing is as accurate as a radar range if you read it right. He drew circles of position on the chart.

"Now come back left those same ten degrees."

When I returned to the screen after passing the message, I saw the bottleneck gap at the bottom of the channel about one hundred yards ahead, and we were on it. All we had to do was hold our present course. He'd set it up beautifully. We had almost reached the open water of Canal Franklin when we struck bottom. Hard.

That sound is appalling. A high, hollow thunk with the pitch of finality about it. Now I don't want to seem an expert on groundings, saying that the sound causes every muscle in the body to contract simultaneously, adrenaline gushing. Then everything turns sharp-edged with a terrible clarity, and events slow as the crucial question—*How bad is it?*—floods in. Has the inrush begun? Are my feet still dry? It took a moment, while the dreadful sound was still bouncing around the inside of the hull, to understand that Hamish was gone. I recalled a blur shooting up the companionway that must have been him.

I snatched a headlamp from a hook on the bulkhead above the nav station, scurried forward into the cold workshop compartment, and pulled up the floorboards to look for water. There was none; her innards were dusty dry. It would take a torpedo to hole *Pelagic*'s hull. But her hull hadn't hit, I realized, because we were still moving, or more precisely because we hadn't come to a spine-snapping halt. I was aboard a thirty-five-foot race boat one morning motoring out of a little Long Island Sound harbor when the sleepy helmsman ran out of the familiar channel and up on a rock ledge. An instantaneous stop, no skidding, even from a slow speed, tends to hurl people down like tulips in a hurricane. That had not happened to *Pelagic*. She'd run right over the rock—

I went topside. Kate stood clutching the wheel with both hands, eyes flashing in the red glow of the compass light, and when I clapped her lightly on the shoulder, she giggled and shook her head. The others were all crowded onto the foredeck, leaning outboard stabbing at the waterline with beams of white light as they moved aft, chattering, laughing at their own dark jokes, because they knew they'd find no holes, dents, or dings. It was clear to us now what had happened. The keel had struck a deeply submerged rock, and the impact had kicked the keel back up into its box, as designed, harmlessly. Had the keel been fixed permanently to the bottom of the boat in typical fashion, one of two things would have happened, both bad. The keel would have been torn off completely, leaving a big hole in the bottom, or else it would have been driven up through the cabin floor, making a somewhat smaller hole in the bottom. But even if neither of these worst-cases had obtained, *Pelagic* would have come to that vicious sudden stop, and only the lucky would have escaped injury.

"There was only one rock, right?" asked Hamish. "We only struck one."

"No," said Kate, "I heard two thunks."

"I think the second was the keel crashing up into the box. Uh, would you kill that headlamp, please?"

"Oh, sorry." I'd wondered why people were recoiling when I looked at them.

"You know what we should do, Kate, we should go back and find the rock with the keel and plot it on the chart—"

"Nooo—"

"Then we'd have the discover's right to name it. Pelagic Rock. . . . Sorry about that untoward bit, gentlemen."

We didn't mind.

"You know, I've been through this pass a dozen times in daylight and never hit that thing. I was just ten feet one side or the other."

"Where am I going," Kate asked. "Could I have a heading, please?"

"Martial. It's right over there—" Hamish pointed at another high, black mass some unknowable distance south.

It was 0200 and, without the heat of emergency, cold again.

"I've never been in there in the dark," Kate insisted.

"I can see by your glare that you want a heading." He put his arm around her and said something private in her ear. "Here, I'll take it."

Caleta Martial on the east end of Isla Hermite lay only three miles away across the narrowest part of Canal Franklin, but it took two hours before we had *Pelagic* securely attached to the bottom. Bleary-eyed but unready for sleep, we slouched around the ship's table, and after passing a bottle of Bermudan rum, Dick proposed a toast to lifting keels. The conversation shifted fluidly, fragmented and reformed, settling on near-disasters and marine absurdities we could laugh at because they were past. So I didn't realize at first when Hamish was talking in his understated mode about this young Norwegian sailor called Jarli, a friend of his and Kate's, that he was missing. It wasn't going to be a funny story, we realized. We discontinued our own to listen.

Kate and Hamish had met Jarli in Ushuaia. He was just eighteen, and, Kate said, he looked like the Hollywood version of a Viking. In this twenty-six-foot cheap plastic boat powered by weak, blown-out sails and a tiny outboard mounted on a rickety stern bracket, he'd sailed down the east coast of South America to Ushuaia. He meant to cross the Drake Passage bound for the Antarctic Peninsula in that toy boat "to see the birds and seals," as he put it in his charmingly accented English. He'd picked up a young California surfer dude, Dave, who had no sailing experience, hanging around the docks looking for adventure. After politely thanking old hands like Hamish and the Poncets on *Damian II* for their warnings against it, Jarli and Dave sailed south.

Pelagic and *Damian* happened to be heading for the same general vicinity, and their captains had arranged a radio check-in schedule with Jarli. That he hadn't checked in or responded to calls didn't surprise Laird and Poncet, because Jarli had only a soggy handheld VHF. Maybe he'd changed his plans or the weather had changed them for him—it was blowing forty knots when *Pelagic* crossed the Drake—or maybe something had broken to force him back to Ushuaia, or maybe he was having a grand time in Antarctica, hidden from radio waves by an iceberg or a rocky penguin rookery. Six weeks passed, and when *Pelagic* returned to Ushuaia, Kate and Hamish searched the harbor and asked around town, but no one had seen Jarli.

"You mean you think he's dead?" asked Jonathan right to the point.

Hamish shrugged, paused, and said, "I wouldn't want to cross the Solent in that bloody Clorox bottle."

Kate peered silently into her empty glass.

We straggled to bed after that, though several of us detoured topside. We saw black islands and the Magellanic Clouds, but the Southern Cross had set. We soon began to shiver.

"A twenty-six-foot boat, imagine," said Tim, "with an outboard motor on a bracket."

"Might as well take a gun to your head."

"Maybe he made it," I said.

No one thought so.

For those waiting ashore, death at sea came in three stages. First there was *overdue*. Vessel such-and-such bound from somewhere around the Horn to somewhere else has not arrived. There was still hope; *overdue* was an official request for information. Had anyone seen such-and-such vessel? Time passed. If no word of her reached her owners or insurers, she would be posted *missing*. There was still a whiff of hope—many ships posted missing down by the Horn turned up, sometimes even at their destination. But most did not. If silence persisted for another chunk of time, then some clerk at Lloyds would rise from his stool, climb the stepladder up to the big blackboard, chalk her name and add the last word to her life: *lost*. Now she was officially dead, with all hands. The Drake Passage swallowed 300-foot steel windjammers in one wave, and when it passed the ship was simply gone, an absence on the surface of the sea.

"Maybe you have more right to go off and kill yourself down here than where we come from," someone said, his teeth chattering.

There has of late been much talk in boating circles (and mountaineering) about responsibility, because if you go missing in other seas, someone is going to search for you, perhaps at risk to their own lives, and therefore you have a responsibility to your would-be rescuers. You own the broad right to commit reckless acts in boats only if they don't endanger others. Trouble is, people expect to be rescued. That wasn't an issue down here. No one would launch a search for Jarli.

A faint glow was visible in the east when we went below.

7

A Glorious Failure

For many and various reasons, it is advisable that this commerce must be conducted by one administration, because if it is left in the hands of a number of companies, then this promising trade will come to naught.

—The Old Company of Amsterdam, 1601

CAPTAIN WILLEM C. SCHOUTEN, A CRUSTY, barrel-bodied Dutchman of few words, wrote this in his log for January 29, 1616: "Cape Hoorn in 57-48. Rounded 8 P.M." That was the first true rounding in history. Drake had already reached the Pacific via the Strait of Magellan when he was blown down to the Horn. He discovered the Horn, but he did not use it as a route from the Atlantic to the Pacific. That was forty-two years earlier. If this was the most significant geographical discovery since Magellan's *paso,* why did it take most of a half century for anyone to make use of it?

Before she knighted him aboard the *Golden Hind,* Queen Elizabeth and Francis Drake spent six hours in private conversation about his circumnavigation. Drake probably waxed eloquent over his exploits, but no record exists, and sadly the personal log presented to Elizabeth has been lost forever. That isn't altogether surprising. Not only was it an incriminating document, it was full of state secrets—geographic knowledge still meant geopolitical power. Elizabeth grasped immediately the strategic significance of the open-water backdoor route to the riches of Chile, Peru, and later the East. After Drake pillaged fat Spanish treasure ships in the Pacific, the viceroy of Peru had ordered one Pedro Sarmiento to establish a fort/colony to plug the strait against English pirates, and the subsequent name, Port Famine, suggests his degree of success. But they couldn't plug an open ocean. Elizabeth swore everyone to secrecy. Publication of *The World Encompassed* was delayed until 1628, fifty years after the event.

The secret leaked, however, because sailors talk. To tell the story of where they'd been, the wondrous things they had seen, the great deeds performed, was part of the point of going. We know that the great talker Drake himself visited the Netherlands in 1586 to buy Dutch ships in which he meant to attack Cádiz, the famous "beard-singeing" raid. There is no evidence that he told anyone, but he must have been sorely tempted as the tavern evenings wore on. Hadn't he done what Diaz had done—discovered that a great continent had a bottom around which ships could sail? Maybe Drake held his tongue. But there is no reason to think his crewmen on the *Golden Hind* were so circumspect over dice and rum in seamen's haunts: "I'll tell you something no one knows if you promise to keep it under your hat. Down at the bottom of the New World, there is another ocean, and there's none like it for storms and seas and cold in the whole world. But if you're as tough and brave as me, there's treasure beyond dreams on the other side." Among those who listened was a canny old Dutch monopolist named Isaac Le Maire.

Crotchety, vindictive, a man of seventy with unstoppable energy, the father of twenty-two children, Le Maire had been one of the founders of the Vereenigde Oost-indische Compagnie, the famous Dutch East India Company, or simply, the VOC. By 1600 Le Maire and the other members had recognized that the East Indies spice trade was a very untidy business. Everyone knew by then that cloves, nutmeg, cinnamon, and pepper could be grown almost everywhere from the Strait of Malacca to the Ceram Sea, hundreds of islands and countless cultures. With so many sources available, trading companies sprang up all over the Low Countries and headed East (via the Cape Of Good Hope), and as the market fragmented, profits withered. Old Isaac and his colleagues knew when a monopoly was indicated. With the Spanish attending to their New World plunder, Portuguese power withering in the Indies, and the English capable only of scattered acts of piracy, the real threat to Dutch control of the spice trade came from other Dutchmen. In 1602 the VOC had convinced the government, an oligarchy of merchants, to grant it an exclusive patent that read: No Dutch ship that is not a member of the VOC is permitted to sail to the East Indies either via the Cape of Good Hope or the Strait of Magellan. That about covered it, they figured; if you couldn't go east around Africa or west through the strait, then you couldn't get there at all.

Isaac Le Maire soon fell out with company policy. He wanted the VOC to seize control of the strait and use it as a base from which to attack Spanish holdings on the Pacific side of South America. Like Drake, he bitterly hated the Spanish. Further, he wanted the VOC to chase them out of the Pacific entirely. An appealing notion, the directors agreed, but that might be going a bit too far. It wasn't that they had any compunction about conquest, no different in that from the Portuguese, Spanish, or English, but to try to control both sides of the Pacific seemed a distraction from the company's purpose, which was to make a lot of money in the spice trade. They voted him down on hemispheric domination.

But Isaac Le Maire took things personally. His colleagues had rejected his position, and so, to Isaac, it seemed justified and reasonable to ruin the VOC in return. He sold his stock short and spread rumors that the company teetered on the cusp of insolvency to induce panic selling, after which he tried to buy up enough of the undervalued stock to gain control of the company, a prescient concept. The VOC was the first publicly held corporation in the modern sense, and Le Maire might have succeeded in this, the first hostile takeover, if the States-General had not stepped in to prohibit short selling. Not about to leave it at that, Isaac formed his own company, and with dreams of turning the Pacific Ocean into an arm of the Zuider Zee, he sent voyagers in search of new routes to the East. He seems to have convinced himself during this time that a passage south of Magellan's strait actually did exist. And that was how he would stick it to the VOC, right through their own loophole: He would use neither the eastern route around Africa nor the Strait of Magellan. He would use this altogether new route—and what could they say to that?

The Dutch never really wanted to participate directly in the East
Indies spice trade. Except for the profits—a reliable 100 percent—it
had no desirable features. Cloves and nutmeg from the Bandas and
Moluccas, pepper from Sumatra, coffee from Mocha and Java—
those places were halfway around the world; it could easily take
three years to send a message from Amsterdam and receive a reply
from Jakarta, which meant that the directors at home had no control over day-to-day business. Moreover, the East was different from
the New World with its primitive savages and vast wilderness. The
East, part of the Old World, was home to venerable, sophisticated
cultures, at least as highly skilled as Europeans at playing both ends
against the middle. These sultans and pashas thought nothing of
selling the same nutmeg, clove, or coffee crop two or three times
over, whether they owned it or not. The trade was dazzlingly complex—Indians, Chinese, Indonesians, Arabs, all with their own
products and wildly fluctuating prices—and utterly corrupt. Only
heavy-duty naval power could begin to regulate the spice trade, and
so overhead was sky-high. Plus, the climate and the mosquitoes
turned white men into hollow husks or killed them outright from a
half dozen different fevers. For a long time, however, the Dutch
profited handsomely from the spice trade without ever having to
leave Europe.

Skilled sailors working the finest ships in Europe, the Dutch im-
ported and distributed timber, amber, fish, furs, tallow, grain, and
everything else produced in Russia, Germany, and Scandinavia. In
Portugal they traded these northern things for spices from the East,
which they sold back in Northern Europe at huge profit. Both Portugal and Spain did their banking in the Low Countries, and in that way
the Dutch gained a cut of the profits from the Spanish West Indies as
well as the Portuguese East Indies. Dutch ports that had been drowsy
inland villages before the Atlantic had filled up the Zuider Zee were
now the busiest, wealthiest, and most cosmopolitan seaports in
Northern Europe. But then came the Reformation and then the
Counter-Reformation to ruin the arrangement.

In 1516, Charles V, the Holy Roman Emperor, inherited the throne of Spain by dint of his father's marriage to Juana ("the Mad"), daughter of Ferdinand and Isabella. Within a thick real-estate portfolio, Charles brought to Spain the duchy of Burgundy, which controlled the Low Countries, where the humanist principles of the Reformation were finding a receptive audience. To Spain, always keen to subvert her own best interests with senseless brutality, Protestant dissent had to be crushed. In 1522 Charles dispatched the Holy Office of the Inquisition and some 10,000 troops under the Duke of Alva. When the holy inquisitors tortured prominent burghers and publicly beheaded the dukes of Egmont and Hoorn, they created martyrs and set off revolutionary war.

The predominantly Protestant northern provinces led the revolution while the Catholic-leaning south, of which Amsterdam was a part, either sat it out or sided with Spain. Isaac Le Maire, a southerner from Antwerp, fled north to escape Spanish terror, and that's where he learned his undying hatred of Spain. As the war swung in favor of the north, the south pragmatically joined up. The north, equally pragmatic, needing its other half, welcomed the south into the United Provinces of the Netherlands in 1609 with Amsterdam as its capital.

In 1581, Spain had annexed the Netherlands' old trading partner, Portugal, thus severing Dutch access to Eastern goods. Now if the Dutch wanted those precious spices, coffee, pepper, tea, silks, they would have to go get them for themselves in their own ships. The Dutch would have to dirty their hands in that mad market or do without. There was no question, of course. But inshore piloting techniques perfected over decades in the trying waters of the North Sea, the English Channel, and the Bay of Biscay would not get them to the Indies. Southern Hemisphere voyages required new knowledge. Where was the best wind? Where should one cross the equator? Where could one find fresh water and provisions?

Then there was the navigation. In the Northern Hemisphere, for instance, you can measure the altitude of Polaris, the North Star, above the horizon in degrees, and that will give you your latitude, no further calculation necessary. By keeping Polaris at a particular angle, you could sail east or west along any latitude you chose. That's how the Vikings and Basques were able to make repeat passages to Greenland and North America. But Polaris and all the familiar stars would not be visible in the Southern Hemisphere, where there is no counterpart to Polaris. The Dutch would need to know new stars, and they'd need mathematical tables to convert raw measurements of their altitude into usable position fixes. The Portuguese knew all those things, having compiled information about the African route since Henry the Navigator in the middle of the 15th century. The Dutch knew just which Portuguese to hire or bribe, and they were very quick studies.

Isaac Le Maire heard that Captain Willem Cornelius Schouten was a man of means and influence in the port of Hoorn, not merely a master mariner and leader of men. A VOC star, Captain Schouten had commanded three voyages to the Indies via the African route. He had made himself wealthy by shrewdly exercising a perquisite of the trade, which allowed the captain to cut his own intra-island shipping deals so long as they didn't interfere with company cargo. Le Maire would have considered any VOC captain who hadn't made himself rich a bit of a dimwit. When he called on Captain Schouten, Le Maire asked him straight out: Did he think there was another route to the East besides the established two? The loquacious captain is supposed to have replied, "There is great reason it might be found." Le Maire had the right man, he could tell.

Conventional wisdom held that Magellan's strait was the only *paso* to the Pacific. What he had called Tierra del Fuego was thought to be part of that Great Southern Continent which carried all the way to the South Pole. The idea got around, however, that Tierra del Fuego was just a big island south of which there was open ocean. The "French Map," 1581 or 1582, of Drake's course shows a bottom to South America, but the continent itself is badly misshapen. Edward Wright's World Chart of 1600 is remarkably accurate, the Beagle Channel, Hardy Peninsula, and Isla Navarino readily identifiable. From a contemporary perspective, however, maps couldn't be called proof. Leaving empty spaces was not in the commercial map-maker's best interest, and so he filled them in; all he needed was a pen. Also, the credible contemporary historian Richard Hakluyt published a new edition of his *Voyages* in 1600, which contained Nunho da Silva's eyewitness account of Drake's voyage, but it mentioned no open-water passage. It was quite possible that this passage was nothing but drunken-sailor palaver and an old man's vindictive obsession. The old man sweetened the deal by promising Schouten the finest sails, running gear, and ships that money could buy. He could pick his own crew and officers, and pay top gilder to get the best of both. Le Maire's only stipulation was that his son Jacob go along as supercargo and business manager. Schouten never really hesitated.

That settled, Le Maire set about cajoling a patent for his voyage from the government, where he still had old and influential family friends, the Prince of Orange, Maurice de Nassau, among them. The States-General decreed: "All persons, inhabitants of the United Provinces, who should make discoveries of new passages, harbors, or lands, shall be permitted and entitled to make the first four voyages to the places by them discovered." Meanwhile, Schouten fitted out two small ships, the *Unity (Eendracht)* and *Hoorn,* with the best equipment aloft and alow, everything shipshape. And he had an idea or two of his own. He had observed what amounted to a vicious circle in previous long-haul voyages. Ships were over-crewed because a mortality rate of about 50 percent was to be expected, but the resulting overcrowding in expectation of disease helped cause disease, and he was not going to make that mistake. Half the normal crew size would be easier to provision for, therefore healthier, and he could compensate with skill what he lacked in numbers.

In June of 1615, the ships stood out into the North Sea, Schouten and young Le Maire aboard *Unity,* while Schouten's brother Jan commanded the *Hoorn.* Where were they bound? Everyone on the Texel waterfront could see that they were fitted out for a long voyage, and that probably meant the East Indies. But not a word had leaked from the principals. And as for the crews, they'd sailed without knowing where they were going, having been paid enough to go anywhere. After a quick stop in England to pick up a gunner and a carpenter, the ships cleared the Channel and crossed the Bay of Biscay in heavy weather, which followed them well into the Trades. They paused at Sierra Leone, where they watered and provisioned—they were offered 10,000 lemons in exchange for a few poor-quality knives. From Africa, Schouten laid a southeasterly course for Patagonia

Suddenly, *Hoorn* struck—or was struck—it wasn't immediately clear—by something below the waterline that shivered her timbers from keelson to cap rail. The off-watch scrambled topside not to be caught below when she went to the bottom. Hands manned the pumps while others readied the boats, but there was no panic; these guys were pros, and *Unity* was standing by. The carpenter sounded the hold. . . . She was bone dry. And she was floating normally. They couldn't have hit bottom; they were in the middle of the Atlantic near 4 degrees North. Still these were uncharted waters. . . . Some sort of "sea mountain" perhaps. They searched with sounding leads, but of course found no bottom. As a sailor leaned overboard to retrieve a lead, he gave a shout that brought the crew to the rail. Astounded, they watched the sea run red, "as if a fountain of blood were gushing up from the keel." A sea monster had attacked them. The *Hoorn* sailed on, seemingly unscathed. Around the New Year, they crossed the equator. It was now 1616.

After a long, painfully slow crossing, they called at the mouth of a Patagonian river near 48 degrees South, which they knew to have a nine-foot tide range, where they meant to careen and clean their ships. After three months at sea, they were dragging a bottom full of stringy green weed, barnacles, and other marine growth, enough to peel off a third of their rightful speed. The age-old procedure was to haul the ship up near the high-tide line, then let the ebb leave her high and dry, which is why a large tidal range was desirable. Schouten knew about this place from a published account of the third circumnavigation (after Magellan and Drake) by an unpleasant fellow called Thomas Cavendish, who after squandering his inherited fortune, set out to replace it by raiding Spanish treasure in the Pacific. And he was successful at it, capturing the *Santa Ana,* which contained the largest single haul ever plundered from the Spanish. He tried to do it again almost immediately, but he died at sea while lost, having hanged his navigator for insubordination. I don't like Cavendish because he wantonly besmirched the reputation of John Davis, one of the greatest of

Elizabeth's sailors and the best man among all of them. Anyway, Cavendish availed himself of Port Desire's tides (Puerto Deseado on charts) in 1586. Drake had been there first, but he had called it the Bay of Seals. If Schouten didn't learn of Port Desire from Cavendish, then it must have been from his countryman Olivier van Noort, the fourth circumnavigator, who careened ("breamed" was the antique term) here. (*Sailing Directions* offers this note about Puerto Deseado: "When strong west winds blow, there may be dust storms which impede visibility; in such cases it is advisable to keep position by radar and [wait] until visibility improves.") Careening the *Hoorn* on a handy sandbar, they solved the mystery of the bloody sea.

There in the bow seven feet below the waterline sticking "through . . . two stout fir planks, through another of stout oak and partly through another rib, where it was finally stopped, to our great good fortune . . . was a horn very similar in shape and thickness to the end of an ordinary elephant's tusk." A "great horned fish," Schouten wrote, "or a sea monster." Some historians say that it must have been a narwhal, but narwhal are exclusively Arctic whales. It was a sword-fish that attacked *Hoorn,* but it had to have been an enormous one to shiver the timbers of a Dutch-built vessel, perhaps fifteen feet long and weighing as much as a mature great white shark, a size unseen today. The profusion of wildlife in the New World back when people were still calling it that is beyond imagining. Later, in Fuegian waters, the *Unity* sailed into an ocean seething with whales from horizon to horizon, "so that we were compelled to be constantly on our guard . . . in order to avoid the whales and not run into them." And of course it was reports just like this by explorers that brought a second kind of conquest of the Americas, this to kill all the whales, seals, otters, and beavers for money. An interesting aspect of explorer literature is the shifting view of nature it reflects. Anyway, after they found the sword, they did a very dumb thing to the *Hoorn.*

This sea growth was really tough stuff, resistant to every method of removal except, well, fire. It was the customary way, but in this case, "the flames unexpectedly and very quickly flew up as far as the rigging and took hold of her, so that in an instant there was no more chance of putting them out, especially as the yacht was beached some 50 feet from the water; and we were therefore compelled to see her totally burnt before our eyes without being able to do aught about it."

They salvaged the nails and metal items from her ashes, and transferred her crew to *Unity*. They prepared her for the heavy weather to come by stripping the upper decks of cannon and other heavy objects they could do without, stowing them deep in the hold to increase her stability by lowering her center of gravity. Morale was high despite the Port Desire disaster and the inevitable ocean violence they expected. The expectation of riches had something to do with that, no doubt. Back in October just after they'd crossed the equator, Schouten had called for the crews to lay aft, and from his quarterdeck he announced their purpose and destination for the first time. It was into the Pacific "by a way other than the Strait of Magellan." The crews cheered, he wrote, "For each one hoped to get something on his own account . . . and to profit by it." Our central source is *The Relation of a Wonderfull Voiage by Willem Cornelison Schouten of Hoorn,* first published in 1619, about which there is some authorship question, but Captain Schouten certainly participated in the writing, and there is no reason to doubt its truth. On September 13, 1616, the *Unity* stood south, either to bump into Terra Australis Incognita or sail around into the "South Sea."

On the twenty-third, they sighted mountainous land to the west, where they expected land to be. But a day later, they saw the same landmass away to the southwest, and then dead ahead—to the south. Was this the end of the line? Had they been right all along, those who believed that Magellan's strait was the only route to the Pacific? The ships were sailing toward the southeast end of Tierra del Fuego, called Peninsula Mitre, which trends well eastward. They turned that way and followed the land, there being no other choice. The wind went light and fluky. When darkness fell, they were on soundings, which is to say the bottom was near enough to measure with a lead line, and a swift current was setting them shoreward. The captains kept the deck all night, double lookouts aloft, anchors catted and ready to drop. In daylight, they sighted land away in the east, snowcapped craggy mountains, "high and frightening," Schouten said, but eastward was still the only way open to them. Schouten managed a quick noon sight of the sun, which put their latitude at 54 degrees 46 minutes.

Then they saw it, the opening, and judging from the speeding current, it was a strait, not a bay or fjord. There were six men on the helm, a tiller in those days, all hands on deck, when the *Unity* turned south with the current, hugging the land on the west side (from Cabo San Diego to Cabo Buen Suceso). Without any reason to believe they were seeing part of Magellan's Tierra del Fuego, they named it Maurice Land. Those "frightful" mountains on their port side Schouten and Le Maire named States Land, not States Island (Staten Island), because they assumed it to be a northern cape of Terra Australis, the Southern Continent, an idée fixe that would not go away for another 175 years. The water in between they named the Strait of Le Maire. It was just beyond the strait that they encountered the enormous pod of whales, and passing through it, Schouten remarked on the profusion of life all around, great shoals of silvery fish, and rolling dolphins; birds of all kinds swooped and circled the ship. No one from *Unity* to *Pelagic* has failed to be impressed or frightened by this Strait of Le Maire.

But, for the record, *Unity* was the second ship to sail these waters. We don't know the name of the first ship, or that of her captain, but we have his log. A member of Don Alonso de Camargo's fleet trying to reach Peru via the Strait of Magellan, this little ship was driven past the entrance and down to the Strait of Le Maire. Her captain tried to escape the storms by anchoring somewhere on Staten Island, but his cable parted, and when the jury anchor (cannons lashed together) failed, he was swept through the strait. As a helpless last resort to keep her upright, he cut down her mainmast, and she survived to shelter somewhere in the eastern Beagle Channel during the winter of 1540, and in the spring, this nameless captain sailed back to Spain and submitted his log. Disregarded, it was lost for centuries. Why preserve the record of a failed voyage?

When *Unity* sailed out of the lee into the head-on brunt of the "mighty waves," they knew that this was open ocean. There was no Southern Continent in the way (though I don't think Schouten and Le Maire were any more interested in the thing than Drake). But now in waters no human being had ever seen before, he still had to find the turning point. He couldn't turn right and head north until reasonably certain that he had cleared all land, but how would he know the end if he saw it? So Schouten was the first captain ever to confront the Cape Horn problem: wind, waves, and current, all heavy and all from the west—when west was where he wanted to go.

Sleet and rain mixed with snow froze in the rigging. The wind surged to gale force, then gasped and died, a pattern that, when repeated, results in a sailing nightmare. Get aloft and shorten sail, quickly, before something carries away ... only to watch the wind die two hours later leaving her to wallow in the plunging waves; then back aloft to release the gaskets, haul the yards around, and sheet the sails, time and time again. (Anyone who's been on a light-air ocean race knows the drill and how old it gets.) The crew was the first to feel that buckshot sleet which would become a staple of Cape Horn literature. Soaked and freezing, hands bloody from clawing at frozen sailcloth, they fought the battle for one hundred hours before the lookouts shouted down to the deck: Land fine on the starboard bow—

Samuel Johnson said something to the effect that if he had to choose between going to jail or going to sea, he'd pick jail, because the food and the company would be better. And there is a common notion that the crews of the day accepted tyranny and underwent extreme fatigue, pain, danger, and disease, because, what the hell, conditions were just as bad if not worse ashore. There was truth to that view, and it obtained throughout the history of sail, but it's not the whole truth. This handpicked Dutch crew, for instance, young hotshot heirs to a long nautical tradition, were probably having the time of their lives. Certainly, as sane men, they were frightened of those churning, towering seas on their bow and the sinister look of the sky, but with this fine ship, a captain made of oak, there was nothing they couldn't handle, the best sailors in the world. It's the same mixture of ambition and adventure that crews up brutal sixty-foot race boats to blast around the world via the Horn flat out for 33,000 miles. I've been outside a little, not worth mentioning compared, say, to Novak or Laird, but enough to be physically miserable and anxious of mind, and then laughing about it with my shipmates, who knew we'd all go again. I can't demonstrate that any of this sea-struck spirit was felt on *Unity*'s deck, but why not? They knew they were making history, and what's a little sleet in the face compared to that, as long as you survive to tell the story? No expedition I recall was canceled for want of crew. Sometimes, however, it seems that the same thing could be said about war.

They sighted an isolated islet about a mile long, green slopes climbing (55 meters by the book) to a stubby black tower of rock with other detached rocks to the north. This could not be the dramatic cape they had expected—it was nothing but an inconsequential outcrop. With smart-ass irony, Le Maire named it Isla Barnevelt. John van Barnevelt, with old Isaac, was one of the VOC's founders, but he was also among those who had disagreed with Isaac's policies—and chief among those this voyage was conceived to undermine and to mock. So he got a rock pile named after him forever. Frankly, I found it magnificent in its isolation, but that's not how Le Maire meant it. Then more land appeared away to starboard. Gray-green and mountainous, they seemed to be islands in a group. Schouten certainly would have seen the southern cape on Isla Deceit only eight miles from Barnevelt. He prudently wore around to the southwest. As the first to do this, he had a unique problem. He needed actually to sight the headland before he could be sure he had rounded it. Otherwise he would have to stand far out into the Pacific to clear his bow. But how could he know?

In less than an hour the thing itself rose through the murk. A small island, low, green, and gently rolling away in the north, but it climbed steeply toward the south end and soared up into a majestic pinnacle. This was the end of the continent. How could a thing that looked so like the end of a great continent be anything else? Everyone lined the starboard rail or hung in the rig for a better view, silent until the captain cried spontaneously, "Hoorn! Cape Hoorn!" And the crew cheered and picked up the call. "Cape Hoorn!"

It was near the end of the first month of 1616. Shakespeare would die that year, and so would Cervantes. The Catholic Church would prohibit Galileo on pain of torture from practicing science.

⌒

There was no thanking of the blessed virgin, no talk of conjurers. The Dutch were as savage as any civilized nation, but they did not try

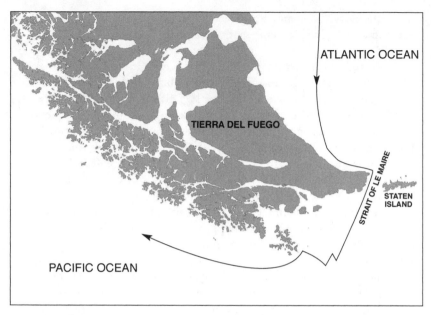

Map 7.1   Schouten's Route

to delude themselves. They knew exactly why they had sailed to these harsh latitudes. It wasn't for geographical discoveries, though they were nice, and it certainly wasn't to convert the natives. Nor was the purpose exclusively to stick it to the VOC, though that too would appeal. And the crew didn't sign on just for the wonder and the visceral thrill. The *Unity* rounded and named Cape Horn because it got them to the East, where they meant to make money in the spice trade. From that perspective the voyage was ruinous. Jan Schouten died crossing the Pacific, but otherwise the ship reached the Indies with a healthy crew. The *Unity* anchored off Ternate, the Moluccas, on September 17, 1616. When people said Spice Islands with caps, they meant the Moluccas and the Bandas, roughly between Sulawesi and New Guinea, the richest of the rich for their nutmeg. The Dutch controlled supply and production for the entire region, to the extent that was possible, at cannon point. The Governor-General of the Dutch East Indies, Laurens Reael, greeted Schouten and Le Maire warmly, and instead of feeling threatened by the incursion, he was fascinated to hear of this new route. Everything pointed to fantastic success when the *Unity* sailed for Batavia, Java, a hub of the Dutch empire.

There, however, they came up against a true believer named Jan Pieterszoom Coen. A VOC star who would take over governor-generalship from Reael, thought too gentle for the job, Coen was a headsplitter in the old Portuguese mold. If the locals didn't want to sell their cloves or cinnamon, that was their right, but it was Coen's right, then, to exterminate them all and take their land. That was the only way to make a rational market in the spice trade. He happened to hail from Hoorn, but Coen wasn't sentimental. And he didn't give a damn whether Schouten and Le Maire had discovered a new route or not. However they'd gotten there, their purpose in coming was to undermine the VOC's monopoly, and besides that, Coen hated old Isaac, "an opponent to the common good," and the whole Le Maire family. He ordered Schouten and Jacob Le Maire to stand trial before the VOC council, which promptly found them guilty of trespass on Company territory. The punishment was confiscation of the *Unity* and everything in her. Her crew was dispersed to other East Indiamen in the harbor. Schouten and Le Maire were sent home in disgrace aboard an Indiaman called *Great Sun,* flagship of Joris van Spilbergen, who was homebound via Good Hope on the last leg of his own circumnavigation. Jacob Le Maire, age thirty-one, had fallen ill shortly after Coen ruined his splendid success, and he died aboard *Great Sun* before she was a week out, from a broken heart, some said.

Back home old Isaac sued the VOC before the States-General, which found in his favor, ordering the Company to make restitution for the ship and her contents. But the company never did.

8

Discovering People

Viewing such men, one can hardly make oneself believe they are fellow-creatures, and inhabitants of the same world. It is a common subject of conjecture what pleasure in life some of the less gifted animals can enjoy: how much more reasonably the same question can be asked with respect to these barbarians.
—Charles Darwin, *Voyage of the Beagle*

"THE YAHGAN WENT NAKED." Someone would say it in the morning before the diesel stove took hold and we could still see our breath in the cabin. On nasty days in horizontal sleet squalls, when we took to our high-tech breathable foulies, hoods and hats and ocean-racing boots, someone would add, "Yahgan infants went naked in this." Here, from *Voyage of the Beagle,* is Charles Darwin on the subject: "In another harbor not far distant [from Cape Horn], a woman who was suckling a recently born child came one day alongside the vessel, and remained there out of curiosity, whilst the sleet fell and thawed on her naked bosom, and on the skin of her naked baby!... At night, five or six human beings, naked and scarcely protected from the wind and rain of this tempestuous climate, sleep on the wet ground coiled up like animals."

The Yahgan astounded, fascinated, troubled, and repulsed Westerners, depending on the period and the Westerner. Francis Drake, who was here in 1578, first reported their nakedness while he and his men suffered in a sleet storm. In 1624, one Jacob l'Hermite paused in Yahgan land en route to disaster in the Pacific. "They more resemble beasts than men," wrote his expedition chronicler, "for they tear men to pieces, and devour the flesh raw and bloody." So barbaric were they, he said, that if you happened to be in the way when nature called, they'd piss on your leg. Even James Cook, the great instinctive cultural relativist, found them to be the lowest order of men in the world. Among Charles Darwin's adjectives are "hideous," "greasy," "miserable," "stunted," "abject," and "filthy."

In 1823, a decade before Darwin, James Weddell, a sealer with the soul of an explorer, rested in Wigwam Cove on Isla Hermite, twelve miles from Cape Horn, after exploring the Antarctic Peninsula and the Weddell Sea aboard his tiny vessels *Jane* and *Beaufoy*. Weddell was impressed by the Yahgans' marine-adapted culture and their survival skills. He studied them for two months, and tried to record some of their language, which he thought sounded like Hebrew, "certainly a question of some interest to philologists." But he also set the tone for the next sixty years of contact between whites and Yahgans: He did not want to exterminate, enslave, or exploit them. What Weddell and the others wanted to do was to "improve" them by converting them to Christianity. Whenever Indians gathered, he would pull out his Bible and read aloud the word of God. They crouched around in a semicircle to watch and listen, Weddell writes, occasionally discussing matters among themselves. "Not that they were expected to understand—But it was proper to show them the Bible, and to read it, in connection with making signs of death, resurrection, and supplication to heaven." One man placed his ear to the book, "believing that it spoke," which of course is what the Christians believed.

"I would willingly, for the honor of human nature, raise these neglected people somewhat higher in the scale of intellectual estimation than they have reached," Weddell wrote in *A Voyage Towards the South Pole*, 1825, "but I must acknowledge their condition to be that of the lowest of mankind." Yet since they were "docile and tractable," they "might therefore be instructed in those arts which raise men above the brute."

I always liked James Weddell, a brilliant high-latitude navigator, an insightful and instinctive relativist, and a self-taught scientific explorer, just like his hero Captain Cook. But times had changed in the forty years since Cook sailed these waters. A man of the Enlightenment, Cook saw his role as an objective reporter of native flora, fauna, and people without judgment or agenda. By Weddell's day, fervent evangelicalism and exploration conflated when explorers showed missionaries the way to new flocks. Not since the 16th-century exploration of the New World had Christians turned up so many non-Christians. Weddell saw Cook himself as an agent of conversion. About Cook's 1769 contact with Fuegians, he wrote: "It would have been agreeable to have ascertained whether from his intercourse with them they had derived permanent improvement, though his stay amongst them was too short to produce any great result." Weddell embodied all the contradictions and paradoxes of the period. His was a scientific mind capable of seeing nature separate from its exploitable resources, and he worried that the introduction of too many metal tools would distort the Yaghan's relationship to their environment—yet he seems incapable of imagining that the introduction of a foreign religion and its mores might cause some cultural dislocation.

As for the Yahgan, they had no room in their minds for any kind of spiritual abstractions, nor words in their language to express them. What the Yahgan wanted was the white man's *objects,* all those wonderful, unfathomable things he carried aboard his cloud canoes. From the white man's point of view, religion shaped the terms of contact. For the Yahgan, to whom it was unintelligible, things—the hysterical desire to have them—resulted in senseless violence. But that's getting a little ahead of the story.

Everyone from Drake to Darwin asked the same question: Why would these Yahgan, why would anyone, settle in such a harsh and stingy environment? Since no one would do so willingly, the reasoning went, they must have been driven down here by stronger, more advanced Indians to the north until they fetched up at the very bottom of the habitable world in a place nobody else wanted. Indeed, the Yahgan did have enemies to the north on Tierra del Fuego—the Ona.

Whites called them "Foot Indians" to distinguish their way of life
from that of the Yahgan, who were "Canoe Indians." The Ona, nomads who occupied the forests, bogs, and pampas on the big island,
were statuesque and elegant compared to the "stooped" and
"stunted" Yahgan, which seemed to prove the point. Ona culture was
in fact richer materially and psychically, partly because they shared
their environment with a plentiful prey animal, the guanaco, a smaller
cousin to the llama, which supplied a full range of human needs,
including clothes.

But that theory breaks down if it implies that the Yahgan were once
Foot Indians who were forced to take up an entirely new way of life after the Ona evicted them from Tierra del Fuego. There is sound archeological evidence that people, presumably Yahgan, were living a
marine-adapted existence some 7,500 years ago. Before that time, Fuegia was uninhabitable, buried beneath an ice-sheet glacier. That doesn't
absolutely preclude the eviction theory, but aboriginal landlubbers
didn't suddenly learn how to build boats and to hunt new prey from
them in an entirely unfamiliar environment. They wouldn't have had
time to learn to adapt before the environment killed them. More likely,
Ona and Yahgan came into the country at nearly the same time, but by
different means; one walked, the other paddled.

In fact, there were four native cultures in Fuegia, two Canoe Indians and two Foot Indians. Cousin culture to the Yahgan, the Alacaluf
lived out on the western islands fronting the open Pacific, where the
climate was harsher, wetter, and windier than in Yahgan territory at
the east end of the Beagle Channel. Alacaluf territory stretched north
from the Brecknock Peninsula to Desolation Island at the mouth of
the Strait of Magellan, and east on both sides of the strait to present-
day Punta Arenas. Also marine nomads, the Alacaluf built bark
canoes of almost identical design and construction to the Yahgan's,
and their diets were identical, but their languages were different. The
signal fires Magellan saw, evoking the name Tierra del Fuego, were set
by Alacalufs. Their unfortunate position on the shore of the *paso*
caused them to incur the senseless cruelty of voyagers such as Pedro
Sarmiento and Olivier van Noort, to name only two of the cruelest.
And in the western islands, they were subject to all the usual deleteri-
ous influences of whalers. In 1885, Thomas Bridges took two Yahgan

who spoke the language, along with his young son Lucas, to pay a friendly visit to Alacaluf territory around the Brecknock Peninsula. Thomas's description of their environment is worth quoting: "Some of the channels we passed through were hardly more than clefts in the rocks, which stood up like irregular walls thousands of feet high on either side of us. The climate there is so wet that moss and trees cling to the faces of these almost perpendicular cliffs. On a still, clear night the stars in the narrow strip of sky overhead shine with double brilliancy and their reflection is multiplied again in the somber depths below." People once thought that the borders between Alacaluf and Yahgan were strict, like those of Chile and Argentina, and their only direct contact happened at a certain Beagle Channel island where both came to collect fire-making iron pyrite. But now experts such as Natalie Goodall think that the borders were porous, and interaction, even intermarriage weren't uncommon.

The Foot Indians occupied all the rest of Tierra del Fuego. The forests, mountains, bogs, and pampas from the east entrance of the Strait of Magellan south to the Beagle Channel, including the Atlantic seaboard and around almost all the way to the Strait of Le Maire—this was Ona territory. But on the far eastern toe of Tierra del Fuego overlooking Le Maire and Staten Island lived the Haush. No one knows exactly how they came to be crammed into that tight extremity, but the guess is they were driven out there by hostile Ona. Like them, the Haush lived on the bounteous guanaco, but, like the Yahgan, they also exploited shoreline resources. However, the Haush probably never built or used canoes, and apparently there was no friendly communication between the Foot Indians and the Canoe Indians. Also, we should recognize that there never were very many of any of these people. Thomas Bridges, for example, estimates that before contact there were about 3,000 Yahgan.

This brings up a broader, older question: How did anyone get down this far, Yahgan or otherwise? Every pre-Columbian person who ever lived in North and South America descended from some shadowy proto-Indian who crossed into the New World from Asia at least 12,000 years ago. From this singular stalk branched the Inuit, Iroquois, Creek, Athabascan, Zuni, Inca, Aztec, Toltec, through a process now called genetic drift. Humans flowed into every part of the

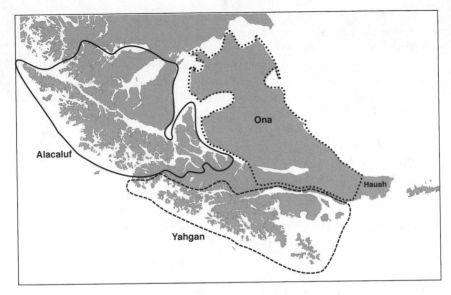

Map 8.1   Tribal Distribution in Fuegia

Americas from the Arctic Circle to Cape Horn, not just the places with nice weather, as if probing at the boundaries of human possibility; and finding none, they pressed on southward to the end of the line—not because they had to, but because they wanted to, because it was there.

However, this issue, the "peopling of the Americas," splits professional opinion into two rancorous camps. The conventional view holds that no humans could have migrated from Asia into North America before 12,000 years ago. Until then, their way would have been blocked—on the Alaska side—by an immense, lifeless ice sheet. It wasn't a question of the Land Bridge from Asia; that came and went with some frequency. After that date, the climate warmed enough to offer an "ice-free corridor" southward into the rest of North America. The fossil record seems to support this view. The oldest reliably dated objects of human origin in North America are finely wrought stone projectiles called Clovis points after the little New Mexico town where they were first discovered—sticking in a mastodon's spine—in

1933. Now that they knew what to look for, archeologists excavating animal sites elsewhere began turning up spear points made by humans all over North America, and then in South America down as far as Patagonia. Clovis technology must have exploded on the scene, revolutionizing the relationship between human hunters and their prey, and therefore accelerating human migration to everywhere. Not a single Clovis point older than 12,000 years has ever been found, and those who believe that the first Americans, the ur-explorers, walked into North America after that date, but not before, are called "Clovis Firsters."

The other side has a most pleasing idea in the context of Cape Horn and its natives: The first Americans crossed the Bering Strait in boats. If so, they could have come anytime, because for boatmen the presence or absence of that ice-free corridor would have been irrelevant. (This side doesn't have a neat name like the Clovis Firsters, and since they accuse archeology of a terrestrial bias, perhaps they wouldn't object to "Mariners.") The Mariners contend that the ice sheet itself would not have precluded navigation, because contrary to previous opinion, it didn't cover the land entirely all the way out to the continental shelf the way Antarctic ice sheets do. It was more like Greenland's, where on the west coast pockets of land, "refugia," remain open along the shore, attracting marine mammals and shellfish, which could quite nicely support transient bands of boat people.

There wouldn't need to have been many refugia, because a bark or skin boat (like the Inuit's umiak) could have traveled much faster and more efficiently than walkers could. Maybe these ur-explorers even employed sails. Some number of people would have drowned in gales or accidents, the age-old disadvantage of water travel. And others would have died of exposure, but boats, say, twenty-five feet long would have had enough capacity to carry supplies and warm furs, upping the odds of survival. Also, a maritime population could grow faster, because young children did not need to be carried. And if they survived the voyage down the ice sheet, the ancient mariners would have found themselves in one of the richest marine environments on the globe, British Columbia and the Pacific Northwest.

The Mariners, however, can't prove any of this with the only evidence that matters in archeology, the fossil record. With reputations and royalties to protect, Clovis Firsters scoff at the Mariners. Doesn't it seem reasonable that if streams of boatmen were crossing from Asia to North America before 12,000 years ago, someone would have found at least one artifact to show for it? Well, no, the Mariners reply, because boats of bark or skin leave no wake in the fossil record, and hard things like scrapers and spear points would be found only out on the ancient Ice Age shoreline, which now lies under 200 feet of cold North Pacific water. Oh, the old submerged evidence, and here the debate turns churlish, sarcastic. Well, the Mariners reply, doesn't it seem a little suspicious, what with all these Ice Age hunters trekking through the ice-free corridor, that not a single Clovis point has ever been found in that region?

But with nothing to offer or lose, I say it's appealing, the idea that bands of voyagers in small boats picked their way south along the west coast of North America down to the equator and beyond, adapting their boats to available resources and local conditions as they went, pressing on, pausing perhaps at the rich marine pickings along the coasts of Peru and Ecuador before they braved the cold waters south of 40 degrees South and then 50 South. Some stopped, of course, to build societies that would last until the conquistadors came. But some, the really hard-core salts, the wanderers who for one reason or another never fit in ashore, paddled on to become—at the very bottom—Yahgan. Though tempted to for the sake of romance and thematic unity, I'm not suggesting that the Yahgan were the same people as those ur-boatmen from Siberia, only that their way of life, marine-adapted hunter-gatherers, was the same, and that they might have voyaged all the way south on the same restless momentum, humans crossing great and perilous distances over water because of practical need, instinctive impulse, or simply because they wanted to. In actual ways and certainly symbolic ones, that's what Cape Horn has always been about.

The Yahgan settled into a vaguely bordered territory shaped like an upside-down pyramid with Cape Horn at its apex. It stretched northwest to where the Beagle splits around Isla Gordon and in the northeast to the mouth of the Beagle Channel east of Isla Navarino, encompassing the Fuegian Archipelago. The southern islands are steep-sided, mountainous, wet, and wind-scoured, useless to humans

above the high-tide line. However, the edges of the land and the channels in between were productive hunting, gathering, and fishing
grounds. The rocky shores were encrusted with limpets, clams, scal-
lops, and the staple of Yahgan survival, mussels. They harpooned
seals and sea otters (now extinct) with help from semidomesticated
dogs, killed birds with slings, snares, and their bare hands, and they
took the occasional guanaco with bow and arrows. Untroubled by
putrid blubber, they scavenged dead whales whenever the opportunity
appeared, an important event in Yahgan life, which attracted canoes
from all over the archipelago. They had a word for going by canoe to
get blubber, *mukka,* but they couldn't hunt whales. When the season
was right, Yahgan men lowered themselves on ropes of seal sinew
over cliffs on the southern islands to harvest sea-bird eggs. They also
gathered several kinds of berries and certain arboreal fungi. But generally speaking, they had no more control over their food supply than
a fox or a wolf.

We found mogul fields of shell middens under telltale patches of
bright green grass on the outskirts of Ushuaia and other places where
the land was reasonably flat. In middens sliced open by watercourses,
layer upon layer of tightly packed shells were visible, culinary stratig-
raphy that spanned thousands of years. Mussels were the Yahgan's
only dependable food source; men, women, and children without
tools or weapons could gather them anytime in any weather. But the
trouble with mussels as a steady diet is that, though rich in vitamins,
salts, and protein, they're poor in fat and carbohydrates. You can eat
a bellyful and still suffer the clutch of hunger. Yet the Yahgan must
have spent prolonged periods weather-bound, hunkering on the thin
berm of some vertical island with only mussels to eat.

Twelve thousand years ago all humans were hunter-gatherers, and
we were that far longer than we've been anything else. Only the invention of agriculture some 3,500 years ago in the Fertile Crescent, a little
later in parts of Asia and the New World, allowed sedentary cultures
to develop. When sedentary cultures expanded into political entities
with boundaries, they spelled the end for nomadic hunter-gatherers.
Nomads passing through are anathema to nations. Hunter-gatherer
populations decreased steadily as they became the minority, until today they exist only in pockets and parks, like the big animals they

once hunted. In regions unusually blessed with abundant natural resources, coastal areas most often, hunter-gatherers who never practiced agriculture, such as the Tlingit and Nootka in the Pacific
Northwest, could quit the road and settle in one place. They could,
therefore, develop layered societies with chiefs, shamans, totems,
tools, and art. Not so in Fuegia, the southernmost extreme of human
habitation in history. Since everyone had to be involved all the time in
the acquisition of food without division of labor except that required
by age and sex, no elites could arise, no hierarchies emerge. There was
nothing for them to control.

Yet even among the nomadic hunter-gatherers, the Yahgan were
unusual in that they were exclusively a marine people. They traveled
the waters down to the Horn in bark canoes, which reminded one
18th-century explorer of the bean-pod boats he'd made as a kid. It's
an exaggeration to say the Yahgan lived in their boats; they spent
nights ashore in dome-shaped wigwams (which reminded Darwin of
hayricks) made of saplings gathered on the spot. But without the
canoes, there would have been no Yahgan—these islands are too
stingy with their resources for humans to settle on any one of them.
In the bottom of the boat, they carried smoldering firebrands in
rock-and-sand nests instead of trying to start a new fire each night.
Fire was crucial to life itself; instead of clothes, they had fire, and it
was the women's responsibility never to let it go out. The Yahgan
had no political or cultural center, no leaders, no permanent settlements, no prefabricated dwellings or tents. They fished successfully,
but they never invented the fishhook. They had no pottery, no cook-
ing implements, no utensils—they picked up a mussel shell if they
needed a spoon or dipper—no domestic items except a basket, no
material object that would have confused a Neanderthal time traveler. They had nothing except fire to alleviate the hard press of their
environment.

Psychically, the Yahgan were similarly bereft—they had no musical
instruments, no dances, little design or ornamentation except for face
and body painting, and few ceremonies other than puberty rites. They
left no abstract representations of themselves or the creatures that
shared their environment, and if a Yahgan ever felt inclined, like a Neanderthal, to stencil his handprint on a rock face as a way of saying "I

am here," no one has found it. That a culture of saltwater nomads who couldn't own anything they couldn't carry in bark canoes would remain materially simple and single-layered isn't surprising. That they adapted to one of the harshest climates on earth by going naked in it *is* surprising. Did the Yahgan, somewhere back in the folds of time, decide to go naked, to adapt rather than insulate, because that was somehow better? The question troubled everyone who encountered them.

In Puerto Williams, Hamish introduced me to his friend anthropologist Maurice van de Maele, director of the Museo Martin Gusinde, in his overheated, book-and-journal-lined office with an incomparable view across the channel to the snowcapped mountains on Tierra del Fuego. I asked him why the Yahgan went naked.

"No one can answer you that," he replied coolly.

"Could they have made clothes from the available fur if they wished to?"

Yes, he said, fur-seal populations were sparser here than on sub-Antarctic islands such as South Georgia and the South Shetlands, but there were enough seals in the archipelago to provide fur, and there were also otters and occasionally a guanaco. Together, these may not have been the finest furs in the world, but they were probably good enough to offer an alternative to nakedness.

Then the director paused and peered at me. His full black beard ascended nearly to his eye sockets, leaving his face in melancholy, it seemed, but there was something more active in his eyes, hotter, something like disapproval. Of me. Without removing his eyes from mine, he spoke in Spanish to Hamish. . . .

"He hopes you won't write more bullshit about the Yahgan." Hamish translated, smiling thinly.

I had similar hopes, and I knew what he was referring to. A recent book by an American had alienated the director and others I spoke with in Ushuaia who cared about such matters. The writer had gotten things wrong, but most egregiously he'd repeated the old cannibalism myth without question. That myth was still hanging around from the 1624 Dutch account. It's just the sort of stuff returning sailors loved to tell the lubbers back home, and during much of the 19th century, tales of flesh-eating natives were all the rage in Europe and North

America. Charles Darwin repeated as fact a story he'd heard from an American whaler in the Falklands about the Yahgan teenager who claimed that his people customarily ate their old women after asphyxiating them in a smoky fire. Asked if they ever ate their dogs, the kid, playing to his audience, replied, "No, doggies good for hunting otter. Old women good for nothing." Their meat, he said, was very tender.

"Have you read *Uttermost Part of the Earth*?" asked the director. It was a test. If you haven't read Lucas Bridges you can't be taken very seriously.

I had, more than once, with pleasure, and trying to demonstrate it, I blathered, but he seemed to relax. After pausing a moment to gaze out toward Argentina, van de Maele began to talk about physiological adaptation to the cold. The Yahgan were short, stocky, waistless, "stunted" to Darwin. One explorer speculated that they'd gotten that way from crouching in canoes all their lives. According to Thomas Bridges's sampling, full-grown men averaged five-feet-two and the women were slightly shorter. Both sexes, much stronger than their European counterparts, had big chests, stubby trunks, large heads with wide, short necks, a general body shape typical of cold-adapted peoples, the Inuit and the Samoyed, for instance. Tall people don't fare so well in cold climates because long trunks and extremities make for larger cooling surfaces, reducing the blood's heat efficiency and stressing the heart.

Van de Maele told us about a then-unpublished DNA study of Yahgan bones by Argentine scientists, which revealed that their normal body temperature was as much as one full degree higher than that of Caucasians. This alone was a huge genetic adaptation when you consider that a sustained drop of only four degrees results in death from hypothermia. Adaptation was also accelerated by behavior. Lucas Bridges watched Yahgan mothers systematically dunking their infants in and out of the sea. And part of the canoe-handling routine for women was to discharge men and dogs ashore, paddle back out, and moor the canoe by looping tough, rope-like strands of kelp over it. Then the women would swim ashore—in forty-eight-degree water—often with an infant riding on their back.

Even so, wouldn't some toasty cloaks or fur blankets have made life a bit more comfortable? Before I figured out how to pose the question in even quasi-scientific terms, the director said, in English, "It is, of course, the environment."

But didn't the environment cry out for insulation?

"No," said the director, "not the cold, but the . . . rain. How do you say it?"

"The wet?" Hamish offered.

"Yes. Wet."

By the time we'd sailed from Ushuaia, we'd been in Fuegia just shy of a week, during which the weather had been fair, not exactly sunny and gentle, but it hadn't rained a drop. We of course knew better than to extrapolate a climate from a week's worth of weather, and even if we didn't, locals told us repeatedly that we'd better enjoy the "dry spell" while we could. I knew from my homework that it rains, sleets, or snows nearly 300 days in an average year. Precipitation comes in intermittent slashes, not rain-forest deluges; so annual amounts are not great, thirty inches on average. (Southern New England, for instance, gets over forty inches in a typical year.) But Fuegia is far wetter than it looks to strangers on bright days, especially strangers who weren't sleeping on the ground.

The Yahgan people had made no warm garments from fur not because it wasn't available, not because they never thought of it, not because they couldn't figure out how to tan hides, but because fur wouldn't work. Once wet, it would never dry in near-daily rain and sea-level damp. Slinging a bolt of sodden fur around one's shoulders after a dip in forty-eight-degree water would afford no comfort at all. And lacking any other viable material, the Yahgan were left with no alternative to nakedness. With nothing between their flesh and the climate, they faced a straightforward proposition: acclimate or die out. I'd intended to approach the topic from an anthropological-environmental stance, but I was going all runny and unscientific for these vanished geniuses of survival, who needed only to be left alone.

"When the first missionaries came, they didn't like people to be naked," said the director. "So they gave them woolen sweaters and clothes of wool." He paused to sigh. "The wool got wet. The Yahgan died by hundreds from chest trouble. What's the word? Breathing."

"Respiratory illness," Hamish offered.

"Yes. Respire."

The Yahgan had survived at least 7,000 years of this cold, wet, windy wilderness, but could not survive even brief white contact. The whites didn't want that to happen, least of all the missionaries. There was no national policy to promote the extermination of the buffalo as a means to eliminate Plains Indians, no smallpox-infested army blankets. There was no Fuegian Wounded Knee, no Trail of Tears; and unlike the Ona, no one shot them down for a bounty like vermin to make way for sheep. The Yahgan's end began as soon as modern cultures turned their gaze south toward Cape Horn, and when they began to stop for their own reasons, the end grew near and inevitable. It would have ended the same way even if the Yahgan had been immune to measles and smallpox. First the explorers, then missionaries and traders, followed by colonial governments—one way or another the natives would have been displaced to make way for Western culture.

The museum was displaying a haunting series of period sepia photographs enlarged to near life size. Originally, they were the work of M. Doze and M. Payen of the 1883 French expedition (Mission Scientifique du Cap Horn) under Louis Martial. Most of the shots were obviously posed—the man squatting on his haunches using his teeth to lash a bone point onto his spear with seal sinew, the hunter with bow at full draw, another with his spear arm cocked as if to ambush a surfacing seal, women and children huddled around an open fire. These images haunt not only because the people are extinct but also because the subjects, who stare at the lens like deer in the headlights, seem to know that the photographs would be documents of their own imminent end.

9

FitzRoy's Fuegians

The Tekeenica are low in stature, ill-looking, and badly proportioned. Their colour is that of very old mahogany, or rather between dark copper and bronze. The trunk of the body is large in proportion to their cramped and crooked limbs. Their rough, coarse, and extremely dirty black hair half hides yet heightens a villainous expression of the worst description of savage features.

—**Robert FitzRoy,** *Narrative*

IN 1829, HOMEWARD BOUND FROM CAPE HORN aboard HMS *Beagle,* Captain Robert FitzRoy wrote this to the Admiralty:

I have the honor of reporting that there are now on board, under my command, four natives of Tierra del Fuego:
York Minster, aged 26,
Boat Memory, aged 20,
Jemmy Button, aged 14,
Fuegia Basket, aged 9 (girl).
I have maintained them entirely at my own expense, and hold myself responsible for their comfort while away from, and their safe return to, their own country.

FitzRoy had nothing to gain, no ulterior motive for taking them back to England. He meant only to help, to "improve" them in the popular term of the day. But he had literally kidnapped Fuegia, York, and Boat; Jemmy he claimed to have bought from the boy's mother for a handful of shiny buttons. "They understood why they were taken," he continued in his report to the Admiralty, "and look forward with pleasure to seeing our country, as well as returning to their own." This began with the contemporary assumption that Christianity could improve all heathen cultures, but the rest was FitzRoy's own ample capacity for self-delusion. These people may have heard campfire tales about white men in their cloud canoes; a few may even have seen a distant ship, and fewer still may have seen a white person in the flesh. But no Fuegian had any idea where England was, and none had the vaguest understanding of this other thing whites took so seriously, this religion, as they called it.

FitzRoy had not been aboard the *Beagle* for the first part of the first voyage. The task of mapping these chaotic islands and channels had been handed to an aging hero of Trafalgar, Captain Pringle Stokes, and it wasn't fair. Stokes had fought sea battles his entire career. He had no surveying experience, no mathematics and little astronomy, and he was too old for such arduous work. But he was under serious political pressure from home to do it quickly.

By the mid-1820s, Spain had essentially packed up and left South America, ending the empire begun in 1492. Now suddenly the whole continent lay wide open for business. Rebel nationalistic movements were pulling down remnants of the old viceroyalties, and new nations were tottering along; there was no predicting the geopolitical upshot. Western nations had a way of saying "trade" when they meant conquest or at least monopoly, but not free-market competition. Here in the new 19th century, they didn't mean to invade, not literally, but they were looking for advantages. They were looking to inflict their will in places where it would produce profit. With manifest destiny on her mind, the United States was eyeing the isthmus and Drake's old stomping ground in Colombia, while France poked around the equatorial regions. England, starting at the bottom, found the southern waters obscure, to say the least. Cape Horn's position was known, of course. Tierra del Fuego was known to be an island—the Nodal brothers had circumnavigated it to verify for Spain that Schouten wasn't lying. As for the islands on the Pacific side of the Horn, almost nothing was charted. Drake had paused here and there, elements of Anson's fleet were wrecked on that coast, and Cook had plotted a few isolated islands, but nothing was really *known*. The first thing England needed, then, was a set of accurate navigational charts. That's where Stokes entered the story, but the old warrior simply didn't know how to make charts.

He tried for fifteen months. Gale after gale lashed the *Beagle,* either driving her into risky anchorages or forcing her to stand offshore for weeks on end accomplishing nothing except saving herself from the same reefs she was there to chart. The crew was suffering from the cold, the storms, the bad diet, brute labor, and constant anxiety—the usual, but more prolonged—and then scurvy set in.

The *Beagle*'s consort, *Adventure*, under Parker King, overall commander of the two-ship expedition, who'd been surveying up in the Strait of Magellan, had already made for winter quarters in Chiloe, Chile, 800 miles north of the Horn. Stokes had orders to join him there, but Stokes lingered long enough to verify the surveyor's worst fears. His charts were riddled with errors, worse than useless. Chiloe is an attractive spot where wealthy residents of Santiago keep vacation homes and boats. The *Beagle* crew must have felt sweet relief heading north for warmer weather. But Stokes had nothing to look forward to in Chiloe except a humiliating reprimand from Admiral King. Unacceptable, Stokes decided. And as for going back down there to try again—that was out of the question. He left orders not to be disturbed, locked his cabin door, and shot himself in the temple. Poor Stokes, even his suicide was inaccurate; maybe he flinched. With the bullet lodged in his skull, he lay for days in howling agony and dementia. Finally, inevitably, he died. He wouldn't have to sail those hateful waters ever again. In his suicide note, referring to the environment, he'd written: "The soul of man dies in him." Word spread through the crew that Stokes's ghost paced the quarterdeck at the midnight hour. Sailors saw it.

Though in command of the expedition, Parker King lacked authority to appoint a new captain except on an acting basis. He had no choice but to take the *Adventure* and the *Beagle* back around Cape Horn to the nearest higher authority, Admiral Otway, chief of the Royal Navy's South American Station in Brazil. King nominated the

Beagle's first officer, a fine seaman with a name right out of a boy's adventure novel, John Skyring. But, no, Admiral Otway had this protégé he wanted to try out, a friend of the family, named FitzRoy. (Today the three men remain linked north of the Strait of Magellan, where Skyring Water and Otway Water are connected by the FitzRoy Channel.)

Robert FitzRoy, then twenty-five years old, was a rising star in the naval establishment, graduating at the head of his class from the new Portsmouth Naval College, a prodigy in math and astronomy, loaded with natural sailing talent, but he'd never been in command of anything. Skyring had more practical experience and the respect of his crew, but FitzRoy had an advantage. He was descended from Charles II, the Restoration king whose father had lost his head to Cromwell and the Puritans in 1649. This Charles, a merry fellow uninterested in the ship of state, kept a string of mistresses, and his union with a certain Barbara Villiers had produced the dukes of Grafton. The fourth duke of Grafton was FitzRoy's uncle on his father's side. His mother also had significant uncles, Lord Castlereagh and the marquis of Londonderry, political powerhouses in their day. FitzRoy would name capes, islands, mountains, and channels after them all over the wild western archipelago.

"What think you of your old brother Bob being a captain of a Discovery Ship?" he wrote to his sister. "We are ordered to collect everything—animals—insects—flowers—fish—anything and everything we can find. . . . Will it not be a most interesting employment?" Despite this insouciance, he must have been deeply anxious. Until that morning in 1864, forty years after his appointment to the *Beagle,* when he got up from bed, kissed his sleeping wife and daughters, repaired to his dressing room, and slit his throat with his straight razor, FitzRoy feared for his sanity. He wasn't free from the "blue devils" at sea, but the social structure aboard ships was simple and his authority absolute. Still, FitzRoy could veer suddenly and without cause into dark depression, turning touchy, sullen, and abusive. While the *Beagle's* crew learned to duck when the funk was on him, they quickly came to respect his technical skills, and his regard for their health, safety, and reasonable comfort. With a practical job to do, and no social or political shoals to navigate, he was in his element and content, for now. No one reported Captain Stokes's ghost after FitzRoy came aboard the *Beagle*.

Surveying was brutish work in the 19th century, yet it required meticulous measurements and sharp intellectual attention. The hard data had to be gathered from small boats while the *Beagle* remained in a safe anchorage, since no engineless ship could actually travel all the narrow, twisting, reef-strewn channels she needed to chart. Crews had to take to the boats and row to work, five or six seamen on the oars, an officer in charge. In addition to all those people and their surveying equipment in a thirty-foot open boat, they had to carry food, tools, utensils, and weapons for an extended period—two weeks was about right—because inevitably they'd get stranded ashore by foul weather. That was the worst of it, huddling on a leeward moonstone beach while fifty-knot howlers tore up the channel. Living like Yahgan, yet lacking their acclimatization and survival skills, the sailors wouldn't have been able to keep a fire going. When the weather cleared, they rowed back out to pick up where they'd left off. By celestial observation, the officer would fix the precise location of a useful point to serve as a benchmark. From it, he would take compass bearings to visible features, the flat-faced cliff at the west end of the island, the headland to the right, that rocky outcrop in the water. He then knew the *angles* formed between his benchmark and the land features, and after measuring the *distance* from the benchmark to the feature, he could begin to construct triangles with known sides and angles. Triangle by triangle, laying a new one contiguous to the last, a raw picture of the region would emerge. Later, back on the ship, FitzRoy and two of his midshipmen would collect the data from the boat crews and actually draw the charts.

But FitzRoy was concerned with land only where it met water, unless the land contained some readily identifiable feature useful to navigators. Captain James Learmont, for instance, an inventive contemporary of Captain Barker of the *British Isles,* obtained a "line of position" from a compass bearing on Mount Aconcagua, the highest peak in South America, visible on clear days from deep in the Drake Passage. When he crossed that with a line of position from the sun's bearing, he'd have a decent fix. (He used the stench of seals to tell him when he was within twenty-five miles of the Falkland Islands on a foggy night.) FitzRoy's task was to draw the water as well as the shorelines. Where did the bottom rear up close enough to the surface in the form of reefs, rocks, bars, shoals, or moraines to impede navigation?

From time immemorial until the invention of sonar, there was only one way to measure depth, by heaving a "lead line." Its business end was a sinker the size and shape of a sash weight, which when dropped to the bottom on the end of a calibrated line (By the mark, twain!) produced soundings, but it did more. There was a concavity at the leading end of the lead into which tallow or another sticky substance was pressed to retrieve samples of the bottom. Whether it was composed of mud, gravel, sand, rock, or kelp mattered and needed to be charted, because the composition of the bottom could help determine position, and also how reliably an anchor would grip, the "holding ground" in boat talk. Also, bottom contours of known, consistent depth could be used to help fix a vessel's position.

The weather had been atrocious for three weeks, a succession of westerly gales that brought survey work to a halt while the *Beagle* ran to sea for safety's sake. Fleeing to sea in a storm for safety's sake might seem paradoxical to land people, but that was the ship's natural habitat. Over the centuries countless ships were driven under by waves in the open ocean, but far more died when for one reason or another they hit "the hard." But of course no surveying got done a hundred miles out in the Pacific Ocean, and this frustration and drain of energy without result helped drive Stokes to suicidal despair. FitzRoy took it in stride, and seeing that, so did his people.

When finally the weather broke and the sun actually appeared, FitzRoy picked his way back into the channels looking for a secure anchorage where he could set up a base of operations. He found a place behind a towering, black-rock headland called Cape Desolation (on Isla Basket) a day's sail northwest of the Horn. Though it lay deep in the core of the wilderness, Cape Desolation had a name and a known position because Captain Cook had paused there homeward bound during his Second Voyage aboard *Resolution* in 1774. Cook had just crossed the Southern Ocean from New Zealand when he came to anchor in fair weather on December 25. In a jovial mood af-

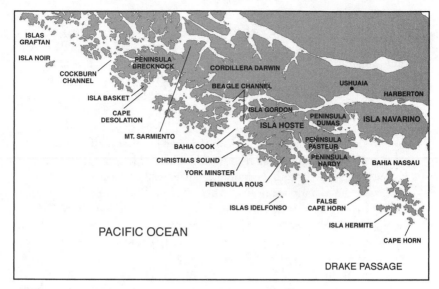

Map 9.1   FitzRoy in Fuegia

ter a goose dinner and the last of his Madeira, he named the water where they sheltered Christmas Sound, and that to the north he called Cook Bay. Though he had no way of knowing it, he'd just discovered the mouth of the Beagle Channel. But almost nothing else had a white man's name when FitzRoy arrived fifty-five years later—except for a spectacular spired mountain to the south of Cape Desolation and Christmas Sound that had reminded Cook of a cathedral. He'd named it York Minster.

The *Beagle*'s anchors were setting fine for now, but FitzRoy wasn't happy there. The holding ground was punk. Plus, he was badly exposed to any wind north of west, and less than a mile under his stern lay a nightmare of fanged rocks over which ocean swells exploded. (One place nearby is called the Milky Way for the waves breaking constantly on the rocks.) If the wind came up from the northwest and she dragged her anchors or if the cables parted, there would be no time to claw their way out of there before the *Beagle* impaled herself on the rocks. FitzRoy ordered his sailing master, John Murray, after whom the Murray Narrows was named, to put over a whaleboat, crew it up with the best boatmen aboard, and go find a better anchorage.

The wind came up hard after Murray and his men had rowed away, built steadily, and by dark a whole gale was howling through the *Beagle*'s rigging. Murray and his men were now stranded out there somewhere. "He could not have been in a finer boat," FitzRoy wrote in his *Narrative*, "and as he knew well what to do with it, I did not feel uneasy for his safety." But the *Beagle* was in deep trouble. Now it was far too late to get under way. Now that her life literally hung on her three anchors, FitzRoy made ready for her death. He equipped and provisioned the lifeboats, ran them out on davits ready to go, organized and rehearsed the abandon-ship drill, then made a little speech about the calm, orderly behavior he expected if the worst should happen. No one slept below. The crew shivered on deck through the long night, but dawn came up clear and bright, and the *Beagle* had not moved. Now what about Murray and his whaleboat crew?

By nightfall, when they hadn't returned, FitzRoy thought about bolting to sea, but he couldn't be certain when—if—the weather would permit him back. Since the anchors were holding, he decided to wait. The weather remained fair through the night and the next day, and as a spectacular sunset flamed out over the Pacific, Murray and his men came alongside the *Beagle*. But they weren't in the whaleboat. They were in a *basket*.

"Reporting on board, sir. But I regret to state our whaleboat was stolen by a band of savages who appeared suddenly." He and his guys had woven a vaguely boat-shaped basket of branches and leaves, caulked the holes with mud, then paddled and bailed the unwieldy thing for nine hours to cover fifteen miles back to the *Beagle*—on the only decent day they would see for the next month. It was intrepid work by an unsung but brilliant seaman blessed by a run of weather luck, and FitzRoy was delighted to see his people safe. But he wanted his whaleboat back. Built by the *Beagle*'s own carpenter, this boat, FitzRoy thought, was the finest example of the genre ever made.

Whaleboats were marvelous things, another instance of how in workboats, beauty and function tended to serve each other, producing the sort of craft one could grow sentimental over. They were big, thirty feet long, double-ended like a canoe, lightly built and easily driven, which made them fast under both sail and oar power. Traditional workboats were conceived and built to perform very specific tasks in narrowly *local* waters and weather conditions, which is why a culture's boats reflect its way of life. Arguably an American invention, whaleboats were made to chase down and kill whales in the open ocean. For that, the boat needed high, sharp bows to cut the waves and wide, flared sides to increase both buoyancy and carrying capacity. Specialized workboats were purpose-built for every conceivable kind of water work, and those that found no recreational adaptation went extinct along with their work. However, there never was an exploration boat, because the ideal exploration boat already existed in the elegant form of the whaleboat. And this particular whaleboat was special because its theft was about to set off a string of unlikely events and decisions that would lead with chilling continuity to the extinction of the "Canoe Indians."

FitzRoy still had another whaleboat aboard and a slightly bigger sailboat (a "yawl boat"), which the *Beagle* carried in stern davits, but he needed both whaleboats. And there was another pressing reason for FitzRoy to get his boat back. It belonged to the *Beagle,* which belonged to the King of England. And ambitious young naval officers on their first command didn't get another by losing His Majesty's gear to thieving savages. He put the other whaleboat over, and with himself at the helm, launched an immediate search before, he said, the thieves disappeared forever into the uncharted channels. He paused only to name the place where the boat had been stolen. He called it Basket Island, and Isla Basket it remains today.

Surveying essentially ceased. The rest of this first voyage was taken up with a chase; at least it seemed to be a chase from FitzRoy's perspective, but it really wasn't. He had no contact with the thieves, never laid eyes on them, and he had no idea where among a dozen different channels they might have gone. To the Indians this was home; to FitzRoy it was geographical chaos. He conducted an aimless, hopeless search, a boy's-own adventure, but not a chase. He decided that the thieves would make for the Brecknock Channel, which as Captain Stokes had discovered led up into the Strait of Magellan, and so FitzRoy made to cut them off before they got that far. Somewhere up in the Brecknock, he further decided, he would uncover their *lair*.

Around one blind turn after another, FitzRoy's party rowed and sailed into deep cul-de-sacs, backtracked until they found a channel, but it led to still another channel, which turned out not to be a channel at all but another dead end. Somewhere (there's no way to know precisely where) he stumbled on an encampment of Alacaluf women, old men, and kids, but no "draft age" men. That was suspicious. Perhaps the men had taken it on the lam with the boat. Then, when he spotted one of the whaleboat's oars nearby, he figured he was hot on the trail. And, further, he concluded that the campers knew the thieves and the location of their lair. So he took two hostages, an old man and a boy, without violence. In fact, they came along with a passivity that was a little confusing under the circumstances, but it looked a lot like consent. If so, then perhaps they could act as guides. The *native guide*—here was an idea dear to the hearts of white travelers, and the literature of exploration is full of stories about guides who offer their local knowledge and survival skills in willing service to the white outsider's aims in tacit recognition of his superiority. But how could FitzRoy have imagined these two as guides? Guides to what? FitzRoy had no way to communicate what he wanted, even if they'd meant to be guides. One night before he and his exhausted crew collapsed on a wet shingle beach, Murray gently covered the guides with spare coats. "Treated as he had so lately," FitzRoy wrote, "one might have thought he would not have been the first to care for their comfort. I mention the incident to show what was our behavior to these savages, and that no wanton cruelty was exercised toward them." During the night, the guides vanished, and so did the coats.

These were the Alacaluf, western cousins of the Yahgan. When whites said "Canoe Indians," they meant these two cultures, but they didn't yet know that there was any difference between them. Drake traded Anjou cloth with the Alacaluf for fish in 1578; the Spanish and Dutch had wantonly murdered them up in the strait. They had appeared in canoes around Cook's *Resolution* on Christmas Day, and even the great relativist was put off. "They were a little, ugly, half-starved, beardless race; not a tall person amongst them," he wrote. They were naked, even the infants, but Cook observed that they carried bolts of sealskin in their boats that they used as cloaks and sometimes as sails. He concluded thus: "Of all the natives I have seen, these people seem the most wretched. They are doomed to live in one of the most inhospitable climates in the world without having sagacity enough to provide themselves with such conveniences as may render life in some measure, more comfortable." It was a band of Alacaluf who had "appeared suddenly" and stolen the *Beagle*'s whaleboat.

The next day another encampment, also lacking young men, hove into sight, and FitzRoy found a lead line, another oar, and bits of gear. *This* must be the pirates' lair. What he couldn't grasp, what no European (until Thomas Bridges) fully absorbed, was the very concept of *marine* nomadism, and witnessing the climate, one can see their difficulty. It just didn't stand to reason that a people would wander these channels in tiny, leaky bark canoes, taking fire with them, that they'd build no permanent structures or settlements, that come dark they'd pull up on some near-vertical beach and huddle around a fire in a wigwam. Still imagining some concerted, organized conspiracy that nomadism precluded, FitzRoy suspected that the impudent savages were playing dumb. However, he did not do what his Dutch and Spanish predecessors had done in the strait. He did not slaughter every Indian he could find. FitzRoy harmed no one, not physically, at least, and certainly not intentionally.

Theft, however, was a constant problem for Pacific explorers starting with Magellan in the Ladrones, the "Isles of Thieves." Two centuries later, when Westerners were exploring the content of the Pacific instead of merely trying to find their way across it, they encountered a staggering diversity of cultures and people with one thing in common—they were cunning, determined thieves. Tahitians stole Captain Cook's leggings while he was using them as a pillow. They picked Joseph Banks clean while he was sharing a feast with them. They were creative and expert thieves, as if they'd been practicing all their lives under some Polynesian Fagin.

It's commonly said that theft was the outcome of a clash between primitive cultures that didn't grasp the principle of private property and Western culture, which was built on the sanctity of it. But this is too simple and reductive. A cultural clash, definitely, but the Polynesians, Fuegians, and the others knew exactly what they were doing. Otherwise they would have stopped stealing when they saw the anger and frustration it evoked in their victims, but they didn't stop. Nor did they confine their theft to useful things, tools and weapons and metal objects. They stole things that had, for them, no intelligible purpose. They stole things because the white man valued them. Theft was a way for primitive cultures to inflict their will on their stronger, technologically advanced visitors. It was a kind of game, comic when no one got killed. It would have been senseless to seek out new peoples in a spirit of curiosity predicated on something like the modern notion of cultural relativity and then slaughter them when, inevitably, they stole your stuff. Yet explorers had to protect irreplaceable equipment. Cook, for instance, sailed to Tahiti on his First Voyage (1768–71) in order to observe the transit of Venus, which if it could be measured might be used as a benchmark for measuring the distance between the sun and earth. Two days before Venus was to touch the sun, the natives stole his quadrant, an essential tool. Cook, who meant to treat the natives "with all possible humanity," devised a gentle hostage-taking policy. He'd go ashore with a squad of marines and sort of invite a prominent Tahitian to return with him to *Endeavour*, where he was treated like a guest, but the message was clear. This became the model tactic for future explorers like FitzRoy, and it worked well for Cook during his First and Second Voyages, but it failed on the Third. Captain Cook was killed on a Hawaiian beach as he rashly attempted to usher King Kalaniopuu aboard the *Resolution* against the theft of a boat.

However, Tahitian and Hawaiian cultures were layered, complex, and sedentary, with kings and queens, royal families, everything that Fuegian culture was not. There were no chiefs in Fuegia. Whom do you snatch? And since there was no central place, no town, only far-flung, roving bands, who would know that a hostage had been taken? Or even that a whaleboat had been stolen in the first place?

FitzRoy's desultory style of hostage taking might indicate that he recognized its futility. He picked them up, but he didn't hold or guard them. They melted away at will. "All our prisoners had escaped, except three little girls, two of whom we restored to their own tribe, near Whaleboat Sound, and the other is now on board," he wrote in his report to the Admiralty. The girl who remained aboard was named Fuegia Basket by someone in the *Beagle* crew.

In the vicinity of Christmas Sound, FitzRoy picked up two young men who "came to us with little reluctance, and appeared unconcerned." They were named York Minster and Boat Memory. After fixing forever a trail of new names on the landscape to mark his experience—Isla Leadline, Cabo Long-chase, Isla Hide, Thieves Sound, Bahía Escape, Thieves Cover—FitzRoy gave up.

Meanwhile, York and Boat, both Alacaluf, somehow communicated to FitzRoy that there were these other people who lived in the east and spoke a different language. (Fuegia Basket spoke Yahgan and Alacaluf, though neither name existed at the time.) FitzRoy was interested to learn that, and he wanted one of this other kind. He ordered the *Beagle* to sail east around False Cape Horn at the tip of Peninsula Hardy into Nassau Gulf searching for a Yahgan. Obviously he was no longer taking hostages against the return of stolen gear—he was collecting specimens.

While exploring the Beagle Channel near present-day Ushuaia aboard the remaining whaleboat, he met three canoes: "I prevailed on their occupants to put one of their party, a stout boy, into my boat, and in return I gave them beads, buttons, and other trifles. Whether they intended that he should remain with us permanently, I do not know, but they seemed contented with the singular bargain, and paddled again towards the cove from which they had approached my boat." This "stout boy" was quickly named by the sailors: Jemmy Button.

Closing his letter to the Admiralty, FitzRoy wrote, "I decided to keep these four natives on board, for they appeared quite cheerful . . . with their situation; and I thought that many good effects might be the consequence of their living a short time in England."

The *Beagle* then rounded the toe of Tierra del Fuego and pointed her bow north, for England and many good effects.

10

"Too Much Skylark!"

skylark 1: to run up and down the rigging of a ship in sport 2: frolic, sport

—*Webster's Collegiate Dictionary*

You care for nothing but shooting, dogs, and rat-catching, and you will be a disgrace to yourself and all your family.

—**Dr. Darwin to his young son Charles**

YOKCHSHLU, ORUNDELLICO, AND EL'LEPARU had sailed across the equator and other imaginary lines in white men's minds, all the way to England, wherever that was, and became Fuegia Basket, Jemmy Button, and York Minster; Boat Memory's real name was never recorded. Upon their arrival at Plymouth in October 1830, they were placed in a boardinghouse near the waterfront. But sailors from the *Beagle* delightedly spread word that they'd brought savage flesh-eaters back from the Land of Fire. Now, deprived of flesh, they'd soon snap, and no Christian citizen of Plymouth would be safe, particularly the female Christians.

FitzRoy moved the Fuegians to a nearby farm when the newssheets got wind of cannibals in town. This was all temporary, anyway. He meant to lodge them with missionaries where they could learn the "plainer truths of Christianity" and thus be civilized—Christianity and civilization being the same thing—but as to where and who would do it, he had made no plans. He left them in the care of Master

Murray and the *Beagle*'s coxswain James Bennett while he went off to
London on navy business, but he was soon called back. Boat Memory,
despite vaccinations at the Royal Hospital, had contracted smallpox.
FitzRoy returned to find him dead. "He was quite an exception to the
general character of the Fuegians, having good features and a well-
proportioned frame. It may be readily supposed that this was a severe
blow to me, for I was deeply sensible of the responsibility which had
been incurred; and, however unintentionally, could not but feel how
much I was implicated in shortening his existence."

The others were revaccinated. Who else would die? Of all the
pathogens brought to the New World since Columbus, smallpox was
among the top three killers. Experts talk about the dead in the tens of
millions, but not many of the smallpox victims died in progressive European hospitals. The others must have been terrified in the hospital,
watching Boat fade away, waiting to die, while strange figures stuck
them with sharp points. But only Boat Memory died. Jemmy, Fuegia,
and York survived for the next segment of their bizarre travels.

FitzRoy tried the Church Missionary Society, one of many such
groups springing up in England and North America, but they were
concentrating on West Africa and Polynesia, too busy for Fuegia.
Someone in the movement passed his plea to another society and another, until a kindly parson named William Wilson found lodging for
Jemmy, York, and Fuegia in a private home willing to take cannibals,
in Walthamstow, north of London. The Fuegians were installed in
what was then called an "infant's school," a charity for the education
of poor kids too young to attend boarding schools. They "were much
pleased with the rooms prepared for them . . . and the schoolmaster
and his wife were equally pleased to find the future inmates of their
house very well disposed, quiet, cleanly people; instead of fierce and
dirty savages."

During ten months at the school, in addition to those "plainer
truths of Christianity," they learned a little gardening—there was always that evangelical link between cultivating the soil and the soul—
and animal husbandry, neither of which would be of any use at home.
But usefulness wasn't the point of this exercise. Jemmy and Fuegia
learned to read and speak English fluently. Fuegia, in fact, turned out
to be a gifted linguist. Darwin would later report, for instance, that

after a brief stop in Brazil, she returned aboard with full sentences of Portuguese, far more, Darwin says, than he could have grasped. York Minster, generally sullen and passive aggressive, refused to read, nor was he much of a gardener. During this entire ten months, no white person made a genuine effort to learn their language, though FitzRoy mentioned that "a good many words were collected" and that York spoke a different language from Jemmy. FitzRoy's idea was that the Fuegians, once Christianized, would serve as the nucleus of a mission, spreading the word of God themselves, so perhaps he thought it was unnecessary for white people to learn their language. But most likely he didn't think about it at all. It was typical of these 19th-century missionaries to travel at great danger to themselves halfway around the world to convert people they couldn't talk to, and Tierra del Fuego would be no exception—until the arrival of the Bridges family in 1870.

Then bad news came down from the Admiralty. They'd lost interest in the southern survey, and the return voyage was off. FitzRoy fell into a funk. He'd brought his charges to England on the proviso that they were just that, *his,* the navy accepting no expense or responsibility. When he picked them up, FitzRoy had no reason to assume that there would be a return voyage. The Admiralty had mentioned it, but nothing was definite. FitzRoy, in the navy since adolescence, had to have known that the firmest of naval plans changed perpetually. If there was to be no navy-sponsored expedition, then he'd have to make private arrangements. He chartered a small commercial ship, the *John of London,* and plunked down a hefty deposit. He then applied for a year's leave of absence for himself and Coxswain Bennett, because he couldn't just load the Fuegians aboard a strange vessel and bid them bon voyage. He'd have to go along to watch over them, since they'd be utterly helpless anywhere except Fuegia. FitzRoy's Pygmalion fantasy was making a significant dent in his fortune, and now he was ready to lose a year of his career to uphold his responsibility. Further, he sent Bennett to buy a flock of goats to stock the Fuegian islands, envisioning ensuing generations of Yahgan as Christian swains with crooked staffs tending their lowing flocks in sixty-knot sleet storms.

Then, in the summer of 1831, Their Majesties King William IV and Queen Adelaide commanded an audience at St. James with FitzRoy and the now-famous Fuegians.

Having been taught to bow and curtsy, Jemmy, York, and Fuegia were got up in their Sunday finery. Jemmy, who, like the others, had grown up naked, was especially delighted with the sartorial aspects of civilization, always admiring his new self in his pocket mirror or any other reflective surface. For this auspicious occasion, he wore yellow kid gloves. His shoes shone. The whole town of Walthamstow turned out to watch as FitzRoy, in formal regalia, cocked hat, long coat, dress sword, gathered the Fuegians into the coach. Bennett climbed into the boot, and off they went to a royal audience. Their carriage was met at the steps of St. James by liverymen and footmen who bowed and called them sir and madam. Butlers ushered them through gilded anterooms to the royal residence. FitzRoy conducted a quick inspection, and in they went, while Bennett stood proudly at attention outside the door.

The Fuegians charmed Their Majesties. Alas, we have only FitzRoy's account of the meeting, published in 1839 in his *Narrative*: "His Majesty asked a great deal about their country, as well as themselves; and I hope I may be permitted to remark that . . . no person ever asked me so many sensible and thoroughly pertinent questions regarding the Fuegians." (William was known, with a sneer, one suspects, as the "sailor king," and he told FitzRoy he'd been to sea long enough to hate it.) "Queen Adelaide also honored the Fuegians by her presence, and by acts of genuine kindness which . . . they never forgot. She left the room for a minute, and returned with one of her own bonnets which she put on the girl's head. Her Majesty then put one of her rings upon the girl's finger." The Queen also gave Fuegia a little silk purse, and the King filled it with coins, saying, according to certain secondary sources, "for your trousseau."

Then suddenly, in the summer of 1831, the voyage was on again. Casually, FitzRoy wrote in his *Narrative,* "A kind uncle, to whom I mentioned my plan, went to the Admiralty, and soon afterwards told me that I should be appointed to . . . go to Tierra del Fuego." That uncle was the duke of Grafton, who, like other dukes in those days, had friends in the lofty echelons of the Admiralty. The duke thought his nephew's voyage a useful and timely undertaking in the national interest. The duke put it to his friend Admiral Francis Beaufort, then in the process of turning the Hydrographer's Office into a dynamic maritime laboratory, and Beaufort thought it a fine idea. If Grafton had not appealed to Beaufort there probably would have been no voyage of the *Beagle*.

Explorers during the Great Age (Columbus, Magellan, da Gama) had found what Fernand Braudel called "the planet's *useful* ocean routes." In the 17th and 18th centuries, explorers went looking for new islands, plants, animals, fishes, and people for the sake of knowledge. It bears repeating that this purity of motive was tinged by the politics of colonialism, paternalistic arrogance, and the unquestioned assumption that white-Western-Christian culture was the highest expression of civilization. No native culture ever benefited from extended contact with Europeans or Americans, but this time explorers *meant no harm*. The shift from the dreary Spanish, Portuguese, and Dutch killers to Captain Cook's gentle instinctive cultural relativism is real and refreshing. The historian William Goetzman—from whom many of us, captivated by the adventure, learned to recognize that there were intellectual and cultural components to exploration—has called this period the Second Great Age of Discovery.

Goetzman pointed out that exploration was inherently subversive. Discovery of the new, the struggle to describe, categorize, and accommodate it, cracked the old structures and assumptions, particularly about wild nature and man's relationship to it. The Newtonian and Biblical explanations for the order of nature, along with hierarchical ones like the Chain of Being, began to erode as contradictory evidence piled up. Before the close of the 19th century, a new ordering principle would replace all the rest. Its author, Charles Darwin, knew what upheaval his published theory would cause, not least to his beloved wife, and so he kept *The Origin of Species* stashed away until 1859. Twenty-nine years earlier, a young man joined a voyage of exploration, and when it was finished, he sat down and wrote what to me is the most pleasing in voice and sensibility of all explorer literature, *Voyage of the Beagle*.

Now that the voyage was actually going to happen, FitzRoy made a special personal request of Beaufort. Could he have a naturalist to accompany him on the voyage? In a ship as small as the *Beagle*, the surgeon usually acted in that capacity, but ship's surgeons were not of a suitable class. What he wanted was a young man of his own social standing, a gentleman educated in the sciences to share mealtimes and talk about natural science. FitzRoy knew the rigors and anxieties of Cape Horn sailing, and he knew what they'd done to Pringle Stokes. Specifically, FitzRoy feared he'd end up like Stokes, a suicide. There was suicide in his family; an uncle, Lord Castlereagh, had killed himself by slashing his throat with a penknife. Also, the *Beagle* would be alone on this voyage, no *Adventure* for support and rescue. FitzRoy alone would be in command, and he feared his "blue devils" might overcome him. Maybe company of a certain upper-class sort would ease his mind. The brilliant Darwin biographer Janet Browne puts it this way: "With touching simplicity, he asked Beaufort to find him a friend."

Admiral Beaufort forwarded FitzRoy's request to Cambridge University. The navy needed educated civilian scientists to serve as naturalists if its scientific expeditions were to be taken as seriously as Beaufort meant them to be. The Cambridge dons, unsatisfied with their "staff" status at the university, saw naval exploration as a source of opportunity and advancement. Cambridge was then the vibrant heart of a new and ambitious class of professional natural scientists known as the "Northern Lights," when the very notion of a professional natural scientist was still novel and somewhat suspect. In *A Preliminary Discourse on the Study of Natural Philosophy*, John Herschel, a leading light, asked how, from seemingly unrelated observations, can we understand nature's unifying laws, her root truths, a line of inquiry, Browne points out, that would lead straight to natural selection. (Isla Herschel lies a couple of miles north of Isla Hornos.) The Cambridge geologist Adam Sedgwick was already posing some touchy questions about the age of the earth and the processes that formed it. Among the lights, also, was a respected generalist named John Henslow.

When Beaufort's letter found its way to Henslow, he thought he might be the very man. A romantic soul, he'd always wanted to go exploring, but a multiyear expedition (five, as it happened) was too much—his new wife was crestfallen at the very suggestion. Henslow had noticed something special in this one young man, Charles Darwin, and wrote: "I suppose there never was a finer chance for a man of spirit. . . . Don't put on any modest doubts about your disqualifications for I assure you I think you are the very man they are in search of."

Charles Darwin, twenty-two, was a good-natured fellow of no particular distinction who liked to ride, shoot, and collect beetles. His father, Robert, who stood six foot two and weighed 328 pounds, thought Darwin was shiftless and undisciplined. He'd studied medicine at Edinburgh, but he was not temperamentally suited to medicine—his father was a doctor—because, among other disadvantages, he couldn't brook the sight of blood. After dropping out of Edinburgh, he went off to Cambridge for a divinity degree and barely graduated. He was hanging around Cambridge after graduation when one day his brother Erasmus invited him to attend a private lecture and discussion on natural history by Henslow.

Darwin's interest in the subject was one of the reasons he'd drifted toward the cloth, since being an amateur naturalist was consistent with being a professional clergyman. That cliché and stock character—the chubby, ruddy-faced, dotty vicar with a butterfly net—was born during this period. Traditional doctrines had long held that nature was God's own book, and the observable order in nature was proof of His existence. The Northern Lights and others were beginning to turn up isolated pieces of evidence that seemed to contradict the Bible, but the scientists recognized that a theological fight over the Creation was in no one's best interest.

Darwin and Henslow grew close, a mutually satisfying father-son relationship. Doctor Darwin genuinely cared about his son's well-being, but he was overbearing and critical, while Henslow made Darwin feel confident. They hiked the countryside "botanizing" and "geologizing" in the terms of the time, and were so often seen strolling about Cambridge deeply engaged in conversation that Darwin's fellows referred to him with some envy as "the man who walks with Henslow."

Henslow's letter arrived at the Darwin family estate, called The Mount, in Shrewsbury while Darwin was on a geologizing trip to Wales with his other idol, geologist Adam Sedgwick. Then Darwin had stopped for some bird shooting at his Uncle Josiah Wedgwood's estate while the letter sat unopened. Darwin almost missed the boat, but he returned to The Mount in the nick of time, read the letter, and thrilled to the possibility. Dr. Darwin, however, thought it the single most damn-fool thing he'd ever heard in his life. Tierra del Fuego? Cape Horn, where people drowned all the time? Absurd, harebrained, just another distraction, shiftless. No, absolutely not, said the doctor, forget it.

Darwin wrote back sadly to Henslow that he would "*certainly* most gladly have accepted the opportunity. . . . But my father gives such strong advice against going." Darwin, it should be noted, wasn't to be paid to sail with the *Beagle;* in fact, the understanding was that he'd pay his own way, including his food. Darwin needed the doctor's money, but he needed rather more his approval: "Even if I was to go, my Father's disliking would take away all energy, & I should want a good stock of that." Biographers of a Freudian bent have looked toward his relationship with his father when trying to explain those strange physical maladies that troubled Darwin in later life. But the old man was really a bit of a softy, and he was touched, it seems, by his son's immediate obedience. He relented, at least to this extent: "If you can find any man of common sense who advises you to go, I will give my consent."

Darwin had just left the estate of a man of common sense who might see it differently. He saddled up and rode the twenty miles back to Wedgwood's. "Uncle Jos" and Darwin, thinking to address the matter in a logical manner that would appeal to the doctor, sat down to produce the famous surviving list of his eight objections, then to counter them one by one. The first objection: "Disreputable to my character as a Clergyman hereafter."

Jos wrote this commonsense counterargument: "I should on the contrary think the offer honorable to him, and the pursuit of Natural History, though certainly not professional, is very suitable to a Clergyman."

Of course, Darwin didn't miss the boat. His father not only gave in, he paid up. Darwin needed a microscope and other instruments, the stuff required to preserve specimens (which would be shipped en route back to Henslow), coats and boots and other personal gear, guns. At least, he told his father, these were one-time expenses, for "I should be deuced clever to spend more than my allowance whilst on board the *Beagle*."

"They tell me you are very clever," the big guy replied.

The voyage of the *Beagle* changed Darwin's life, and then he changed everyone's view of life on earth. He couldn't have done that without the voyage; no one who stayed home could have understood natural selection. But back then, in the late summer of 1831, Darwin's participation was still not definite. He still had to meet and be accepted by the man with whom he would spend the next several years in very close quarters. A dinner date in London was scheduled.

FitzRoy had prepared himself an out by saying that he'd already offered the post to a Mr. Chester and was waiting to hear back. But the dinner meeting went splendidly, and the two men hit it off immediately. The captain, however, saw potential trouble reflected by the shape of Darwin's nose. (FitzRoy had taken his Fuegians to his favorite phrenologist, who concluded that their "propensities," the "barbarian" part of the brain, were overdeveloped.) Phrenologically speaking, Darwin's nose just didn't indicate the high level of inner resolve and fortitude this voyage would require, but FitzRoy liked the rest of Darwin. The *Beagle* was tiny, FitzRoy kept stressing, only ninety feet overall; there would be seventy-four people aboard, and Darwin would have almost no space to call his own. Normal states of cleanliness were out of the question, and the violence of a little ship like the *Beagle* in a heavy seaway was unimaginable to a landsman. He could be seriously injured at any time by any one of a dozen different *common* accidents. And then there was the gloom and the cold winds of Cape Horn, the williwaws, and other unforeseeable "inconveniences." Could Darwin put up with this life?

Oh yes, indeed, Darwin said, without a clue. He knew he'd been chosen not because of his proven accomplishments but because he was a nice guy of the right social standing, and that was fine with him, recognizing the storybook opportunity that had fallen in his lap. He came away from the dinner date extolling FitzRoy as the "beau ideal of the naval officer," but this was before he'd witnessed any of the captain's blue devils. "Woe unto ye beetles of South America!" Darwin exclaimed to his family when the actual offer arrived.

By the time landsmen learned about the tight quarters and the brutal motion, they had already learned another fact of sea life: ships almost never sailed on the scheduled day, or month. His sisters had
rushed to prepare his clothes and organize his kit; his Cambridge
sponsors had tutored him in the latest techniques for preserving specimens; Henslow had collected books and equipment and offered last-
minute instruction; his father had written checks. Darwin, giddy with
excitement, reported aboard the *Beagle* at Plymouth docks—along
with Jemmy, York, and Fuegia—in September. But the *Beagle* wasn't
ready. She wouldn't be ready in October, nor in November. Engaged
in a major refit, the captain had no time for Darwin, who had nothing
to do but wait and worry.

The *Beagle* was still sound, but Cape Horn waters had taken their
toll. Most of the standing rigging was shot, there were some rotten
planks below the waterline, and her decks needed to be replaced completely. FitzRoy took the opportunity to raise the decks almost a foot,
making her drier forward and more livable below. Now she'd actually
have standing headroom in the after cabins, if not in the crew's quarters. He redesigned Pringle Stokes's old cabin, using part of the space
as stowage, carving his own cabin from what remained. He found a
little extra space for the midshipmen's cabin and crew's mess, and he
discreetly offloaded a few cannons to lighten her.

The *Beagle* had originally been rigged as a *brig,* that is, she had
two masts with square sails on both, but brigs seem to have had balance problems. If the press of wind in the sails can't be balanced, the
vessel will always be cranky and recalcitrant, failing to perform when
performance was crucial, as when trying to claw off a lee shore in
heavy wind. Before FitzRoy took command, a third mast, a "mizzen,"
had been stepped aft of the other two on which a triangular sail, like
Pelagic's mainsail, was set. Technically speaking, this turned her into a
bark. (A *ship,* technically speaking, is a vessel with three or more
masts, all square-rigged; *ship* designates rig, not size.) The mizzen
made her more maneuverable by helping to turn her stern. FitzRoy
tweaked his rig incessantly, partly because it needed tweaking, but
there was also a neurotic component to his technical mindedness.

Darwin learned that FitzRoy's warning about space was palpably
true. There was none. Darwin was to share the aft cabin with the two

young men who would be responsible for actually drawing charts from raw surveying data, John Lort Stokes (no relation to Pringle), who had been a midshipman on the first voyage, and Phillip King, the fourteen-year-old son of Parker King, overall commander of the first voyage, along with their big chart table. "The corner of the cabin, which is my private property, is woefully small," he wrote to Henslow. "I have room to turn round & that is all." Darwin was allotted a few drawers for his belongings. Taller than most of his shipmates, he removed the drawers before he went to bed to make room for his feet.

FitzRoy, an instrument nut, also commandeered space in the aft cabin and elsewhere for his chronometers, accurate clocks necessary for determining longitude. The central purpose of the expedition was to complete the survey of Fuegian islands and channels, but secondarily, FitzRoy was charged to proceed west across the Pacific and systematically fix points of longitude. Whalers, regularly rounding the Horn since the 1790s and fanning out over the Pacific, had discovered new island groups, but their positions were way out of whack. John Harrison, by inventing a clock that would work on a ship, had solved the longitude problem in the previous century, and Captain Cook himself had proved that Harrison's chronometer worked on his First Voyage. But chronometers were still too expensive to be in general use, and by 1830, no one had been around the world taking longitude measurements to clean up centuries of guesswork.

Here, briefly, is the problem and the solution. Lines of latitude are parallel, and the equator is the reasonable natural benchmark, but there is no such benchmark for longitude. Meridians of longitude are not parallel; they converge at the poles, so a degree of longitude decreases the farther one sails north or south of the equator. Since there is no natural "equator" of longitude, an artificial one, a "prime meridian," had to be established. Because Britain had the chronometer and the power, the prime meridian was set at Greenwich, England. Since the earth completes one 360-degree rotation every twenty-four hours, the passing of one hour marks one twenty-fourth of a full rotation, or fifteen degrees. Therefore, a navigator can convert time into distance by comparing local apparent noon, the time when the sun is at its zenith, measurable by sextant, with the time at the prime meridian kept by the clock. Every hour's difference then equals fifteen degrees of distance at the various latitudes.

This longitude business was one of Beaufort's pet projects, and in FitzRoy he had his man, an anal-retentive. Beaufort issued FitzRoy a dozen chronometers, but he cadged six more, and still thinking that wasn't enough to average out slight inaccuracies, FitzRoy bought six more at his own expense. And he hired a professional instrument maker, also at his own expense, to babysit the clocks around the world.

Waiting anxiously to sail, Darwin fell ill. Sores broke out around his mouth, and his chest ached with what he surmised to be fatal heart disease, but he kept quiet about it for fear he'd be invalided out of the voyage before it began. Then, finally, by early December, the waiting was over. The *Beagle* cast off her links to home and sailed—only to be blown right back into Plymouth, just like Drake, by westerly gales blasting up the Channel. On December 7, 1831, the *Beagle* put to sea for real, and for Darwin new misery set its teeth: he suffered chronic seasickness. Incapacitated, he tells how Jemmy Button would come to his bedside, bring him things, and say, "Poor, poor man," then turn his face aside to laugh. In his diary, FitzRoy predicted that Darwin would jump ship at the first opportunity. And maybe he would have if his first chances hadn't evaporated when FitzRoy skipped scheduled stops at Funchal, Madeira Island, and at Tenerife. Tenerife would have been a tempting place to bolt. Darwin's hero, and Henslow's, the naturalist Alexander von Humboldt, had made Tenerife famous. "Oh misery, misery . . . we have left perhaps one of the most interesting places in the world, just at the moment when we were near enough for every object to create, without satisfying, our utmost curiosity."

But here in the tropics, Darwin, like thousands of seasick sailors before and after, withdrew his longing for the stillness of death. And to his delight, FitzRoy called for a stop at St. Jago in the Cape Verde Islands for a round of celestial observations. There Darwin saw his first volcano, his first palm tree, tasted a banana for the first time. "I returned to the shore, treading on Volcanic rocks, hearing the notes of unknown birds & seeing new insects fluttering about still-newer flowers. It has been for me a glorious day, like giving sight to a blind man's eyes."

The principle under which Darwin, his mentors, and his heroes operated had been established during the Enlightenment by Captain Cook, Joseph Banks, and a few others, including Thomas Jefferson and Lewis and Clark: Because nature is so vast, complex, and various, you first must collect specimens, make objective, strictly descriptive observations. You must stick to the facts, be careful always to filter out emotional reactions or a priori assumptions or anything else that might color objectivity. Only later, after all the raw data have been thoroughly digested, do you even consider drawing conclusions about causes or patterns, or especially meaning. Enlightenment naturalists more or less stopped at the fact-gathering stage, perfecting the scientific method as they went. Beneficiaries of this work in the next generation, the Romantic-age explorer-naturalists, embraced their own emotional responses to nature (Humboldt was the new model), and they began to encourage speculative theories about the whole of nature and the processes that formed the world. Only then, at the conclusion stage, did the conflict between science and the literal Bible become inevitable.

Bedazzled by St. Jago, Darwin got a bit giddy. He found an octopus in a tide pool, and flabbergasted when it changed colors before his eyes, Darwin concluded that he'd found an unknown natural phenomenon. He wrote a trembling letter to Henslow informing him of his great discovery. Nope, Henslow wrote back, calm down, everyone knows that octopi change colors to match their background.

However, armed with the first volume of Sir Charles Lyell's *Principles of Geology*, a departure gift from FitzRoy, Darwin noticed that the rock strata on the slopes of St. Jago's volcanoes were lying horizontally, suggesting gradual uplift instead of explosive fracturing, which jibed with Lyell's view that the earth's features were fashioned by uniform forces, such as erosion, uplift, subsidence, and sedimentation, that were still in process. To compress geologic time into the seven-day Creation and to fit a world that was only 6,000 years old, according to biblical scholars, who'd counted the begats or something, geologists had jumped through intellectual hoops to come up with the idea of "catastrophism." The world could be just 6,000 years old only if its formative events had happened suddenly, cataclysmically. Lyell frontally challenged this view with his "uniformism," and if his theory were true, the earth must be many millions of years older than the Bible allowed.

But that wasn't exactly what troubled Sedgwick, Henslow, and the other liberal minds at Cambridge. What troubled them was Lyell's view that those uniform world-shaping processes were not progressive. The earth didn't "improve"; it only changed, flying directly in the face of Christianity, and of course man's ordained position as the most progressed of all living things. Darwin noticed that Lyell's uniformism worked to explain the rocks on St. Jago, but chastened by the octopus business, he kept his mouth shut about it for now. But on that volcanic slope, thrilled sensually and intellectually, all Darwin's ambivalence about the trip evaporated, and he decided that just maybe he'd write about geology based on his *Beagle* experience. "If it weren't for seasickness, all the world would be sailors!" he effused.

The *Beagle* sailed on south across the equator and stopped at Bahia (now Salvador), Brazil, where Darwin and FitzRoy had their first serious fight—over slavery. The Portuguese were still actively importing West African slaves to work Brazilian plantations, and seeing a slave culture for the first time, Darwin was appalled. The Darwins, going back to his grandfather, the poet and evolutionist Erasmus, and to the first Josiah Wedgwood, had been active abolitionists. Wedgwood's plaque depicting a chained, supplicating slave, crying, "Am I not a man and a brother?" had sold millions. Doctor Robert Darwin and Uncle Jos had picked up the abolitionist banner, and the moral struggle had become part of Darwin's heritage.

But FitzRoy, the aristocrat, wasn't so appalled. He didn't support slavery, but he patronizingly pointed out to Darwin that when the Bahian slave master asked his assembled slaves whether they were happy being slaves, they'd all said yes.

Of course, Darwin shot back, what else would they say to the man who *owned* them?

FitzRoy flew into a rage. If Darwin so disrespected his views, then they couldn't share the same room. The officers, Wickham and Sulivan, who'd been wondering how long it would take before their mercurial captain alienated Darwin, invited him to mess with them. But before the day was out, FitzRoy tendered an extravagant apology, and the routine in the after cabin returned to normal. For Darwin, though he remained grateful to FitzRoy all his life, the blush had faded from his "beau ideal" of a naval officer.

As for the Fuegians, speaking of paternalism and specimen collecting, neither FitzRoy nor Darwin has much to say about them during the passage. They dressed up in their royal-audience best for the captain's long, pious Sunday services. As part of the bargain for housing them, the missionaries got to send one of their own to help set up the mission, an utterly inexperienced young catechist named Richard Matthews, who'd never been out of England. Matthews is a vague figure, brave but dumb, who never learned a word of the Yahgan language, though he had a full twelve months with the Fuegians on the *Beagle* with nothing else to do.

York Minster and Fuegia Basket had become a couple. Whenever Fuegia was out of York's presence, he'd grow even more sullen than usual, and he'd visibly tense whenever any of the crew got too close to her, which must have been constantly. Both Darwin and FitzRoy were a little frightened of York, because he was so big and so much stronger that any man aboard, and there seemed a cunning quality about him. For instance, he understood far more English than he let on. No doubt the crew, who seem more interested in the Fuegians than FitzRoy or Darwin, took every opportunity in those close quarters where nothing went unnoticed to razz York.

Jemmy, his consistently happy, good-natured self, was having a grand trip. He loved to wear his natty clothes, shiny shoes, and gloves, and he still admired himself in reflective surfaces at every opportunity. He loved to joke with the crew as long as the jokes weren't on him, which, given his vanity, they often were. Jemmy, like most Yahgan, had the eyesight of a raptor, far more acute than any European's. So when Jemmy grew tired of being kidded, he'd say to the officer of the watch, "Me see ship. Me no tell."

An Indian boy, "merry-faced," Darwin calls him, from the Río Negro came aboard in Rio de Janeiro and stayed until the *Beagle* touched at Montevideo. The boy immediately spotted Jemmy's love for mirrors and mocked him. Darwin wrote: "Jemmy, who was always rather jealous of the attention paid to this little boy, did not like this, and used to say, with rather a contemptuous twist of his head, 'Too much skylark!'" But he hadn't seen anything yet.

II

Back Home Again

We could hardly recognize poor Jemmy. Instead of the clean, well-dressed stout lad we left him, we found a naked thin squalid savage.

—Charles Darwin, *Diary*

GIDDY, EXCITED, JEMMY BUTTON SHUTTLED ALONG the starboard rail watching the land slide by, telling anyone who'd listen about how beautiful his homeland was and how happy his people would be to see him, they must have missed him sorely, and they'd celebrate the *Beagle* for bringing him home again. This was the Atlantic side of Tierra del Fuego, a gravel steppe stretching westward to a range of treeless mountains in the distance, not Jemmy's homeland. But Fuegia and York were excited as well, if not so volubly. There was something familiar in the air.

When the *Beagle* came to anchor in Good Success Bay (Buen Suceso), a bite-shaped cove at the very toe of Tierra del Fuego overlooking the Strait of Le Maire, she was greeted by "a Fuegian yell from a party of natives . . . on a projecting woody eminence, who were seen waving skins, and beckoning to us with extreme eagerness. Finding that we did not notice them, they sent up a volume of thick white smoke." (FitzRoy) These people were the Haush, sometimes called the Eastern Ona. This would be Darwin's first contact with "men in a state of nature."

FitzRoy, in full uniform with dress sword, went ashore along with Darwin, Jemmy, and some marines and sailors to meet the naked savages. But the natives had melted back into their environment. Then, tentatively, six men, their eyes ringed with white paint, slashes of ocher on their lips and foreheads, guanaco skins draped regally over their shoulders, emerged from the forest. Both sides stood staring at each other across the cultural chasm until FitzRoy offered them strips of red cloth. An old man stepped forward to accept, and then others followed. (I wonder why red cloth particularly delighted aboriginal people. It wasn't only the Fuegians. Joseph Banks, with Cook on his First Voyage, reports that red cloth was the favorite among the Polynesians, and early 19th-century Arctic explorers say the same about the Inuit.) They proudly tied the cloth around their necks and then showed it off to each other. The old man, the spokesman, patted each of the sailors' chests as a sign of friendship, then bared his own for the same. Chests patted, everyone relaxed. The children were brought out of hiding to see these strangers from somewhere. The spokesman, concerned that Jemmy was stranded among these odd bearded fellows, invited him to stay and live here if he wished. Jemmy mocked the old man behind his back.

After dinner, FitzRoy returned to shore with York and more *Beagle* crewmen in two boats. More native men gathered but still no women. One of the sailors shocked the Indians by singing a popular song and dancing a waltz on the beach. They quickly recovered from their surprise, murmured among themselves, and then joined in as if they'd been waltzing for generations in Tierra del Fuego. The Haush shared with the other Fuegian groups an inexplicable talent as polished and precise mimics, as if they sat around their campfires rehearsing their acts. If a sailor coughed or yawned or scratched his forehead, an Indian would do the same. They could mimic a man precisely, his walk, bearing, gestures, even his accent, and his shipmates would laugh with recognition. It wasn't just one or two with some natural talent; they could all do impressions. And they could mimic language. To English ears, the Fuegian tongues were impenetrable. To Cook, Haush sounded like a man clearing his throat; Yahgan reminded Darwin of the sounds people make "out the sides of their mouths when encouraging horses or feeding chickens." Yet these Haush, to a man, could repeat verbatim strings of English sentences, including the speaker's facial expressions, his intonations, and gestures—and they did so constantly.

Europeans usually found the Ona and Haush pleasingly proportioned, proud, tall, aristocratic, all a noble savage was supposed to be.
As opposed to the squat, stubby, skinny-legged, short-waisted Yahgan. And there on the beach, one of FitzRoy's officers exclaimed,
"What a pity such fine fellows should be left in such a barbarous
state." To FitzRoy, who was feeling some doubt, the man's sentiments
demonstrated "that a desire to benefit these ignorant, though by no
means contemptible human beings, was a natural emotion, and not
the effect of individual caprice or erroneous enthusiasm . . . which had
led me to my undertaking the heavy charge of those Fuegians whom I
brought to England."

The next day, after a farewell visit ashore, the *Beagle* left Good Success Bay and laid a course southwest for the Horn. In his *Narrative*,
FitzRoy coolly announces his plans: He would round the Horn and
then make for Whaleboat Sound to return York Minster and Fuegia
Basket, his "betrothed," to Alacaluf territory. From there, FitzRoy
would sail back east through the Beagle Channel, charting its western
reaches, to return Jemmy to his people in Yahgan land. . . . And his confused reader starts flipping pages for something he must have missed.
What about the mission at Wulaia? Wasn't that the whole point of this
exercise? Back in England, he'd proclaimed, as if he knew what he was
talking about, that the mission could succeed only with a nucleus of
three native converts. Now he was taking two of them somewhere else.
He doesn't say that York had a change of heart, requested to be ex-
cluded from the plans and returned to his homeland instead. It begins
to dawn on the reader that nothing had been settled or arranged. The
Fuegians didn't have the foggiest idea what was expected of them. Nor
did they understand even vaguely what this religion thing was all about.
They'd done their kindly keepers' bidding, passed catechism to please
them, but to imagine any understanding or commitment beyond that
was self-delusion. No, the whole thing was exactly what FitzRoy said it
wasn't, "individual caprice and erroneous enthusiasm."

The *Beagle* was chewing up the hundred-plus miles between
Bahía Buen Suceso and Cape Horn in a rare north wind, broad-
reaching under blue skies. FitzRoy meant to sail in close, have a
good look at the Horn, and fix its longitude. But typically, thick
black clouds boiled up over the western horizon to change those

plans. The north wind stumbled and died. FitzRoy, who later pioneered the use of barometers to forecast weather, didn't need one, he wrote, to know that a big blow was coming on. He decided to run for it, taking shelter in a bombproof natural harbor called Caleta St. Martin. On the east side of Isla Hermite, St. Martin is totally protected from westerly storms—but it's prime williwaw geography. One after another blasted down the hill, until FitzRoy, deciding he'd better take his lumps out in open water, resumed his attempt to round the Horn. This, however, was another of those times when the Horn wasn't allowing anybody around.

The *Beagle* pounded herself against the wind and the waves for two solid weeks, barely making any westing at all. A small wooden ship, about one-third the size of the *British Isles,* the *Beagle* was stout and well sailed, but not meant for this kind of punishment. And neither was Charles Darwin, utterly incapacitated by seasickness again, curled in his bunk, longing for death. His wish nearly came true in the early afternoon of January 14, a typical summer's day with a hurricane blowing.

FitzRoy "was anxiously watching the successive waves, when three huge rollers approached, whose size and steepness at once told me that our sea-boat, good as she was, would be sorely tried. Having steerage, the vessel met and rose over the first unharmed, but her way was checked; the second deadened her way completely, throwing her off the wind; and the third great sea, taking her right a-beam, turned her so far over, that all the lee bulwark, from the cat-head to the stern davit, was two or three feet under water." After a moment of indecision, she rolled upright again. The *Beagle* was still game, and FitzRoy wasn't ready to give in. She actually managed to cross Cape Horn's longitude and even made some westing, and FitzRoy "flattered himself" to think that he'd bested the Horn, but with a sudden gust the wind came on harder than ever. There was nothing to do but strip her down to bare poles and try to keep her stern to the wind as the storm drove her back, just like the *British Isles,* to from where she'd come. FitzRoy tucked her into a safe lee near False Cape Horn behind the high Hardy Peninsula and waited for the thing to relent. But it didn't.

Then, to everyone's surprise, York announced that he and Fuegia would like to live with Jemmy and his Yahgan relatives. Hearing this,

FitzRoy, who had all but admitted failure, was fired with new zeal. Now, with all three converts, the mission might work out after all. Darwin, who always viewed the project as an absurdity, wondered if York had changed his mind because he'd had enough of Cape Horn seafaring. Darwin certainly had, and he was relieved not to go back out there again. But, he added ominously in his journal, "I little thought how deep a scheme Master York had in contemplation."

From the anchorage on the Hardy Peninsula, FitzRoy ran across Bahía Nassau to her old, safe anchorage from the first expedition— Goree Roads—between the southeastern rump of Navarino and Isla Lennox. They would leave the ship there and journey to Wulaia by small boat. He would, he wrote, "establish the Fuegians, with Matthews; leave them for a time, while I continued my route westward to explore the . . . arms of the [Beagle] channel, and part of Whale-Boat Sound; and at my return thence decide whether Matthews should be left among the natives . . . or return with me to the *Beagle*."

He lowered the three remaining whaleboats (the fourth was lost in the Cape Horn knockdown) along with a small yawl-rigged sailboat. There was much to carry. About thirty people would go, including Darwin, a couple of officers, an artist, and twenty-four seamen and marines. In addition to provisions, supplies, weapons, and tents, the surveying gear had to be safely stowed—along with a load of ridiculous contributions from well-meaning people back in England, which FitzRoy diplomatically calls "the stock of useful things." Wineglasses, beaver hats, tea trays, butter bolts, a portable commode, good stuff for canoe nomads. On January 19, 1833, the boats sailed away from the mother ship. The simplest culture in the world was about to meet the most complex boat-for-boat in the Fuegian channels. They had met before, but the difference this time was that the intimidating, incomprehensible center of power, the ship, was absent. Both cultures were riding close to the water.

The Englishmen saw no natives the first night out, camping in a "snug little cove, concealed by some surrounding islets" (Darwin) at the eastern mouth of the channel, which sounds a lot like the cove behind Punta Eugenia. But the next day, as the four-boat fleet pushed westward, smoky fires began to appear on the headlands of Navarino. By the afternoon, a band of Yahgan appeared on a cliff jumping up and down and waving their arms, sending "forth the most hideous yells," wrote Darwin, who never did warm up to the Yahgan, much preferring kelp and tussock grass as points of interest, but he never in his life forgot the people.

That night the *Beagle*'s boats approached a cove among a gathering of Yahgan, who, after spiriting the women and children into the forest, met the visitors with loaded slings, but FitzRoy cut the tension by distributing that reliable red cloth. Then the "yammerschoonering" began. It means, essentially, "I want" or "will you give me?" That word crops up time and again over the next fifty years of contact, and in a real sense characterizes the relationship. Darwin explains: "After pointing to almost every object, one after the other, even to the buttons on our coats, and saying their favorite word in as many intonations as possible, they would then use it in a neuter sense, and vacantly repeat 'Yammerschooner.' After yammerschoonering for any article very eagerly, they would . . . point to their young women or little children, as much to say, 'If you will not give it to me, surely you will to such as these?'"

Fuegia, Jemmy, and York were ashamed of these people's behavior. Fuegia took it particularly hard. This was not how English ladies and gentlemen acted, yammerschoonering all over the place. She ran off in tears and hid herself. Jemmy and York were troubled and embarrassed, calling them "monkeys—dirty—fools—not men," though FitzRoy says, "it turned out that Jemmy's own tribe was as inferior in every way." But these *were* Jemmy's people. FitzRoy mistakenly thought they were members of the Yaapooh tribe, whereas Jemmy was a Tekenika, neither of which existed. Lucas Bridges points out that Yaapooh is a corruption of their word for otter. It happened like this, he surmises: FitzRoy had pointed to some feature of the geography and asked, "What is that called?"

Jemmy or whoever it was spotted an otter, and said, "*Iapooh*."

Which FitzRoy took as a reply. "Yaapooh? Yaapooh Bay?"

"Yes, *iapooh*."

Likewise, "Tekenika" was the result of confusion now permanently fixed on the charts, that fjord our Chilean friends had granted us permission to visit. The word, Bridges says, meant "difficult or awkward to see or understand."

"What's that place?"

"*Teke uneka.*"

The Yahgan, incidentally, never called themselves Yahgan. They had no name for themselves except the general Yámana, the "people." When Thomas Bridges undertook his formal study of their language for his dictionary, he chose the Murray Narrows region lying roughly in the geographic center of their range where, he reasoned, he'd hear the purest form. The Indians called the Murray Yahgashaga, for "Mountain Valley Channel," and its inhabitants Yahgashagalumoala, which Bridges shortened for obvious reasons.

The next night, FitzRoy ordered his boats across to the north shore of the Beagle to escape the importuning and begging, but by dawn flotillas were arriving. The weather was holding calm and sunny, so he could see them coming from miles away, and he noticed that they paddled with furious, frenzied strokes. While they were still hull-down over the horizon, he could make out the streamers of smoke. Their boldness increased with their numbers, yet they weren't exactly threatening, and they hadn't tried to steal anything, not yet, but the expedition was growing edgy because these people seemed unable to control their excitement. Waving their arms and babbling, they were nearly hysterical. So FitzRoy decided to quell their ardor and to dispel any confusion over who was strongest by staging a demonstration.

He cocked two pistols and fired them near a native's head. . . . Silence. No one moved. The astounded subject blinked, shook his head, rubbed his ear, and turned to his companions for a discussion. No one fell down before his superiors in awe and respect. FitzRoy waited for the awe and respect. . . . Maybe he'd been too subtle. He began to shoot holes in things. He shot water; he shot mud and trees, and made rocks dance. The Yahgan watched while FitzRoy fired as fast as the marines could hand him loaded guns. If he'd seen an animal, he would have shot it, and that might have grabbed them, but the exhibition was fizzling before his eyes. The natives were rapt, squatting on their hams, watching every move he made and talking things over among themselves, imitating the bang, but not once making the link between the noise and the bullet's impact. No one wanted to hurt the Yahgan, nor did they feel particularly threatened by their number, but everybody was bloody sick of this yammer-schoonering. "On leaving some place," Darwin wrote, "we have said to each other, 'Thank Heaven, we have at last left those wretches' when one more faint halloo from an all-powerful voice, heard at a prodigious distance—'Yammerschooner.'"

Among other advantages, the expedition had sails. The whaleboats could quickly throw up a lug rig, and the yawl made decent speed in a stiff breeze. The expedition, to the delight of all, sailed away from the paddlers, recrossed the *Beagle*, and stopped at a well-sheltered cove, probably present-day Puerto Navarino at the northern entrance to the Narrows. It appeared to be free of locals. But as the white men were making camp, a delegation of natives appeared from the forest and approached cautiously, perhaps having spotted Jemmy, whom they knew. He went to speak to them.

But something was wrong. These were Jemmy's own people, yet he couldn't communicate with them.

Slowly it dawned on FitzRoy and Darwin: Jemmy had forgotten his language. Jemmy was barely a teenager when he first came aboard the *Beagle*. He had submerged himself far deeper than Fuegia or York in English life and culture. He loved "Inglan," especially its clothes, yet there he stood in his sailor suit on a moonstone beach in the heart of his homeland, fumbling for words, bewildered and estranged. Darwin was moved by the sad scene, and FitzRoy felt guilty. York, an Alacaluf who spoke only a smattering of Yahgan, stepped up to help translate, and finally the news came clear.

Jemmy's mother and brothers were well, and probably heading this way, but his father had died. Jemmy shed not a tear, went off by himself—"Me no help it," he said, passing FitzRoy—started a smoky fire with green branches, and sat down for a time to watch it smoke. When he stood up again, "he talked and laughed as usual," FitzRoy observed.

That night Englishmen and Yahgan families sat around the camp-fire. "We were all well clothed," Darwin says, "and though sitting close to the fire, were far from too warm; yet these naked savages, though further off, were observed to our great surprise, to be steam-ing with perspiration at . . . such a roasting." The sailors sang chanties, and the Yahgan imitated them in unison, a bar or so behind.

Next morning there came, faintly at first, from too far off to locate, an echo: "Yammer . . . schooner, yammer—" then another, nearer, more distinct, and another, layers of approaching calls and shouts. The canoes were coming in fans from west, north, and east. Then from behind, from inland, four men sprinted down the mountain screaming and leaping and flailing their arms. They were frothing at the mouth and bleeding from the nose due to sheer exertion, having run from who knows where, Wulaia maybe, in a headlong frenzy to see these strangers and the wondrous *things* they carried. Darwin thought they looked like "demoniacs." It was clearly time to shove off again.

Out in the channel, thirty to forty canoes, each with a column of blue smoke wafting into the still air, met FitzRoy's boats, bark boats and wooden boats congealing gunwale to gunwale, the clothed and the naked shouting at each other. The whites fended off the canoes, then lay to their oars, trying to shake the canoes among the islets and skerries. But without a breath of breeze, the lighter canoes were faster. Tempers were fraying as the combined fleets turned south into the mouth of Murray Narrows. A breeze blew up, light at first, but favorable from the north and building. With a cheer the rowers became sailors, stepped their masts, set everything flying and trimmed for speed. The helmsmen straightened, concentrated, and began to stretch it out on the paddlers. Burdensome in the history of exploration is the modern understanding that no contact between whites and aborigines was ever harmless, that for the natives every discovery triggered decline, but at the time it must have been thrilling for both parties, and on that sunny summer day in January, 1833, the boat race down the Murray must have been fun. Fun seldom crops up in the Cape Horn story.

The racecourse was as exotic as the competition. This crack between two chunks of the earth's crust is an exception to the austere and somber aesthetics further south. Nowhere wider than a mile, its sides slope gently down to still water, and in the reliable lee, trees can stand straight instead of cringing from the westerlies. The mood is gentle and tranquil, but the Murray is literally a crack, which, one imagines, occurred with sudden violence. About thirty million years ago, after the uplifting and crustal folding, the mountain building had ceased, some imbalance deep in the earth remained, and Navarino broke away from Peninsula Dumas. I admit I don't know that it happened suddenly, like a glacier calves an iceberg, but there is circumstantial evidence on the chart: On the west side halfway down there is a ball-like protuberance of land (used today as a lookout post by the Chilean navy), and if the two parts could be reconnected, that ball would fit perfectly into a socket-like cove directly across on the east side.

The wind freshened from dead astern, and FitzRoy's boats flew before it, leaving the canoes far behind, so far behind that when the sailors cleared the southern mouth of the Murray and turned left behind a small but high island, which FitzRoy named for Jemmy Button, no natives were in sight. When the whites landed at Wulaia, they found a handful of natives, who dissolved into the forest. Winning the boat race by a big margin gave FitzRoy time to case the cove, determine the best site for the mission, and begin off-loading the gear, the butter bolts and tea trays, before the locals caught up.

Wulaia by Fuegian standards is downright sylvan. Level, green meadows—with *flowers*—ease down from the inland mountains, and four freshwater streams gently course through the flats and empty into the harbor, itself snugly protected from the westerlies by a scattering of islands and peninsulas. Jemmy beamed as FitzRoy extolled the virtues of Wulaia. The sailors hurriedly unloaded their gear, the practical and the absurd, along with lumber and tools to build three huts for Matthews, Jemmy, York and Fuegia. They laid out a site for the garden, and then with a shovel FitzRoy scratched a boundary line in the grass around the would-be mission grounds, which the flock was not to cross.

The Yahgan, 150 of them, FitzRoy estimated, beached their canoes several hundred yards away from his boats and his mission claim. (In 1908, one Charles Furlong on a private anthropological expedition found what he took to be canoe-launching ramps at the south end of the cove, but we couldn't find them.) The women and children remained with the canoes, but the men advanced on FitzRoy's line in a clearly aggressive manner. Sentries leveled their rifles when the throng surged into the no-go zone. Gifts of red cloth cut the tension temporarily. FitzRoy and Darwin observed that even in the heat of excitement the Yahgan paused to tear the cloth into equal pieces so that everyone could have at least a little bit. Distributing nails and tools and trinkets, Jemmy and York tried to explain why they'd come and what this boundary line meant without much success.

Jemmy suddenly stopped, looked around. He'd heard a familiar voice in the next wave of canoes.

"My brother!" he exclaimed, leaping up on a rock to wave.

Jemmy's entire family landed—his mother, two sisters, two brothers—and Jemmy walked slowly down to the shore to meet them. FitzRoy described the wrenching scene: "The old woman hardly looked at him before she hastened away to secure her canoe. . . . The girls ran off with her without even looking at Jemmy; and the brothers stood still, stared, walked up to Jemmy, and all around him, without uttering a word. Animals when they meet show far more animation and anxiety than was displayed at this meeting. Jemmy was evidently much mortified, and to add to his confusion and disappointment, as well as my own, he was unable to talk to his brothers, except by broken sentences, in which English predominated." Darwin also thinks of animals; this reunion between mother and son after a three-year absence was less demonstrative "than that between a horse turned out into a field when he joins his old companion."

Was this the Yahgan way of it? Having talked with Jemmy's mother, York told Darwin that she had been inconsolable after her son's disappearance and that she'd searched everywhere for him. FitzRoy "bought" Jemmy for a button or two fair and square; he had no trouble at all assuming that mothers in Fuegia sold their children for trinkets. But why had his mother paddled away and left Jemmy aboard the *Beagle?* There is so little to go on. Even Lucas Bridges, who grew up with the Yahgan, and who eighty years on tells the *Beagle* story with sympathy to the missionary motive, doesn't offer any explanation, saying about this troubling reunion only that "there was no sign of pleasure or surprise, but rather a cool indifference. Many of the natives, having satisfied curiosity, retired." Yet he also writes that the notion that Jemmy's mother sold him for anything is absurd. But that still leaves Jemmy standing at the lonely shore between two unbridgeable cultures, snatched from his own at an impressionable age and dumped into an utterly alien culture. Its trappings and its luxuries had seduced him, and now he had forgotten his language, and seemingly his mother had rejected him. Darwin and FitzRoy both assume that familial love in so unimproved a state of man was simply absent, eroded by the climate and harsh realities of aboriginal life. But if that were so, his mother wouldn't have been "inconsolable" at his disappearance. Lucas Bridges tells us that the Yahgan way of dealing with grief was never to speak of the deceased again. Jemmy, for instance, was unable to learn any particulars about his father's death because none of his relatives would discuss it. Was it something about death? Jemmy's mother would have given him up for dead, and here he was back again. . . . If it were a matter of social style, the Yahgan version of the stiff upper lip, Jemmy might not have been so surprised and hurt. We can't know.

The *Beagle* party started work early the next morning, building the huts and digging the garden, while more canoes arrived. Jemmy, York, and Fuegia had gone among the people the previous evening to explain, and this morning the Yahgan squatted to watch the work. Everyone, as FitzRoy put it, seemed "well-disposed." But to be on the safe side, he ordered that a hole be dug under Matthews's wigwam, then floored over to stow valuables including guns and ammunition. Some of the natives helped carry wood down from the forest to make the huts and rushes from the streams to thatch them. Mostly it was the women who helped. The men squatted on their hams.

The sailors planted potatoes, carrots, turnips, beans, peas, lettuce, onions, leeks, and cabbages, the first-ever sowing of seeds in Fuegia. There would be no reaping, but for now, things were proceeding amicably, and FitzRoy's mood was buoyant. Jemmy's brothers, now the richest men south of the Beagle Channel thanks to his gifts, were friendly and helpful, and the sailors promptly named them Tommy and Harry Button. FitzRoy sent Jemmy's mother a "garment," which she came to model, bringing a bundle of fish. Jemmy was proud of his wealth and spread it around the bosom of his family. York liked Jemmy's eldest brother, "much good friend," and he repeated his wish to live with Fuegia Basket in Yahgan land.

The thieving began almost immediately. Everything had to be guarded or it was lost. For lack of an alternative, FitzRoy conducted another demonstration of his awesome power by shooting up the place while the natives watched, apparently without making the intended connections. That night, sentries chased off a shadowy figure skulking along the tree line. The next day, the Indians returned as usual and hung around watching the *Beagle* party thatch the wigwams, like cottages in the Cotswolds. But then at some unseen cue, the natives, all of them, including Jemmy's family, packed up and paddled off. Even Jemmy was baffled at this behavior. Were they taking the women and children to some safe place in preparation for an attack? Or perhaps they were afraid of FitzRoy's awesome firepower. Anyway, something was changing. Waves of people had been arriving, strangers to Jemmy, who were, FitzRoy says, "intent only upon plunder."

He'd seen a man pluck a watch from Jemmy's pocket while another man distracted him. Even York, cautious and large, had lost things. And there had been an ugly little incident the evening before. Several old men among the strangers had made to cross the boundary line, and when "gently, though firmly" rebuffed, one of them spit in the sentry's face and "went off in a violent passion, muttering to himself, and every now and then turning round to make faces and angry gestures." Perhaps, FitzRoy speculates, Jemmy's people feared they'd be caught in the line of fire when the strangers provoked a violent incident. If so, why didn't they tell Jemmy? Besides, the strangers had left as well. By dark, no natives had returned, and FitzRoy used the opportunity to stash some tools and other items under Matthews's floorboards.

Through all this, Matthews had maintained what Darwin observed to be "his usual quiet fortitude (remarkable in a man apparently possessing little energy of character)." Neither Darwin nor FitzRoy much liked Matthews, but they'd come to respect his determination to make a go of it. Though they couldn't explain the people's hasty departure, York and Jemmy didn't think it presaged an attack. They seemed so certain of this that FitzRoy decided to give Matthews and the mission a trial run if Matthews concurred, which he did. FitzRoy loaded everyone except the missionary and "his Indians" into the boats and sailed a few miles south and around the corner into Bahía Tekenika, where they spent an anxious night. To the men it was obvious—the natives would tear Matthews limb from limb, then eat him—and after they said so a few times, FitzRoy ordered them to belay it.

FitzRoy had them at the oars before dawn, and as they rounded the last point, they saw Matthews carrying a kettle to the fire. Nothing untoward had happened overnight. A few natives had returned,

Tommy Button among them, and the rest of Jemmy's family was expected back that day. As for the strangers, "the bad men," the "Oens
men", they had left and weren't expected back. FitzRoy found this all
very gratifying. Perhaps it was time for a longer trial period. He had
planned to explore the western reaches of the Beagle Channel and the
region around Whaleboat Sound. He waited out the day, finding that
"nothing could be more friendly than their behavior," so he decided
to go, to leave Matthews there alone for a week or two.

He ordered the yawl and one whaleboat back to the *Beagle* in
Goree Roads, and the other two boats headed west. Despite the rigors
of open-boat travel in that climate, this trip might have seemed a vacation. Without the burden of human psychology, they could get on
with what they had come here to do, observe and describe nature,
chart geography, always easier, and to Darwin far more pleasing. He
had become by now a trusted shipmate. He'd always been good company; his affable nature had gotten him aboard in the first place. But
now he'd grown tough and capable, confident he could handle any
hardship except seasickness. This was the adventure he'd longed for.
You can see it in the wit of his prose style in *Voyage of the Beagle*.

While exploring the glacier country in the north fork of the Beagle
Channel, he literally saved the expedition. Thrilled by the scenery,
towering snowcapped mountains, by that magic Fuegian light glistening on beryl-blue ice, they beached the boats and went on foot to ex-
amine one of the glaciers. At the very moment when FitzRoy and
some sailors were saying how sublimely wonderful it would be if the
glacier calved a berg for their delectation, a house-sized block of ice
cracked from the face and hung for a moment before it plunged into
the water. The explorers whooped and cheered like boys—this was
what exploring was about at its best.

However, when glaciers calve big bergs, waves result. As the falling
ice settled, it displaced tons of water, sending three high, steep waves
running directly toward the beached boats. Thinking faster than his
mates, Darwin and several seamen sprinted down the beach and
reached the boats just as the first wave broke over them. Darwin and
the others were tumbled and banged up, but they managed to hold on—
that was the important thing, don't let the boats be washed away. By the
time the trailing waves broke, the rest of the crew had arrived to help.

Darwin made light of this seamanly act, barely mentioning it in favor of remarking on the curious occurrence of glaciers reaching sea level here in 55 degrees South, whereas in Europe none do so south of 70 degrees North. But FitzRoy says, "had not Mr. Darwin and two or three seamen run to [the boats] instantly, they would have been swept away from us irrecoverably," in which case survival would have been in dark doubt. As a tribute to his friend, FitzRoy named the high peak down which that glacier flowed Mount Darwin, and then he named the whole range of mountains after him: the Cordillera Darwin.

Pushing west into unknown channels, FitzRoy continued naming features, an island here, a sound there, "after my messmate, who so willingly encountered the discomfort and risk of a long cruise in a small loaded boat." The captain didn't intend to map every bay, channel, and fjord, a lifetime's work that would probably remain undone today but for satellite photography. Instead, FitzRoy meant to make broad geographic connections between this unexplored part of the Beagle and the part he'd charted on his first voyage. In a remarkable stretch of fine weather, they rowed and sailed all the way to the Pacific just north of Londonderry Island, but they didn't tarry long, because FitzRoy was anxious about his charges back at Wulaia. On the return trip east, the party cursorily explored the southern arm of the Beagle, the first whites ever to see those waters.

When still a good day's run west of the Murray, they spotted the first sign of trouble, an old woman in a canoe wearing a dress that belonged to Fuegia. Other Indians were wearing strips of new cloth in their hair or tied around their heads. FitzRoy noticed among the canoe people "an air of defiance . . . which looked as if they knew that harm had been done, and that they were ready to stand on the defensive if any such act as they expected were put into execution." (FitzRoy's prose was as tightly wound as his psyche, and to his lifelong chagrin, his version of the story was ignored, while his messmate's book became a best-seller.) Then, speeding through the Narrows before a stiff breeze and a fair tide, they encountered a small flotilla of natives all festooned in tartan cloth and white linen. These people peered at the whites with that same defiance.

There are a lot of lurid variations on what happened next. One historian repeats the story that when the party rounded the point, they saw Fuegians holding Matthews down while others plucked the hairs from his beard with mussel-shell pincers. As a source for that version, the writer cites the *British Baptist Reporter* of 1859. Another writer reports that Matthews, sighting the whaleboats, ran hysterically to the beach, dove into the water, and swam for his life to meet them. Great melodrama. But I'm remembering the heat from Dr. van de Maele's gaze back in his Indian museum and my promise to avoid the obvious bullshit. I don't think there's any reason to doubt FitzRoy's own account. It makes sense, and it largely agrees with Darwin's.

Painted Indians all wearing ragged remnants of English clothes gathered around the boats as they landed. "The Indians came hallooing and jumping about us, and then, to my extreme relief, Matthews appeared, dressed and looking as usual." Darwin added without elaboration that they arrived just in time to save Matthews's life. Jemmy and York also appeared looking "as usual." Fuegia, they said, didn't want to come out of her wigwam. For privacy, FitzRoy took Matthews in his boat and shoved off into the bay, while the Fuegians ashore "squatted on their hams to watch our proceedings, reminding me of a pack of hounds waiting for a fox to be unearthed."

All had been tranquil for three days, Matthews said, until the strangers returned, and then the harassment and thievery began in earnest. Matthews hadn't a moment's peace. If the natives weren't dashing in to snatch his stuff, they crowded around and into his wigwam yammerschoonering for it. When refused, several flew into wild rages, and one returned with a large rock making signs that he would smash Matthews's skull if he didn't cough up his goods. In only one instance had he actually been touched—when a man grabbed him and bent back his head to show how easy it would be to snap his neck—but there were plenty of threats. At night natives screamed in his ears to exhaust him.

Matthews's only refuge was with the women. They made room for him around their fires while he got some sleep with Jemmy watching his goods. The women asked for nothing in return. York had lost nothing, perhaps because York was bigger than everyone else or perhaps because he sided with the natives. Jemmy, however, had lost almost everything. Even members of his own family had stolen his stuff.

The garden was trampled, and when asked about it, Jemmy just shook his head and sadly said, "My people very bad, great fool, know nothing at all, very great fool."

The mission project was clearly a complete failure. Leaving Matthews here was out of the question, though he bravely offered to give it another try if FitzRoy wanted him to. No, sooner or later they would kill him. Distributing strips of cloth, knives, and nails, FitzRoy managed to create enough diversion for some armed marines to collect the stuff and load it into a boat. Then he bade farewell to Jemmy and York (Fuegia never came out of her wigwam), promising to look in on them again in a few days.

He left at dawn, his boats running fast before a manageable west wind around the south shore of Navarino, and by dark they had reached the *Beagle* still anchored in Goree Roads, shipshape and ready to weigh. He beat her back across Bahía Nassau against that same breeze, which, by the time she found a lee behind Peninsula Hardy, had increased to a whole gale. After a night pummeled by williwaws, better weather came with daylight, and FitzRoy sent a party overland to have a close look at False Cape Horn. He took another boat north ostensibly to explore a piece of Ponsonby Sound, but his real purpose was to return to Wulaia.

There had been a fight between Jemmy's people and the strangers, each throwing "great many stones" at the other—the Yahgan flung grapefruit-sized rocks at high velocity with deadly accuracy, major-league arms, by all accounts. No one had been seriously injured in the melee; however, the strangers had stolen two women, and Jemmy's people had taken one of theirs. The strangers driven off, all was quiet now. Jemmy had been building a dugout canoe from a single log like those he'd seen in Brazil. York was also building a canoe, an uncommonly large one, out of the boards from the huts. Neither one feared for his safety, and neither wanted to return with FitzRoy to the *Beagle*. There was nothing further for him to do except to say good-bye to those three people, who in his own way he actually loved; it was, FitzRoy says, the hardest thing he'd ever had to do. He finally recognized and was able actually to state that their trip to civilization and back had done them no good and, further, might cause them unhappiness. But he then added, as if with a sad sigh, that perhaps one day sailors shipwrecked in the islands would find succor from Indians who remembered the kindnesses paid them by the men of the *Beagle*.

There's a coda to the story of FitzRoy and his Fuegians. After leaving them at Wulaia, he conned the *Beagle* back around the toe of Tierra del Fuego into the Atlantic and spent the next fourteen months surveying the coast of Patagonia. It was grueling, precarious work along this flat, exposed shore, a lot of anchor hauling and small-boat toil in dirty weather. The dark moods, the "blue devils," overcame him more frequently now. He grew thin, his face gaunt. The man was only twenty-seven years old, but Darwin said he looked "aged."

Part of his tension was due as always to the war of contradictions raging in his psyche, but part also had concrete nautical cause. This violent climate and tortured geography had made the survey by a single ship all but impossible even for a gifted explorer like him. He might have cut it short and headed out across the Pacific to undertake the rest of his assignment, including that fateful stop in the Galápagos Islands. But his retentive, perfectionist streak wouldn't permit that. Instead, FitzRoy decided that what he really needed was another ship, and he assumed baselessly that the Admiralty would concur and reimburse him for it.

He bought a decent schooner from an American sealing captain he'd met in the Falkland Islands for 1,300 pounds and named her *Adventure,* after the *Beagle*'s original consort. Then he informed the Admiralty of this by letter, which he mailed via a homebound ship. She did prove useful, but she essentially doubled the technical, nautical demands on him. FitzRoy was no good at delegating authority. Over a year later, the Admiralty's reply caught up with him in Valparaiso. Forget it, the lords said, we never authorized the purchase, we're not paying a guinea for it, and what's more, get rid of it right now. FitzRoy, in the navy since adolescence, should have known that first-time commanders don't buy extra vessels and send the bill to the Admiralty. But the letter didn't stop there. The Admiralty added a reprimand for taking so damn long on the Tierra del Fuego survey. Among those who signed the letter was his patron Beaufort. FitzRoy dropped into a deep funk. He wrote a letter resigning his commission, but Lieutenant Wickham, who had been taking care of FitzRoy, talked him out of sending it.

While FitzRoy was toiling to map the shores of Patagonia, Darwin was having the time of his life. He spent most of that year adventuring ashore in Argentina and Uruguay, riding with the gauchos, observing nature, and collecting specimens, which, when he reached civilization, he'd send home to Henslow. And though Darwin didn't know it, the specimens, some previously unknown in Europe, were making him a star at Cambridge and something of a romantic figure in the style of his hero Alexander von Humboldt. During this time, Darwin also made a personal life-changing decision—that he would forgo the clergy and devote himself entirely to natural science. FitzRoy was fascinated to hear about his exploits when Darwin rejoined the *Beagle,* but sadly admitted that he was jealous. Darwin was finding new sustaining energy, while FitzRoy's was flagging.

Finally, in the austral autumn of 1834, FitzRoy completed the Patagonia work, and again he laid a course south for the Horn. Everyone was delighted to get the hell out of Fuegia before winter, but FitzRoy had a stop to make. He worried about his friends in Wulaia. This time, instead of anchoring at Goree Roads and proceeding by boat, he boldly took the *Beagle* west in her namesake channel. For the natives and the crew, her presence changed everything. "I was amused," wrote Darwin, "by finding what a difference the circumstances of being quite superior made in the interests of beholding the savages." Now it was "the more the merrier, and very merry work it was. Both parties laughing, wondering, gaping at each other; we pitying them, for giving us good fish and crabs for rags; they . . . at finding people so foolish as to exchange such splendid ornaments for a good supper."

FitzRoy sailed her right through the Murray Narrows, and on March 5, 1834, the *Beagle* came to anchor in Wulaia Bay. The old wigwams were still standing, but clearly abandoned. In fact, all of Wulaia seemed abandoned, but then, only the white men had ever thought of it as a permanent settlement. The Yahgan, however, were keenly aware that the *Beagle* had entered their little world. Canoes soon straggled in from the south and gathered around the ship. There was Tommy Button, waving.

Then FitzRoy recognized another face, but only vaguely. The figure smiled up at FitzRoy, touched two fingers to his brow in a sailorly salute—it was Jemmy Button.

"But how altered!" FitzRoy exclaims in the *Narrative*. "I could hardly restrain my feelings, and I was not . . . the only one so touched by his squalid, miserable appearance. He was naked, like his companions, except for a bit of skin about his loins; his hair was long and matted, just like theirs; he was wretchedly thin, and his eyes were affected by smoke. We hurried him below, clothed him immediately, and in half an hour he was sitting with me at dinner in my cabin, using his knife and fork properly, and in every way behaving as correctly as if he had never left us."

Over dinner FitzRoy told Jemmy that he'd be welcome back aboard the *Beagle,* and that he could if he wanted return to England.

No, Jemmy said, he would cross no more oceans. His place was here, not there, and besides, he had taken a wife. In fact, as Jemmy and the captain ate, they could *hear* his wife down at water level in her canoe, keening, wailing with despair and fear for her man. No one could induce her aboard, not even with rich gifts, and nothing could convince her that Jemmy would not be taken away.

Where, FitzRoy wondered, were York and Fuegia?

Gone. Jemmy told FitzRoy that when York had completed his big canoe, he'd invited Jemmy and his mother to accompany him and Fuegia to Alacaluf country. They piled their goods into two canoes, and everyone paddled west as far as Isla Gordon, where the Beagle Channel bifurcates. While Jemmy and his mother were sleeping, York stole everything they owned and made off with it during the night. He'd disappeared into those same uncharted channels as FitzRoy's whaleboat, the incident that had set this whole story in motion, leaving Jemmy and his mother in their original bereft state. "I am now quite sure," FitzRoy writes, "that from the time he [York] changed his mind, desiring to be placed at Wulaia, with Matthews and Jemmy, he meditated taking a good opportunity of possessing himself of every thing."

They took a last sentimental walk ashore, and Jemmy pointed out in a childlike way the old boundary line, the places where tents had been pitched, "and where any particular occurrence happened."

Every day Jemmy had watched the garden to see if the vegetables were sprouting, but they never did. He said that the three huts, though still standing, were unusable because, built too high, they were cold in the winter. He said also that Wulaia had been abandoned because of the Ona. The Yahgan's old enemy, hearing of the white visitors and their riches, had staged a raid some months before, crossing the Beagle in pirated Yahgan canoes, which they'd lashed together for stability. They'd landed on the north shore of Navarino, then traveled overland through the forests to attack Wulaia from the rear. Jemmy claimed to have killed one of the raiders, but because the Ona might return at any time, he and his family had moved to Jemmy Button Island (as FitzRoy had named it).

As a final gesture of good-bye, Jemmy brought FitzRoy two carefully preserved otter skins. He also had a gift, a bow and a quiver full of arrows, for the schoolmaster back in Walthamstow, and as a parting gift for Darwin, he'd made two bone spear points. That, then, was the end of it, at least as far as the *Beagle* and her people were concerned. She weighed, sailed slowly and forever from Fuegia. Ashore, watching, Jemmy lighted a signal fire, threw on some green boughs, and, as Darwin describes it, "the smoke curled up, bidding us a last and long farewell, as the ship stood on her course into the open sea."

No white man would ever see York Minster again, but forty years on, Fuegia would return to the eastern part of the Beagle and there meet Thomas Bridges. About fifty-five years old, she was strong and healthy, if toothless. In Yahgan, Bridges asked her what she remembered of her *Beagle* experience. London, she said, and the people at Walthamstow, their kindnesses to her. She remembered FitzRoy and the *Beagle*. Fuegia remembered a little English, a few nouns, *knife, fork,* and *bed.* She had forgotten almost all else, including everything about the "plainer truths of Christianity." When Bridges offered a chair, she squatted on the floor beside it. Fuegia was traveling with her new, much younger husband, typical of Yahgan marital practices. York, she told Bridges, had been killed years earlier in a vendetta by the family of a man he had killed. She had two sons by York, and anxious to get back to them, she soon left for the west.

Thomas Bridges saw her once more ten years later, in 1883, in her own home range when she was old and near death. He'd assembled a small-boat expedition to the western channels, and hearing of her whereabouts from natives near Isla Londonderry, went to visit her. She was weak and "unhappy," but she had her sons and other relatives to care for her. Bridges, "confident she would not fall victim to *tabacana*," the Yahgan practice of killing the very old and infirm (shared by other nomadic cultures), he offered her Christian comforts and said good-bye.

For Jemmy Button, who did not disappear into the remote western channels, the future would play out quite differently, and his contact with white missionaries was far from finished.

12

To Cape Horn

Our horizon was limited to a small compass by the spray; the sea looked ominous; there was so much foam. . . that it resembled a dreary plain covered by patches of drifted snow. Whilst we were heavily labouring, it was curious to see how the albatross with its widely expanded wings, glided right up the wind.

—**Charles Darwin,** *Diary*

I AWOKE WITH A START FROM A NASTY DREAM, no idea where I was except that it was a cold place. . . . Caleta Martial, the morning after we'd struck in Paso Bravo. That settled with some effort, I pulled on a coat and climbed topside in the cold, pale dawn to have a piss off the stern. During our first night, in Puerto Williams, I'd made the mistake of using the head, instead of the stern, in the middle of the night. Flushing, I heard the captain on the other side of the bulkhead begin to moan and mutter troubled gibberish in his sleep. The sound of gurgling water—the sound of sinking—had loosed a flood of anxiety, attuned as he was to the untoward waking or sleeping. I heard thuds. He was manning the pumps. Kate said, "Shhh, it's okay, it's only the head," in a soothing whisper. I never did that again.

Caleta Martial, a safe, deep semicircular notch in the leeward side of Isla Herschel, was postcard beautiful, like a Caribbean come-on in a snow-belt train station. The water was downright pellucid, the sky dark blue and endless, and against it, the green and brown islands were so distinctly delineated as to seem abstract. I tried to call up the chart. Away to the north was Paso Bravo, the gorge between Wollaston and Freycinet, where we'd touched last night. Isla Deceit, steep and rocky with vertical shores, lay several miles to the east. Up behind Martial Cove's symmetrical crescent beach, a soft, rolling meadow climbed at a gentle hiking angle to a scattering of greenstone boulders and on to the brown, vertical remnant of a shattered mountain. The buttery light, the glassy blue water, the white beach suggested repose, a softness in the environment. Famous last words. But there actually are these sessions of tranquillity when the sky lifts behind yesterday's depression. They're not common, but they're a real part of the environment, and I wanted to bask in this one alone while that dark dream wilted in new light.

I dreamed I'd seen Jarli die out there in the Drake Passage. I watched from a stable, elevated viewpoint, an albatross eye at masthead height off his starboard quarter. The seas were lethal, seething forty-footers with streaks of crazy spume tearing down their faces. Jarli sat at the tiller of his little boat—it had blue topsides—running under bare poles before the wind and seas without a chance of survival. Jarli knew it, I knew it. A breaking wave higher than the rest soon lifted the stern, pointed the bow at the bottom, and for an instant the boat hung there. Jarli glanced astern, his face calm, watching the wave curl with a seaman's interest. He didn't seem frightened, that's what struck me, as if he'd known his whole life that he'd die young at sea, and now with the moment at hand he was curious about the shape of the wave. He released the tiller—no more steering to be done—and leaned back against the lifelines as it broke over his head. From aloft I saw a flash of red bottom paint in the white froth, and then nothing, gone without a trace.

People were stirring below, laughing at something, Dick making toast on the top of the cabin heater. He was a meticulous toaster. The stove hadn't quite done its work on the toast or the boat-wide chill, breath still visible on the fringes. But the steel boat warmed up, the toast turned out excellent, and the marmalade, and the crew. One could go all sentimental here amid this excellence, this pellucidness ten bird miles north of Cape Horn on an exquisite gift of a day. We were going to get there. Today. Hamish was firing up his laptop for the morning weather map, but I didn't look, preferring to remain adrift in the present. There was probably something brewing in the west, but there was always something brewing in the west.

Caleta Martial was named for the kindly captain of a French expedition aboard the steam-assisted naval vessel *Romanche* to observe the transit of Venus on December 6, 1882. They spent a year at Bahía Orange on Peninsula Hardy studying the Yahgan, surveying and naming everything that the Dutch and the English hadn't already named, peninsulas Pasteur and Dumas, for instance. Their stay was one of the high points in Lucas Bridges's childhood. He was fascinated by these men of science with their pointed beards and eyeglasses with different-colored lenses, and best of all, they paid Lucas and his brother Despard to collect plant and animal specimens. As we were hauling up the long anchor chain, Hamish said that Caleta Martial is one of only several coves in the entire archipelago where a boat can lie safely to one anchor without having to be tied to the shore. The holding ground, mud and sand instead of kelp and rock, is excellent. But also the topography, its long, gentle up-slope, is not conducive to williwaws.

It should have come up before now, this subject of williwaws, since we talked about them nearly every day. Williwaws, in their very nature, reflect exquisitely the spirit of this place. What happens is sublimely diabolical. Cold, therefore heavy, air blows in and encounters a steep mountainside. Instead of just bending up over the summit and carrying on, the heavy air pools like a liquid on the windward side. If nothing changes in the atmosphere, the pool continues to fill—until it overflows the top of the mountain. At which point it avalanches down the other side and drops on your deck like a cartoon safe. But what makes the williwaw so diabolical is that it flies in the face of nautical common sense, which says that if you expect bad weather from the west, then you want to seek shelter on the east side (the leeward side) of something substantial, something like a mountain. But here anchoring in the lee of a mountain puts you beneath the williwaw. Later, on Peninsula Hardy, for instance, we would tuck into places utterly protected from all points of the compass—but not from above. A williwaw is an air strike. Further, williwaws aren't necessarily foul-weather phenomena, though they often accompany storms. On a fine, sparkling day like this, the monster can dive over the mountain and lay you on your beam ends like a bathtub toy, mast in the water, re-arranging your kitchen. Hamish, who tensed whenever we approached "williwaw country," said that 100 knots wasn't at all unusual.

"A *hundred* knots?" said Jonathan.

The *Beagle* was knocked down twice by williwaws. She survived because the anchors held and because, battened down against the event, she took no water. If no water finds its way inside during the first onslaught, she'll likely survive the experience, and if her people escape injury, then she's had an inexpensive lesson in katabatic behavior. Williwaws are short-lived; that's about their only positive aspect for the mariner. Once the bowl of wind empties over the mountain, which doesn't take long at 100 knots, the williwaw is finished. For the moment. And sometimes the environment warns of williwaws, as Joshua Slocum noticed aboard his home-built thirty-seven-foot yawl with the immortal name *Spray*. In the Strait of Magellan, 1896: "The day to all appearances promised fine weather and light winds, but appearances in Tierra del Fuego do not always count. While I was wondering why no trees grew on the slope abreast of the anchorage, a williwaw came down with such terrific force as to carry *Spray*, with two anchors down, like a feather out . . . into deep water. No wonder trees did not grow on the side of that hill! Great Boreas!" (*Sailing Alone Around the World*)

Planning the trip, we took every occasion to say the word, *will-i-waws*, great Boreas, perfect emblems of Cape Horn. The Spanish word is *rafaga*, and when he was a kid, Lucas Bridges called them "cloudies" for the spindrift they kicked up, but williwaw is a tough word to beat. We wanted to see one up close, though we never mentioned that to the captain, lest we seem overexcited lubbers, the sort who, watching waves from a beach chair, claim to "love the ocean when it's rough." Hamish is level, smart, imperturbable, probably the best all-around sailor I'd ever had the pleasure to sail with, more than capable in extremis, no doubt, and that he held williwaws in such deep respect enhanced our desire to witness one or two up close.

"One *hundred* knots?"

Will-ee-waw.

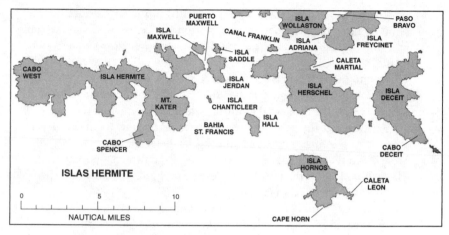

Map 12.1   Islas Hermite

A little northerly breeze filled in at about twelve knots, the result, I suppose, of thermal activity on the islands, just enough wind to move *Pelagic* at a pleasant sight-seeing pace as long as the wind stayed over the beam. Reaching along comfortably in Paso Franklin between Herschel and Wollaston, the wind over our starboard side, *Pelagic* felt happy. She seemed slippery in the water. All sailboats are happy on that point of sail, but we'd soon be turning south between Herschel and Hermite, which would put the little northerly dead on our stern, a point no sailboat relishes in light breeze, especially steel boats loaded with expedition gear and a metal shop. And without any gradient activity overhead, the northerly wouldn't last. We were going to visit Cape Horn in a calm. A white-knuckled struggle along the edge of control, fifty-knot sleet bullets, would better fit the image, but we'd see nothing beyond the bow in those conditions. We wanted to see Cape Horn. So, gratefully, we lazed along on a general southerly heading, keeping her as high as practical without running afoul of rocks and reefs around little Isla Chanticleer.

Hamish glanced abruptly to starboard—a big bluff on the shore of Isla Hermite—and said quietly, "There's one now—"

Like rotor wash from a low-hovering helicopter, but three times the diameter, a cylinder of cold air slammed the water, punching in a distinct, lingering depression, a round scoop from the flat surface. Dense white tendrils of spray flew outward from the center up over the rim and high into the air as pirouetting swirls and miniature waterspouts which, spent, fell back as rain. "Did so violently fall . . . that they would pierce into the very bowels of the sea & make it swell upwards on every side," said the Reverend Fletcher in *The World Encompassed* about williwaws. By the time we'd grabbed at handholds it was over.

We watched the shorelines on either side hoping for more. I was steering at the time, or sort of, and I'd let *Pelagic* fall to her left, "by the lee," in the general direction of long kelp streamers buoying rocks. Hamish nodded at the bow to suggest I watch it every now and then.

"A small one," said Hamish.

"That was a *small* one?" David exclaimed.

We wanted numbers, velocity in knots in order to transpose it into forces we understood, that is, horizontal forces. What was it, fifty knots?

"Oh, more."

"Seventy?" That's hurricane velocity.

"Easily."

We always encouraged Hamish to tell us high-latitude war stories. Here's one about being the ice pilot aboard the magnificent *Adix*, a long, thin three-masted schooner owned by a South American pluto-crat who likes his privacy. They'd been to the Antarctic Peninsula, Desolation Island, and it had been hell on Hamish, the ice pilot. He said he had to sit around in the mahogany salon under the round sky-light sampling rare vintages. Occasionally, he'd go topside, look around, and say, "Ah, helmsman, mind those growlers, now." Return-ing to Ushuaia, the ice astern, the schooner was reaching along in a stiff breeze carrying a lot of sail as she entered the east end of the Bea-gle, a place Laird and Novak called Williwaw Alley. (A place nearby is named Punta Remolino, Whirlwind Point.) Hamish suggested to the captain that he might want to shorten down for that reason. The cap-tain looked around and saw clear skies and this fine fresh wind, and said no, we'll carry on. She carried on about three boat-lengths before a williwaw, careening down from the mountains on the Tierra del Fuego side, knocked her flat, masts in the water. She came back to a level keel, no one injured, but about $200,000 in sails had been turned into streamers.

We stood around the side decks, trying to absorb the landscape, waiting for williwaws. The big islands around us—Hermite on starboard, Herschel close aboard on port, Wollaston astern—made the Beagle Channel shores seem temperate, verdant, lush, rich in resource and variety. In scar-like ravines and watercourses, copses of beech trees huddled, while others in small bands grew out of the vertical cliff face, but none peeked over the crest of the cliff. Both the deciduous and evergreen beeches *(Nothofagus antarctica* and *betuloides)* grew tall in dense forests between the mountains of Tierra del Fuego and the Beagle shore. These in the southern islands, ducking behind the cliffs and hanging on against the williwaws, were predominantly dwarfs *(Nothofagus pumilio),* gnarled and nearly leafless. Leaves were probably unaffordable luxuries down here at the southern fringe of chlorophyll production. These trees looked like torture victims.

Isla Hermite fell astern, taking our lee with it, and we could see westward for the first time, out into the Drake Passage. Everyone went for the handholds as a six- or seven-foot swell pitched the bow skyward, and *Pelagic* hobby-horsed down the backside. Between the swells, the sea was dead flat. There was no wind—the dribbling northerly didn't count—and there had been none for four days. But that's the nature of swells. They are spent waves that roll on beyond the influence of the wind that made them, and theoretically, they can keep on moving indefinitely. Southern Ocean storms edging along the Antarctic Circle radiate swells that turn into extreme-surfing waves when, 6,000 miles later, Hawaii trips them up. The old salts used to call swells "the dogs before their masters." We had all seen swells from boats in open oceans, but none of them looked like these swells. Hamish, who'd seen these swells many times before, said that there are none like them in any other ocean.

First, they were extremely long, a quarter mile from crest to crest, maybe longer, easily a minute and a half between crests. (I meant to time them, but I got unscientifically lost in the feel of the scene, the menace beneath the horizon, the psycho killer's squeaky shoes from off camera.) Swells naturally lengthen the farther they travel from the wind source, but in other oceans, they bump into land before they get this long. That wasn't the only anomaly. These swells were moving fast, as if urgently fleeing from something. I wasn't sure if they actu-

ally moved faster than normal swells or if they only seemed to, until
Hamish said no, they're very fast. The sea had gone slate-gray now,
the sky pale like drowned flesh, which those of a romantic temperament might see as signals of latent menace—"you will see everything
that is sublime," said Captain Eric back in Puerto Williams. We all
knew the Drake's reputation for menace, captivated by it since childhood, but now, decades on, the surprising thing was that it *looked* so
menacing on a fair day.

We looped south into the open Drake until we'd passed the latitude of Cape Horn, where Hamish gestured for a left turn.

"Careful of the jibe," said an ironist up forward, as the boom
lazed across to the starboard side. Only then did we begin to believe
that the weather would hold. Patches of blue came and went in the
east above the Horn. The swells, now on her starboard quarter, hefted
Pelagic's stern time and time again, sunk her bow to near the toe rail,
and dropped her back in lake-flat water. We were heading due east
(104 degrees magnetic) toward the pitch of the Horn, and from five or
six miles off, we could see that distinctive pointed crest, the brown-
grass slope easing away to the north. But we were still not seeing the
seaward face.

Two rocks called Robinson and Bascunan stand like sentinels
astride this near-shore approach from the west, and our present heading would take us between the two. The *Sailing Directions* says in
supreme understatement that the "rocks are marked by breakers."
They're marked by something, but not the sort of breakers you see in
normal oceans. When the swells reached first Bascunan, then Robinson, they didn't break so much as explode with a spectacular violence
wildly disproportionate to their size. The volume of white water and
the altitude to which it was flung suggested, someone said, depth-
charge attacks in Battle of the Atlantic documentaries. The black glistening rocks had barely surfaced, white water still cascading down
their flanks, when the next swell bore in. If eight-foot swells made
such a fuss, what would thirty-foot waves look like?

"Can we go between them?"

"Yes, stay in the middle."

. . . There it was, now barely a mile away to the northeast, the face
of Cape Horn. It rears abruptly from the ocean in an elegant sweep to

a rounded summit. Cape Horn is graceful in shape, statuesque. Kate thoughtfully stepped to the helm, and I took a place with the others on the rail, swell-braced against the shrouds. It was due to blind geologic chance that South America ended this way, in a sublime upswung black-rock cliff, instead of, say, a low, flat, featureless beach. Or even a hilly meadow. Centuries of ships would still have had to round it; it would still have been "the hard" as far as navigators were concerned, but it wouldn't have been the same. It was likewise a random botanical evolution that produced *Nothofagus* to look like a scene painter's evocation of a creepy forest and then hung it with rotting-lace lichens in case you missed the mood. Look around in all directions, look at that leaden sea and the outsize swells, the moody clouds, the Southern Cross, the light itself. Nature, making extravagant statements and gestures everywhere, would not have missed the opportunity to put appropriate punctuation at *el fin del mundo*.

The Cape Horn of legend, the Old Ogre, was in league with the wind and the waves, more cause than symbol, who decided which sailors got around unscathed and which were driven under. But those to whom the legend applied, the sailors fighting it out down in the Drake, seldom laid eyes on the face of Cape Horn. If they had, the legend might have been cast differently, for this is a badly beaten and beleaguered ogre. And suddenly, before I knew it was there, no chance to pinch it off, a williwaw of powerful feelings washed over me. If I'd had some warning, I might have ducked behind scientific objectivity. The rock face is denuded into sharp vertical ridges and deeply eroded ravines. The rock is faulted, crumbly, and cracked from eons of alternate freezes and thaws. The low, green vegetation that somehow found root on this most exposed of places seemed to be holding back its disintegration. I made sure to avoid eye contact; expedition members shouldn't be seen to dissolve into Romantic tears every time the sublime hoves into sight. Still, having lost all moorings to objectivity, I was about to burst out weeping for the Old Ogre and his brave stand in the face of the wind. Weather-beaten and wave-battered, Cape Horn was a colleague of the sailor, not an agent of the wind. I hadn't expected that, and now it seemed poignant beyond words.

I hadn't gone too far adrift on personification and pathetic fallacy to notice Hamish emerging from the doghouse—we'd not seen him go

below—with a bottle of champagne and an ancient Boy Scout
hatchet. He leaned these items against the cockpit combing and
reached back inside for a tray of glasses. After distributing the glasses
he held the bottle outboard and lopped off the neck with a clean
hatchet swipe. "Old *Pelagic* custom," he said, pouring, after having
splashed a dollop into the sea. "I don't think I was aboard for its ori-
gins, but it must have had to do with a lost corkscrew. To Cape
Horn."

"Cape Horn."

Toasting the Old Ogre in the sunlight, I recognized that this would
be one of the fine, purest moments of my life.

Only a lucky fraction of those who seek to land on Isla Hornos
actually manage it, because the only reasonable anchorage, Caleta
León, offers scant protection and poor holding ground, but at least
it's secure from the westerly swell behind a stout peninsula. Novak's
sketches and notes from 1991 say, "Drop anchor at edge of kelp in
8–10 meters, use only in low swell conditions, no wind." We understood how lucky we were. Because the rocky, kelp-covered bottom
sheds anchors and because things change quickly, Kate remained
aboard while Hamish and the yachties dinghied ashore. (Kate, however, was treated to the sight of a minke whale doing a couple of laps
around *Pelagic*.) The landing was a bit tricky, a beach of impossibly
slippery, bowling-ball rocks, and we crawled above the tide line
where dry rocks could be walked on—to the foot of a mossy wooden
stairway.

Caleta León lies on the east side of a short, hooked peninsula
hanging from the southeast corner of the island. This peninsula is the
only part of Isla Hornos (3.5 miles from here to Cathedral Rocks at
the northwest corner by 2.5 miles at its widest east-west point) open
to the public. In other words, you may not walk to the crest of Cape
Horn. This may be to protect the tussock grass that covers most of
the island, or maybe the Chileans decided that Cape Horn should not
be trod upon because it's Cape Horn. One suspects that the prohibition has something to do with Argentina. Antipersonnel mines, you
know, Bouncing Betties to discourage Argies. I don't know if there are
still land mines, and I didn't want to know, so I didn't inquire. But
there were definitely land mines here when New Zealander Gerry

Clark, hopelessly sea-struck and captivated by high-latitude seabirds, anchored his little sloop *Tortorore* in a cove at the northeast corner and walked overland to the "naval station" located right here at the top of the stairs. "The approaches . . . were a maze of barbed-wire fences and entanglements, with many trip-wires," he wrote in 1984. "No doubt they would have been an obstacle at night, but it is no trouble to us to negotiate them by day—"

Isla Hornos is a member of the Hermite group (including Deceit, Hermite, and Herschel) about which the *Sailing Directions* has this to say: "The shore of the islands are bold and steep-to; the mountains are pointed, with steep ascents, and are thickly overgrown with shrubs and evergreen trees to about 91 meters of their summits." Islas Hornos is so steep-to that without the stairs, there would be no way up. Cape Horn itself lies southwest of the public point a mile and a half away across a short bay. From the top of the stairs, only the back-side of the Horn is visible, nothing of the seaward face. Off to the northwest at the crest of a gentle hill, we could see the monument to drowned sailors which I knew to stand twenty feet high, yet it ap-peared a minute speck that caught the eye only because it contained straight lines. I never quite understood why this southern-island land-scape dwarfed distant objects even when the scale of the landscape was not very large.

The Armada de Chile maintains a string of wooden boardwalks to protect the tussock grass from human boots. Beginning at the top of the cliff stairs, the boardwalk branches right in a sinuous trail toward the monument, and to the left it ends at the naval station, where a sailor and his family are stationed. It was a single-story, shed-like dwelling with a peaked, corrugated-metal roof outlined in rust stains. Built of redwood-stained, heavily weathered clapboards, the central house was surrounded by addenda to make habitation reasonably civ-ilized. A blue plastic tub elevated to roof level on a rust-streaked wooden scaffold delivered running water. A noisy generator in a ven-tilated box brought electricity. Erector-set towers, like old-time TV antennae, kept the station in touch by radio—passing vessels are re-quested to report their nationality and destination by VHF. Drain-pipes, rusted at their couplings, ran from the rain gutters down the front of the house, met other pipes, and merged into a single pipe, which emptied into an ugly plastic tub big enough to drown in. It's not really fair to say it looked like a desert rat's double-wide because nothing man-made fits here. When Gerry Clark was here, this house, clearly visible for twenty miles in every direction, was painted in camouflage colors. An Orlikon anti-aircraft gun was mounted near the tiny chapel, and inside ammo was stacked in belts and boxes from floor to ceiling. A Madonna kept the powder dry. Now peace reigns. No guns are visible.

There was no sign of habitation except the chugging generator and white wispy curtains in the little window, so we walked on, not wanting to disturb. A rangy black dog spotted us, however, and came bounding joyfully over the tussock tufts to greet us, licking and jumping. This was no doubt a fine place to be a dog, and dog joy is fun to be around, but it was not conducive to wildlife sightings. We hoped he had orders to remain on base as we headed down a dirt trail into the tussock forest, but no, he sprinted ahead. Higher than our heads, this really was a forest of tussock. The roots harden into a ball aboveground, and in the older plants the root ball can grow six feet in diameter. The saber-shaped leaves growing up from the center, curving gracefully downward at the tips, look like water spurting from a fountain, and they make a sibilant sound when the wind blows through. But this is a tough plant, this *Poa flabellata*. Other salt-resistant flora like holly and a sort of beach plum hide in and among the tussock, the only plant that stands up completely exposed, a feat of hardiness not even the beeches can pull off. Tussock grass in the Falkland Islands has been radiocarbon-dated at 300 years.

The dog had found something down the trail, excited, high-pitched yapping, and we hurried to see what. Shearwaters and a variety of petrel make nests by burrowing beneath the root balls, and so do Magellanic penguins, the only burrowing penguin. The dog, brave tracker, was down on his haunches barking into a burrow. I told him to stop, get back, and he waited a little while for congratulations before he ran off in search of other wonders. I crawled between two fat root balls to see into the third. It was moist and warm in there, the smell of ammonia and the nutritious rot of peat intoxicating. A little Magellanic penguin was sitting on her nest in a shallow depression lined with decaying tussock leaves and white downy feathers. I could see the black band under her chin, the distinctive black chest band, and beneath her belly the bulge of one white egg. She cocked her head sharply from side to side, showing the white ram's-horn slash of white against the black, her reddish eye flashing. I watched for a little while, trying to determine whether that head movement was a threat gesture or a function of monocular bird vision, until I felt too guilty and backed away, murmuring soft and reassuring things as if addressing an agitated pet parakeet. Magellanics are called jackass penguins for their call, a mournful bray followed by a series of short honks and loud inhalations that crescendo in a long, dramatic howl. The Chileans, hearing human cries, call it *pájaro niño*, the child bird. (Gerry Clark, *The Totorore Voyage*)

Hamish thought that it was too late—autumn—for the egg to hatch or if it did for the chick to survive. Though there were tracks, feathers, and burrows on either side of the trail, we saw no other penguins in the tussock. Nesting season had passed. I was suddenly overtaken by a fast-moving cloud of Cape Horn melancholy, for the penguin trying so hard, Jarli dead in the Drake, for the lonely windswept exposure of Cape Horn itself. Something about this place, the light or the wind or the weird landscape, dissolves protective coatings, and the explorer wears his heart on his sleeve.

Nonetheless, we pressed on along a narrow path terraced into the shoulder of the hill until the path began to tilt downslope even as the angle of the slope steepened, and we started to take the walk more seriously, one hundred feet to the black rocks below. The peninsula ended with a pointed hill about four stories high, but hanging under the hill was a peculiar hook-shaped lobe of land, the point of which curved back toward the shank to form a tiny, round cove with a beach of small rocks. The point of the hook was our destination, a spire of soft gray rock that looked climbable by non-climbers, because that was the closest we could get to the seaward face of Cape Horn. But before we arrived, we could tell that the sight angle was wrong. We could see the grassy plain running up to the precipice but only a tiny part of the plunging face. Somebody said he thought that was appropriate—you have to see it from saltwater. The spire had a flat spot of crumbly rock and glacial litter and a patch of grass at the top, where we took pictures and basked in the mood of the place.

Francis Drake anchored at two different spots on only one island, which he named after Elizabeth (the archipelago he named the Elizabethides), and he stayed only four days, October 24 to 28, 1578. He walked to the crest of a high headland, and there he "cast himself down upon the uttermost point, groveling, so reached out his body over it." Then when back aboard the *Golden Hind* (anchored within talking distance of *Pelagic*), he proclaimed that he had just been farther south "than any man yet known." It was a very Drakean move, part of the legend, like the game of bowls, illustrative, and people wanted the headland to be Cape Horn. But in 1926, the Drake expert Henry R. Wagner threw cold water on that great-moment-in-exploration. No, the professor said in *Sir Francis Drake's Voyage Around the World,* Drake stopped on Henderson Island. After comparing the firsthand accounts (which don't agree) with the known geography, Wagner found that they reconciled only on Henderson Island. Where the hell is Henderson Island? . . . It lies sixty-two miles west and twenty miles north of Cape Horn. So we're left with Drake performing that showboat, *fin del mundo* move on some no-account island nowhere near the southernmost? When the dean of maritime historians Samuel Eliot Morison came along and with a flip of his hand declared that it was Henderson, the fizzle was fixed in history.

Raymond Aker, professional navigator and lifelong student of the voyage, however, spent years comparing modern nav charts to reports of courses and distances and the lay of the land with the contemporary sources. He also factored in the set and drift of the Cape Horn Current, which had not been done accurately before. He was kind and patient enough to walk me through the evidence step by step. Afterward, it seemed obvious. It could only have been right up there on the crest of Cape Horn that Drake groveled. Only there do all (or most) of the sources reconcile. But there's another piece of evidence for Cape Horn, not real evidence, not the sort to stand up in court, but still a compelling argument for those who have seen this place. It just *looks* like the end. Everything you see all around the compass, from sea level and from high land, says this is the end. This is the last gasp of South America. Only ocean from here on out. It's nakedly apparent, and it would not have been lost on Francis Drake.

I had another small objective. I wanted a rock from Cape Horn. I don't remember who said that it was customary, but I liked the idea. I wanted something tangible from this place, a small rock, baseball-sized, but reflecting the complex local geology, that I could display on a surface, dust. Something around a billion years old. That little cove down there would be a perfect source, a beach composed entirely of rocks beaten round by wave action. Even now, eight-foot combers were breaking on the rocks, clattering as each wave receded. I made my way down without injury, walked halfway around the steep crescent, and as I made my selection, fat brown shapes moving in the waves caught my eye. In a moment just before it dissolved in foam, the crest of the wave caught the light and turned translucent green. There were seals in the green layer, and they seemed to be bodysurfing. Brown heads peeked from the face of the wave, picking the precise moment to peel out before it broke. And then they went back to do it again. No, too anthropomorphic, a temptation we pinniped experts have learned to resist. They must be feeding, they had to be doing something practical, as further observation would reveal. . . . There was no feeding urgency among the seals, no hurry at all. A dozen or so were gathered bobbing around seaward of the break. Time after time, several would dive at once and reappear in the wave, riding the curl, for what seemed clearly to be the hell of it.

"What are they doing?" I called up to the guys watching from above.

"Playing."

"Surfing." It was obvious to my colleagues.

Standing on rocks and tussock, several caracaras eyed us with bold conceit as we headed back through the grass forest. These hawk-like birds of prey, black except for their cinnamon bellies and thighs, are without fear. They didn't flinch as we walked past at arm's length, and it was clear they thought they were smarter than us, anyway. There are five other varieties in South America, but we saw only striated caracaras on the southern islands where they are fairly common, lurking around penguin rookeries.

The dog picked us up on our way, and still delighted, led us back to the boardwalk path by a shortcut around the decommissioned light and the chapel/ammo dump to the little house. The air was moist and muggy, almost tropical, even along the high spine of the peninsula, where the grass had been cropped to kneecap height by the wind. But there was no wind, none at all. The sky had lost its features under a growing monotone gray. The ocean was empty.

A short, dark man in jeans and a sweater emerged from behind the corrugated metal shed as we clopped up the boardwalk toward his house. He greeted us with a short military bow, said his name was Ramón, and shook our hands, averting his eyes shyly. He asked in Spanish if we would like him to take our picture, a group portrait, around the Cape Horn sign. The sign, mounted right in front of the tin shack beside the plastic catchment tank, was made from white-washed beech-tree boles in the shape of a hitching post. From the horizontal piece, about the right height to lean on, hung three white boards on which was hand-painted in black:

WELCOME
CAPE HORN
CHILE

Hamish took a few shots, and we invited Ramón to join in the picture. His son, a twelve-year-old replica of Ramón, showed up, and we got him in as well. We were happy tourists, posing.

Ramón invited us into his house to stamp our passports, which Hamish had gathered in a zip-lock bag in case of a dunking. We removed our boots and went inside, where the temperature hovered around eighty-five degrees. Every building I entered in Fuegia, no matter its type or purpose, was stiflingly hot. On questions of controlled environments, Chileans and Argentines are in accordance—it should be hot enough to incubate reptiles. I removed my fogged glasses and saw Mrs. Ramón enter through a curtained doorway, a short, strong woman wearing a flannel apron over a cable-knit sweater. She carried a tray of water glasses which she placed on a low table, then gestured for us to sit, on a couch against the front wall and two adjacent armchairs with fringed doilies. She backed out through the curtain, nodding all the way.

Ramón said he was sorry the water didn't taste so good because it came from the roof tank. He had pulled out his pad and was inking up a big, curved face stamp, rolling it back and forth, and careful not to drip, he rolled the imprint onto each of our passports with a practiced hand. It was a blue-ink map of Isla Hornos with the Chilean flag in the middle and a pair of emperor penguins looking in from east and west. From the armchair, I glanced at my shipmates in a row. They could hardly hold their heads up in the heat, so I wasn't alone in that. Then Ramón Jr. and his beautiful younger sister came to the parted curtain, both looking shy but excited, holding trays containing their objêts d'art with Cape Horn themes. Their father, grinning shyly himself, gestured them in. They put their work on the coffee table and stepped over to their father as we extolled its virtues. Rocks painted as penguins or seals, banners that said *Cabo de Hornos, Tierra Austral,* a multimedia albatross on a driftwood plank.

Tim asked if they would take American dollars for their work.

"Oh yes," said Ramón, "dollars they love."

If this was a tourist trap, it was the sweetest we'd ever fallen into. And as we pulled our boots on to leave, Ramón said in Spanish that we should not miss the memorial. He sighed softly and touched his heart with the back of his fist to indicate its emotional impact. Kneeling in the short tussock tying our shoes, treating our lungs to air, we saw that another sailboat, a sloop about her size, had anchored near *Pelagic,* and it wasn't *Golden Hind.* It was the German boat. Or French.

"French," said Hamish. The Frenchmen were standing in a semicircle peering up at the monument, moved, specks in the distance.

If there must be a man-made monument on Cape Horn, and there probably must, I don't see how there could be a more appropriate or a finer one than this. It is a huge, which is to say life-size, wandering albatross in a steep bank standing vertically on the tip of its outstretched wing. Brilliantly, the albatross is formed in negative space, an air albatross, cut into a sheet-steel square balanced on one point. Drawing nearer, climbing the hill on the boardwalk, we saw that the sculpture was made not from a single sheet of steel, but several laminated together, each layer cut with abstract patterns suggesting the waves and clouds around the soaring bird. And as the real clouds moved behind it, the albatross flew with them.

13

From Hermite to Duck

Although it was early summer neither the song nor the twitter-
ing of birds was heard, and one could well believe the merriest
songster might be subdued by the gloomy solemnity of its sur-
roundings.

—H.W. Tilman, *Mischief in Patagonia*

PUERTO MAXWELL IS A DEEP NICHE in the northeast corner of Isla
Hermite. I'm looking at Skip Novak's hand-drawn chart (a "rutter")
of Maxwell from 1991 when he and Hamish were beginning to acquire their local knowledge. "Storm-proof anchorage—" he wrote in
the margin, "best in the archipelago—" His sketch shows *Pelagic* in a
wedge-shaped cove tucked in behind and tied by the stern to a couple
of "obvious" rock islets, another line tied to trees on Hermite, plus
the anchor. And that's exactly where Hamish put *Pelagic,* with the
same heavy mooring precautions—though storm-proof, Maxwell is
not williwaw-proof. We left her alone and took the dinghy ashore to
hike the interior plateau of Isla Hermite. Motoring slowly alongshore,
however, we could see no route up the densely forested mountainside.
A watercourse or a rockslide would have been useful, and since both
were fairly common, we expected to bimble right up there, as Hamish
put it. But Hamish was silent behind his skirted, opaque mountaineer's sunglasses, watching the forest go by.

The Yahgan used to cruise like this close to shore while their dogs trotted along the beach or ranged through the thickets, hunting. But these dogs, about the size of a large fox terrier, were not bred or trained, they were barely domesticated, and they were hunting for themselves. The people had to hurry if the dogs actually caught something desirable, for "the ravenous pack did not bother to kill [the guanaco] before beginning to devour as much of him as they could swallow, whilst the Yahgans hurried to reach the spot before their share of the meat should be too greatly diminished," wrote Lucas Bridges, eyewitness. In these outer islands where guanaco were exceedingly rare, the dogs most often flushed otters, extinct now, like the dogs and the Yahgan.

Speaking of hunting, Lucas Bridges tells about an amazingly elemental means of catching cormorants. While the birds fished far at sea during the day, the Yahgan planted two guys in their roosting site, which was often nothing more than a treeless islet or even an offshore rock pile. The hunters hid under ledges or vegetation, while the canoes, which would have scared away the returning cormorants, had to be paddled out of sight. The men were marooned. They lurked under cover as the birds returned from sea near dusk, settled in, and finally tucked their heads under their wings to sleep. "Dull and rainy weather was always chosen, and when it was quite dark the men would creep forth . . . and seize an unsuspecting bird firmly over the wings so as to keep the head imprisoned, thus preventing a flutter or a cry, and kill it by biting its neck or head, holding the bird till it was quite dead. They then laid it down, and treated another and another in the same way. . . . Sometimes several hundred might be taken." But if the weather took a turn for the worse, and the canoeists couldn't get back, then these hunters were stranded without cover. Of course, they had plenty of food. Whites were repulsed by the oily flesh of cormorants.

Isla Hermite is the largest of the Hermite Group. The name is Dutch, after Admiral Jacob l'Hermite, who led the "Nassau Fleet," eleven ships and 1,600 men, on its way around the Horn in 1624, intending, as old Isaac had proposed, to drive the Spanish out of Chile and Peru. Another fleet was scheduled to attack around Brazil, and together they would take over the whole continent, then the isthmus, and maybe the entire Pacific to go with their domination in the East. The fleet had made it this far intact, a genuine accomplishment in the 17th century, but the admiral had fallen ill with an unknown disease. In February 1624, the ships anchored in the lee of Isla Hermite around the corner from Puerto Maxwell to wait for him to die or recuperate, but he did neither. Smaller ships and boats, which had to go out every day for wood and water anyway, explored Bahía Nassau, leaving Dutch names on Windhound Bay and Goree Roads, Schapenham and Orange bays on the Hardy Peninsula, as well as the Hermite Islands here in the south. Otherwise the trip was an utter disaster. They straggled around the corner into the Pacific, but they missed the northbound treasure fleet. L'Hermite finally died, but by then discipline had totally dissolved, and so had the fleet. Bands of marine hoodlums stormed ashore here and there on the Chilean coast, wantonly slaughtering any Spanish men, women, or children they happened upon. Fragments of the fleet called at the Juan Fernández Islands, which, since their discovery in 1563, had served as a standard rest-and-provisioning stop for Horn-battered mariners. These mariners killed so many seals "for diversion" that the stench of rotting corpses forced them back to sea.

But before all of this, while still anchored in Caleta St. Martin, the Dutch had the first-ever contact between Europeans and Yahgan. A party of seventeen sailors gathering wood and water were stranded ashore on the Hardy Peninsula when their little ship had to make a run for open water as a sudden storm swept in. The Yahgan attacked them without provocation, murdered fifteen, mutilating some of the corpses, but two men who managed to crawl off into the forest lived to tell the tale. A barbaric act, all agree, but it was largely the same thing the Dutch did to the Spanish.

For us, from our outboard-powered, hard-bottom inflatable, there seemed no way to reach the interior plateau, but we didn't want to give up while the weather was holding fair. Isla Hermite seemed particularly important. Only a dozen miles from Cape Horn itself, Hermite is ecologically identical, except that people land on Isla Hornos,

weather permitting. Now I'm not suggesting for a moment that Cape
Horn is overdeveloped, its primordial integrity stained by a few
boardwalks, a little chapel, the albatross monument, some Frenchmen, us. On Hermite, however, there is absolutely nothing of human
influence, and no one stops here. Hamish spun the dinghy, doubling
back, willing to settle for a sparser patch of forest in the absence of an
easy route. But it was uniformly dense, so we settled for an easy
landing place on the moonstone beach, dragged the dink above the
high-tide line, and tied it off.

Peering up at the vertical forest, Hamish said, "It's often easier
than it looks," but he didn't seem convinced that this would be one of
those times. Lucas Bridges was encouraging, writing that "on the
exposed coasts, . . . there are thickets nourished by abundant moisture
and closely pruned from above by continuous gales. These are often
so dense that a person may walk on the top of them. . . . It is surprising to find after walking thirty or forty yards from the beach on
what appears to be a coarse and springy turf, that in reality one is
treading on tree-tops, six or eight feet above the ground." But I think
he was referring to thickets on reasonably level ground, whereas this
one was growing out of the side of a sixty-degree pitch.

Hamish and Kate approached the trees, paused, then plunged in,
and we lined up to follow. It wasn't so much a matter of climbing the
cliff as climbing inside the trees, using roots and low branches like
ladder rungs. The live trees barely flinched under human weight, but
the dead ones (it was hard to tell the difference in the tangle) broke
with syncopated cracks as first one of us, then another, dropped into
knee-deep, sometimes hip-deep, leaf litter and detritus. I stuck my arm
down to rock bottom where the stuff was warm and wet. These trees
were drawing their sustenance from the rot of their relatives rather
than from anything like soil, and for stability they had interwoven
their roots basket-fashion. Every trunk and branch was spattered with
gray-green lichen that looked like decaying lace, called *Usnea,* I later
found out. Another arboreal parasite named *Cyttatia darwinii* after
the man who first described it was a seasonal staple to the Yahgan,
though we didn't see any here among these bonsai *Nothofagus.* Compared to Hermite, sheltered valleys of Tierra del Fuego along the
Beagle Channel are like fecund, vital subtropical rain forest where

trees can spread out and grow tall. Down here, everything is nipped close, stressed to the limit, forced into hiding, reduced to the miniature.

Scratched, sweaty, we topped the cliff where, one by one, the scene brought us up short. The plateau, as the *Sailing Directions* called it, was endless. Undulating slabs of gray-white, coarse-grained rock piebald with lichens and veined with streaks of black igneous rock formed the floor. From it, rocks in naked clumps, lobate extrusions, and sharp spires like bone shards stretched westward to where crumbly, miniature mountains of brown sedimentary rock rose, said the *Directions,* 1,700 feet above sea level. But they looked like Matterhorns. Isla Hermite seemed continental in scope. Nearby in the dips and rills that punctuate the bedrock grew copses of shrub-sized beeches, calafate, holly, tussock grass, and a prickly heath the Yahgan called *gush.* The lower places were covered by green and rust-colored sphagnum moss beds, and in the very lowest places here and there, round depressions had turned into ponds.

Kate and Hamish decided to climb this pyramidal peak, the highest in sight off some inestimable distance to the southwest, for the view back to the Horn. Thinking they could do with some privacy, we set off on a diverging track toward a set of four identical ponds in a line some other inestimable distance west. We covered a lot of easy-going ground, but I had lost all sense of time as well as distance. Had we been at it forty-five minutes or an hour and a half? I took pleasure in the fact that I felt vaguely anxious in the *fin del mundo* strangeness of the place and the total absence of human presence. Occasional gusts whistled among the rocks and shrubs, but there was no other sound, and nothing else moved except Hamish and Kate, specks in the distance.

Dick said it first. There was no life up here except plants. Nothing scurried through the leaf litter, no birds, sounds, no movement.

We walked on watching for movement, listening for natural sounds that weren't caused by the small, moist breeze, until we arrived at the edge of the first pond. The glacier left these depressions, called kettle ponds, but why were they identical, round and regular about the size of a golf green, and why did the four of them lie in a dead-straight line? Did four separate blocks of ice cause these depressions or was it just one moving somehow in stutter step? Russet and brown moss bogs with green bromeliads and ferns poking several inches above the sphagnum surface separated the tannin-black ponds. We avoided walking on the bogs, but kneeling beside them, pushing gently, we set the bogs undulating, as if in a sea swell, twenty feet around. The depressions and the lower reaches of the island were awash, which leads one to think that annual rainfall is extreme, but it's not. It's just that very little evaporation takes place.

Freshwater ponds and wet places like this at the same latitude in the Northern Hemisphere, say in Labrador, would teem with dragon-flies, water spiders, horse- and deer flies, clouds of mosquitoes in spring and summer. Insects would attract wading and perching birds, as well as waterfowl. One would expect to see frogs, salamanders, and other amphibians. But even if this is to overstate the fecundity of a Labrador kettle pond, there would undoubtedly be billions of mos-quitoes. Not here, not on the top of Isla Hermite, at 55 degrees, 49 minutes. I poked at the opaque water, stirring up clouds of vegetable decay, but nothing else.

Dick was turning over flat rocks, exposing dark and moist places where bugs and beetles hide, but there were none, no worms or milli-pedes, not even those little gray segmented things that curl into a ball when their place is disturbed, nothing at all, lifeless.

"Maybe without insects," I proposed weakly, "there's no bottom to the food chain. And so there are no birds."

"Maybe," said Dick. "But why are there no insects?"

We left the ponds, walking a circuitous route back toward the dinghy. If an environment contains things normally conducive to life, but there is none, then climate must be the cause. What else is there? Conditions here, while far from gentle, are not extreme, due to the moderating influence of the ocean. The average summertime tempera-ture up in the Beagle Channel hangs around fifty-one degrees, and the ocean never freezes in winter. Boston's climate, for instance, has a far greater range in annual temperatures. Birds, mammals, shellfish, and crustaceans flourish in the waters between Cape Horn and Tierra del Fuego, but inland the southern islands are devoid of life except for a few plant varieties. Why, when birds and animals have established themselves in every terrestrial niche except the highest mountains and the ice sheets, was this vegetated, well-watered island empty of them?

Was it the wind? Did the Cape Horn snorters denude the place?

We speculated on this question for the remainder of our trip and beyond. We poked and probed all around it, getting close, but I didn't learn the precise answer until I found that perennial favorite, *The Biogeography of the Southern End of the World* by zoologist Philip Darlington. Writing about plant and animal distribution, Darlington points out that myriad species are found in the tropics, but relatively few individuals within each species. In the Northern Hemisphere, the number of species able to withstand winter decreases as the latitude increases, but there can be vast numbers of individuals in a single species, the caribou herds in the Arctic, for instance. But species distribution does not work that way in the Southern Hemisphere. There, *all* terrestrial life diminishes as the latitude increases toward Cape Horn.

We were standing at the absolute bottom of a nearly continuous forest stretching a thousand miles down the Chilean seaboard. At its northern end, there are multiple species of trees, but here there are only *Nothofagus* and Winter's bark (named, incidentally, after the captain who deserted Drake). There are, Darlington showed, fifty-five species of snakes at the northern end of the forest. At the latitude of Santiago/ Buenos Aires, around 35 degrees South, there are twenty-two snake species. But in Tierra del Fuego, there are zero. Take ants: 222 species are found at 25 degrees South, around São Paulo, Brazil, and 103 at Buenos Aires's latitude. In Tierra del Fuego, there are two, and down here in the islands, zero. No amphibians and no reptiles live south of the Strait of Magellan. There are land birds on Tierra del Fuego, hawks, owls, one parrot, one woodpecker, and some perching songbirds, but down here there are none.

The reason for this southerly decline in land species turns out to be elegantly simple. It's not a matter of extreme cold, but the sustained absence of warmth. Killing blizzards are common in midsummer. It can blow sixty knots with a few pauses for weeks on end, and if it skipped to eighty knots and blew for another week, no one would be astonished. In the far Northern Hemisphere where summers are relatively warm, life explodes, and other animals move in to exploit it. They must hurry, but they have time to feed and breed before the freeze. Down here, there is not enough warm-time to do that. Nothing can begin. Strategies for survival, no matter how willful, simply don't work, and so nothing grows or changes except from erosion.

In our knobby boots, high-tech, primary-colored wind-wickers and fuzzy hats, rock-hopping over the bogs, I began to feel faintly absurd. I didn't bring it up; one's shipmates don't relish being thought absurd, even faintly, but I couldn't shake the notion. . . . I didn't feel absurd on Isla Hornos or aboard the boat beneath the pitch of the Horn. Only here, something in this weird, lifeless, rock-and-bog landscape, and the light. We climbed a slab-sided mass of greenstone and looked south over Islas Hall and Chanticleer toward the sloping backside of Cape Horn clearly visible ten miles away. The Drake Passage was as empty as when he arrived, nothing but the roll of long swells and the cascading explosions against the foot of the Horn and its off-lyers.

It took me a moment to realize that we were looking over the rim of Wigwam Cove (Caleta St. Martin). Everyone stayed in Wigwam Cove. Weddell and Matthew Brisbane in *Jane* and *Beaufoy* rested here in 1823 after sailing those tiny wooden vessels farther south than any humans had ever been before—74 degrees 15 minutes South—in what would be called the Weddell Sea. (Brisbane was that unfortunate governor of the Falklands whose feet FitzRoy would find protruding from a shallow grave.) The *Beagle* was heading westward around the corner to York Minster's home waters when Cape Horn stiff-armed her aside, much to seasick Darwin's relief: "when squalls of rain, with hail, swept by us with extreme violence so that the captain determined to run into Wigwam Cove." And that was the other desirable feature of the cove in addition to its solid protection from the west—it was easily accessible from the Drake Passage, perfect for bail-out purposes, and it was simple to enter in a pinch.

Darwin's lifelong friend and one of his pallbearers, the botanist Joseph Hooker, was enthralled by the wildness of Wigwam Cove and eastern Hermite. Hooker came here in 1842 as assistant naturalist (to that Dr. McCormick who left the *Beagle* in a huff because this whippersnapper Darwin was receiving preferential treatment from the captain) on the *Erebus* and *Terror,* part of the famous British scientific expedition. In command was James Clark Ross, a dashing officer-explorer who was said to be the handsomest officer in the Royal Navy. But he didn't just look the part. He was already a star of Arctic exploration before he sailed to the Antarctic with the same two ships and same second-in-command, F. R. M. Crozier, captain of *Terror*. They were searching for the south magnetic pole along with the usual scientific objectives, but mainly they were there to claim for the navy the "farthest south" record. It was then held by this civilian sealer James Weddell, and that just wouldn't do. Ross and Crozier sailed brilliantly in Antarctic waters, far more difficult than Arctic seas, discovered the present Ross Sea and Ross Ice Shelf, and named those icy volcanoes Mount Erebus and Mount Terror, but they could not break Weddell's Farthest South. (*Erebus* and *Terror,* with Crozier still in command, were doomed to vanish in the High Arctic with John Franklin, and Ross would return to search fruitlessly for his old friend.)

The two ships and 128 men stayed a happy month in Wigwam Cove. Arriving here after a season probing the ice shelf, they exulted in the existence of trees and other green things. That they found the east edge of Hermite soft and welcoming indicates the level of misery 19th-century Antarctic explorers endured. Officers set up a magnetic observatory on the plateau somewhere nearby. Hooker looked at the trees and began to ask questions about plant distribution in the Southern Hemisphere. How is it that *Nothofagus* and Winter's bark grew everywhere in the sub-Antarctic region, including islands such as the Falklands, South Georgia, and Kerguelen isolated by thousands of miles of Southern Ocean? And looking at it the other way, how did plants like celery and dandelions find their way to Tierra del Fuego, if not to these harder southern islands? Darwin pointed to the bright green grass that flourished on Yahgan shellfish middens. Wigwam Cove is still ringed with these bright green spots.

Hooker, who slept with Darwin's *Journal and Remarks* under his pillow that he might go right at it in the morning, dismissed the natives as "degraded savages." The Yahgan were troubling, and no one wanted to look too closely at them. But everyone who came here in the 19th century wanted to convert them, which was a good way not to have to take them in. We know about Weddell and FitzRoy; Ross wished that they could receive "the blessings of civilization and the joyful tidings of the Gospel." Even Darwin chimed in, at the Conclusion of *Voyage of the Beagle:* "From seeing the present state,

it is impossible not to look forward with high expectation to the future progress of nearly an entire hemisphere. The march of improvement, consequent on the introduction of Christianity throughout the
South Sea, probably stands by itself on the records of history. It is
the more striking when we remember that only sixty years since,
Cook, whose most excellent judgment none will dispute, could fore-
see no prospect of such change." I think Cook wouldn't have
wanted such change.

There was one undesirable aspect to this otherwise excellent
refuge, and it was no secret: williwaws. The *Beagle,* to cite one, ran
into Wigwam Cove to escape the waves in the Drake, until a series of
williwaws made Cape Horn waves the safer alternative, and FitzRoy
bolted. You could see williwaws in the environment, scoured clean by
100-knot blasters sweeping over this narrowing neck of land and
plunging over our heads into Wigwam Cove. I turned and faced inland, west, from where it would come, but it was no use trying to
imagine a wind like that in a sudden gust. However, I noticed that
now there was actually wind, a twenty-knot sailing breeze. Were we
too distracted by *el fin del mundo* to notice? Or had it just come up?

"Look," said David, "whitecaps."

Unless one can't help it, one never wastes a sailing wind.

Pelagic liked it, twenty knots from the west, a close reach on our
north northwest heading. Open to the west, Paso Franklin is a maw-
shaped bay, with the north coast of Hermite as the lower jaw and the
Wollaston Islands the upper. Our wind had a bit of south in it, so we had
plenty of room to ease the sheets and let the sails breathe. *Pelagic* sighed
and took off. And then the sun came out, sparkling on the facets of the
waves. We were all giddy and light. Kate beamed, and the captain put his
arm around her shoulders. Cape Horn bliss; it comes up in the literature.

Hamish nodded away to port to say, there it is. False Cape Horn.
We'd been talking about Cabo Falso de Hornos, what a sinister *falso* it
was, and how of all the nautical adversities lurking in these waters this
one seemed excessive. As you can see on the chart, False Cape Horn
and the real thing don't look so deceptively alike, the latter a high

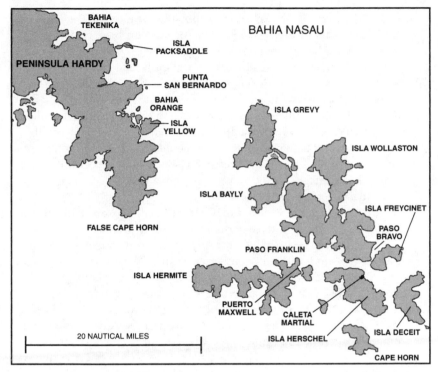

BAHIA
TEKENIKA

BAHIA NASAU

ISLA
PACKSADDLE

PENINSULA HARDY

PUNTA
SAN BERNARDO

BAHIA
ORANGE

ISLA GREVY

ISLA
YELLOW

ISLA WOLLASTON

ISLA BAYLY

ISLA FREYCINET

PASO
BRAVO

FALSE CAPE HORN

PASO FRANKLIN

ISLA HERMITE

PUERTO
MAXWELL

CALETA
MARTIAL

20 NAUTICAL MILES

ISLA DECEIT

ISLA HERSCHEL

CAPE HORN

Map 13.1   From Hermite to Orange

promontory at the bottom of a small island, the former a big bulge at the bottom of an enormous peninsula. On a day like this, the difference between the two would be crisply visible. The sinister part lies not in the accuracy of the impersonation (good enough in foul weather), but in the relative location of the two. False Cape Horn is situated seventeen miles north and thirty miles west of real Cape Horn. This was no problem for a westbound ship from the Atlantic, because after digging far enough south to round the real thing, the fake would pose no threat. But consider the problem of the eastbound ship.

Say it was a big four-master, maybe *Moshulu* or *Herzogin Cecilie*, with a load of grain from a south Australian port "running her easting down" toward the Horn; but it may have been *Potosí* or *Pamir* with a hold full of Chilean nitrates looping out into the Pacific for a straight-on shot at the Drake Passage, or it might have been a tramp from Hawaii. An eastbound ship may have been sailing fast before the west wind for weeks on end without a glimpse of a celestial body or the horizon. Out in the lonely reaches of the Southern Ocean where there was nothing to hit, an estimated position was good enough. But now there was the sawtooth coast of Chile to hit. She had to be sailing along a track south of at least 56 degrees South to clear the Horn, but the navigator couldn't be certain. He could dip far to the south, relieve some of the anxiety, but there were solid arguments against overdoing that strategy. He didn't want to shave it close, but nor did he want to subject his ship to the ice.

All anxiety would vanish if they actually sighted Cape Horn. Doubled lookouts strained their eyes. . . . All aboard were terrified of seeing land or, worse, breaking surf anywhere on the right side of the bow. Downwind sailing in Southern Ocean following seas brought a distinct danger along with the exhilaration. Once she had pinned herself on that wind, she gave up most of her alternatives in a way that vessels beating to windward need not. Running before a big sea, she might turn a few degrees one way or the other, adjusting course. But a big alteration like ninety degrees was out of the question. If she turned hard one way or the other, the waves would find the side of the ship and try to capsize her. That's why everyone was terrified of land anywhere to the south. That would mean they had missed the Drake Passage, that they were about to drive full speed into the side of the Andes Mountains, and that it was too late to stop or turn her.

"Land ho!" called the lookout at the fore topmast, and the crew froze. *Where!* "Away three points off the port bow!"

Thank Christ! Some of the watch cheered, but the officers and captain went forward to see for themselves, and peering though the sleet, together they agreed: Cape Horn. Stand on. If it was Cape Horn, and if the wind held, they'd be around, and ready to head north for better weather in twenty-four hours. If this were but False Cape Horn, and if she carried on at, say, ten knots, for one hour, then it would be too late. She would have sailed into the maw of Paso Franklin.

Pelagic was taking a little water over the bow to show she was serious. We tuned and trimmed and tweaked and steered the tell-tails with race-day concentration, and she responded to the attention. At least a little bit. Kate sighed at the luxury of not being needed, stretched back against the cabin trunk, while the punter/yachties adjusted leads and traveler position.

"Right in here," said Hamish from the stern pulpit where he and Dick had been talking computer gibberish, "there is a magnetic anomaly." He looked around to be sure of his bearings.

"It was right in here—due south of Isla Bayly." (Bayly was an astronomer on *Adventure* with Cook.)

There's no telling how many eastbound ships and crews died on the teeth of Paso Franklin after mistaking False Cape Horn for the real thing, but only one ship I ever heard of made the mistake and survived to tell about it. The *Peri,* an ungainly, unlovely three-master en route to New York from New Zealand, made what must be the weirdest west-to-east rounding in history, February 28, 1905. Lookouts spotted a bold headland through a break in the endless fog. Cape Horn it was, the officers all agreed, and they carried on before a west wind, fortunately light. Then the fog parted again to reveal a chilling sight—land away to starboard—to her south. Then more land to the north. And both were closing in fast around the *Peri.* Captain Phillips ordered the lifeboat provisioned and run out as he tried to turn her to starboard, but it was too late for that. She was hopelessly trapped, so he put her back on the easterly heading, and began looking for a flat place to beach her. Giving calm, crisp orders when he must have been in despair, he sighted what looked like an opening dead ahead at the hinge of the jaw. . . . If the water held deep and if he could fit her through two kelp-marked reefs guarding the opening, she might just make it. Captain Phillips (who changed his shirt and tie three times a day fair weather and foul) squared her yards, put his best guy at the helm, and aimed at the chink in the land. She literally scraped between the reefs, her hull plates groaning, while no one breathed, and then she popped out into the open sea east of Deceit.

Tim tapped the clear dome over the compass card. "I think we're here."

We looked in. The compass was slewing drunkenly through about ninety degrees. The card, the part with the numbers on it, rolled eerily from side to side. This ancient essential instrument was only semiconscious.

"What causes that?"

"Could be the helmsmanship."

"Is it something beneath us? What's that island there?"

"Bayly."

"Is it because Bayly Island has a great vein of iron running through it? I mean, is it something in the earth? Or is it something in the earth's magnetic field."

Some people attribute magnetic anomalies to extraterrestrials, but not us. We turned to Dick, since most questions of that sort went his way. But a couple of dozen dolphin suddenly formed up on our bows, changing the subject. We'd seen dolphins in Bahía Nassau and just west of the Horn, but in pairs or small groups when *Pelagic* was chugging along under power. There were twice as many as I'd thought, and beneath the bows we could see layers of dolphin four deep. They jinked and zipped and crisscrossed, and we whooped encouragingly. (I don't know any sailor too jaded or crusty to ignore dolphins when they ride his or her bow.) Each of the four varieties that frequent these waters are beautifully marked in black-and-white variations, but those of us new to the Southern Hemisphere had been finding it hard from deck level to distinguish a Peale's from a dusky or a Cruciger or, for that matter, a Commerson's. But this time we were ready. I had the book in my coat pocket. It didn't take a moment to know they were Peale's dolphins, clear from their all-black faces and elegantly backswept dorsal fins. These animals, it was also clear, were examining us visually. I've seen dolphins do that at sea in the lower latitudes, and in the same way—taking turns. Those nearest the bow rolled onto their sides to bring their eye out of water, and we could plainly see the eye rove aft and back to focus on the humans hanging over the lifelines making faces. After a while that set of observers banked off, and several other animals swooped in to take their place, checking out the cut of our jib from close aboard. Among the local weather sayings cited by Natalie Goodall in *Tierra del Fuego* is one about whistling dolphins. When you hear them whistle, you know heavy weather is on the way. These remained mute.

When they rolled they made a distinctive splash, with their tails, I think, that earned them the name ploughshare dolphins. Few details are known about the lives of Peale's dolphins—they weren't even de-scribed for science until Titian Peale, a naturalist and artist on the United States Exploring Expedition, did so in 1839—because their habitat is so remote. They're found only in South American waters from about 50 South in both oceans down into the Drake. These are Cape Horn dolphins.

The binnacle compass remained unsure of itself for a couple of hours, until we had sailed into light and fluky wind under the snow-capped lee of the Hardy Peninsula. Something was brewing on the other side, black cloud stacked up in terraces over the spine of the peninsula. It began to drizzle. The weather mood had changed theatri-cally, and the lighting design now called for gloom, melancholy, dolor. It seemed a bit heavy-handed. Melodramatic. But the temperature actually plunged twenty degrees, and snow flurries began bending with the breeze around the curve of the mainsail.

Our destination was Bahía Orange, twelve miles up the Hardy from False Cape Horn, about thirty-six miles northeast of real Cape Horn. By the standards of the Fuegian Archipelago, Bahía Orange is another important anchorage, along with Wigwam Cove and Wulaia, but Orange is the best of them all. Orange is a natural masterpiece of a harbor.

The two-mile-wide mouth of the bay makes for easy entry in thick weather or at night, but it also means exposure, to the northeast, in this case. Exposure here, however, is diminished by thick kelp beds at-tached to reefs and two little islets (Burnt and Goose) that act as po-tent breakwaters. But if it really blows up from the east, and kelp can't still the waves, there are three long, finger-shaped, deepwater coves nestled into the west and south sides, where a squadron of Chilean gunboats could ride out a hurricane in peace. Also, Bahía Or-ange is rich in fresh water from a couple of small rivers and several streams draining the 500-meter Cadena Garitas Centinelas.

Conditions are very different over here on the east side of Hardy compared to the close-cropped, wind-scoured Isla Hermite. Orange by local standards is lush and fecund, and the trees, a mix of decidu-ous and evergreen beeches and a few Winter's bark, stand relatively strong and straight. But it can still blow like hell in here. In 1979 Hal Roth visited the two Armada de Chile sailors who used to be

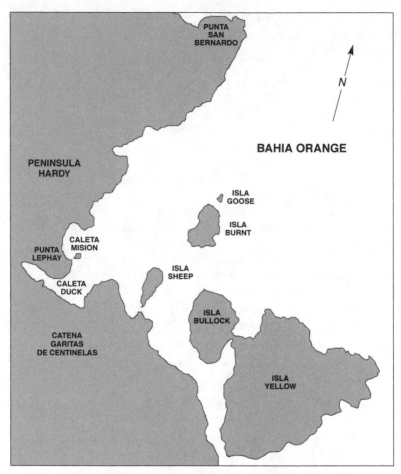

Map 13.2   Bahía Orange

stationed in Orange to report weather conditions (and Argentinean fleet movements) back to the base at Puerto Williams. They told Roth that until a few days before, the wind had been blowing seventy knots for a full week without reprieve. Novak and Laird had been here before because Orange was the only place on the Hardy Peninsula that wasn't *prohibido*. Members of l'Hermite's fleet named it for the House of Orange, and the next bay south, Bahía Schapenham, was the site of the massacre of those fifteen Dutch sailors by Yahgan in 1624.

We had cooked up an objective in Bahía Orange. We wanted to find the plaque of bronze left behind by the Expédition Scientifique de la France, or the *Romanche* expedition. Under the able command of Louis Martial, its central objective was to measure the transit of Venus of 1883, but they did much more. They collected specimens of just about everything, surveyed and named two of the three eastern peninsulas of Isla Hoste, performed enthusiastic if not totally scientific ethnographical studies of the Yahgan, and the expedition surgeon, Dr. Hyades, saved Thomas Bridges's life.

"Where is it, this plaque?"

Hamish, who was at the wheel piloting her into the bay, dodging a huge patch of kelp off Isla Bullock, wasn't sure. Upon further inquiry, it became clear that Hamish wasn't entirely sure that it *was* a plaque. It may have been a cairn or some other sort of monument. Something likeable French scientists might leave behind in 1883.

"And you don't know where?"

We passed Bullock on port, then Isla Sheep, and between the two was one of those fjord-like holes in the land, where the water carried ten meters deep right up to the trees. But if the feature had a name, it didn't appear on any chart, not even the big-scale charts by El Instituto Hidrografico de la Armada de Chile.

"I know that it's in Caleta Misión. Or that it's supposed to be. That's Misión dead ahead." It was a pleasing bite-shaped cove at the back of the bay, but it had a bad eastern exposure. We weren't going there, however; we were heading for Caleta Duck. Duck was a dogleg left, then back right, penetrating deep into the forest at the base of bold, wooded hills that rose no higher than ninety meters above the deck—but their steep ascent, their bare-rock crowns and dusts of snow made them hulk like giants overhead. We dropped anchor in about five meters near the shelving, kelp-covered beach at the toe of Caleta Duck. According to williwaw routine, we winched the dinghy over the side, and Kate and David motored off to shore with the mooring lines. Once they had the lines tied off to immovable objects, we took up slack and cleated them off.

Hamish, approving, thanked us and went below to make popcorn (he says Americans don't know how to make popcorn), a much-awaited evening ritual. Around the ship's table, we talked about Captain Cook, Antarctic exploration, and the race for the South Pole. Hamish and I took a cruel delight in fracturing David's illusions about Robert Falcon Scott. We told David that Scott was an arrogantly unprepared amateur and egotistical screw-up on a suicide march. We had to do it—for our shipmate's own good. This was no time or place for illusions of "heroic exploration." . . . I was awakened by williwaws in the night. They took *Pelagic* by the masthead and set her trembling. For a half-waking moment, I thought this was what happened to churlish revisionists of Scott. I could see my breath when I looked out my curtains wondering if anyone else felt the williwaw.

The United States South Seas Exploring Expedition (the "Ex. Ex."), a depressing affair of missed opportunities commanded by a paranoid martinet called Charles Wilkes, stopped here in February of 1839. It was late in the season for a dash to Antarctica, but that's what Wilkes was preparing for in Orange Harbor. He meant to set a new record for Farthest South, and he was in a rush, because serious competition lurked. There was a French expedition out there somewhere, led by Captain Dumont D'Urville, the man who had found the Venus de Milo and who loathed high-latitude sailing. D'Urville had called James Weddell, holder of the record he would fail to break, a "mere sealer." Then there was Ross in *Erebus* and *Terror*. He was supposed to be looking for the magnetic South Pole, but Wilkes knew he was out to steal the record.

The United States needed to put forth something in the way of a federally funded scientific expedition, a circumnavigation. Not only was it a matter of national prestige, it was a matter of national expansion. The British had been poking around the Oregon and California coastlines, but by charting those coastlines and showing the flag, President Andrew Jackson could demonstrate just whose destiny was manifest. Jackson ramrodded the appropriations bill through Congress shortly before the end of his presidency, leaving the Ex. Ex. in a slough of politics, prejudice, bungling, and stupidity. North and South couldn't agree on anything, and the navy was riven with nursed grudges, jealousies, and hostile cliques, and its officer corps was a pretty dim-witted lot. But they became brother officers of a single mind and unified voice on the subject of the civilian scientist. They didn't want any. They called naturalists "clam diggers" and "bug catchers."

However, this was, as Goetzman writes, "a new age in which, while trade, plunder, and imperial designs were still relevant to exploring activity, a new dimension had been added—the search for pure knowledge, scientific knowledge for the benefit of mankind in general." Without scientifics, real ones, not jumped-up ensigns, the navy knew, nobody would take them seriously. They'd look like rubes who didn't exactly grasp the point. The best scientists in the country scrambled to sign on—James Dwight Dana, Charles Pickering, Horatio Hale (whose mother wrote "Mary Had a Little Lamb"), as well as artist Titian Peale. The trouble was, they got for a commander this "petty tyrant," in Peale's words, who treated the scientists with unveiled mistrust and contempt while doing all he could to make their work impossible. He knew they were conspiring against him. Just like the officers—they were conspiring against him too. Wilkes was no Captain Cook.

The French expedition anchored the *Romanche* in Bahía Orange, but they built their observatory in Caleta Misión. This we knew. And Hamish seemed certain that's where they left their monument or cairn or something meant to last. The chart showed that Caleta Duck and Caleta Misión were separated by a teardrop lobe of forested land called Punta Lephay, and it looked very steep from the cockpit. We rowed the dinghy ashore, because it was too close to bother running the motor, and climbed in the treetops to the ridgeline.

There was an acre or so of flat land behind the rocky beach, almost a meadow of tussock grass with little stands of calafate, holly, wild currant, and prickly heath, I determined from the plant book. At the bottom of the hill, a brown stream draining the high spine of the Hardy Peninsula emptied into saltwater, darkening it. Someone, the French scientists, or the Chilean navy much later, had built a bridge over the stream, but only the iron-rail frame remained. We tightroped the inch-wide rails with some success and gathered on the sickle-shaped beach to reconnoiter. Besides the rails, a few rusted bolts and desiccated boards, there were several concrete cubes the size of refrigerators. The top had broken on one, but there was nothing inside except rubble. We had no idea what they were, and we saw no other monument to the works of man.

"If you were a Frenchman, where would you put your monument?" Hamish wondered.

The eclectic French built corrugated iron huts for themselves and their astronomical and meteorological instruments. Probably some of the metal things belonged to them, but not the concrete cubes. Thomas Bridges, respected by the Yahgan, made it possible for French ethnographers to do their work. With Bridges's word, some Yahgan allowed Frenchmen to take full plaster casts of their faces, breathing through straws. Dr. Hyades accompanied Bridges to Ushuaia, where he treated the sick and performed several surgeries without anesthetic. He performed eye surgery on a man called Palajlian, removing one infected eye and operating on the other to save his sight. Palajlian took it without showing "even by a moan, any sign of pain."

We split up. Some of us inspected the north shore of the cove, others poked around the concrete things, while Kate and Hamish took to the hills for an overview.

How big is the solar system? That was the question that the transit of Venus could answer, and it captured the public's imagination in a way no astronomical event (except imminent asteroid impact) ever will again. Isaac Newton, Johannes Kepler, and other powerful minds theorized that the distance between the earth and the sun could be calculated by timing the passage of Venus across the disk of the sun, which happens twice in a decade and then not again for 122 years. If you had that distance, you could extrapolate the dimensions of the solar system. For greatest accuracy and to up the odds of clear weather, ships carrying astronomers and their telescopes and measuring devices needed to spread out all over the globe, and of course only a national navy could afford that. But these were *good* explorers, enlightened, not like before, not like, well, you know. Captain Cook's career began as a voyage to Tahiti to observe the transit of Venus in 1769.

At the end of the beach, a near-vertical slab of rock dropped straight into the water, and on the otherwise black slab was a nearly square patch of white. To get to it, I'd have to edge along a boot-size, wave-washed ledge, an oddly inaccessible site for a monument. . . .

Hamish and Kate had spotted something on the opposite ridge. That made sense, the ridge overlooking the main part of Bahía Orange, that's where you'd want your monument. I almost decided to go look at that white rock, a little "geologizing," as they used to say, but this would be a poor place to break an ankle. I realized later that it wasn't a white rock, but a rock covered with white lichen. I suppose I should have known.

Some 120 observers from sixty-two separate viewpoints around the world made observations of the 1761 transit, and about twice that many tried again in 1769. England and France, at war in North America, gave safe passage to transit ships, among them of course Cook's *Endeavour*. In the United States passions ran so high, William Goetzman notes in his brilliant *New Lands, New Men,* that the nation's foremost astronomer, David Rittenhouse, lying in a field of mud peering up through his telescope, fell into a swoon, overcome by the moment when Venus touched the disk of the sun. But he came to in time to measure the moment, at least as well as the day's rudimentary technology allowed. However, Goetzman writes, what really mattered was that he had "participated meaningfully in a ceremony that Western man in the eighteenth century had come to regard as holy."

The French astronomers observed the 1883 transit in clear weather. By that time they were packed up and ready to go home, and they probably stood around here on the ridge after they had set up their monument. It was a flat sandstone slab the size of a large portfolio standing upright. The navy, I suppose, had built a redbrick wall to support it from the leeward side. Chiseled into the monument's face in dignified sans serif, it says simply: SEPT. 1882–SEPT. 1883. Over the years, a few idiots had scratched their own names and their loves' in the face.

14

The Death and Life
of the *British Isles*

"Down hellum! DOWN HELLUM! DOWN! Haul yards! Le'go
port braces! Let 'm rip! Quick, Mist'r! Christ! What ye standin'
at? Ice! Ice, ye bluidy eedi't! Ice! LE'GO AN' HAUL! All hands,
there! Up, ye hounds; up if ye look fur dry buryin'!"

—**Captain W.S.**
"Old Jock" Leask aboard the *City of Florence*

APPRENTICE JONES CURLED fully dressed in his berth and tried not
to move. If he lay perfectly still, condensation dripping from the overhead wouldn't run down his neck, and then he'd be warm and dry. A
foot of frigid Southern Ocean water sloshed back and forth while
sunken sea chests rode from wall to wall with each unceasing roll. Listening to her creaks and cracks, her prolonged groans, he strained to
determine whether he was awake or asleep. That wasn't so easy these
days. He'd been falling asleep on deck, sliding into some kind of bad-
dream state while coiling a line or dragging himself along the lee rail.
He was frightened to find himself doing something on deck without
an inkling of how he got there. Maybe it would be better if the ship
cracked open and went straight to the bottom. If they were going to
die, it would be best to end this grim fatigue quickly. Wouldn't it?
That question had never come up in his boyhood sailing fantasies.

The storm wasn't passing. It was strengthening. A lifetime ago he'd watched the building waves with something like admiration, but that was before they'd grown into seething blue-black monsters higher than the topsail yards. He remembered when he first saw the *British Isles*. He was still young then, not like now, and she seemed such a giant, grand, and invincible thing. How could wind and water reduce her to this? He no longer looked at the waves; he no longer looked at anything beyond the deck planks three steps ahead and the next hand-hold. And sometimes he felt like sobbing, but he lacked the energy.

"All hands on deck!"

He'd had another food dream, so he must have been sleeping, four eggs, bacon, bread to sop it up, and a dry tablecloth, checkered. He'd heard the call for all hands, but that was only a dream, they couldn't be calling all hands again. . . . But what was that other sound? A throbbing. Then dimly he remembered. As he'd gone off watch, the mate had ordered the new watch to take sledgehammers and beat back the ice accumulating on everything.

"ALL HANDS ON DECK!"

Suddenly he was topside on the main deck and slammed to his knees by the wind. This was not like air at all, you couldn't breathe it, you couldn't stand up against it, you couldn't— Stop, he told himself, and *think!* That's what Paddy had said, never stop concentrating on what you're doing. The man, or boy, who stops thinking goes over the side. The mate and the captain were screaming at the exhausted men and boys from the quarterdeck and pointing overhead, but it was too late.

The lower topsail on the mizzenmast exploded. The windward half disintegrated into streamers and vanished. But the other half, still intact, began to flog, sag, and flog again, time after time, a ton of frozen number-one canvas cracking like artillery fire. The mizzenmast, the deck, the entire ship from mastheads to keelson shuddered. Maybe the damned thing would blow itself to ribbons, and they wouldn't have to go up to subdue it. But it didn't. And up they went, because they all knew that if the flogging sail took down the mizzenmast, they'd lose the ship. The *British Isles* was barely holding her own now. Crippled, out of balance, she wouldn't survive two watches. Besides, Barker and the sailmaker wanted to save what they could of the ruined topsail to build a new one. Topsails were the only sails she could carry in extreme weather, and this was the third topsail she'd lost.

Jones and the rest of the watch pulled themselves up the ratlines against the press of wind. Always climb up the *windward* side in heavy weather—Paddy Furlong had drummed that into their heads. If you fall from the windward rigging you might land on the deck. You'd probably be dead, but if you went over the side, you'd definitely be dead. Somehow, this fifteen-year-old boy and his mates climbed to the lower topsail yard and edged out on the footropes beneath the leeward side of the yard while the *British Isles* rolled rail to rail. After two hours' clawing and dragging at the canvas, they had it under control, loosely bundled beneath the yard, but now they had to lash it there with ties called gaskets. This was the procedure: A sailor would sit or crouch on the footrope and try to sling a gasket up from under the bundle of sail to a watch-mate lying out over the yard. An experienced seaman named Davidson was lying on his belly far out over the yard to catch a gasket just as a strong gust struck. The sail billowed with a sharp snap, flipping Davidson like a rag doll forward over the yard into thin air. Jones saw him hang there for a surreal moment before he flailed his arms and legs and fell forty feet into the sea.

"Man overboard!" Paddy Furlong screamed from the yard.

"Man overboard!" his mates screamed as they scrambled down to the deck, while the sailcloth they'd fought so hard to subdue flogged once, exploded, and vanished downwind.

The rest of the crew, who'd been fighting their own battle with the fore topsail, laid aft when they heard the cries and huddled beneath the break of the quarterdeck, where the captain and the mates joined them. The ship, struggling to recover her head after that heavy gust, now lay nearly dead in the water. The crew could *see* Davidson when he came onto the crests, and they could hear him crying to them over the roaring wind. But Davidson, who had been to sea all his life, must have known that nothing could save him.

The *British Isles* carried two lifeboats lashed to the fo'c'sle roof with steel strops, but Barker gave no orders to deploy them. Instead, as a matter of form, he asked for volunteers. The huddling ring of wet, ashen faces, icicles in their hair, stared back at him in silence. These men who lacked so many traits approved of by shore-side civilization—Paddy Furlong, for example, the caring crew leader and teacher, turned into a senseless drunken brawler as soon as he stepped ashore with money in his pocket—did not lack courage. Nor were they inured to or fatalistic about the loss of a shipmate. Without hesitation, they would have risked their own lives to save his, but seamanly risk was separate from suicide. No wooden lifeboat would survive seas threatening the life of a 300-foot steel ship, even if somehow they managed to launch it without squashing themselves. And the *British Isles,* essentially out of control, could not be stopped or maneuvered in any way that would help Davidson. She could only sail away from him.

"Jaysus have mercy on his soul," said Furlong, crossing himself. "He's gone, and nothing can divil a one of us do to help him now."

And before that day was done, the *British Isles* lost another man, when Able Seaman West, one of the older, experienced crewmen, got caught out on the long open main deck by a bad boarding sea. *Never run from a boarding sea*—that was another of Paddy Furlong's precepts. Leap instead to the nearest solid object, get as high as possible, hug it, hang on for you life. No one knew whether West broke that rule, since no one saw him go, but at the change of watch, he'd tried to take the direct route to the fo'c'sle house instead of making his way from handhold to handhold along the leeward rail, as his mates had done. Maybe he thought that just this once he could beat the sea. (Seawater weighs three-quarters of a ton per cubic yard, and windjammer experts estimate that a bad boarding sea could bring 500 to 600 *tons* of it over the rails.) Or maybe West was too exhausted to think at all. Someone caught sight of his glistening oilskins in the leeward scuppers as the sea cascaded out through the freeing ports. His mates linked arms, for the second time on this voyage, to drag one of their own, limp and broken, from under the leeward rail. As they carried him aft, they saw that the cap of his skull was flapping in the wind, his frothy blood vaporizing downwind.

Barker met them, led them to the spare officers' cabin, now a sick bay where Witney lay with his shattered leg. The captain and the carpenter lashed West to the table, and working in the light of a swinging oil lamp, they shaved his head and cleaned the wound. They could see the cleft between the two lobes of his brain. There was nothing to do but bandage his skull and wait for him to die.

Now the crew, shorthanded before they'd left the dock, was down three experienced seamen, and the rest were moving like zombies, morose and silent. That silence frightened Jones and the other apprentices most. The old salts were no longer saying things like "Seas? You call these seas? Why, you should've been around the Horn on *Monkbarns* in '97, you want to see seas." Until now, no matter what it was, the cold, the pully-hauly labor, even the lousy food—some voyage had been more so. "Hot? Don't talk to me of hot unless you was on *Olivebank*, thirty-eight days in the doldrums." No one was comparing this Cape Horn weather to other Cape Horn weather. Paddy Furlong, for one, had been rounding the Horn since clipper ships, and if he'd seen worse than this, he wasn't saying so. And if this was the worst the salts had seen, how bad could it get?

The mate knew what he'd do if he were in command, and he made no secret of it. This storm was obviously something extraordinary, and instead of beating themselves to death against it, Rand wanted to turn and run for shelter in Port Stanley in the Falkland Islands. He said so too many times for the captain's liking.

"I'm bound for Pisagua, Chile, Mister Mate," said Barker with his withering stare. "Not Port Stanley."

But the mate had a nautical point. Port Stanley lay *down*wind. They could be there in three days, they could wait out the storm in some quiet shelter, clean up the mess, dry out the galley, and care for the wounded. After all, they were going backwards as it was. Captains hated to put in anywhere because their crews would very likely desert. But this was another argument in favor of Port Stanley—nobody deserted in the Falkland Islands. At that very time, other ships driven back from the Horn were dropping anchors in Falkland lees and Staten Island; there was no disgrace in it.

The mate, though he'd shown himself an excellent technical sailor time and again, had no tact and plenty of hostility. "How's your family?" Rand shouted over the din. "Cape Horn's no place for women and children—or men either." Ignoring Barker's obvious growing anger, Rand pressed on. "Captain, what's the matter with the Falklands!"

"Mr. Rand, we're bound for Pisagua!"

In his book published thirty-one years later, Barker writes: "I decided then and there that under no circumstances short of a dismasting or mutiny would I falter in my determination to make westing, double the Cape, and successfully arrive at our destination. I now knew that Mr. Rand was not of the same mind as myself, and that only under pressure could he be prevailed upon to carry out his duties." Barker mulishly meant to round the Horn, no matter what.

You couldn't say the ship was *sailing* during this time, carrying nothing but a few triangular sails between the masts to keep her bow pointing vaguely to windward, but she was still afloat, still rising to the waves. Three weeks after Davidson was lost, three weeks of unrelenting hurricane-force wind, the *British Isles* had slid all the way down to 65 degrees South, 550 miles south southeast of Cape Horn, barely 100 north of the Antarctic Circle. To touch anything made of steel—everything was made of steel—was to sustain instant "frost burn." Gloves were useless; wool was all they had, and wet wool was worse than nothing. Besides which their lives routinely depended on their grip, and even dry gloves impeded that. Boots filled with water and froze. Nine of her seventeen able seamen had been crippled by frostbite, and now the stench of gangrene wafted through the ship.

With one man and a mate at the wheel, another man standing lookout on the bow for ice, the rest of the watch reported to the aft mess room to help the sailmaker build new topsails from salvaged scraps. Short, rectangular sails set low on the masts, topsails could be flown in winds too heavy for any square sail, and they could still power the ship. The crew didn't mind this indoor work one bit—the mess room *contained a stove*. They stoked it red hot, stripped half naked, and gathered around. Paddy started telling stories again, thank God, because a silent Paddy signaled death. Everybody knew they were in a sewing race for their lives, and there was still that other grim factor. If the wind didn't moderate, it wouldn't matter whether they had topsails or not.

One night the grinding misery was relieved by a moment of pure glee for the crew: the Stove Incident.

"Captain Barker! The stove's adrift, and the cabin's afire, sir!" screamed an apprentice eyewitness. The only other stove on the ship besides that in the after mess room/sail loft was this one in the captain's quarters where his wife and children were holed up. The savage rolling had torn the stove from its mounts in the middle of the night, and now in flames it was hurtling from port to starboard doing dreadful things to the mahogany wainscoting.

The second mate's watch rushed in one door while Barker went down the aft companionway. "The scene which met my eyes was one of heart-rending devastation," he wrote. "Red hot coals were scattered about the carpets, furniture was overturned and broken, and the air was full of smoke and soot. There were great holes in the port and starboard wall, while in the bedroom the big iron stove, still smoking like a dying dragon, was lying over on its side."

Barker told the second mate to get his men around it, haul it topside, and throw it overboard. The crew picked it up with wet sacking, and striking up a rousing version of the old chantey "There's fire in the main top, and water down below, hi-ho, hi-ho," muscled it on deck and with a cheer heaved it over the side. Morale soared.

They finished the sails on the last day of August, and the still-ambulatory crewmen (minus two at the wheel helm), the cook, carpenter, both officers, and the sailmaker shouldered the topsails, over a ton apiece, and lugged them up on deck. It was still blowing some unnatural velocity, and tons of water still poured over the rails with each roll. The mate had each step planned, sails laid out at the foot of their masts while hoisting lines were rigged and run to haul the bundles up to the topsail yards. Barker fired up the donkey engine for the heavy lifting, burning a ton or two of his owner's coal. Once the sails were hoisted, the crew had to go aloft, arrest the swinging bundle, and lace the head of the sail to the yardarm. That part of the job took three days, but sails were affirmations of hope. The crew still had to rig and reeve on the control lines. Each sail had hundreds of meters of ropes attached to it. There were tacks and sheets, braces, buntlines and clew lines, garnets and reef tackle, almost all of which had to be led through various pulleys down to the deck and belayed to one specific belaying pin. When the chores were done, Barker invited everyone aft to take a tot of rum.

However, there was still no chance to set the new sails, because the wind would reduce them to streamers the instant they were sheeted full, and with them all hope would vanish. The *British Isles* and her people would have to wait for the blow to moderate or shift favorably, but time and distance were running out.

It wasn't the slant of their dreams, but with the shift in direction, the wind diminished somewhat, and everyone knew it was time. Loosed one by one and gingerly sheeted in, each sail held its own, drawing—the ship felt alive again.

Now what about the wind angle? . . . It had definitely gone southerly. You couldn't call it southwest, but it was definitely south of west. Should they go for it, or hold for a more favorable shift? That was the classic Cape Horn question, but it was urgent now. She wouldn't get too many chances with ravaged crew and sails. As it was, they might have too few crew to pull it off—

"We'll wait for a smooth, then we'll go over."

When a really big plunging wave rolls through, it leaves a sort of slick behind, a smooth, that doesn't last long but can still be useful. "Mr. Atkinson, call all hands."

Atkinson hauled himself forward along the lifeline over the main deck to the fo'c'sle, and when he opened the door, another four feet of seawater washed over the elevated sill. "All hands on deck!" Men moaned. The stench of gangrene struck him like a solid thing. "Come on, you farmers, and haul for your lives! . . . Smartly now, this ain't a funeral, not yet!"

But only three men were answering his call. He'd already rousted the two off-watch apprentices, and now he summoned the carpenter, sailmaker, and cook. With about a century and a half of deepwater experience among them, they knew what was up and they knew the stakes. They were dressed and ready. Atkinson led them aft to join the on-watch at the break of the quarterdeck.

"On the deck there, Mr. Atkinson!"

"Sir?"

"You will take the foremast. Mr. Rand, you the main. Divide your watches and assign positions! We shall wear ship upon my orders." Shielding his eyes with his fingers, he squinted to windward in search of a smooth. . . .

In order to get their bow, now pointing south, to point north, they would fall away from the west wind until they were sailing east. Then when the waves permitted, they would continue the left turn until they were pointing north, and of course the sails had to be adjusted in tune with the turn. Wearing was a complex maneuver requiring precise timing and communication, and the danger would come when during the turn she presented her vulnerable side to the waves. That's why Barker looked for a smooth. "Stand by the weather braces! . . . Helmsman, take her down, gently as you go."

Spoke by spoke, the helmsman turned her left, *away* from the wind—

"Square the weather braces!" Barker ordered.

Led by Paddy Furlong, the crew broke into a hauling chantey, pulling in unison on the braces to bring the yardarms "square" to the centerline of the ship. So far so good. She was now heading east, running before the wind and seas.

"Helmsman, mind her head!"

"Aye, sir!"

A steering error here would be fatal.

"Hold her there!"

"Aye, sir."

"Aye, sir? Then do it, damn you! There on the deck, are you ready?"

"Ready here!" came a call from the darkness. "Ready on the main." Someone passed the word aft that they were ready on the foremast.

"Helmsman, on my order, take her up."

"Sir!"

"On deck! Stand by weather sheets and braces!"

A new wave train was bearing down on them.

"Helmsman, begin your turn. . . . Ease weather braces!"

Continuing her left-hand turn from east toward north, Barker had no choice but to present her flat side to the elements. If her people couldn't bring her bow up smartly, if something fouled or broke, if the crew lost control of her yards under tons of load, if any of a dozen things went wrong—"Helmsman, take her *up!* On deck, ease weather braces to the shrouds, smartly now!"

Up she came. And the big ship, as if in gratitude, pointed her port bow into the wave train. She rose and seemed to shoulder them aside in her delight with the port tack. Finally, for the first time in a month, she was heading north toward the living.

"All hands lay aft!" Barker bellowed. When his crew had gathered below him on the main deck, Barker said, "Well done," and ordered one watch then the other into his mess for a tot of rum.

Apprentice Jones wrote, "It is surprising how a little success will encourage human beings to further efforts. So in our mood of optimism, we thought that we had the Greybeards of Cape Horn beaten at last—but they were only chuckling at us."

Barker went to comfort his wife. Her face had gone gray, and his young daughter stared blankly at the overhead. But his infant son slept peacefully, imperviously.

"We'll be all right, won't we?" she asked in a thin voice.

"Of course we will." He kissed them, and told his wife that this weather couldn't last forever, especially now they'd come over on the other board, heading north. It could only improve.

But it didn't, it worsened. Seas were running sixty feet on average, and the only way to move on the elevated quarterdeck was by crawling on hands and knees. And when no one could imagine worse, an impossible gust tore through the ship. It was 0400 on September 12, 1905. A shattering crash, louder than the wind, echoed through the ship. Something forward and aloft had carried away, but in the darkness, through fire-hose spray and driving sleet, they couldn't see just what it was.

No single-piece mast 150 feet tall, not even a steel one, could stand up to the great press of sail in heavy weather. The practice, therefore, was to section the mast into three shorter spars and overlap them at top and bottom, mating the pieces with thick steel sleeves and caps. From lower to upper, the sections were designated mainmast, topmast, and topgallant mast. The fore topgallant mast had broken at the coupling, and along with its three yardarms had fallen. Hanging by a tangle of rigging, the wreckage now slammed the side of the ship with each roll, setting off explosions of yellow sparks. But there was nothing to be done. To approach within half a deck of the flailing steel tubes and fat cables would be gory suicide.

The fore and main topsails, over which all hands had slaved, were shredded. Jones, on deck when the explosive gust struck her, wrote: "With utter dismay, we saw large pieces of canvas, torn from the yards, flying to leeward in the howling wind to be swallowed up in the welter of foam and spindrift."

All day the new storm raged. With no sail to hold her head up, the ship fell away from the wind, only barely in control. And the waves pursuing her were breaking all around. Still her luck held through the brief daylight hours, until six o'clock when, suddenly, it ran out.

Barker, who'd just arrived topside, saw it coming through a break in the clouds when moonlight fell briefly on its crest, a scene, he wrote, "which caused me to gasp with astonishment and awe. There, stretching endlessly north and south, a mighty wall of water, towering high above its fellows and making them appear insignificant by comparison, was rolling towards the *British Isles* . . . at a speed not less than forty miles per hour."

Barker shouted, "On the main deck there! Let everything stand. Jump into the rigging—quick! Climb high and hang on for your lives!" Then he joined the helmsman to help control the rudder. The hollow face of the wave looming, he wrote, "like a frowning cliff and blotting out the moon, cast us for a split second into deep shadow. . . . The end of the voyage for us all. The old ship's gone." Then the great Graybeard broke over her. "The ship fell over so far and so deep . . . that I expected her to turn turtle. There was a terrific roar. Then— chaos. The ship was completely engulfed in the swirling maelstrom. Overwhelmed by that depth of water, not a single elevated structure along the whole length of the decks could be seen. That the helmsman and myself were not swept overboard like match sticks seemed miraculous." As the ship labored to recover, Barker writes that he "heard faint cries of a man in distress," though not from aboard but "from out of the darkness far down to leeward."

"Where's Nielson!" someone shouted.

The wave had stove in the steel wall of the fo'c'sle as if it were made of chocolate.

"Where's Nielson!"

There had been two boats mounted on the rails port and starboard near the stern, but they were gone, leaving twisted davits. There had been two other lifeboats aboard, lashed bottom-up with steel strops on the fo'c'sle roof. A much-liked Danish sailor, Nielson, standing lookout on the roof, had lashed himself to the lifeboats. Both boats and Nielson were gone.

But that wasn't the end of it. Jones writes that in the smooth after that monster's passing, as the water cascaded out through the freeing ports, the survivors found another of their shipmates crumpled in the scuppers, a Greek sailor they called Jerry. These ships were rigged with heavy steel doors in the bulwarks (the sides above the deck) to let the water run off the deck. The freeing ports were hinged on the top so that they could only open outboard, and Jerry had been picked up by the wave and washed halfway out the port. The door, banging open and closed, had smashed Jerry's leg, as Jones put it, "to a horrible gory mash." The human toll could have been worse. The entire watch could have been swept away. It happened. But as it stood, with Nielson and Davidson gone, Witney, Jerry the Greek and West grievously injured, and ten others decaying with frostbite, the crew was reduced to six seaman and four boys, everyone spent.

Finally Barker gave the order to fall off from the wind, steer northeast for Staten Island. Jones says that he saw a "flicker of a smile of triumph" in the mate's eyes. "But the victory was not his. The Greybeards of Cape Horn could shout in derisive laughter, shattering the sky with their uproarious mirth, as they compelled a gallant ship to turn tail and run for shelter from their too-long sustained rage."

Now the seas were coming on her stern, her port quarter, to be precise. And now she was a nearly crippled ship, her rigging in a shambles. The carpenter found that the breaker had smashed through part of the latch cover and left three feet of water in the hold. The pumps, which were mounted aft of the mainmast in the most exposed position possible, had to be manned day and night.

After she had been running for four days, blown along at four or five knots under whatever scraps of sail they could find, they came in sight of Staten Island. During that time, they had built a new hatch cover, battened and "frapped" it down; they had lowered the broken mast section and yards to the deck, cut away the twisted cables. While aloft, they discovered that the mainmast was cracked near the top. And they pumped and pumped "until life seemed no longer worthwhile making such an effort to preserve it." When they neared Staten Island, they saw "at least twenty-five" other ships with men aloft sending down broken gear, licking their wounds. The *British Isles* was among the last. The air and the surface of the sea were alive with albatross of all kinds, petrels, shearwaters, and prions, also seeking a quiet lee.

Tired men in pain performed brilliant pieces of seamanship aboard each of those vessels, but the *British Isles* seemed the most severely damaged. The biggest job was to repair the masts and, as it turned out, the jib boom, which was cracked and pointing skyward. The jib boom was that spar sticking out from the point of the bow. The reason for its existence was not to look elegant, but to supply a place where stays supporting the foremast could be attached. They fixed the masts and boom by a technique called "fishing and frapping." The process is to double the break with something like a pole or spar or a strip of steel and lash it with chain or rope and drive wedges into the structure to tighten it up. Easy to say, less easy to do with a steel tube six feet in diameter. While these crews slaved to put their ships back in order for another go at the Horn, a German four-master, one of those "Flying P" ships, hove into sight, and everyone looked on enviously as she sailed past the island flying six topsails doing a nice turn of speed on starboard tack "with not a rope-yarn out of place!" That scene was indicative of the windjammer period.

On September 20, three days after she'd anchored under Staten Island, an east wind came up, and Barker couldn't resist. They set what they could and sailed toward the Horn. But there were grievously injured men aboard. West and his hideous head wound, Witney's compound fracture, Jerry's pulped leg, gangrenous frostbite cases. An east wind is also fair for the Falklands from Staten Island, two or three days. There were by this time medical facilities in Port Stanley. But the injured, lashed in their berths (everyone now in the starboard fo'c'sle), delirious with pain—they were going to round the Horn, and then sail the rest of the way, a matter of weeks to Nowhere, Chile, which didn't even have a dock, let alone a doctor. What's perhaps more remarkable than Barker sailing for the Horn was that Jones doesn't even mention it. The idea of sailing two or three days in the opposite direction to save them was so far out of the question that it didn't bear mention.

The easterly didn't last long before a wind filled in from the northwest and quickly freshened to a gale. It began to look like the nightmare was returning. Jones calls the seas "confused."

It's a technical term, as well as descriptive, and it's an important member of the Cape Horn mix.

The leftover swells from that endless storm were still high and still running easterly. Now this new wind from the northwest was setting up its own seas, and when they overran the slower-moving swells, liquid chaos erupted. Even when they're relatively small, as in normal sailing conditions, confused seas can make the ride exceedingly lumpy. Jones said that waves were breaking on deck from both sides of the ship. The wind climbed to a "strong gale" in the language of the antique (but really salty) Beaufort Scale (that's the same Beaufort who befriended FitzRoy), between 41 and 47 knots in modern usage. The "crests of waves start to topple and roll over; spray may affect visibility," says Beaufort. Icicles formed in the rigging. It was just too cruel.

Barker kept sail on, trying to gain as much ground as he could while the wind remained reasonable. It was a defensible gamble, but the ship lost when a hurricane blast caught her with the mainsail up. In square-rigger usage, the mainsail was the largest of them all. It was set lowest on the mainmast from a yardarm over 100 feet long, 3,700 square feet of board-stiff canvas. The gust smacked her flat, and there she remained until the mainsail blew apart. Up the rig they went, six seamen and four boys—Jones said it blew so hard, they could barely drag themselves up the windward ratlines—and out onto the giant, frozen steel yard to haul in what they could save of the shredded sail.

They'd been at it for hours when a seaman named Henderson lost his grip, and "with a piercing cry of utter despair that chilled the souls of all who heard it," he fell sixty feet into the sea.

"Man overboard!" sounded through the ship for the third time. But everyone knew it was hopeless, including Henderson, of course, and no one left the yard, because scraps of sail could be saved. Henderson could not.

However, that hurricane gust "was the last blast of hate." Wind and seas gradually moderated. The wind remained shifty, requiring a lot of work on deck and aloft, but plain sailing work seemed a gift to this shattered crew. In the falling light of September 28, Cape Horn came abeam, out of sight, but they had crossed its longitude, exactly fifty-two days after they had done so the first time with such high hopes. They sailed on slowly westward in the fluky winds for ten days.

The fo'c'sle house was divided into two rooms in order to separate port watch from starboard, a typical arrangement that made the change of watch more efficient. But the port side of the house, stove in by the wave, had to be abandoned, and the entire crew lived in the same charnel house, reeking of gangrene. That was due mostly, but not entirely, to Jerry's leg. The carpenter, who'd been tending Jerry, went to the captain and said, "Cut him der leg off, or he die pretty quick!"

Jones was on deck during the operation, but he knew that it was over when he saw Cronberg come topside carrying the leg, run to the rail, and throw it overboard. Without benefit of anesthesia or medicines of any kind, Barker had amputated the Greek's leg using the cook's meat saw, a butcher knife, and a hot poker to cauterize the stump, while ankle-deep water sloshed around the stinking fo'c'sle. The patient actually survived to return home by steamer. Thomas Shute, owner of the *British Isles,* put Jerry the Greek on a pension for the rest of his life.

However, Seaman West, the man with the hideous head injuries, died on October 9 after hanging on as a "living corpse," Jones said, for several weeks. They committed his body to the sea "in the sure and certain hope of Resurrection. . . ." The captain closed his prayer book and said, "Haul the mainsail up, Mister, before that squall hits us."

That was the last squall, and nearly the end of the ordeal. The *British Isles* had gained the Pacific and turned the corner at the cost of four dead, and she was still 2,000 miles from her destination at Pisagua, Chile. At noon on October 16 she crossed 50 degrees South latitude (at 82 West), northbound. She had finally rounded Cape Horn. It had taken seventy-one days.

Operating on the slimmest of margins, windjammer owners were famously frugal. Among the many items they hated to spring for was the cable communications with their captains. When Captain Gustav Erickson bought the *Thomasina McLellan,* he chopped off her surname to save the expense of an extra word (Alan Villiers, *The War with Cape Horn*). Therefore, Captain James Learmont, arriving Honolulu aboard *Brenda,* 127 days out from Hamburg via the Horn, was surprised to find a long cable from his owner, John Rae, one of the most frugal of the frugal, who typically kept his cables to three words. Captain Rae was enquiring, at length, about a ship owned by his friend Thomas Shute, the *British Isles.*

"Why, that's Barker's ship," said Learmont to his mate, "the fellow who says he beat the *Pruessen*. He hasn't beaten much this time. Poor fellow, he must have taken a real beating—has his family aboard the brute too." Word traveled fast in this small world of shipmasters. In his own book, *Master in Sail,* Learmont quotes *Sea Breezes* magazine of October 1947: "During the months of May, June, and July (1905) no fewer than 130 sailing vessels left European ports for Pacific coast ports of North, Central and South America. Of this number, 62 were British, 34 French, 27 German, 4 Italian, 2 Norwegian, one Russian and one Dane. Out of this number 52 arrived at their destinations, four were wrecked, 22 put into ports in distress after Cape Horn damage and 53 had not arrived or were unaccounted for by the end of July." That was a bad year, but Learmont and *Brenda* had been out there. The passage from Atlantic to Pacific that had taken Barker two and a half months, Learmont delights to say, took him two weeks.

The *British Isles* made it to Pisagua and discharged the coal, but the Germans had taken all the nitrates. She tramped for whatever cargo her agents could find, twice across the Pacific, four years and 87,000 sea miles before she returned to Britain. Jones stayed at sea until retirement age.

15

How to Round
Cape Horn

It is nearly always very bad. . . . The winds blow almost continuously from the west, and although gales do not last so long in summer as in winter, they are more frequent and stronger. On the other hand, the winds are more variable in winter, the cold is bitterer, and the hours of daylight are much reduced—lasting at most from nine to three—and there is mist and snow to make things even worse. In short, navigation is nowhere more difficult than in these waters.

—**Instructions to Captains**
from shipowners A.D. Bordes et Fils

ROUNDING THE HORN WAS A RECOGNIZED badge of honor with certain rights, privileges, and visual displays, an earring of some special sort, for instance, a tattoo. But a sailor who'd been around the Horn could, most usefully, piss to windward and not get wet. Symbolically, he could urinate on that west wind. By 1855, Cape Horn had become a busy shipping lane. You could get in a collision if you didn't keep constant vigilance. Shipowners, officers, captains, and able seamen came to view rounding the Horn as a special segment of the voyage, like the trade winds and the doldrums, and as such, it was measurable. Sailors love to measure things, particularly speed.

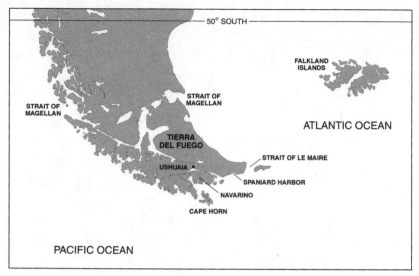

Map 15.1   50 South to 50 South

"How many days rounding, Captain?" the owner would ask.

"Twenty-two, sir."

"Ah, well now, Captain Johanson beat that by six days."

But just what was it, this rounding of the Horn? If the professionals were going to measure it, and if it was an indication of sailing skill, then everyone had to agree on just what it meant to round the Horn. Rounding had to be more than merely crossing Cape Horn's line of longitude in the Drake Passage. You were "off the Horn" when you passed 67 degrees 16 minutes West, but you were not around, not by a long shot. By sound nautical logic, rounding the Horn came to refer to that passage from 50 degrees South in the Atlantic down around the Horn to windward and back up to 50 South in the Pacific. That made sense because when you passed south of 50 degrees South, you were deep in Cape Horn weather, under the influence of the Southern Ocean and Antarctica. Fifty-South-to-50-South was a unity from a sailing perspective.

Cape Horn's latitude—55 degrees 59 minutes South—is only one mile short of 56 degrees, so let's call it that for simplicity's sake.

Fifty-six degrees South. There are sixty minutes in one degree of latitude, and each minute equals one nautical mile (or 1.15 statute miles). Therefore, a ship had to sail 360 miles of straight-line distance from 50 South just to get down to the level of Cape Horn at 56 South. Then there was the other 360 miles back up to 50 South in the other ocean. That's over 700 miles already. Of course, the ship couldn't just sail down there, swing around the rock and head back up north as if it were a turning mark in a yacht race. Cape Horn skewered ships caught trying to cut the corner close when the wind shifted or died. (Please remember that Cape Horn ships never had engines.) Once she'd cleared the Horn itself, she still had to run well out into the Pacific to put some water between herself and the heartless Chilean coast, the worst lee shore in the world. To protect their investment from this death trap, shipowners stipulated in writing that their captains carry on westward into the Pacific some 200 miles before they were allowed to turn north toward their destination. In practice, the sail from 50 South to 50 South covered 1,200 to 1,500 hard sea miles, depending on weather luck, on sailing skill, and on the ship.

We're talking for now about east-to-west roundings, from Atlantic to Pacific, windward roundings. When in waterfront bars (Rasmussen-the-Dane's in Hamburg, Big Nellie's in Newcastle, or that place in Tacoma where the proprietor shanghaied his own sons) old salts claimed to have been around the Horn, man and boy, two dozen times, they were referring to windward roundings exclusively. Downwind, well, that was nothing to brag about, a sleigh ride, almost like *yachting*. Generally, downwind sailing was easier on the ship and the sailors, and it was strategically simpler than beating west against contrary wind, seas, and current, but it was no yachting holiday going the other way, running wild on the edge of control. That sleigh-ride stuff was mere cant. Plenty died with the wind from behind. The old salts knew there was no easy way around—nobody relaxed south of 50 South.

The windward rounding was a sailing problem of the most basic sort: How do you get a big square-rigger to go west when everything— wind, waves, current—was coming hard from the west? If the west wind held, she would never make it. The very best direction she could make against the west wind was south, and if she wanted, she could turn around and try it the other way, but then the best she could do was north. Back and forth, getting nowhere, happened all the time. A constant fifty-knot west wind would have plugged the Drake Passage. But constant isn't in the nature of wind; it gusts and lulls, backs and veers. Sooner or later it would shift to the south or even the east, not for long, but it happened. So what to do? Many stripped her down and waited, sort of hunkered hoping for a new weather pattern.

The alternative was to sail aggressively, put her nose up as close to the wind as she'd go, pile on sail right to the edge of rationality. If the wind should shift south of west, a favorable slant, then seize it at once. Turn onto port tack without delay. In other words, drive this three- or four-hundred-foot square-rigger like a fifty-foot ocean racer, which is exactly what the best ones did. But turning a square-rigger from one side of the wind to the other was tricky business when a big sea was running. It required a piece of high-stakes choreography which if mistimed or otherwise screwed up could bring the masts down around the crew's ears. The men were cold and wet, and the sails and the lines were frozen, and that made the maneuver even chancier. It's no wonder the more timid captains just held starboard tack headed away from their destination, waiting, hoping for the big shift to bring them north again and west. The captains whose names we sea-struck kids grew up on hadn't a passive bone in their sailorly bodies. They never hunkered from the wind when it was still possible to use it to sail the hell out of there. But some other captains crumpled under the pressure as they crossed 50 South and the thermometer and barometer plunged in unison. It was one thing to be a "hard driver" in the trades or even in the forties, but it took a particular kind of man to keep her driving in Cape Horn waters.

Captaincy of a commercial square-rigger, out of touch with civilization for over 100 days at a time, carried utter authority like no other civilian job. The captain's character and competence, his temperament, and even his little foibles defined the tiny world his officers and crew lived in, which is why ships make good literary microcosms. Under the burden of absolute authority, the captain was terribly alone. It wasn't proper to fraternize with his mates, and certainly not lowly crewmen. Some captains talked to the specialists, the carpenter or sailmaker, who may have been with him on other voyages, but no captain would have confided anxiety to anyone. The hull began to creak under the press of wind aloft, the cold bit down, and sleet rattled against the steel masts—just as those savage fangs on Staten Island hove into sight. It's not hard to empathize with the man who ordered shortened sail. That's what happened to the *Denbigh Castle* in 1908. Her captain sailed her so timidly that the crew sent a delegation to complain, but it was too late. He had missed his only opportunity to escape before the westerlies closed the gate. After a three-week hammering south of the Horn, she turned tail and ran east along 40 degrees South halfway around the world to Fremantle, Australia, after eight and a half months at sea. The crew was literally starving. But some other captains freaked out entirely and took to their beds and/or their bottles. James Learmont, one of the windjammer stars, came suddenly to command when as a young officer his captain went rigid with shock and terror.

The fast guys, the artists, knew just how much sail to carry, not a stitch more or a moment longer than she could handle. That was the art, to sense her limits. Any maniac could carry too much sail, and any weak-kneed lubber could strip it off. The idea was to skate along the edge but never cross it, go fast as hell around the Horn, but don't break anything and don't kill anyone if you could avoid it. Speed mattered a lot, but what mattered most was speed in the desired direction, to "make westing," they used to say. The fast guys typically kept the deck for days at a time waiting for the favorable slant. Sailing aggressively, wearing around on every decent slant, shortening sail to protect the rig when the wind piped up, but putting it right back up again in the lulls—sailing under a hard driver meant a lot more work for the crew, but they appreciated it and respected the sail carrier. They resented timidity because laggardly sailing increased their exposure to Cape Horn miseries.

Captain Learmont, who was brilliant and had no doubt about that, made his view plain in *Master in Sail:* "Distance made good in the vicinity of Cape Horn was all-important. Any change in the wind that stopped her making westing or northing had to be attended to, otherwise you were making easting or southing and losing ground, and the remedy was to wear ship without hesitation. It was difficult and at times dangerous. . . . The danger lay in the turning, when the sea was full on your beam and the weight of it struck the full length of the ship. Once around, you had the sea on your bow but it was prudent to have the crew off the main deck before you brought her to." (That's because there could be six feet of seawater running over the main deck.)

This illustrates what may be the chief difference between the east-to-west windward rounding and the downwind run from the Pacific. To make progress to windward the ship had to change tacks—she had to wear. And wearing, by its nature, required the ship to present her side to the waves, the worst possible thing to do in a big sea. At no point in her long run across the Pacific did the eastbound ship need to show her side to the waves. That happened only by terrible error.

Throughout the literature, when the famous fast guys talked about how to round the Horn, they spoke of their crews and officers, the people who actually executed the maneuvers. Back in the Gold Rush clipper days, a 200-foot-long ship might carry a crew of fifty, excluding officers. Generally, however, these were not sailors. Most aimed to desert as soon as she docked in San Francisco and light out for the goldfields; that's why they'd signed on in the first place, to hell with Cape Horn. And that's why a captain needed thugs for mates who could instill some sailing enthusiasm with a rope end or a belaying pin. They weren't sailors, the circular logic went, but shoreside scum, so why treat them like sailors, and if anybody talked back, kick him in the nuts. Many of the mates deserted right along with the men, and far more crewless clipper ships rotted away at their moorings in San Francisco Bay than were lost down by the Horn.

By 1900, everything had changed. The ships had gotten bigger, doubling in size while carrying less than half the crew in number. But a professional-seaman class had developed. Sailors were still among the most tyrannized and exploited of all workers, paid a joke of a wage and fed on slop. But many of these men did not need to go to sea in a sailing vessel. There was plenty of work in steamships, where wages were higher and living conditions far less squalid. These crews had chosen to go in sail, partly because steamships never rounded Cape Horn. They were real sailors, not merely another variety of exploited laborer. The names of the mean and stupid captains who disregarded their crews are forgotten, because they didn't go fast. It was easy for a crew to thwart a captain they didn't like just by doing a sloppy job, say, of lashing the main topgallant and letting the wind shred it. The smart captains respected their crew's professional pride, looked out for their health and, though the word barely applies, their comfort. Captain Learmont, whose crews signed on with him voyage after voyage, wrote, "I'm not going to say that my actions in this were purely sentimental. I realized that a well-cared-for crew would help me make good passages, and this was my one and only ambition." (*Master in Sail*)

Windjammer crews came literally from everywhere in the world. Tahitians, for instance, were valued seamen. Polyglot crews were nothing new in the history of sail, but by the end there were a disproportionate number of Finns. I like this moment from *Master in Sail*: "... I had given the order to furl the fore and main topgallant sails, and the second mate, coming back to the poop from being aloft with his watch, said, 'My God, sir, I never saw anything like those Finns tonight on the yard! The way they muzzled those sails. You had to see it to believe it! I don't believe they are human!'"

Two weeks was a respectable time for the windward rounding from 50 South to 50 South. The all-time record remains an incredible five days, fourteen hours set in 1938 by Captain Adolf Hauth in the four-masted bark *Priwall*. Author and master mariner in his own right, Alan Villiers recorded a talk with Captain Hauth about that rounding after he had retired:

> I had a lot in my favor. It was summer. She was in nice trim, not down to her marks. I still had a stiffening of the good old sailors—six A.B.'s, four mates, a carpenter, sailmaker, blacksmith, and bos'n. Up to 1938 we still had some seamen who had never been in a steamer. They knew the sailing-ship work and life, and they preferred that. They didn't like steamers or motor ships. There wasn't enough sailorizing work. It was all hurry-up and worry about the cargo.... We didn't have any single days of great sailing all that voyage. The best twenty-four hours was 236 miles. The *Priwall* was not the fastest ship.... But it seemed as if this time she was determined to get past Cape Horn as if she never wanted to be taken there again. (*The War With Cape Horn*)

Captain Robert Hilgendorf commanded nine different windjammers over a twenty-year career for the Laeisz ("Lights") Company, the so-called Flying P Line, because all its ships' names began with the letter *P*. Known as the Wizard of Hamburg, Hilgendorf, his colleagues said, had supernatural insight into wind, knew what it was going to do before the wind knew—and, further, that the wind knew he knew. They weren't entirely kidding. But as Alan Villiers points out, Captain H. was not a wizard, he was a scientist. By his time—he retired in 1901—plenty of information was available about wind and weather patterns down by the Horn to help a studious captain sail fast, and one of the best sources was still Matthew Fontaine Maury's *Wind and Current Charts* and *Sailing Directions*. (Maury, who more or less invented the science of oceanography, would be far more famous in his own country if he hadn't sided with the South in the Civil War.) Captain Hilgendorf rounded the Horn sixty-six times, and never once did he need more than ten days to thrash from 50 South to 50 South.

The clipper ships owned the flat-out, straight-line speed records until fairly recently, when brutal, brilliant catamarans sailed by the heirs of the old Cape Horners (including Slip Novak) took aim at their records. But all the fastest roundings from 50 South to 50 South are still held by windjammers. It's not really fair, though, to compare the different kinds of vessels. For windward thrashing, summer and winter, steel construction and great size had it all over the lightly built clippers. Without disrespecting those magnificent anomalies, it stands to reason that wooden masts couldn't take the same loads and strains as steel, and so the clipper ship had to shorten sail, to sail defensively, long before the windjammer. It's said windjammers could carry on to windward in 50 knots of wind. Still you hear those dreadful stories. The *British Isles* is one, and that same winter, the *Susanna* beat herself half to death south of the Horn for ninety-one days, falling at one point down as far as 62 degrees South. I've never heard of a firsthand account of that rounding, but it must have been horrific.

A lot of ships died no doubt on the windward rounding when the heavy westerlies never relented or shifted favorably. They were driven south, unable because of conditions or injured crew to wear, into the ice. The northern extent of sea ice is clearly charted, but in fact it's notoriously irregular, and some years ice squeezed the Drake Passage in half. Yet for a while in the early 19th century, there was talk among Cape Horners about dipping down south far enough to pick up the newly discovered, narrow belt of easterlies that circle Antarctica. That east wind could be used to gain ground to the west. But experience showed this to be a bad strategy, because the east-wind belt was too far out of the way and too deep in the ice zone. In the winter of 1904, a French bark, *Emilie Calline,* sighted a three-masted full-rigged ship sitting upright high and dry like some fever dream on an iceberg with scraps of canvas snapping in her broken rigging. *Emilie Calline* passed as close as she dared, finding no sign of life, but not close enough to pick a name off the ghost ship's stern. In 1906, the ship *Monkbarns* got stuck in an ice field for sixty-three days, killing her captain and half his crew before a lucky wind shift saved the ship.

No, as Maury wrote, the best course was to stand and fight it out up in the Drake, closer to the Horn than to the ice. And that's why the captain often stayed topside day and night waiting for a favorable southerly slant; everything depended on the slant. The greats always found a way. In 1905, while *Susanna* and the *British Isles* were beating against the brick wall, Captain Learmont in *Brenhilda* slipped around with relative ease. He must have had different conditions. Could he have sailed himself out of the weather Captain Barker saw on the *British Isles?* I don't know, but the great ones never had those hideous experiences, they were never driven into the ice, they seldom broke expensive gear or sails, almost never lost a man, and not once did it take them over two weeks to clear 50 South in the Pacific from 50 South in the Atlantic.

Whalers were the first around, beginning with *Amelia,* a British ship manned by expatriates from Nantucket, in 1787. There were the fur traders bound to the Pacific Northwest and on to China with pelts. There were the miserable little brigs in the hide-and-tallow trade to Mexican California, R.H. Dana's *Pilgrim,* for one. But it was the clipper ships that brought Cape Horn to public attention. They were the bright and shining moment—long, thin hulls with sharp bows and yacht-like sheer lines, masterpieces carrying more sail on taller masts than anyone had ever seen before, skysails above the royals, around Cape Horn. These were Gold Rush days, the 1850s, the days of the hard driver, Creesy in *Flying Cloud, Sea Witch* when Waterman had her, when nothing mattered but speed, around Cape Horn we'll go bound for Cal-a-forn-i-o. *Flying Cloud* crossed the Golden Gate eighty-nine days out from Sandy Hook, New York, logging an incredible 374-mile day in the bargain. But the magnificent clippers were born to serve a gold rush (in 1849 it cost $13 to ship a ton of goods from New York to San Francisco; in 1850 a ton cost $60; one egg cost a dollar in San Francisco, $100 for a pair of boots), and so by definition they couldn't last. More level-headed cargo carriers called Downeasters picked up the California trade for a while, until the transcontinental railroad turned American attention westward, instead of seaward, at least as far as long-haul commercial sail was concerned. Lacking a new continent to exploit, Europeans carried on in deepwater sail because they still had heavy things to import. And out of that need for grain, wool, nitrates, at one time guano, came this wonderful brute of a ship, the windjammer.

One of her last jobs was to haul coal or general cargo from Britain or northern Europe around the Cape of Good Hope, across the Indian Ocean to southeast Australia (Adelaide, Melbourne, Port Lincoln, or Sydney), where she exchanged her outbound cargo for several thousand tons of wheat or barley. Those ports lay near 40 degrees South on the edge of the Roaring Forties, and so the route home was clear— ride the wind all the way to Cape Horn, 7,800 miles east. That was almost half the distance to England, and it was all downhill. Now instead of pounding her brains out to windward, which square-riggers were never meant to do anyway, she had everything, winds and waves, to her advantage. Even the current was heading her way. In this long stretch of the Southern Ocean, as in the trades, this sailing ship, an antique in her heyday, made sound practical sense; never mind the poetry and gooey voyages of personal discovery, this vessel made clear-eyed commercial sense. Three hundred free, fuel-less miles each day, totally independent of land for months at a time, an efficient pelagic thing big enough to carry more bulk tonnage farther and cheaper than a steamship—it only happened to be an aesthetically stirring object.

But there was a price to pay for this downwind delight in the Roaring Forties. It usually comes up when racing sailors congregate, and as the evening wears on, the pisco flows immoderately, they begin to tell war stories that end up focusing on knockdowns, savage round-ups, and mast-in-the water broaches. These terms describe basically the same completely avoidable event, that is, the loss of control while running before the wind. The boat heels too far, the keel and rudder lose their grip on the water, the boat spins out sideways to the wind, and over she goes. The cause is too much sail. (Those of us who sail other people's boats don't really mind, but if I had a boat, I'd never let exhilarated hooligans like us set big spinnakers in way too much wind.) This kind of wipeout doesn't happen much beating to windward, because the boat has a less slippery relationship to the water than when running. We need to add one additional, semi-technical principle to appreciate the difference between the two points of sail: apparent wind.

If a sailboat is going seven knots into a twenty-knot breeze, the sails, rig, and crew are experiencing a wind speed of about twenty-seven knots, because a moving boat makes its own wind. A moving automobile also makes its own wind, but that doesn't matter to the driving. It matters a lot to the sailing, because a twenty-seven-knot wind packs more force than a twenty-knot wind. On the other hand, the boat sailing at seven knots in a twenty-knot breeze from behind is feeling only a thirteen-knot breeze. This means that a downwind vessel can carry a lot more sail than an upwind boat, and it means also that she can get in more trouble much quicker, when we expand the numbers out to Cape Horn velocities. Fifty knots of west wind surprised no one. Seventy knots would have surprised no one, either, but that was too much; the waves would have been untenable for fast sailing. Fifty from a few degrees south of west would have been celebrated. Pile on the sail. If the wind blew up twenty knots higher in sleet and freezing rain, then sail would have to come in. But speed was no problem, speed to burn; the problem would be control. And the danger of losing it came not from the wind, but from the following seas.

The ship might be doing fifteen knots through the water (maybe more over the bottom, since she had the current with her), but the waves could easily be rolling in at twenty-five knots. "When we previously had mountainous seas," wrote Ray Wilmore, who rounded downwind in the four-masted bark *John Ena* in 1911, "we were heading almost directly into them. I thought they were bad when they broke over the bow, sending spray and foam up into the rigging, but these following seas are worse and they make steering a nightmare. I spent the hardest and most terrifying two hours of the trip during my trick at the wheel this afternoon." *(Square Rigger Around the Horn)* As each of the waves passed, they hefted her stern such that the rudder came out of the water, and the force of the wave then directly attacked the rudder surface. There was a simple, direct wire-and-pulley linkage between the steering wheel and the rudder, so any shocks and strains on the latter were sent directly to the helmsman. Windjammers carried double wheels rigged in tandem to a single axle, and in extreme conditions, it took four men, two on each wheel, to control the rudder. "I was in a lather of perspiration the entire time, notwithstanding the near freezing temperature," Wilmore wrote. "It was work, work, work, every second. The ship would yaw and run off before the wind with every following sea. She seemed to slip and slide, first at the stern, then at the bow, then sideways with the wind. Before I could do anything about it, the ship would be off course a couple of points. There she would hold and hold and wouldn't come back. Then all of a sudden . . . she'd overreach the mark by a couple of points. So it went all afternoon, . . . two points north then two points south of the course, wallowing in the trough, climbing the side of a mountainous sea, sliding down the other side, completely awash most of the time." Stories of helmsmen being flipped right over the top of a runaway wheel and flung clear across the deck are common.

A steering wheel spinning like a deranged thing with spokes, flipping people, clearly indicated that the vessel was no longer under control. First, her stern would fall away from the wind, and if no one caught her, she'd career around, and when she presented her side to the wind and seas, they would likely knock her down. If her hatch covers held, no water got into the hold, then she could come back up—many did, we know—but almost certainly her cargo would have shifted. Listing cripples didn't last long before the pounding seas found a way in.

The other scary thing about following seas was their tendency to break over the stern, "pooped," in the language. Not only were sterns badly shaped to take a wave, they contained that vital steering gear. When waves broke over the stern, they smashed the wheels, the binnacle and compass, as well as the helmsmen and the captain, because that was his place. Sometimes boarding seas swept her stern to stem, taking out the lifeboats, the deckhouses, and anyone who couldn't hold on—and then drove her down by the sheer weight of water on deck. Rex Clements described the experience during his 1911 passage as apprentice on the small bark *Arethusa:*

> High above the taffrail—forty or fifty feet—it loomed, and the next minute it fell. . . . Through instinct more than exercise of will I hung on. I felt my shoulders were being wrenched out as demon-fingers plucked at me; then the weight of the avalanche lifted and I knew the blessed feel of light and freedom again. . . . As the water passed we looked up. The great roller that had pooped us had swept for'ard and buried the ship deep under a green swirl of water. Even as we looked, two walls of water rushed in over the submerged bulwarks and collided down the length of the ship. The hull settled and felt dead beneath our feet.
>
> "My God, she's gone!" said the bosun. (A *Gypsy of the Horn*)

In *A Two Years' Cruise off Tierra del Fuego,* that Captain Snow who sailed for the missionaries until they alienated each other wrote, "If it should appear that I speak too much of gales and stormy weather, it must be remembered that I am writing of a part of the world where it is rare to have a fine day; and consequently, if I depict—truly—more of gloom than sunshine, albeit some of the latter will, I trust, be found to occasionally appear." Some of the latter, yes, the literal and figurative sunshine. There were broachings, founderings, collisions, dismastings, and catastrophic losses of buoyancy. Everyone knew that who read the shipping news. The food was garbage, living conditions abysmal, the work unrelenting and routinely dangerous. That was no secret either. By, say, 1915, everyone knew that square-rigged Cape Horners were about to vanish from the sea. People went to have the experience before it was too late. I might not have gone twice, but I would signed on for one voyage had the time been right. I'd have done it for the pure sailing of it. For the half-mindless, yah-hoo exhilaration of running before a whole gale west of the Horn.

There may be a handful of men who remember what it was like, the awesome power of heavy wind in big square sails set on steel masts and yards, but the ships will never sail again. Those lovely, sentimental "tall ships" trundled out for patriotic events are only semblances of the original windjammers. To serve as cadet-training vessels, their rigs have been cut down to manageable size, their decks built up to accommodate civilized quarters, and, terminally, diesel engines and propellers have been plunked in. Occasionally, on a race boat flying a spinnaker too long in rising wind as the boat loaded up with scary force and control grew iffy, I thought, it might have been like this, the power up there, but not really. We were dealing with a fraction of the horsepower contained in one upper topsail on *Passat, Pommern, Moshulu, Peking, Viking,* just to name those preserved in museums.

The hard-body Swede from the Aaland Islands, Elis Karlsson, was at sea since about infancy, and when he was chief mate on the four-masted bark *Herzogin Cecilie,* he had a moment of understanding while debating whether to quit the sea or not: "I was watching spellbound the most awe-inspiring, and at the same time the most magnificent, sight I shall ever see. I knew then that nothing would carry away; nothing would stop this marvelous ship in this her hour; as she was carried eastward in the heart of the gale, ship and elements were one. The spectacle was so overwhelming in its display of power that ordinary awareness, stark fear, or even apprehension vanished and were replaced by an exultant feeling of oneness with the elements and the ship. I knew then that all was well and stood there reveling in it all. A spectator yet a part of it." For moments like that, pure sailing moments, the sea-struck willingly absorbed misery, privation, and danger down by the Horn.

16

The Undiscovered Land

"Sod this for a game of soldiers."

—Captain Hamish Laird

"I don't wonder you love boating, Mr. Allnut."
—*African Queen*, James Agee screenplay

BAHIA ORANGE. HAMISH had just brought up the morning edition of the weather picture on his laptop, a major occasion in our routine, and when he whistled softly at the image, we crowded around the nav desk, leaning in. I couldn't see from my oblique angle at the edge of the crowd, but I could tell from the exhalations, another whistle, that it was worth seeing.

"I've never seen anything like this before," said Hamish in that level British-mountaineer-expedition tone. . . . Clearly something serious was bearing down on us, and after that first surge of excitement, it dawned on me that they might be looking at the end of our trip. Drake's storm, the one that blew the *Golden Hind* down this way, lasted a month. It wasn't unusual. The *British Isles* fought near-hurricane winds for two months. Cape Horn reality coming our way.

"Have you ever seen anything like this, Dick?"

Dick, who used to be a professional meteorologist, said, "Never."

I ducked and fidgeted and jockeyed for a cogent sight line.

An immense mass of low pressure, a fully formed spiraling storm. We'd seen it before in its adolescence, but now it had matured, tightened, twisted and intensified. Its wind bands seemed to cover the entire ocean, and there in the middle was that tiny black dot, the center of rotation, the eye. What we were seeing was a satellite image, an actual photograph of the storm. Hamish switched to the map page, the one that showed the isobars. . . . They were so tightly packed they blurred into a single smudge. We stood in silence staring at our future. Dick reminded us that the isobars were really only estimations based on the look of the storm from aloft. Nothing out there in the wilds of the Southern Ocean was actually measuring barometric pressure.

"So you mean it might not be so bad?" Jonathan asked.

"Yes. Or worse," said Dick. "But look here, the depression has hardly moved in, what, forty-eight hours. It's deepened, strengthened, but it hasn't moved. Now look here, and here, here—" He was pointing to these cells of high pressure, four of them, neatly encircling the much larger depression at northeast and northwest, southeast and southwest. *That's* what he'd never seen before.

"Nor I," said Hamish.

It looked like a cartoon, brave and stalwart little highs had hurled themselves at the marching storm, digging in their heels, straining to stop it before it hurt somebody, but I tried to pose the question in something like scientific terms. Could that happen, could the highs actually be retarding the easterly march of a Cape Horn snorter?

"I don't know."

"Could it just sit there and blow itself out?" Jonathan wondered.

"Not likely," said Hamish with a shrug. Who knows what manner of wild phenomena go down in the Southern Ocean that no one ever sees.

"Want to get under way?" I asked

"Let's."

We hustled into our layers and up the ladder to release *Pelagic* from the land. Though Laird and Novak had devised smart systems, getting under way was an elaborate procedure. First, the shore lines had to be detached by two people in the dinghy, one to drive while the other clambered up-slope to untie the four lines from rocks and trees. If the shore-side kelp was too dense, then the boatman had to raise the outboard and row in. Once free, the lines were wound up on the separate spools bolted to *Pelagic*'s deck near the mast. Then the dinghy had to be winched aboard on the spinnaker halyard and lashed to its chocks on the foredeck, and that left only the big plow anchor to haul aboard and secure. We were getting pretty good at it.

Hamish backed through a narrow channel in the kelp until he could get his bow turned toward the mouth of the cove. We moved deliberately, the way one moves in heavy seas. Hamish had called for a reef in the main. But the weather outside was fairer than it looked from inside, clear blue sky overhead, young cumulus growing above the mountain peaks. And we discovered a nice sailing breeze once we'd cleared the hefty lee of Peninsula Hardy. Hamish nodded at the mainsail. We shook out the reef, trimmed it up, then rolled out the jib. *Pelagic* liked that.

Kate was sitting in the cockpit grinning broadly, sipping maté from her gourd. "It's so luxurious sailing with you guys," she said. "We need something done on deck, and you do it in a flash."

"Oh, I bet you say that to all the punters." They'd been calling us punters and yachties.

"Uh-uh," she insisted, crossing her heart. "It's particularly nice, since today is my birthday."

We'd already noticed and complimented her earrings, a gift from the captain, who beamed.

"Then I'll make something special for dinner," Jonathan, a fine boat cook, offered. "Lamb would probably be in order." We glanced as one at the sad little carcass curing on the backstay.

The Hardy Peninsula is an enormous lobe of land, thirty miles from False Cape Horn north to the narrow stalk near the head of our fjord. Though many were topped by isolated, naked crags, the mountains on Hardy were rounder, more dome-like, than the Dog Jaw Range on the north side of Navarino, Mount Olivia and Cinco Hermanos on Tierra del Fuego. As we rounded the imposing promontory called Punta San Bernardo and crossed Bahía Scotchwell, the breeze gasped, sputtered, and everyone stopped in mid-sentence to notice. It veered about forty-five degrees, then returned to its original direction and velocity.

After two hours, minding the helm and the trim, trying to sail fast, we entered a channel, clearly marked by kelp, between the Hardy shore and an island aptly called Packsaddle, then rounded the point. The land fell sharply away to the northwest, and the water opened to the north. This was the mouth of Bahía Tekenika, the rim of the funnel-shaped bay, which at the narrow end became our fjord. We were close now, though still too far to identify the entrance, and the weather was holding fair. On Peninsula Pasteur, hulking mountains shouldered their way far above the snow line, and I scrambled to take it in, to imprint it. But it dazzles. I couldn't grasp the scale except by accumulation—the mountain, the snow line, forest, shoreline, channel—or I'd lose it to overload.

That's why it took me a while to notice the sudden profusion of wildlife. Every little raft of rock, every high-and-dry islet and half-tide pile of glacial rubble seethed with thick brown bodies and waving flippers. They rolled over on one another, nestling out some personal space where a pinniped could expose itself to the sun, while others brayed in protest. Some gave up and slithered over the edge into the water. We could smell them, dank, musty, and wild, when we passed downwind. These were South American sea lions and southern fur seals, and frankly we needed the *Field Guide* to tell them apart at first. Both are eared seals, as opposed to true seals, which are seldom seen in these waters. (In addition to having external ears, eared seals differ from true seals in that they propel themselves through the water with breaststrokes from powerful fore fins, while true seals such as Weddell's and crabeaters swim by sculling their hind flippers.) Male sea lions sport the dense mane that earned them their name, but fur seal males also have manes. The bulls of both varieties, with their massive muzzles, thick necks, and blubbery bodies, typically weigh in at over 700 pounds, twice the size of the more graceful and streamlined females. Both were hunted to near extinction by sealers from England and New England, and the naturalist Natalie Goodall believes that the sealers' bloodthirsty greed contributed more to the disruption of the Yahgan culture than most sources credit. We noticed after a while that there was always a posted lookout, head held high, sniffing and scanning the water for ghostly Yahgan or Quakers. At *Pelagic*'s approach, they honked and shook themselves, sending a twitter of alarm from body to body, waking the others, who watched us pull abeam. Yet only a timid or prudent few fled to safety in the water. The rest peered at us with big, black, sad eyes. Some of those seals, said Hamish, might have witnessed the lethality of humans in boats, since less than a decade ago, Chilean crab fishermen were killing seals and sea lions for bait. They strung nets straight out from shoreside points and headlands to catch *centrolos* when they migrated. But since the shores plunge so steeply into very deep water, all migrating crabs were forced inshore, where inevitably they'd scudder into the nets. That method would have exterminated every crab in the islands if the authorities hadn't banned it. Fishermen, forced to switch to wire traps and seeing no percentage in buying crab bait when the environment was full of free bait, began shooting seals. When populations plummeted to a state of emergency, the government banned that practice, so the fishermen began harpooning porpoise for bait as they played in the bow waves. Ornithologist Jerry Clark, seeing empty rookeries, suspected that the fishermen were killing penguins for bait in the mideighties. (We didn't see a single fishing boat.)

Every rock and islet unclaimed by seals was packed with Magellanic cormorants and penguins, sometimes sharing the same rock perch, but always in segregated groups. I think we saw four kinds of cormorants, heads pivoting in unison as we passed, but I couldn't distinguish, for instance, the blue-eyed cormorants from the kings. These were big birds, far taller and heavier than their northern cousins, and all were vividly marked in variations of black and white. So were the penguins, and at first we confused the two, which, I was glad to hear Ms. Goodall later say, is typical of newcomers. Once our eyes adjusted, we wondered how we'd ever failed to see the difference, even from a distance. These Magellanic penguins stood shoulder to shoulder, pivoting nervously en masse watching our approach. Hamish and Kate have seen the very rare macaroni penguins, as well as rockhoppers and gentoos, but none except Magellanics are common here. Black-and-white kelp gulls hopped around among the penguins on the edges of the roosts trying to see what was in it for them. Two or three hard-looking skuas were doing the same thing from orbit one hundred feet overhead.

Peninsula Pasteur towered on our starboard side. Away to port, the Hardy Peninsula's mountains dove straight into the water too steeply to have anything like a shore, not even a fringe of rocks.

Ahead the fjord bent slightly north of west and seemed to constrict to nothing.

A squadron of black-browed albatross appeared astern wheeling, banking, and jinking in the light breeze, where minutes ago there were none, and others were gliding in to join them, sliding off the mountain updrafts, swooping down the flanks to sea level, then gyring up to the most popular altitude, about 200 feet above the deck. Were they following *Pelagic* like expectant herring gulls in a stern-dragger's wake? Or did it only seem that way? We'd seen albatross around the Wollastons, Hermite, and the Horn, but singly or in pairs, at some distance off. Here the air was layered with those marvelous high-aspect wings that never need flapping. I wanted to believe that they had never seen a boat before, and it was our novelty that brought them close aboard. It probably wasn't so, yet nothing else seemed to be going on, no feeding frenzy; no fish roiled the surface, and the birds never touched the water. Kate and Hamish have occasionally spotted other varieties of albatross passing over, and Bridges says two are indigenous (there are nine varieties from the River Plate to the Antarctic peninsula), but these were all black-browed albatross, sleeker-bodied and smaller than the famous wandering albatross, with a six-foot wingspan against the wanderer's fourteen. Hamish, who's seen plenty of both, observes that the black-brows are more nimble, more beautiful on the wing. Coleridge's albatross, hung around the narrator's neck, was a wanderer, but Coleridge was no mariner. That killing an albatross brings a shipload of ill fortune was his own poetic construct. The old salts dragged a baited triangular wooden frame behind their ships to snare albatross by their beaks. Many latter-day voyage accounts contain photographs of captured albatross—with six guys supporting its out-stretched wings—but albatross catching had more to do with amusement than food, because most sailors found the flesh too oily and fishy to eat, and some albatross were even released unharmed.

Cape petrels, gorgeous little birds with black-and-white checkered plumage across their backs, wings, and rumps, bold white undersides, pirouetted and soared with the albatross. There were other varieties of petrels in the air, but even with bird book in hand, we could seldom distinguish diving petrels from Wilson's storm petrels, too many swirling birds. Brown and great skuas broke off their orbiting patrols at several hundred feet, dropped to masthead height, and zeroed in on our lamb carcass. Big dull-brown, gull-shaped birds with four-foot wingspans, skuas are primarily predators (of gull and cormorant chicks) and scavengers, but they're best known for their piracy on the wing. They wait circling above the hard-working gulls and terns until a successful fisherman tries to fly home with his catch, then they sweep in and attack, like Francis Drake on a fat Spanish treasure ship, until the victim drops his fish. The skuas up in the Beagle have grown used to sailboats with lambs lashed in their rigging, and they lurk until the crew goes below before diving in for a bite. We'd played the skua game, ducking below, leaving the boat on autopilot—five minutes later the skuas would arrive in a line astern waiting to be sure the coast was clear. But these skuas had no guile or subtlety. Swooping in for the attack, their wings popped in the air, and we could feel the whoosh on the backs of our necks. We took down our lamb before one of us got a face full of skua claws.

Fat kelp geese waddled along the shores—the males are bright white, the females an unobtrusive brown—pecking and probing strands of tide-line kelp. Several varieties of ducks bobbed on the seaward fringes of the kelp groves. We also saw steamer ducks, hands down the strangest bird in these strange waters. Though unmistakably duck-shaped, steamers are goose-sized, weighing over twenty-five pounds at maturity. Flightless, the steamer duck skims across the surface by rapidly, loudly rotating its stubby wings like paddle blades. Estimating its speed at fifteen knots, Captain Cook called it the racehorse duck. But Captain Pringle Stokes, FitzRoy's predecessor who shot himself, delighted by the birds, gave them the name that stuck. Sailing fifty years before Stokes, Captain Cook had never seen a paddle-wheel steamboat. Steamer ducks (also called flapping loggerheads), alone among the avian extravagance, seemed frightened by *Pelagic*. They'd shoot off, wings moving too fast to see, leaving a stutter-like wake behind, but if they still felt unsafe, they bowed their bodies and dove like a cormorant. The Yahgan ate steamers, catching them with snares, but whites found their flesh repellent.

Why was life here, especially bird life, so much more profuse than elsewhere? Was today an aberration, our one-time good luck? Hamish's deep local knowledge couldn't help, because he'd never been here. . . . Gulls, skuas, penguins, petrels, cormorants, seals, and sea lions are all fish eaters. Did that mean there was better fishing in our fjord, or was it just safer here? Did isolation from humans draw them here, thanks to Chilean *prohibición?* No one really knew. I couldn't find anyone who'd been here. In *A Two Years' Cruise off Tierra del Fuego,* Parker Snow wrote, "The sea birds swept round and round us, each time narrowing their circle, as these birds almost always do when a severe gale is approaching."

The wind died without a sputter or a gasp, as if struck down by a massive coronary. Shedding her momentum in two boat lengths, *Pelagic* sagged to a stop, sails hanging in that ugly way of becalmed sails. Everyone looked aloft. The sky had gone bony pale, studded with ice clouds. High, white flakes of cirrocumulus had arranged themselves in a ripple pattern—the "mackerel sky"—and even as we watched they began to thicken and turn gray. Low, dense stratus slid in fog-like layers over the tops of the western mountains. The surface of the bay turned black and oily. The inevitable was about to befall us. . . . But we were fascinated by the sky show, a textbook demonstration of foul-weather warning with the pages turning at high speed. We would have felt quite different about the show, however, if we were wallowing in the Drake Passage a couple of hundred miles south, instead of in these narrow waters.

"Let's get the jib in, please."

"Want the main down?"

"Just sheet it in for now." Hamish fired up the engine, monitoring his rpms. But then turgid black cloud climbed over the western mountains and avalanched into the fjord right down to the deck. "Never mind, main down, please."

Someone popped the halyard, dropping the full-battened main into the lazy jacks, and we lashed it down. The clouds were all on the move, boiling, agitated, bullet-colored, wedging themselves beneath billows black as an oil-field fire, while stringy, bone-white wisps flew eastward, mesmerizing. Sublime. Prudent mariners, however, don't stand around in slack-jawed pantheistic reverie, but make ready for heavy weather. Hamish did a once-over from bow to stern, yanking at the dinghy lashings, taking a couple more sail ties around the main. He always moved at high speed around his boat, but always with a dead-certain step.

The wind leapt to twenty-eight knots in one boat length, paused only briefly to collect itself before skipping into the mid-thirties with higher gusts. The high, steep walls of the fjord, its fjord-ness, would make this wind very gusty. The seas were still flat, but they wouldn't stay down for long. It began to rain hard. Hamish revolved his index finger in the air, and I advanced the throttle while he listened to the rpms with the soles of his feet. I stopped when he signaled. It began to sleet. Take the briefest dip into Cape Horn literature and you'll come across sleet. It's infamous.

About the size of BB pellets and just as hard, this sleet doesn't fall from the sky like normal sleet, but flies—horizontally—before the wind. This hail hurts. It hits exposed, upright things (like the helmsman), bounces a couple of times on the cockpit floor, tinkling and accumulating in the corners. I held my ski glove against my face and tried to peek through the fingers. It was dark, with nothing but deeper darkness beyond the bow, and the contrast made the white incoming bullets glow for a moment before impact. The wind climbed into the forties. I considered excuses for relinquishing the helm, but none seemed remotely plausible.

Kate and the others nestled in the lee of the doghouse laughing and chattering with heavy-weather excitement.

"So. Who wants to drive?" I wondered loudly enough to beat the wind.

No takers, pretending not to hear. Sleet/hail was pinging off my forehead, probably pitting my glasses. The mountains were obliterated in the blackness, and our visibility was reduced to the negligible. Evincing no desire to steer, my shipmates had sensibly moved inside the doghouse, and soon, without deck work to do and nothing to see, they'd begin to trickle below. . . . Kate would probably make a spot of tea.

Hamish squeezed through the spectators and ducked below to look for alternatives.

The waves had caught up with the wind. They weren't big waves, there wasn't enough time or fetch for that, but they were standing straight up, stiff with determination, three feet high, like rock walls in Vermont. *Pelagic* couldn't find any room to relax between crests, hobby-horsing in short, sharp plunges. I could no longer see the speedo or any of the other instruments, but glancing overboard, I could see that we lacked forward progress. We were at a standstill. There were no more usable revs in the engine, and of course the sails were useless with the wind dead in our teeth. We could go no faster—but the wind could. There was little point in this kind of travel. The wind, not the Chileans, had denied access to our fjord, for now.

Hamish came topside, looked outboard for a little while, then said something I didn't quite hear, but I think it was "Sod this for a game of soldiers." He leaned closer and shouted, "Head thirty degrees to port."

Bullets were bouncing off the compass glass. Thirty degrees left pointed us at land—high, hard land—but nothing of it was visible. Only those wildly shifting variations of gray. The whine of the wind through the rigging rose a notch or two at the new angle. In *Two Against Cape Horn,* Hal Roth wrote: "It was the sound of the wind that got to me after a while. The continual moaning. The crescendos. The hollow roar. The scream when it was on us. But these words are meaningless because they merely describe the edge of the wind. No one can talk about the squalls of Cape Horn. You must experience their color and shape and size and intensity yourself."

Hamish said, "Come left another twenty degrees, please. And slow her down."

The turn and change in revs woke the slacker-watch below, and they crowded into the doghouse like a comedy team, heads swiveling, to see what was going on.

"So who wants to drive?"

Suddenly land hove into sight, individual trees. A wicked, wind-assisted ebb tide was setting us backward. Hamish said, "That's all right, we'll fall down to that headland. There's a likely-looking cove behind it." I could see no headland.

"We're anchoring?" David asked.

"No. We're turning downwind to set the spinnaker." For an instant, I think, he almost believed me. He would have done it.

It looked like we were going to be blown right past the cove. Hamish asked for the staysail to come out, and Tim trimmed it to our heading. "There," said Hamish, "that should give you some lift."

It did. The bow was pointing straight for the cove, and with the help of the headsail, I could easily lay the headland. It was a high rocky lobe, exposed to the east, but a bulletproof lee in this westerly.

David stepped beside me. "Would you have thought of doing that, setting some staysail? For lift? In forty knots of wind?"

"No, but I will now."

A cold, steady rain was falling from a bank of oily clouds no higher than the masthead as we entered the cove.

Hamish took the wheel, turned in slow circles until he found a spot he liked, and with his bow pointing away from the beach, he called for the anchor.... "Snub it, please." He slowly backed toward the shore so that the bow anchor pulled uphill against the steeply shoaling bottom. Anchors pulling downhill seldom hold. He gunned the engine in reverse to set it. "How much is out?"

"Twenty meters. On the deck." Kate called back.

Hamish had marked his anchor line, called a rode, with bits of colored nylon in order to know how much he had out. The rule of thumb says that the rode should be seven times the depth in order that the pull on the anchor always remains horizontal to the bottom. But because *Pelagic*'s rode was all chain, it could be shorter. "Put twenty-five meters on the deck, please. Let's see how that holds."

Outside the lee, the wind howled, whipping ragged sheets of rain and driving whitecaps before it.

Hamish went forward to inspect, leaving the engine ticking in reverse. "How about Cape Turnaround?" he proposed, coming aft, pointing at the forested headland. Hamish liked pretending that we had the right to name places without charted names.

"How about Chickenshit Point?" Tim proposed.

Our stern lay only twenty feet from the beach, low tide, anchor holding, when we winched the dinghy over the side. Kate and David climbed down and drove it ashore to tie off the stern lines. Since the trees were not stout enough to trust, Kate took cable strops with eye splices in either end around two well-placed boulders and tied on the shore lines. Approving their choices, Hamish shut down the engine.

"How about a crown roast?" Jonathan wondered. "With mint sauce." Kate had found some wild mint near the *Micalvi* in Puerto Williams.

"Cape Crown Roast."

"Or I could braise a shoulder." He went below to plan the birthday menu.

David and Kate came back aboard and went directly below.

"How about Caleta Zarpe?" Hamish proposed as he went below. "I like that. Caleta Zarpe." In their instructions to FitzRoy, the Admiralty wrote, "The name stamped upon a place by the first discoverers should be held sacred by the common consent of all nations; and in new discoveries it would be far more beneficial to make the name convey some idea of the nature of the place ... than to exhaust the catalogue of public characters or private friends at home. The officers and crew, indeed, have some claim on such distinction, which, slight as it is, helps to excite interest in the voyage."

Dick hauled slack out of the port stern line and made it off.

The driving rain blurred our view. In an 1857 pilot book called *A Sailing Directory for the Ethiopic, or South Atlantic Ocean,* a stimulated A. G. Findlay wrote, "In Tierra del Fuego, the rain is so violent and incessant that one might suppose the waters of the firmament were again falling in shape of a second deluge." But every now and then, the waters of the firmament parted enough for us to see the wind, which had increased since we'd bailed, ripping up the channel, whitecaps everywhere. It was certainly no place to be in a stitched-together bark canoe. The short, steep, belligerent breakers had brought this steel-built, diesel-powered, fifty-three-foot boat to a dead stop. A bark canoe loaded down with a family of four, their dogs and their weapons wouldn't last three waves. . . .

No. That couldn't be true, and I was glad I hadn't voiced the dim observation to Dick, also standing in the rain pondering the weather. If every squall in this home of squalls took down a canoe with all hands, no Yahgan would have survived to be wiped out by white people's germs. Second, while the wind came on hard as suddenly as I've ever seen, the sky had been sending warnings since first light. If greenhorns like us could read the sky signs, then no sensible Yahgan would have been caught out by the wind. They'd have done what we did, ducked behind something high and hard, but they would have done so sooner.

Marine nomadism, the only possible means of survival, required a suitable boat. Engravings by Conrad Martens aboard the *Beagle,* a description by James Weddell, and sharp photographs by members of the *Romanche* expedition, among other sources, show the same, singular kind of boat: a bark canoe about seventeen feet long with very high free-

board, long up-swung bows, and short waterlines. Except for slight differences in length—sources report twenty-foot-long canoes in the more-
exposed Wollastons—the proportions and shape were nearly identical
throughout the Yahgan range. Vice Admiral Schapenham in the l'Hermite expedition of 1624 was the first European to describe the canoes at
any length, but he is a bit misleading, comparing their shape to Venetian
gondolas. Their ends weren't quite that high.

The Yahgan had about 7,000 years to think about their boat, and
plenty of motivation. It evolved like any other specialized workboat,
like FitzRoy's stolen whaleboat, in response to a specific need in a particular environment using the building materials available. The whaleboat builder used aged wood and steel-edged tools to shape the ribs,
steam boxes to bend the planks, and metal fasteners to hold it all together. The Yahgan had only bark from a single tree, the evergreen
beech (*Nothofagus betuloides*, or *shushchi* in Yahgan) sewn together
with seal sinew, no tools except a bone barker and an awl. A whaleboat required such a high order of skill and experience that only professionals could build one, while the Yahgan, constantly on the move
in order to eat, had no time for specialization. Everybody had to be
his own boat builder or die. Despite these vast differences—that between technological and Stone Age cultures—both the plank-on-
frame whaleboat and the bark canoe were perfect in a relative,
evolutionary sense. If one builder altered or added something to the
design that experience showed to be better, other builders quickly
copied it. If something broke, builders beefed it up, and if someone
discovered how to make the boat lighter without sacrificing strength
or stiffness, then everyone else would incorporate the innovation. The
design evolved over time until no further improvements were needed
or possible. That's why by the time of contact, all Yahgan canoes
looked the same. Archeologists delight in finding a vanished culture's
boat because it illustrates adaptation to need and locale. To row a
Gloucester dory, a St. Lawrence skiff, or a peapod, to name only those
I've known, is to recognize oneself aboard a masterwork. I wonder
what it was like to paddle a Yahgan canoe.

The last canoe was built in 1924 by a Fuegian called Pedro Viejo,
who was hired to do so by missionary-anthropologist Martin
Gusinde. Since by then the old ways had faded into memory, it's

impossible to know whether Old Pedro was winging it or not. But when we get right down to it, ignoring dugouts, there are only two ways to build a small boat in the whole history of boat building before fiberglass. You form the skeletal frame first, attaching ribs to a keel or bottom board, then you cover the frame with wood or animal skin to form the sides, but the shape of the boat is predetermined by the skeletal structure. Or, you shape the boat by building the sides first, then you shore them up with internal stiffeners—ribs, thwarts, stringers, gunwales. This, called the "clinker method," was the best for bark canoes wherever they were used, from the North American birch bark, the highest expression of the genre, to the Yahgan beech-bark canoe. But specifically how the Yahgan built their canoe is not known. How did they obtain the bark? Almost every witness states that the sides of the canoes were made from a single piece of bark. What kept the bark strip from breaking? (Gusinde described the barking process in his book, but something happened in transcription or editing, leaving the text hopelessly garbled.)

There is not a lot to go on. Oddly, few of the professional captains who stopped here climbed into a Yahgan canoe and learned to paddle it out of plain nautical curiosity. As far as I know, only James Weddell, the sealer with soul, did that. Martin Gusinde went for a few rides in Pedro's canoe, but he was a landsman who wouldn't have understood what to look for. Even Lucas Bridges, a true boat person always interested in Yahgan ways, gives the canoes small mention, perhaps because by the time he'd reached his teens, canoe nomadism had largely come to an end.

But in 1988, anthropologists Carlos Vairo, Ernesto Piana, and Hernan Vidal, a team from the Museo Territorial in Ushuaia, and Oscar Zanola, director of Museo del Fin Del Mundo, set about to build a canoe from scratch as a way to understand Yahgan culture though intimacy with the thing that made it possible. Dr. Vairo and the others used Old Pedro's boat, in the Museo Histórica Nacional de Santiago de Chile, as a reference point, but not a model, and when the historical eyewitness sources left them hanging, which was often, the builders had to resort to their common sense and their sea sense. The result, displayed at the Museo Maritimo de Ushuaia, is thoroughly convincing. It's sixteen feet long, three wide, probably medium-sized.

Each side is made from a single strip of bark as long as the boat, rough side out, sewn with seal sinew to a stiff bottom piece also made of bark.

Vairo and the builders learned by trial and error how to bark a tree in long, boat-sized strips without breaking them; breaks would have required an extra leaky seam. Leaks were the bane of bark canoes. The Yahgan caulked theirs from stem to stern with clay, but apparently they still leaked constantly. There is a famous engraving by Annie Brassey showing an Alacaluf canoe alongside a whaleship, a man standing in the bow apparently trading with men up on deck. The woman in the stern is too busy bailing to participate. Among their few material objects, the Yahgan had that universal boat tool, the bucket. (The fastest bailer ever invented, the saying goes, is a frightened man with a bucket.) Vairo wrote that, though the team always treated their canoe gingerly, never exposing it to rough water, the bark cracked every time someone sat in it. Several historical sources say that along with fire and weapons, the Yahgan carried spare bark, and heavy patching is evident in Doze and Payen's photos from the 1883 French expedition. Vairo et al. also learned how to bark a tree without killing it, a crucial requirement for the Yahgan, since bark canoes, easily holed and prone to rot, did not last long. If every barked tree died, then the loss would have extinguished the Yahgan themselves. Stupid aborigines don't last 7,000 years.

But from a nautical viewpoint, Vairo and the team's most interesting discoveries exploded old popular myths. After making sure I was alone in the museum, I ever so gently lifted the bow a few inches off its cradle. This canoe was heavy. Stiff. No rickety, delicate cockleshell, but a stout, strong boat well-matched to the environment as long as the owner didn't press his luck. The boat is heavily ribbed with saplings about the size of a pool-cue butt split lengthwise and bent U-shaped, then placed flat side down to support the sides and bottom. The surprising thing is that the ribs are laid in contiguously from bow to stern. In other words, the entire inside is ribbed—I counted about one hundred ribs on one side. That's a lot of ribs. Their canoes were not conceived with the open ocean in mind, but there is firm archeological evidence (shell middens) that the Yahgan camped on Staten Island, which means that they paddled across the Strait of Le Maire.

Perhaps the canoeists went there to exploit some seasonal migration of birds or seals, or maybe because they were curious about this fanged island visible sometimes beneath the rising sun. After all, it was some combination of acquisitiveness and curiosity that brought the Western explorers here in the first place. The Yahgan must have found something worth the trip to Staten Island, staying long enough to leave a lasting pile of discards.

Crouching to see it in profile, I could tell that the boat rode high in the water. The high ends and sides combined with low wetted surface suggested instability, and many visitors—who never went aboard—implied that instability suggested nautical backwardness. "They know not ballast," clucked one. But there's no sense in designing a deep-riding boat in the interests of stability if you're going to load it down with people and things. It's the same with a Gloucester fishing dory—an empty one, bobbing like a toy, will dump you in the drink if you're not careful, but add a load and she becomes a rock. Certainly high sides would have been desirable in these flailing waters, but they must have made paddling uncomfortable. The Yahgan weren't long of limb to begin with, and it was usually the shorter women who did most of the paddling and boat handling. How did they reach the water, I'd wondered. A paddling culture would not have built a boat that couldn't be paddled efficiently. Vairo had been asking that question as he tried to figure out the utility of the design before building the canoe, and when it was finished, when he actually paddled it, he discovered the Yahgan technique. They induced heel by shifting their weight to one side or the other, lowering a gunwale and shortening the paddler's reach. Heeling put the flared side deeper in the water, increasing stability ("form stability" to boat designers). This technique would also have been useful when dragging a harpooned seal or otter aboard, or when discharging people, dogs, and things ashore. This was a smart, strong boat. Too bad there was no way to experience one.

Dick and I went below, where the others, sitting around the table eating popcorn, were making a list of potential names.

17

A Fjord for the Naming

It has been a bad habit of mine generally to write an account of journeys made by land or by sea.
—H.W. Tilman, *Mischief Goes South*

TIME TO BECOME A MOTORBOAT AGAIN. It was the only sensible response with twenty-five knots of cold, gusty wind in our face from the depths of our fjord, which we named Seno Robinson after the naval attaché. We'd named last night's shelter Caleta Zarpe, behind Cape Turnaround, not Chickenshit. After two or three tacks, we were still abeam of Turnaround. It was delusional to think we could get anywhere against a stiff breeze in tight quarters, and we were as delusional as the next sailors, so we tried one more tack before we took in the jib and turned on the engine. The raw, driving rain helped in that decision. The conditions in these channels constantly reminded us of the technical sailing skills that were required just to get out alive in an engineless sailing ship. Not to mention the absence of charts. FitzRoy had taken a chance sailing the handy little *Beagle* into the Beagle Channel, but he wouldn't have considered sailing into the fjord. He named Bahía Tekenika, and he spent several days exploring this general area. If they ventured into our fjord, they would have had to go by boat. I couldn't find any reference to the trip in FitzRoy's journal or in Darwin's.

During the several minutes it took four guys to lash the main to the boom, the low cloud parted to unveil a spectacular mountain landscape. In a few places, the heavily wooded slopes draped into the water at a shallow angle, but most dove in vertically and continued down to a depth of between sixty and seventy meters, according to our gauge. The tree line was lower on these mountains than elsewhere in the archipelago, and there was more ice above it on the black fissured rock. Snow blowing from horns and spiked arêtes glistened in the stark sunlight. Layers of mountains stepped inland on Peninsula Dumas toward the highest visible peak, a great dome of black rock, unnamed on the Chilean and the Admiralty charts. From a cleft at the summit, a blue-ice glacier dropped several hundred feet, split into two tributaries around a jagged rock pyramid, and below rejoined into one. But the glaciers expired short of the tree line, turning into silvery waterfalls. In tinsel streams and real torrents, the mountains seethe with water.

Darwin remarked on it, as did FitzRoy and Weddell, I believe: These mountains were not tall by Rocky Mountain standards, only 1,000 to 1,500 meters, but they seemed gargantuan, tricking the eye with their sheer flanks and great snowy bulk above the tree line.

From his usual place at the rail on the starboard quarter, Hamish said, "I'll bet not a one of them has ever been climbed." He stared out longingly through his opaque glasses. Then he lapsed into his crass-American-climber character. "Hell, we could bag 'em all in four days, tops." (His other character was the crusty clipper-ship captain who says things like, "What I want from you, Mister Mate, is silence, and not too much of that.")

The temperature dropped a good ten degrees in two boat lengths as the passage constricted and new wind slid down the mountains. Other blue-ice glaciers popped into view, glowing as if with a light from deep within.

"You don't want to take water from a glacial stream," said Hamish. "It contains rock ground to a fine powder. Glacial flour, it's called."

I admit, sitting back there on the stern pulpit, I reveled in the privilege to sail, hell, even motor, in a place where glacial flour flowed. But then with the same light-switch suddenness, oily black cloud rolled in from the west to obliterate every mountain in the world. And of course the sleet bullets followed. The new pattern was growing clear to us greenhorns. The complexion of the sky changed about every twenty minutes. Black cloud down to the deck, whiplash squalls of rain turning to sleet, then clearing to crystalline blue, a rainbow arcing from peak to peak, sometimes two, and back again, a week of weather in a single morning. The sides closed in, visibility dropped again. "If you wouldn't mind, Kate?" asked Hamish, indicating the mast, as in, climb it, please, and watch.

"I'll go," said David. "It's her birthday."

"Wasn't that yesterday?"

Short ladder rungs were riveted to the side of the mast reaching to the first spreader about thirty feet above the deck. Spreaders are flattened tubes of aluminum attached horizontally on opposite sides of the mast. Shrouds from the masthead pass through the outer ends of the spreaders before they run down to the deck; they "spread," thus strengthen, the shroud's angle of support. David sprang up the ladder and took a seat on the portside spreader.

We were concerned about the two identical and incongruous points on either side. The shoreline was steep-to almost everywhere else, but these points were anomalies. They ended in flat, gravelly bars reaching well out into the channel. A pair of kelp geese was poking at the edges of the bar on starboard.

"Slower, please," Hamish requested of the helmsman, Dick. "How's it look up there?"

"Fine, carry on," said David.

Flowing ice makes fjords. Every island in the archipelago has been shaped and characterized by flowing ice, but peninsulas, Hardy, Pasteur, Dumas, are most deeply and extensively gouged. As the ice inched downslope, it split open natural fault lines and ancient streambeds, grinding bedrock to flour. And the leading edge of the glacier pushed before it high hills of broken rock and boulders. But these gouges didn't become fjords until the climate changed, and the ice melted and sea level rose. Melting ice dropped all that material it had been pushing in a giant heap to form moraines. You can still see a shadow of the old moraine in the soundings on the Chilean chart. Depths of between fifty and sixty meters drop abruptly into the 180s just outside the mouth of Tekenika. But glaciers advance and retreat spasmodically, leaving moraines along the way. Could these twin points and their flat sandbars be remnants of a moraine, and therefore shallow?

"All clear up here," David called.

The rest of us watched the depth gauge climb gradually as we neared the line between the points, then quickly, twenty meters in a snap, and there it stopped. Hamish had left the keel half down to act as sounding rod, but we didn't need it with fifteen meters of water under her when we crossed.

"Kelp ahead," David called. "Come a little to port. . . . Good, straighten her up."

Hamish and I looked over the starboard rail. I didn't see any kelp. If Hamish saw any he didn't mention it.

Bending around this bulge of land, essentially the base of a plunging mountain, on the starboard side, we saw that the fjord branched north and south around another magnificent mass of rock and ice. Which way? (Pretend explorers, we were trying not to use the chart.) No, a short way on, it became clear that the southern branch was actually a bay.

"Still," said Hamish, "it looks like a bombproof anchorage. Might come in handy. But we'll have to name it."

Dick turned north into another constriction with gravel bars, another moraine, perhaps, our third now; we no longer worried about them.

"Forty degrees to starboard," David directed. "Kelp. . . . Okay, come back to course."

We looked for kelp passing to port.

"Would you call him a stable man?" Hamish asked.

Tim chuckled at the idea.

Kate climbed up and took a seat on the starboard spreader.

Another big bay opened on the port side, but ahead our fjord seemed to end. Rounding another mountain, we saw that it carried on another three miles in a southeasterly direction. Two steamer ducks powered off as our bow approached, but they had done that time and again, skittering straight ahead fifty yards. Then they stopped, floating like normal ducks, as if they had outrun the threat. We caught up, they sprinted ahead, stopped again. Good thing for the steamer duck that they tasted lousy.

It was midday now, but the temperature remained in the low thirties. Another squall tore through almost like a prolonged gust, leaving behind a dark gray sky but fair visibility.

"Condors!" called Kate, pointing to a mountain on port (which happened to be charted, La Corona, 917 meters). A pair of them wheeled lazily in its updrafts, and even at that altitude against a featureless sky we could see that these were truly enormous birds, the largest alive today, with a wingspan of fifteen feet. With their long, square-tipped wings, they looked like a couple of Piper Cubs circling. They soared close enough that we could see their primary feathers, the flight-control feathers, splayed like fingers at the back of the wings.

"There!" Kate shouted. "A baby!"

God, we'd been lucky. The baby appeared from behind a mountaintop and wheeled in formation with the adults. The only difference between them, except for size, was that the baby occasionally flapped its wings, while the adults never did. Condors, big buzzards with their naked heads, bent necks, and flopping wattles, are strictly scavengers. Dead birds and seals are probably their main food source. We didn't see a single seal in this fjord, but of course we had a sea-level point of view, not the best for scavengers.

Then Kate moaned disgustedly. "Dead ahead—a buoy. A daymark, green."

That was distasteful. This was no place to put aids to navigation, the bloody wilderness. It was a rust-streaked green diamond made from sheet metal braced and bolted to a rock right at the end of the fjord. The Armada de Chile had been back here, and we were momentarily deflated, like Scott sighting the Norwegian flag at the South Pole. As we drew nearer we saw that the diamond did not stand at the end of the fjord but at a sharp left-hand turn, which we probably would have noticed without the nav aid. We were still over two miles from the end.

The head of the fjord was a wonderland lake utterly surrounded by domed snowcapped mountains, another higher layer of mountains beyond. The water was clear, flat, and deep. There was even an ideally situated islet with its own miniature forest to tie off to. A light, wet fog rolled in and blurred the snow peaks, enhancing the sense of remove and gigantic scale. After we had *Pelagic* securely bound against

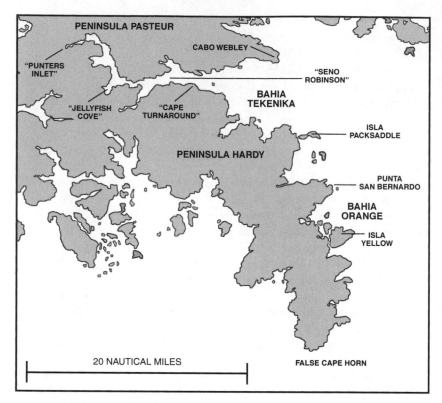

Map 17.1   Undiscovered Land

williwaws, we stood around the deck grinning, shaking our heads with awe and delight. We had sailed (motored) into the core of a mountain range.

"A cracking spot," said the captain, rubbing his hands together.

It began to snow.

We picked as our landing site the delta of a little river, but because it was a delta, the water was too shallow for us. After we'd found a deeper approach, beached the dinghy, and walked back toward the stream, we came upon a whale's backbone, a piece of it, anyway, bright white against the black-rock beach. It was about eight feet long, just the linked vertebrae, no ribs or skull. The bone was probably old, pitted, with a stony feel. As we inexpertly examined the remains, the snow faded to flurries. A wet breeze brought thickening fog and the intense, unmistakable smell of anchovies. Following it upwind to the mouth of the stream, we found hundreds of silvery corpses strewn among the rocks, sea lettuce and other algae at the high-tide line. Each fish was identical, five inches long with straight spines, up-swung mouths, and fat silvery bellies. I picked one up and smelled it. The dying had happened only a little while ago, perhaps not more than a day. Other corpses bounced languidly along the bottom in the thin current.

Autumn was a special time in the Yahgan year when great schools of sprats arrived and were pursued by penguins, petrels, gulls, cormorants and other birds, as well as seals. The Yahgan called this time of plenty *Iacasi*. The smelts and mullet tended to follow the flood tides into the narrow mouths of rivers and streams. Before the fish arrived, the natives built stone ramparts to constrict water flow to a small gap. After the fish swam through, the fishermen blocked the gap with branches or nets if they had them. "Sometimes, in this way, a ton or more fish might be taken at once, but it would be a long time before a like number would assemble in that same creek." (Lucas Bridges)

We were here in autumn, perhaps near *Iacasi,* but these were not smelts. Freshly caught smelts smell like cucumbers. Though popular names of fish vary widely, I think these were anchoveta *(Engraulis ringens)*. The Peruvian anchoveta fishery was the largest in weight in the world during the 1970s until overfishing and El Niño temperature fluctuations put an end to it. In Maine, for instance, bluefish and other predators including dolphin chase capelin, a kind of smelt, up narrow bays where they crowd into shallow, oxygen-depleted water and die in such number that the locals are forced from their homes by the stench of rotting fish. Perhaps something similar happened here. And maybe that whitened spine on the beach belonged not to a small or young whale but to an overexcited dolphin that chased fish too far into the shallows. We took pictures of the bones to show Natalie Goodall, but the photos were lost. In any case, we named this Whalebone Cove on our private chart, even if the bones were of something else. Marine Mammal Cove had no ring to it.

We tramped the wet woods for most of the day, following the river upstream as far as we could. In places, the rushing tea-colored water had cut deep vertical chasms in the marine sediments, and at the bottom there was no daylight. Hamish, always seeking the higher elevations, climbed at his accelerated pace, which only Kate could keep up with. When our paths crossed farther on, they told us that the condors had circled them no more than twenty feet away. We climbed a rocky spur, hoping for our own close-up condor sighting, but we saw none. Glossy black clouds had topped the mountains in the west, perhaps warning the condors to head for their hangars. Heading downslope ourselves, we came upon a large berry patch. The Yahgan ate several different kinds of berries, and we'd been hoping to sample them. Hamish called them *chua* berries, but I'm not sure where that name comes from. The bushes were thorny, and the berries dark blue, so I think they were also called barberries, the most common in Fuegia. The Yahgan word is *umushamain,* which meant "thorn berry." These were bitter and hard. There are no poisonous berries in the islands, though Lucas Bridges says that the *spisa* ("diddy-dee" in the Falklands) is a powerful laxative if eaten in immodest quantity.

The Yahgan also ate a berry they called *belacamain,* which look like small raspberries, but they grow in tree mould, so we probably walked over them without noticing. Francis Drake and the crew ate what the Reverend Fletcher called "a kind of wild grape," much to everyone's enjoyment. Bridges says that these had to be *goosh,* a plentiful berry on the outer islands, including Isla Hornos, that came ripe in the spring when Drake was here. In his middle age, Bridges visited the London Flower Show, where he saw a fruited *goosh* bush. "The man in charge told me that they were . . . highly poisonous. I thanked him for the information and, with permission, collected several fallen berries. Then, under his horrified gaze, I ate them and departed."

We were finished here, alas. We pressed on awhile, crossed to the other side of the "lake" by dinghy in a sleet squall, confident it would pass. It did, but there was another close astern, and it showed no signs of passing. That was fair enough. We'd seen our fjord, a gift of nature few have seen, a privilege now over. We hoped for a last glimpse of the condor family, but if they were still up there, they soared on instruments in blind black cloud. Still we were grateful for our luck, even as we climbed back into the dinghy, our shoulders hunched, hoods up against a cold, hard rain. It had turned to snow by the time we came alongside *Pelagic,* snug, warm, soon the happy sound of popping corn.

I read that afternoon in *Uttermost Part of the Earth* about the bright green grass that grows nowhere else but on Yahgan shell middens. They called it *ucurhshuca,* or "house grass," because where there were discarded shells enough to make mounds, there had also been wigwams. Lucas Bridges had become an admired figure aboard *Pelagic,* where on foul-weather days he was widely read. We thought him a great man, and *Uttermost Part of the Earth* is a true delight. I wish it were available everywhere. Without the Bridges family, living and dead, Fuegia would be a far more dimly understood place.

"Corrientes, Corrientes, Corrientes. *Pelagic.*" Every evening at 1700, I think, Hamish was required to check in with the Chileans, our hosts, by radio and report our position and our intentions for tomorrow. He'd been trying without success to raise the naval outpost at Corrientes on the Murray Narrows. We were surrounded by mountains that no VHF waves could escape. But he gave it an honest try before switching off. Hamish was interested in the deep cove we'd passed coming in, the one we mistook at first for a branch in the fjord. He suggested that we duck in there—though he thought it looked like williwaw country—and set out for some fresh sight-seeing if the weather broke. After we got the anchor up, Hamish and Kate named this beautiful mountain water in our honor. Punters' Inlet. That had a ring to last the ages.

We had a quick ride under main alone back to the cove in question. We found that the mouth was wider and the cove deeper than we'd thought as we felt our way in. The water was deep, and all the rocks were marked by thickets of kelp, some of which could be marking rocks 100 feet down. Critics have clucked at Darwin because while on the *Beagle* he evinced more interest in kelp than in the natives. And that was of course because he *was* more interested in kelp. "I know few things more surprising than to see this plant growing and flourishing amidst those great breakers of the western ocean, which no mass of rock ... can long resist. ... I can only compare these great aquatic forests ... with the terrestrial ones in the intertropical regions. Yet if the latter should be destroyed, I do not believe nearly so many species of animals would perish, as, under similar circumstances, would happen with the kelp." Fish, birds, otters, seals, dolphin would all vanish, and "the Fuegian savage, the miserable lord of this miserable land, would redouble his cannibal feast, decrease in numbers, and perhaps cease to exist." (*Voyage of the Beagle*)

The cove narrowed to a little river in the farthest corner. Kate assumed lookout position on the spreader, and, dead slow, we entered another remarkable place. The channel doglegged left, and then we could see at the end a peculiar round island with about four beech trees growing on it, and behind the island, a small boggy delta. Quarters tightened down, the hills steepened, and the channel narrowed so that another *Pelagic* couldn't have passed beam to beam.

"Look at the jellyfish," Kate called down.

Millions of small milky jellyfish were riding the ebb-tide current. The water from bank to bank and seven or eight feet deep was viscous with jellyfish.

Pelagic trembled and vibrated all night to the williwaws' tune. I didn't get up to look at the numbers, but the wind made that combined howling-whining sound heard only when air moves through wire rigging at highway speed. She surged against her lines. It was cold in the cabin. One thinks of the Yahgan sleeping on the ground in a mud-caulked wigwam. I mused on the power of the human will to survive from inside my toasty top-of-the-line borrowed sleeping bag. The wind noise was too loud to sleep through. It was still blowing the next morning, sleet and snow, and we took our time with the toast—Dick had perfected his stove-top technique—and though we geared up at a desultory pace, we were resolutely motivated by self-interest, sensual pleasure, and hygiene. We meant to fill her tanks with fresh water, run the engine to heat it, and use it all for hot showers!

"The Yahgan went naked in this," someone said on cue from the next williwaw whine and shudder.

We'd been talking about hot showers for a couple of days, and even now Hamish was preparing the gear topside. We quit faffing around and joined him for job assignments. We winched the dinghy overboard, pulled it aft to the gate in the lifelines, and Hamish loaded the watering gear aboard. It consisted of a garden hose and a funnel. We wondered why he had four coils of hose, enough to reach halfway to Wulaia.

"Because they'll probably break. You just can't get good garden hose in Ushuaia." (Which the Yahgan must have found inconvenient.) "But I think I have enough fine British Empire hose to do the job."

The easy availability of fresh water must have eased the press of the environment for all concerned, even if they didn't shower very often. There seemed to be running water in rain-forest profusion, yet, we reminded ourselves, no more rain falls in Fuegia than in Boston. Yet here, unlike Boston, little water evaporates, a remarkable concept, new to us all. We had four streams to choose from within hose-length on the starboard side alone. The steep shoreline was so close aboard that to reach it we just gave the dinghy a shove. Tramping on the tree-tops, Hamish inspected the streams. Sampling the waters in the cup of his hand, he selected the nearest, and set up his catchments. It was a pleasingly simple system. After mating funnel to hose, he wedged and lashed the mouth of the funnel into the flow. The Chilean hose did a stalwart job. Water gushed from the onboard end. It was my job to place the hose into the water tank, and I made seamanly work of it.

No, our weather luck had run out. It was rain, sleet, or snow with a hard steady wind or else a hard gusty wind. A few of us tried a walk up the hill, but we could see nothing, literally in the clouds. We waited, hoping for a break, jellyfish flowing in, flowing out. Hunkering in the cabin, breathing each other's exhalations, we fell back on our inner resources, essential for a tranquil life in confined spaces. The great Norwegian explorer and Nobel recipient Fridtjof Nansen said that as polar explorers Norwegians had an advantage over other nationalities because they could sit around on the same block of ice all winter quite contentedly without speaking a word. Certain European and American expeditions, wintering over, put on plays and published a ship's newspaper, and they still went nuts.

18

The Martyrs Insisted

A sailor had given a Fuegian a tin pot of coffee, which he drank, and was using all his art to steal the pot. The sailor, recollecting after a while, that the pot had not been returned, applied for it, but whatever words he used were always repeated in imitation by the Fuegian. At length, he became enraged, and placing himself in a threatening attitude, in an angry tone, said "You copper-coloured rascal, where is my tin pot?" The Fuegian, assuming the same attitude, with his eyes fixed on the sailor, called out, "You copper-coloured rascal, where is my tin pot?"
—James Weddell, *Voyage Towards the South Pole*

THEY HAD NO AMMUNITION. If it wasn't among their crates of gear, then it could only be aboard the *Ocean Queen*, now heading for San Francisco. She'd diverted from her course to deliver missionary Allen Gardiner, his six devoted followers, their two small boats, and crates of supplies to this cold, empty beach on the north side of Isla Picton. She even lingered awhile in case the missionaries changed their minds, but now she was gone. The rifles useless, there would be no hunting to sustain their stores. Other people might have experienced a twinge of apprehension at the absence of ammo, but not these people, because they knew that the Lord would provide. Or not.

Allen Gardiner had been a highly competent Royal Navy officer who, like FitzRoy, attended the Naval College at Portsmouth at age fourteen, and by sixteen, he had seen naval combat. During the War of 1812, the U.S. frigate *Essex* rounded the Horn and tore through the British whaling fleet in the Pacific. A British squadron caught up with her off Valparaiso on March 28, 1814, and after a short, vicious battle against a superior force, Captain Porter surrendered the *Essex*. Allen Gardiner, a midshipman aboard HMS *Phoebe,* was selected as a member of the prize crew that sailed the *Essex* back to England. Handsome and charismatic, he rose quickly through the ranks to captain. How could an experienced, practical naval officer forget to unload the ammunition? Why hadn't he kept a checklist or something?

He was fifty-four when he landed on Picton and no longer in the navy. His career on a fast track, he'd abruptly quit to become a missionary, a zealot, really, a quiet fanatic who traveled the world trying to save savage souls. First, it was off to South Africa to convert the Zulu, arriving just as war broke out between the Zulu and the Boers. A string of absurdities followed, characterized by an utter lack of planning and organization. He just wanted to save souls; it didn't matter where or whose, and God would take care of the checklist.

He tried Bolivia, a Catholic country in the throes of revolution where Protestant proselytizers were not welcome. Next, he headed for New Guinea, full of savages. But the Dutch, among the most savage, still ruled the region, and seeing no profit in an ex–Royal Navy officer preaching to natives they'd systematically subjugated for about two centuries, sent Gardiner packing. Failure fueled his determination. He headed back to South America to convert the Araucana Indians, who were fighting a long, losing war of genocide against the Argentineans. The local Spanish priests, untroubled by genocide, didn't like Protestants saving souls in their parishes. The Argentine officials agreed, and drove Gardiner away. Again he returned to England without even meeting the people he'd hoped to convert.

His hot eye then settled on Tierra del Fuego. He'd read his Darwin and FitzRoy, and he'd already encountered the Yahgan while rounding the Horn as a midshipman. Here were savage souls that really needed salvation, and better still, there were no Dutchmen, no papists, nobody at all to interfere. But again his impetuous departure without plans doomed the effort. He chartered a leaking wreck of a schooner with a crazy captain and a crew of drunken scum who stole most of his stuff. And once he arrived, the Yahgan stole the rest of it. He and his followers slunk back aboard the schooner and left with their lives.

After that failure, Gardiner and a catechist named Hunt moved the "mission" north to Cape Virgins at the east entrance to the Strait of Magellan. They built a rude hut on the pampas and waited for potential converts to show up. It's a darkly comic scene—these two brothers in Christ, reading their Bibles aloud, calling each other Mister Hunt and Mister Gardiner. But no Indians arrived. Flockless, the missionaries built fires to attract savages. Days passed, but no one came except a treacherous half-breed called Wissale and his hygienically neglected string of children. Gardiner fed them because that was the Christian thing to do, so they stayed on to freeload, but when supplies ran short and he asked them to leave, Wissale turned belligerent, menacing. The Allen Gardiner story probably would have ended right there, with a blunt-impact trauma to the cranium, but for the chance arrival of a westbound ship. Again, Gardiner picked up stakes and returned to England. But he had liked the looks of Fuegia, and before setting off this time he formed the Patagonian Missionary Society and chose for its motto, Hope deferred, not lost. He appointed a meek, devout pastor from the North, the Reverend George Pakenham Despard, to oversee the mission and to try to raise some money.

The party that landed on Isla Picton without their ammunition consisted of three devout fishermen from Mousehole in Cornwall, John Pearce, John Badcock, and John Bryant; a catechist, John Maidment; Richard Williams, a surgeon; and a carpenter, Joseph Erwin. All had been inspired by Gardiner's towering faith and golden rhetoric. Erwin, for instance, wrote that "being with Captain Gardiner was like a heaven upon earth, he is such a man of prayer." Gardiner exhorted them to fret not about the useless guns. They had ample food, and there were fish in the seas, shellfish on every rock. Besides, Gardiner had left instructions with Despard to send additional supplies by ship in two months' time. That settled, kneeling with his men in prayer, Gardiner named the site Banner Cove after a line in the fourth verse of Psalm 60: "Thou has given a banner to them that fear thee, that it might be displayed because of the truth." The party pitched tents, while the carpenter set to work assembling the mission building.

Others broke ground for the inevitable garden with all the symbolism attached, planting vegetables and spring bulbs, tulips, a proper Protestant garden. They named it Garden Island; it's now called Isla Gardiner. After the natives had driven him off the last time, Gardiner wrote to Despard, "From what I have now seen, it is my decided opinion that until the character of the natives has undergone considerable change, a Fuegian mission must of necessity be afloat." Yet here they were on land, planting. Eighteen years earlier, FitzRoy had planted his bulbs at Wulaia.

By the next day, however, smoky signal fires had gone up all over the surrounding shores, and by afternoon, waves of Yahgan literally invaded the mission. Gardiner and the big strong Cornwall fishermen held them off for a time with gifts, but as Darwin had written, the natives were "easy to please but impossible to satisfy." When the gifts ran out, they began to steal anything they could get their hands on. The missionaries ran from one pile of stores to the next yanking back their belongings as best they could. It was ignominious; this was not the way of the light. And these savages were *savage*. And they stank.

For the next two nights, during respites from the Yahgans' increasingly hostile onslaughts, the missionaries slaved to build a log barricade around their camp to keep out the flock they'd come to save. But it was no use. The Yahgan men—and women—plowed right through the barricade to get at those wondrous things these white people— unprotected by a ship—had brought into their land. This behavior, which came as a rude shock to his followers, should not have surprised Gardiner, who'd seen it before, yet he had made no plans to address it. In a letter for Despard he'd sent with the *Ocean Queen,* Gardiner wrote that he'd been thinking and come to certain decisions about the future shape of his mission. He would *learn the Yahgan language,* he announced as if it were an epiphany. He would go about doing that by taking Yahgan volunteers from Fuegia (too many distractions) to somewhere like the Falklands or Staten Island, where he would establish mission central and begin language lessons. But for now, they couldn't stay on Garden Island. Now all they could hope for was to get out with their lives.

They broke camp, reloaded what they could of their necessities aboard these damn-fool boats they'd brought, and buried the rest of

their supplies. This brings us to the nautical component in the evolv-
ing debacle, since escape by water was now their only hope. Back
when Captain Gardiner had concluded that due to Yahgan bad behavior, only a floating mission could succeed, he'd had a proper ship in
mind, a two-master, a schooner or brigantine, in the 100-foot range,
but there was no money for that. The society might have raised
money for a more modest vessel, but Gardiner couldn't wait. He
found in an advertisement a boat twenty-six feet long, eight feet wide,
built of wood, but the sides and bottoms were shod in iron, and there
was a decked-over section of iron plate. Perfect, Gardiner said, iron
was far better for the rocky shores of Fuegia, *and* it would be more
maneuverable in the twisting channels than any large vessel. The
bucket was advertised to be a sailer, with masts and things, so Gardiner didn't slow down long enough to test it in English waters. He
bought two and loaded them aboard the *Ocean Queen,* anything to
get going. And now they learned that their boats, heartbreakingly
heavy, were sluggards under sail, and they could barely be made to
move by four strong guys named John laying on the oars. Now it was
too late, now they were stuck with lunkers, and not even the grace of
God could turn them into good boats. Furthermore, *Pioneer* and
Speedwell, as Gardiner named them, were too deep to penetrate the
kelp beds fringing the shores, and so they had to tow dinghies behind
in order to reach land. They were also towing a long, heavy plank the
captain of the *Ocean Queen* had donated as repair material. It constantly got hung up in the kelp.

They piled a portion of their irreplaceable supplies into the
dinghies, lashed them together, and Gardiner, with three men, towed
both behind *Pioneer,* while the remaining men, in *Speedwell,* towed
the plank—out into the open water of the Beagle Channel. Inevitably,
the weather turned foul, rain and sleet, a stiff westerly setting up
short, steep waves, and in no time the boats became separated. The
idea had been to seek out an uninhabited cove on the south shore of
Tierra del Fuego where they could hide from the Yahgan. Gardiner's
boat pressed on to windward a few miles and came upon a bent finger
of land with flat water behind it. But before he could enter, the towline parted, also inevitably, and the dinghies—with the supplies—were
swept away. *Pioneer* made it into the cove, which Gardiner named

Blomefield Harbor for one of the society's contributors (it's now called Cambaceres, part of the Bridges homestead). But what about the *Speedwell?* Her crew, if they were still alive, would never find the *Pioneer* in Blomefield Harbor. After lightening their boat by offloading and burying still more of their supplies, they shoved off after dark in search of their people. Among the folly, irony, and black comedy that underpin the story, there is also poignancy. These men genuinely cared about and selflessly tended each other right up to the end.

The wind was down, not calm, but too light to sail, so the men rowed the *Pioneer* back eastward in the Beagle toward Picton, where'd they'd last seen their friends. It was killing work, but they made it, and they sighted *Speedwell* drifting offshore. Was she abandoned, the men drowned? Or were they lying in the bilges with their skulls stove in? "It was an awful suspense," Gardiner wrote in his diary, "not a word was uttered among us. We were now actually alongside, but no movement or sound was heard on board the *Speedwell*. I confess my blood ran cold."

Williams, Badcock, and Erwin were lying in the bilges all right, but they weren't dead or injured. Exhausted, they were sleeping. The squall, they reported, had blown them back toward Picton, where that plank had fouled hopelessly in the thick kelp, and they had to cut it away. The Beagle Channel waves had found still another flaw in the boats. They leaked like old baskets, and everything the men owned, including more of their food supplies, was soaked.

They tried to hole up in Banner Cove to retrieve some of their cached supplies, but Captain Gardiner—a professional seaman in his other life—anchored too close to shore, and the ebb tide left him high and dry. He awoke to find two hostile brown faces with matted black hair peering over the gunwales at him. Several more Indians emerged from the woods. They were behaving differently now, not begging or hopping with excitement, but staring silently, coldly at the white men, at their saviors. The Christians brandished their guns, but the Yahgan never even flinched, as though they knew the ammunition was bound for San Francisco. Then the missionaries, who probably wouldn't have shot the Indians anyway, dropped their guns, fell to their knees in prayer, and, says Gardiner's diary, "committed ourselves to the mercy and protection of our heavenly Father. [The Yahgan] stood still, without uttering a word, while we were in prayer, and seemed to be held in some degree of restraint."

At dawn, canoes approached Banner Cove with bundles of spears propped in the bows. Here and there along the shore, Indians were gathering throwing-size rocks in baskets, and passing the baskets aboard waiting canoes. There seemed no question about it. These Yahgan meant to murder the missionaries. *Speedwell*'s people landed to help shove *Pioneer* from the beach, and then everyone scurried back aboard their respective boats, rowing for their lives—slowly. The Yahgans had marshaled about a dozen canoes, and they paddled in pursuit, chillingly silent. Their canoes were overloaded, only marginally faster than the boats, but the missionaries didn't stand a chance. This was hunting; this was what the Yahgan did with their lives, and their canoes were steadily closing in. Zephyrs began to ripple the surface. Would it build to a sailing breeze? It did, from a light, patchy breeze to a stiff wind moments before the canoes had pulled within spear-throwing range. Sails up, the fat boats began to leg it out on the hunters, who broke off the chase. Why bother to get all fatigued? Time was clearly on their side. They knew every cove, bight, and cape on every island down to the Horn. They'd find the white men and their objects no matter where they went.

However, the missionaries had only their boats; there was no hope on land. The only chance for them to take an active hand in their own survival lay at sea. Gardiner and his followers might have sailed away from Fuegia to the Falkland Islands. It would have been a long, tough haul in unsuitable boats, but they could have done it in stages. They could have picked their weather, coast-hopping east along the shore of Tierra del Fuego to its extremity, where they could have rested in Good Success, like so many before them, waiting for favorable conditions. It's 300 miles from Good Success to Port Stanley in the Falklands, and the odds of drowning would have been high, but professional seamen—who were behaving as such—might well have made it. Gardiner, however, seems not to have even thought of the idea.

Under cover of night, they sailed back to Blomefield Harbor to pick up the food Gardiner had stashed, but the natives had already found it. Nothing was left. For the next couple of weeks, they bounced around the Beagle Channel shores, among the eastern islands, and the same thing happened almost daily wherever they went. A smoldering signal fire would appear on a nearby headland, then another, others in the distance, and then canoes would converge on the missionaries' hiding place. They'd flee again. Ironically, they'd been reduced to the lifestyle of the culture they had come to change, but the white men weren't very good at it. They threw rocks at the kelp geese. Starvation loomed.

Finally, they decided to flee before their flock murdered them. The only hope for escape lay eastward, out toward the toe of Tierra del Fuego. The landscape flattens along this empty, exposed coast, and the thick beech forest grows right down to the tide line. The missionaries picked their way along looking for a place called Spaniard Harbor about sixty miles east of the Beagle. The weather held fair, and on January 31, 1851, they found it, a perfect place for doomed missionaries. Instead of impenetrable forest, there were gentle meadows at the back of the bay, and a handy freshwater stream, now called Río Cook, flowed into it. In fact, the stream flowed right into a snug little cove in the northwest corner of the bay. Gardiner named it Earnest Cove. And best of all, there were no Yahgan anywhere. Here the missionaries would wait in peace for a ship to happen by. The Reverend Despard would dispatch that relief ship; all they need do was to stay alive. God would provide a ship, and leaving it to Him, they settled in to wait.

They couldn't wait long. They were starving. There were no Yahgan around Spaniard Harbor or anywhere else along the southeast coast because it offered nothing of what they needed. And soon a southerly gale coughed up big seas, which, when squeezed between the narrow shoulders of the bay, grew enormous, and Earnest Cove was ideally situated to absorb the worst of them. *Pioneer* was thrown ashore and wrecked by the waves, but worse, more of their very limited supplies were ruined or washed away. "But all this is well," Richard Williams actually wrote in his journal, "the mission has been thereby begun." They waited while February passed, then most of March, and as winter loomed, they made no move to save themselves. They languished in some kind of religious-starvation state for nearly six weeks, surviving off of whatever putrid bird corpses happened to wash up, before it occurred to Gardiner that since the weather was often overcast, foggy and such, they might miss a passing sail. Besides that, no relief ship would look for them out this way—it would go to Banner Cove back in the Beagle Channel—and a captain setting up his approach to the Beagle would give this coast a wide berth. Therefore, they had to return to Banner Cove, Yahgan or no Yahgan, and leave a message for the relief ship. By then, however, scurvy had set in. Gardiner and several who were still able shoved off in that piece of junk and clawed their way back west in appalling conditions.

Foul weather covered their approach to Banner Cove, and the next morning when the skies cleared, they saw no canoes, no smoke signals from either shore. A single family camped nearby was willing to trade nails for fish, and better still, the missionaries found their last buried cache of supplies unmolested by the Yahgan. While the others loaded their bonanza into *Speedwell,* Gardiner lettered this message in white paint on a bare rock face at the mouth of the cove: GONE TO SPANIARD HARBOR. Then, curiously, below that, he added, YOU WILL FIND US IN SPANIARD HARBOR. Of course the natives spotted them, dozens of canoes bored in, and again only a timely breeze saved them from their flock. But at least now, for the first time in weeks, their bellies were full as they sailed back to Spaniard Harbor.

Soon they were starving again. There were still mussels by the billions, but they could not stomach any more mussels, not even mussel broth. If no carrion washed up on the beach, they didn't eat. And yet they waited. Months passed before Gardiner thought about attracting the attention of a passing ship—by hanging a white tablecloth in a tree. April and May passed, winter bit down, and by then, ravaged by scurvy and prolonged starvation, the men were too weak to walk. Babcock, one of the Cornishmen named John, was the first to die, on June 28. With his last breaths, he joined Dr. Williams, his cabin mate in *Speedwell* (the others were lying in a cave and under the upturned wreck of *Pioneer*), in singing, "Arise, my soul, arise/ Shake off thy guilty fears. . . "

One by one, the others died, all beautifully, comforting one another and sharing every dwindling morsel to the very end. Perhaps that was Gardiner's purpose from the outset, to die beautifully in

poverty with the word of God on his last breath, evangelism as a
mode of martyrdom. The others, playing the Apostles, followed en-
thusiastically. On September 3 the last of their food ran out. Gardiner was the last to die, we know from his journal, where he
recorded the deaths of everyone except Dr. Williams. Thinking he
was still alive, though he probably wasn't, Gardiner wrote: "My dear
Mr. Williams, the Lord has seen fit to call home another of our little
company. . . doubtless he is in the presence of his Redeemer, whom he
served so faithfully. Yet a little while, and through grace we may join
that blessed throng to sing the praises of Christ throughout eternity. I
neither hunger nor thirst, though five days without food! Marvelous
loving-kindness to me a sinner! Your affectionate brother in Christ,
Allen F. Gardiner."

The story of mulish determination, empty-headed planning, lubberly comedy, grandiosity, as well as brotherly devotion and tender-
ness, really had little to do with the Yahgan or their souls. It's a
white-man story, part of the gold-and-God theme that runs through
the larger Cape Horn story. The Yahgan were nothing but converts to
be chalked up on God's score sheet. They could just as well have been
Zulus or Araucanas or any old savages as long as Gardiner could die
trying to save their souls.

On October 21, 1851, chill and dark with something serious festering in the west, Captain William Smyley gingerly dipped the *John
E. Davidson*'s bow into the mouth of Spaniard Harbor. Smyley, a grizzled veteran of these latitudes, had come straight from Banner Cove,
where he had seen the writing on the wall. Exposed to the big
southerly swell, Spaniard Harbor was no place to be in a blow. He
dropped the hook, put a boat over, and quickly pulled for shore.

There was a corpse mostly devoured by birds sloshing back and
forth in the shore break, another corpse in the *Speedwell,* and a grave
with something indecipherable written on a plank marker. The boat
crew barely had time to take it all in before the new wind arrived, setting his ship bucking against her suspect anchor. Smyley snatched up
some sodden, scribbled pages—Gardiner's journal—and barely beat

the storm to sea. En route to the Falklands with the news, Smiley read the journal, found it sad, but he had a question, that same frustrating question: Why didn't experienced seamen sail the hell out of there, to the Falklands, say, anywhere? Three months later, HMS *Dido,* bound west around the Horn, diverted to Banner Cove to look in on the mission, saw the painted message, and hurried to Spaniard Cove. Hard-bitten salts were heard sobbing as they dug graves.

When word reached England, more bitter tears were shed over good men who wanted nothing for themselves, exemplars of the faith lost in the service of the Lord, but when Gardiner's journal with the facts came to light, the story didn't seem quite so black and white. Some people suggested that those lives had been thrown away. Opinion split around the question of whether Gardiner was a martyred saint or a damn fool. Newspapers, opinion sheets, and rags heaped calumny on the Patagonian Missionary Society, while others celebrated it. Here in Victorian times when editors and prime ministers were learning the principles of modern publicity, the one that says there is no such thing as bad publicity was vividly demonstrated: Contributions poured into the mission. Suddenly all things were possible, but who could pick up the standard for Allen Gardiner?

There was that Reverend George Pakenham Despard, who had been appointed "honorary secretary" by Gardiner. Despard had been paid almost nothing. On the other hand, the job wasn't all that demanding, since there were about four members of the mission, and there had never been any money to manage. Despard, who had six children, could keep his day job as a Nottinghamshire minister. But now everything changed. Now the mission had all the cash it needed, and that was directly due to Gardiner's death. Did Gardiner die so that his mission could live? The devout, middle-class cleric who'd never been anywhere stood up, straightened his vest, and set the future course for the Patagonia Missionary Society—and to a real extent, the future of the Yahgan people.

Despard knew just what to do. He would establish his mission's base in some remote part of the Falkland Islands, now solidly British, 400 sea miles from Cape Horn. He would bring a few Yahgan at a time—of their own free will—to the Falklands, where Indians and missionaries could live together, garden, worship, and the missionar-

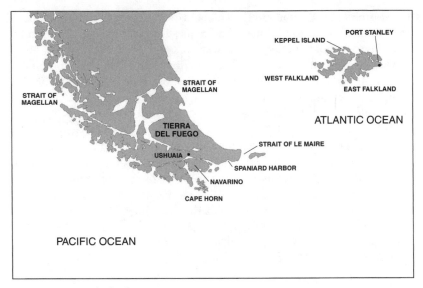

Map 18.1   Keppel Island

ies could learn the Yahgan language. This was the revelation Gardiner had explained to Despard by letter from Fuegia, as if it weren't frustratingly obvious. Despard arranged a grant for a little backwater called Keppel Island seventy hard miles from the tiny town of Port Stanley. This would be mission central. Then he bought a topsail schooner (some sources keep calling it a brigantine) over 100 feet long, the very ship Gardiner had envisioned before lack of money and his own impatience let him settle for those clunkers *Speedwell* and *Pioneer*. Of course, the schooner was christened the *Allen Gardiner*.

But there was a second part to Despard's plan. To wit: Jemmy Button. Jemmy would serve as the nucleus of the mission; Jemmy would be the one to explain to his people why they should go to Keppel Island and become Christians. Despard would pick up where FitzRoy left off, never mind that FitzRoy's "mission" was an absurdity, or that no white man had laid eyes on Jemmy for almost twenty years. No, he was alive and he was willing to serve. There was no question about it.

To command the *Allen Gardiner,* Despard, who would remain in England for now, hired an interesting odd duck named Parker Snow.

Snow was a lifelong adventurer of a distinctly British sort that would become a stock stage character by the end of the century. He'd searched for the lost Franklin expedition in the Northwest Passage, and now he'd become an expert in these waters south of 50 South. Ninety days out from England, they landed on Keppel Island, which Despard had acquired sight unseen. Snow was appalled at the place, with its swamp, windswept heath, and rockbound shoreline where every landing was an adventure. There had been the predictable dissension between captain and missionaries over just who was in command, and a catechist named Garland Phillips didn't think Snow's crew was as devout as Snow had claimed. They unloaded the prefabricated house that would be mission headquarters, and then they sailed in search of Jemmy Button.

In Banner Cove they saw their first natives. Smoke signals wafted up from prominent headlands and the canoes converged. We know the events of this voyage, by the way, from Snow's journal, a rare volume heavily titled *A Two Years' Cruise off Tierra del Fuego, the Falkland Islands, Patagonia, and the River Plate: A Narrative of Life in the Southern Seas,* published in 1857. Snow didn't find them threatening, but he knew from FitzRoy's *Narrative* that these people were intimidated by white men's ships. As they pressed on west in Beagle Channel, Snow pondered the problem of how to find one Indian who looked like every other Indian among these fractured channels, and it came to him while rereading FitzRoy: Jemmy Button was different from all the rest because he had an English name. He might find Jemmy simply by shouting his name.

In present-day Ushuaia and Puerto Navarino on the other side, in the Murray Narrows, Ponsonby Sound and Bahía Tekenika, then back toward Wulaia, he shouted for Jemmy. And though it's unclear precisely where, somewhere near Wulaia, a voice from among the dozens of canoes gathered around the *Allen Gardiner* called back.

"Jam-mus Button, me! Where's the ladder?"

Though Jemmy was naked, greasy, and smelly, a "stout, wild and shaggy-looking man," Snow could still recognize him from FitzRoy's sketch, which shows Jemmy wearing a stiff Victorian collar and cravat. Snow threw over a rope instead of a ladder, because he didn't want a deck full of the indigenous, and Jemmy climbed aboard. When he learned there was a woman aboard ("Ingliss laday?"), he called for clothes. But the pants were too big, he called for suspenders ("Need braces"). Then Jemmy, Snow, and his wife went below for a proper Christian luncheon.

Snow showed Jemmy pictures of England. "Yes, me know—Ingliss conetree. Vary good. . . . All good in Ingliss conetree—" And Snow showed him FitzRoy's book. "Me know Cappen Fitzoy—Byno—Bennet—Walamstow." It appeared to Snow that the images "made him laugh and look sad alternatively, as the two characters he was represented in, savage and civilized, came before his eyes. Perhaps he was calling to mind his combed hair, washed face and dandy dress, with the polished boots it is said he so much delighted in: perhaps he was asking himself which, after all, was the best—the prim and starch, or the rough and shaggy?" Jemmy could break your heart. However, he flat refused, Snow said, to go to the Falklands, wherever they were, or anywhere else. So that was that.

They went topside, and Jemmy pointed out his canoe and his wife, who, cradling their baby, was calling out to Jemmy in English words. He also pointed out this canoe and that—they contained bad men, "not of my conetree," and he called them *Oens* men, the same word he'd used with FitzRoy for the thieves at Wulaia.

Jemmy paddled out to the ship the next morning accompanied by a couple of dozen other canoes. To Snow, it was clear that Jemmy was the leader. Snow let aboard a few additional Yahgan whom Jemmy vouched for. His wife came aboard at Mrs. Snow's invitation, but Jemmy again refused to leave on any more English ships. Then, when this gentle meeting was over, and the Yahgan were leaving the ship, the last two made a sudden grab for Snow's coat. Snow threw one to the deck. The other broke off the attack when the crew came at him with belaying pins. The natives sprang over the side. And on that parting note the *Allen Gardiner* laid an easterly course across Bahía Nassau bound for the Falklands.

It took months for word to reach him in England, but when it did, Despard was livid. Snow had found Jemmy, but failed to bring him back to Keppel Island. That was unthinkable. Despard, who'd always been suspicious about the depth of the captain's devotion, recognized that he, Despard, would have to do it himself. He loaded his wife and six children, their household goods, another prefab house, lumber, tools, and the kitchen sink aboard a chartered vessel called *Hydaspes,* and sailed to the Falklands in eighty-seven days.

Among his three adopted children was a thirteen-year-old named Thomas Bridges. The story goes that an infant in a basket was found abandoned beneath a bridge and taken to Despard's church. The baby, clean and cared for, wore a fresh tunic with the letter *T* embroidered on the chest. So Thomas Bridges he became, and Despard took him into his home. Bridges would prove himself the only true humanitarian among a lot of zealots and egotists.

Despard fired Captain Snow after Snow refused to carry a herd of cattle from Port Stanley to Keppel Island—on the *Allen Gardiner*'s deck. And rather vindictively for a man of the cloth, Despard not only refused to pay return passage to England, he hit Snow up for two pounds for his mattress and bedding from the ship. Despard replaced him with Robert Fell, a competent sailor who was more devout, or at least more willing to follow orders. Then the reverend whipped his mission into shape, building homes, sheds, a school, and when the garden was in, he had Captain Fell run him and some disciples over to Spaniard Harbor, where they stood around the graves and sang and prayed, after which they went back to work on Keppel Island.

Everything ready, Despard dispatched the *Allen Gardiner* to Wulaia to fetch Jemmy Button and don't take no for an answer. Without Parker Snow's presence, we have only missionary documents, and they record only bare facts of the following events. Word went out from Wulaia for Jemmy Button, and soon he paddled up to the ship. Just like that, as far as we can know, Jemmy said sure, Keppel Island, fine. Why Jemmy changed his mind is unclear. He may have been induced by gifts, or it might have been whim. It's possible that Snow didn't try very hard. What seems clear enough from the bare events is that Jemmy was not coerced or forced in any way—he agreed to go of his own volition, and to take his wife and kid along. For the second time in his life, Jemmy boarded a sailing ship and left his homeland to learn white men's religion in some foreign place so that he might then pass it on to his people.

Jemmy, however, was not the same pliant, pudgy, eager-to-please charmer who'd met the king and queen of England, but a grown man of about thirty-five, maybe even an unofficial leader of his people. Jemmy was not happy on Keppel Island. Perhaps he had been expecting something like the delights of England instead of a treeless bog. He wanted to go home. Despard agreed because Jemmy's sour attitude was a bad influence on the others. Jemmy and Despard cut a deal by which Despard would take Jemmy home on the *Allen Gardiner,* and Jemmy would encourage friends and relatives to attend, help keep the flock flowing. So the ship with the martyr's name, both Despard and Jemmy aboard, sailed back to Yahgan land. Despard was looking for a site to build his permanent mission once the Keppel Island preliminaries were complete. He picked Wulaia, like FitzRoy, because it offered a snug harbor with gently climbing meadows behind a fine stretch of flat land. Wulaia was perfect. So while Jemmy filled his part of the bargain, enlisting nine willing Yahgan, including one of his sons, Billy Button, Despard measured off the exact dimensions of the mission to come and marked it with string. Then back they went to Keppel Island.

This was a good batch of Yahgan, pliant, participatory, and they liked to garden and sing hymns. Before their ten-month stay was up, Thomas Bridges had grown fluent in their language. Maybe it was during this period, before he'd even set foot in Fuegia, that Bridges began to perceive an inherent problem. The Yahgan language, rich and sophisticated in vocabulary and syntax, was rooted in the immediate and concrete, just like their lives. There were, for instance, a half dozen words for snow. There were more for beach, depending on its direction and whether there was water between it and the speaker. A thing seen from a canoe might have a different word when seen from land. However, Yahgan had not a single syllable to express the notion of spirituality or any other sort of abstraction or symbolism fundamental to religion. But this wouldn't have been something Despard wanted to hear.

Confident and pleased with his progress and with the Yahgan's devotion, Despard was ready to take the next step by establishing the permanent mission on that green meadow at Wulaia. Thomas Bridges wanted to go, but Despard said no. Bridges was far more useful working on his Yahgan-English dictionary. Garland Phillips, the catechist who had disapproved of Snow and his crew, was designated leader by

Despard. His orders were to construct the mission building as Despard had laid it out in his last trip, hold a service to demonstrate what this religion was all about, and finally to return to Keppel with the next batch of would-be converts. But the trip got off to an angry start, over objects, over theft.

Members of the mission complained to Despard that some of their personal property was missing, and that those items would doubtless be found right there in the bundles the nine Yahgan were carrying aboard the schooner. What to do? Forget it, or search the bundles? Despard felt he had no choice, and he ordered the bundles searched. The Yahgan were furious, howling in protest—they clearly understood the concept of private property when it came to *their* private property. Of course the missing stuff turned up in their bundles, and getting caught further outraged them. I wonder if Garland Phillips saw the beginning of the end in that incident. He had asked Despard to leave the bags unsearched. The ship sailed for Wulaia in rotten weather and arrived without incident in Wulaia bay. By the time the anchor had set and sails were furled, she was surrounded by canoes. Calling for his son, Jemmy Button paddled alongside, and Billy appeared at the rail, then the rest of the Christianized Yahgan. They were still aggrieved, shouting and waving their arms. Phillips asked Jemmy to come aboard to help calm things down, and he might have done so had there been a pile of wonderful gifts waiting for him on deck. But there were no gifts at all. Given that the missionaries' religion was meaningless to them, the Yahgan who journeyed to Keppel Island may have been motivated by a sense of adventure, curiosity or other intangibles, but mostly it was the gifts, white man's stuff. Nobody thought to bring gifts to Jemmy Button, who was supposed to be the cornerstone of the mission. Though Despard didn't like Jemmy, or the idea of bribing the flock, this was a dim and completely avoidable oversight. Phillips tried to cover it by pulling together a gift bundle of tools, trinkets, whatever came to hand, but it was too late. Jemmy was offended, irate, in fact, fomenting anger on deck, and by the time the natives had lined up to leave the ship, they were trembling with rage.

Then, to make a bad scene worse, a sailor stepped forward and complained to Captain Fell that some of his stuff was missing. Stop!

Fell ordered their bundles searched. Again. And this time their clothes as well. Now it was turning really ugly, women and children wailing, sailors trying to wrest away the bundles—Yahgan rage could not be contained in language, either language. They bellowed and screamed, stamping and waving, and Billy Button frothed at the mouth. A Yahgan named Schwaiamugunjiz who'd been endearingly nicknamed Squire Muggins, a willing fellow who'd been everyone's favorite back on Keppel, hurled himself at Fell's throat, but the squire was wrestled off. Bags and bundles were searched by force, and all the stolen objects emptied onto the deck. Then, before they left the ship, the Yahgan made a simple, brilliant gesture to demonstrate the state of the relationship—they tore off their Christian clothes and jumped naked over the side.

Fell and crew, armed with guns and two small cannons, stood watches through the night, while ashore the natives wailed and shouted until a cold rain quelled their ardor for the time being. The next morning, in the same rain, the missionary party began to shuttle tools and material ashore. Fell posted several armed men to guard the stuff, while others covered them with rifles from the schooner. They worked all the next day in the rain, and repeated guard duty that night. The little chapel was nearing completion when the skies cleared, and the Yahgan turned out in number. They crouched around for a while watching, just as their fathers had watched FitzRoy assemble his mission on the same spot, before they pressed in to steal whatever they could lay their hands on

Then Phillips decided that one thing alone would soothe the savage breast, and that was the light of the Lord. The next day, Sunday, the missionaries would march unarmed into the chapel and hold a service, they would pray and sing the old hymns, and the scales would fall from Yahgan eyes. So it was decided. Bibles and hymnals in hand, Phillips led Captain Fell, the Swedish carpenter called Agusto, and the devout sailors up the meadow toward the mission house. The crowd, estimated in the hundreds, parted for the men to pass, then closed up behind. Seemingly dozens of Yahgan pressed into the little house, and the service began. It was November 6, 1859.

Only the cook Robert Coles remained aboard the *Allen Gardiner*. Watching from the rail, he saw several Yahgan scamper down to the beach, snatch the oars from the longboat, and shove it off. The first snippet of song was cut off by Yahgan screams. Bloody, Garland Phillips staggered from the chapel toward the boat. Agusto also made it out of the chapel and ran for the boat. As Phillips waded in after it, Billy Button threw a rock that hit him in side of the head. He sagged underwater. They killed Agusto at water's edge, bringing him down with rocks and harpoon thrusts, and then a Yahgan smashed his skull with a boulder. The others were already dead in the house of worship. Then the Yahgan boarded their canoes and paddled for Coles and the schooner.

19

At Wulaia

He told [my mother] of the unkind climate, of the long dreary
nights, of the solitude, when one was completely cut off from
the outside world. In this wild and desolate region, he had told
her, there were no doctors nor police nor government of any
kind: and, instead of kindly neighbors, one was surrounded by,
and utterly at the mercy of, lawless tribes without discipline or
religion.

—Lucas Bridges,
Uttermost Part of the Earth

"Mind the nav?" Hamish asked, long enough for him to have his
shower. We had all had exquisite hot showers without need to con-
serve water, and now it was the captain's turn; by that old tradition of
the sea, he was the last to shower.

We'd been to the pitch of the Horn and traveled the length of our
fjord, and now we were inbound, heading for the hitherto *prohibidos*
Murray Narrows to rejoin the Beagle Channel—with a stop for the
night at Wulaia. I had been dreamily watching the environment and
the changing weather, not bothering to identify or reconcile anything.
Minding the nav required a different kind of focus, and while minding
it, I didn't want to sail right past Wulaia.

We had just jibed onto port, turned north around Cape Webley on
the eastern point of Peninsula Pasteur. The wind was west, a trifle

light for *Pelagic*'s liking, but now on a beam reach we were doing almost five knots. I had had a glimpse of Cape Webley astern before a black woolen cloud slid down the mountainside to cover it. We had just entered the constriction between the southwest toe of Navarino and a large island called Milne-Edwards on the west side. Henri Milne-Edwards, born 1800, and his son Alphonse, who died in 1900, were French naturalists during that century of scientific exploration— Henri has a lemur named for him—and their name was left on the local environment by the *Romanche* expedition in 1883. Henri had joined Pasteur, of whose peninsula Isla Milne-Edwards is really a part, on the scientific side of a nasty argument over spontaneous generation that went for years. In the wide-open spaces of Ponsonby Sound, the wind turned gusty and it began to rain. The snowy mountains on peninsulas Pasteur and Dumas vanished. If you still don't mind comparing Isla Navarino to a walrus facing west, then the tusks are a wedge-shaped, steep-sided island FitzRoy named for Jemmy Button. It was dead ahead, due north five miles, and I could still see it. At the point of the tusks, we'd turn hard right, and there, behind two or three islets, would be Caleta Wulaia, the scene of the crime.

Despard, Captain Fell's wife, Mrs. Garland Phillips, and the others had waited on Keppel Island in growing distress for the *Allen Gardiner*, now five months overdue, and something had to be done. Everyone worried about those 350 open-ocean miles between the Falkland Islands and the Strait of Le Maire, where well-found ships regularly vanished. But communications were nonexistent—there was still hope that the schooner had been forced into a harbor of refuge with damage to repair. That might account for two months, and with other delays they could be three months overdue, but five—that had the feel of death about it. Despard sailed around to Port Stanley, the tiny colonial capital about seventy miles away, to inquire, but no one had seen or heard from the *Allen Gardiner*. He hired Captain Smyley, who had found the bones of Gardiner and his devotees at Earnest Cove, to go to Wulaia, and if he found nothing there, to conduct a search of the archipelago.

Sailing up the chest of Navarino, *Pelagic*'s present heading, in his small topsail schooner *Nancy*, Smyley and his crew spotted the masts, incongruous straight lines, behind the sheltering islands at Wulaia. But the masts were naked poles, stripped clean of rigging, fittings, and

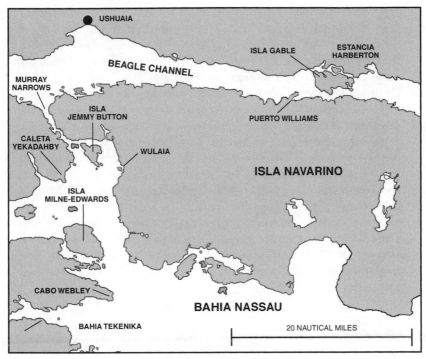

Map 19.1   To Wulaia

sails. When *Nancy* cleared the northern point, turning into the flat bay, they saw that the *Allen Gardiner* was adrift. Though there wasn't a single Yahgan in sight, Smyley knew they were there, watching from the forest. After anchoring close aboard, Smyley and a well-armed boat crew rowed over and boarded the *Gardiner*. Her deck was as bereft as her rig, and the spaces below had been pillaged of everything down to bare frames and bulkheads. Now it was time to go ashore and inspect the remains of the chapel.

As Smyley and his crew made their way up the meadow, a white man stumbled from the trees. Screaming and flailing his arms, he ran toward the sailors, then when he reached them, when he was safe, he collapsed at their feet. It was the cook, Alfred Cole. His naked body was covered in cuts, bruises, and festering boils. So was his face, and he could barely speak through lips encrusted with sores. It sounded at first like insane babble, but the message came through. They had all been murdered in cold blood, Captain Fell, Phillips, Agusto the Swede, and the others—all dead. Killed six bars into the first hymn of the first Sunday service. Two sailors picked him up—he weighed nothing—while two others covered the trees, and they hustled him back aboard the *Nancy*. Cole was literally starving. He had reached that point, the same as Gardiner's party, where it was impossible to eat another mussel even if it meant starving to death. Smyley slowly fed the cook, salved his boils, and the rest of the story had unfolded before the lookout called—canoes were approaching. Smyley rushed topside, told everyone to hold fire. One canoe came alongside. A man climbed aboard without invitation. He stood at the rail, and with the old smile introduced himself. He was Jemmy Button.

There was probably a moment, a double take, another weird Fuegian tableau. Then Smyley snapped out his orders: Make sail, get the anchor up. They were sailing for Port Stanley immediately, and Jemmy Button was going along, under guard if necessary—let the authorities work it out.

⌒

"Look at that," said Jonathan, pointing over the bow. "A light."

It was, an actual lighted aid to navigation.

"How do you want to pass it?" asked Tim at the wheel.

"Keep it to port," I said. It marked the end of a run of rocks, broken islets, and reefs stretching south from the point of the tusks. Three miles later, we came abeam of the steep-sided, forested island called Conejos that protects Wulaia from the west, essentially forming the bay. I leaned down the companionway to tell Hamish, working on his anchorage database after his hot shower, that we were here.

A new misty drizzle and low-hanging fog isolated *Pelagic* and Wulaia. Hamish, who'd never been here before, picked his way in with his usual calm dexterity. He had a Chilean pilot book, the *Ver Carta*, with sharply drawn little charts of certain bays and coves of which he was prudently skeptical. On the chart Wulaia looked like an easy in, no obstructions, twenty feet of water almost everywhere. Hamish picked a spot where the bay constricted between a small island and a bulging point to drop the hook. He saw no need for shore lines because the

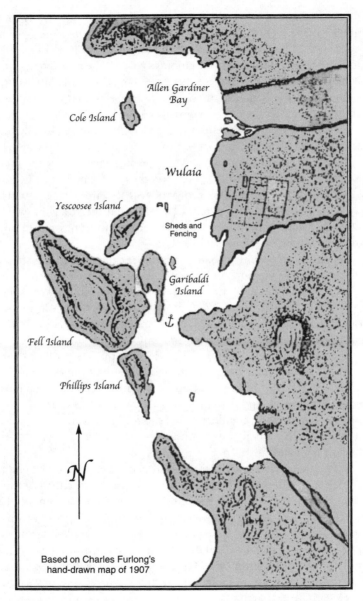

Allen Gardiner
Bay

Cole Island

Wulaia

Yescoosee Island

Sheds and
Fencing

Garibaldi
Island

Fell Island

Phillips Island

N

Based on Charles Furlong's
hand-drawn map of 1907

Map 19.2   Scene of the Crime

holding ground was good and the lay of the land was not conducive to williwaws. We were here, in Wulaia where no foreign boat had anchored in decades, but the "exploration impulse," so keen in Punters' Inlet, was absent. The mood was gloomy. We launched the dinghy from the foredeck efficiently, but there was little spirit behind the procedure.

The weather was gloomy, if you wanted to see it that way, but gray weather had not darkened the mood aboard before. We were aware of the sad history, but I don't think the events of 1859 were immediate in our imaginations as we approached the shore in fog. And the geography was cheerfully expansive, wide-open spaces. A level green meadow, four running brooks, lush forest, and friendly hills behind, Wulaia is sylvan, the gentlest geography in the archipelago. Wulaia may be the southernmost parcel of usable real estate in the world. Naturally, white men looking to build permanent things where none had ever been before chose Wulaia.

We landed on a gently shoaling beach near the mouth of a stream, and stepped over the bow onto the meadow. It's not clear to me from the sources where exactly the chapel was situated, but we were standing near the most obvious site, and it was occupied by a large two-story house. Built of plastered brick moistened by moss, with a mansard roof, French windows, and tall wooden doors with glass panes and lintels, this looked like a down-at-the-heels villa in rural Spain. Beside the villa, predating it, white men had built a sprawling network of split-rail corrals with internal pens and chutes. The house seemed abandoned, and though we'd seen cows on the north shore of Navarino, there were none here. But the first guy ashore discovered that they had been here and recently, too. We weren't ready for the works of man and cattle.

In 1907 Charles Furlong led a small private expedition intending to observe the Yahgan culture and write an essay on tribal distribution in Fuegia. But 1907 was too late. The American Museum of Natural History had kindly allowed Tim and me to view the artifacts donated by Mr. Furlong. They were stored in crumpled cardboard boxes in a row of metal shelves directly beneath the eaves of the oldest building, pigeons murmuring. The Yahgan are not hot tickets. But then, these artifacts were really tourist items. There were bows and a quiver with several arrows, two miniature canoes made of bark and twigs; there were bark baskets of the sort used as bailers, age-browned, cracked, and forlorn objects of little distinction. The arrowheads were fashioned from broken bottle glass. The canoe models differed widely in design, and neither looked like a Yahgan canoe. The basket was far too flimsy to be real, a knock-off quickie made for the cash economy by Indians with wet coughs. When Furlong landed here in a thirty-five-foot sloop chartered from Ushuaia, he found corrals, fencing, sheds, and a hut owned by an Austrian settler, Antonio Vrsalovich, who came in 1896.

Furlong drew a decent map published with his article (in *The Geographical Review*). In the notes to the map, he states, "In the absence of charted names of the bay and islands, the writer has named them as follows: Allen Gardiner Bay; . . . Garibaldi Island, after the sloop of the expedition; Yescoosee Island; which Vrsalovich said the Yahgans called it; Fell and Phillips Islands, after the victims; and Cole Island, after the cook who escaped in a small boat past this island and by taking to the woods on the opposite point."

Vigilance was required to avoid the volcanoes of cattle shit and establish a beachhead. Someone pointed out the stark iron hooks hanging from trestles and crossbeams under a lean-to shed. This was a tannery. That accounted for the galvanized tanks and coffin-size vats with bad-looking black liquid at the bottom.

News of the murders and the person of Jemmy Button in Port Stanley posed a problem for Governor Thomas Moore. Because the crimes didn't happen in his jurisdiction, he had no legal authority to prosecute, even if he'd wanted to, which he did not. But since the victims were residents of the Falklands, the circumstances so sensational, and since Jemmy Button was present in Port Stanley, he couldn't ignore it. The governor was no friend of the missionaries, however. Bringing Indians into the country was an unnecessary threat to peace and prosperity, in his view, and he didn't care for Despard's imperious attitude, as if Keppel Island were a private country.

The Falkland Islands had only recently settled into a stable outpost of the British Empire. European sea powers since Elizabeth's time had recognized the strategic potential of Port Stanley as a base astride the route to the Horn, but none could overcome the remoteness, the treelessness, or the wind to actually settle there. Argentina tried it by sending a rugged breed of cattle and a similar band of gauchos. Argentina even today sees Islas Malvinas as an offshore extension of her natural territory. Maps and public images of Argentina still include the Malvinas, as if the Falklands War never happened. Britain staked a simultaneous claim back in the 1820s with naval power, not cattle, to back it up. But it was only the promise of power. No ships were present, only a sort of unofficial representative named Matthew Brisbane. And one day the gauchos murdered him, and then dragged his body around by the neck behind a horse.

Brisbane, captain of the tiny *Beaufoy,* with Weddell in the *Jane,* had established the record for Farthest South in 1828. FitzRoy, Darwin, and the *Beagle* spent some weeks in the Falklands while Brisbane served as the lone symbol of Britain's authority. The two captains became friends, and FitzRoy encouraged Brisbane to stick it out, show the flag, not to worry about the gauchos; they'll fall into line. When the *Beagle* next called at Port Stanley, FitzRoy found Brisbane's animal-gnawed feet protruding from a shallow grave. By 1859, the year of the Wulaia murders, the gauchos were gone, and Port Stanley was still too small to resemble a bucolic little village in the Scottish Highlands, but it was trying.

Governor Moore (also an ex-polar explorer, captain of HMS *Pagoda* in James Clark Ross's second Arctic expedition) empaneled a board to take depositions from the witnesses, and then he'd write a report to London that would take months to arrive, longer for a reply, and maybe the whole sordid affair would fade away.

First, Albert Cole was deposed. He repeated that he saw two Indians take the oars from the longboat just before the massacre began. Afterward, he leapt into the dinghy, rowed to a nearby point, and bolted into the forest. Yahgan pursued in their canoes, but after collecting the abandoned dinghy, they didn't bother to chase him any farther. For the next two weeks, he hid in the woods by day, and at night crept down to the shoreline to gather mussels and limpets. One day, starving and sick, he lingered too long after first light and was spotted by several Yahgan. Apparently in a mood more sporting than murderous, they chased him down, sat on him, and began to pluck out his facial hair with a pair of mussel shells; the Yahgan didn't like facial hair. They grew bored before the job was done, drifted off, and Cole followed, hoping they'd take him in. They didn't exactly do that, but neither did they drive him off. Some ridiculed him, others ignored him completely, but no one harmed him. Some shared their wigwams and food with him and daubed mud on his boils. Cole further testified that he had witnessed Jemmy's son throw the rock that dropped Garland Phillips as he waded out to retrieve the boat. Cole, however, did not see Jemmy at the scene or for weeks afterward.

It's curious and probably revelatory of something fundamental about the Yahgan that they didn't kill Cole as well. He was, after all, an eyewitness to their crimes. And though vengeance killing was a part of Yahgan and Alacaluf society (that's how York Minster died), the Yahgan at Wulaia seemed unworried that other white men would come to avenge the missionaries. If they'd been thinking like ruthless criminals, they would have disposed of Cole and burned the *Allen Gardiner*. Cole, who communicated with the natives through sign language and the smattering of English they'd picked up at Keppel, testified that they freely referred to the murders, and when talking about looting the *Allen Gardiner,* they kept saying, "Jam-mus. Jam-mus Button." The name came up a lot. At dusk on the day of the murders, the looting of the *Gardiner* was not quite complete, but the Indians were afraid to stay aboard after dark. Not Jemmy; he wasn't afraid. In fact, he led the others to Captain Fell's quarters and declared that he was going to sleep right there, in the captain's bed. And so he did. That was all hearsay, but Cole believed that Jemmy had instigated and organized the attack on the missionaries.

Then it was Jemmy's turn. Though FitzRoy's *Narrative* had tanked, Darwin's *Voyage of the* Beagle was a huge seller (*On the Origin of Species* was published in England in 1859, the year of the killings), so Jemmy was still something of a celebrity. And he was still cute; that had always been an advantage for him in white culture. For a member of one of the simplest cultures on earth, Jemmy had experienced a lot of English institutions—the church, the navy, education, *and* the crown. His English was slipping away, but he could still make himself understood. The gist of it was that the natives had been taken to Keppel against their will. And as for that fracas with Fell and Phillips aboard the *Gardiner*—that started because his people thought they were being taken back to Keppel. It wasn't about theft at all. Jemmy flatly denied having anything to do with the murders. And he most certainly never slept in the "cappan's" bed. No, Jemmy was deeply upset by news of the slaughter, and completely innocent of it. Furthermore, he said he knew who the guilty parties were: none other than those *Oens* men. The Ona, the dreaded enemy from the north.

Moore summoned Despard to Port Stanley to tell his side of the story, but Despard flatly refused. The governor's board deliberated on the available testimony and determined that the Patagonian Missionary Society was entirely at fault. They had more or less kidnapped those Fuegians, and the subsequent tragedy stemmed from that, the bondage at Keppel Island. That's the end of that, Moore blustered in the absence of authority, no more Indians may be brought into the islands, period. Lucas Bridges has no doubt that Jemmy instigated the "treacherous attack on those who had befriended him," and he surmises that it was prompted by a "combination of resentment and jealousy." Yet even without Jemmy's "leadership," the outcome would have been identical, he says: "The unguarded schooner and the defenseless party ashore offered too tempting an opportunity to be resisted by such undisciplined children of nature as the Fuegian Indians."

A few of the Christians in Port Stanley were murmuring about a punitive expedition to Wulaia, correcting those children's behavior, but Governor Moore absolutely forbade any such thing. He'd been trying to keep this whole ugly matter quiet, whereas blowing bark canoes out of the water was loud. Besides, how would they know whom to punish? Did they mean to kill any woman and child they came upon? . . . Well, yeah.

Despard was finished as a missionary. All his efforts and inspiration, all his certainty had led here, to this, and in despair, he sent word to England to find a replacement. But he could not of course leave the *Allen Gardiner* to rot at Wulaia. Despard hired Smyley to buy whatever cordage, hardware, sails, and other gear he'd need to rig the *Allen Gardiner* for sea and sail her home. Jemmy Button was aboard when the (well-armed) *Nancy* sailed for Wulaia. Smyley made a seamanlike job of rerigging the schooner, and the natives pitched in to help. Soon Smyley sailed the *Nancy* and the *Allen Gardiner* back to Keppel, where Despard was packed up and ready to sail for England.

Recognizing his adopted son's physical and intellectual gifts, Despard asked whether he wanted to go home with the family or remain to continue the work at Keppel. (No one intended to accede to Governor Moore's prohibition.) Thomas Bridges, only nineteen years old, fluent in Yahgan, elected to remain and run the mission until the new superintendent arrived. Thomas had plans of his own. It was time, he thought, to go to Fuegia and establish a physical presence. The difference between the previous attempt and this one was language. For the first time in nearly three centuries of sporadic contact, a white man would speak to the Yahgan in their own language. The new superintendent, the Reverend Wait Stirling, a brave and competent man, surprised by Bridges's fluency, agreed that it would make all the difference. Both men sailed to Fuegia aboard the *Allen Gardiner* in 1863.

Lucas Bridges, using his father's private diary as a source, writes in *Uttermost Part of the Earth*, "Since the massacre at Wulaia the natives had lived in constant dread of reprisals, and it was with evident trepidation that they approached the vessel," interesting in light of the fact that they could have covered the traces of the massacre had they been so ruthless. In any case, the natives were astonished to hear a white man call out and address them in their own language. The trip had several purposes. The first was reconciliation, showing the natives that there would be no reprisals, only Christian forgiveness. They had nothing to fear from whites. As the schooner traveled west in the Beagle Channel, Thomas rowed ashore alone at various Yahgan "settlements" in order, his son writes, "to encourage sociability and avoid ostentation." The missionaries called this the "Trip of Pardon."

The other purpose, the search for a suitable mission site, was pursued with "a view to a white settlement in the country." Lucas Bridges lists his father's criteria: "It must be a place where a large number of small farmers could live and prosper, with decent gardens and a few cows and goats. It must have a roomy harbor. . . . And it must be near the very heart of Yahgan country and easy to reach from all sides by the natives." They stopped to inspect the Beagle shore north and east of Gable Island, which would become and remains today the Bridges

family homestead, Estancia Harberton. It had a good harbor and ample land, but for the present purposes it was too far from the Murray
Narrows, "Yahgashaga," which Thomas considered the apex of Yahgan land. It was Thomas Bridges who named them Yahgan.

The missionaries appraised present-day Puerto Navarino on the
northwest side of the island, on the walrus's skull, centrally located,
but the harbor was tricky in reduced visibility. Wulaia was out because of its dark history and limited space. Ushuaia, however, was
perfect, within sight of the Narrows, on a fine deep harbor with ample
flat land for farming. So there it was, the future. Thomas Bridges was
terribly wrong—the Yahgan had everything to fear from whites, even
those of unalloyed goodwill. Even Thomas Bridges, a man of depth
and kindness beyond duty, continued to assume without question that
Christianity and civilization were a unity, and that aboriginal people
would be improved by conversion and exposure to both.

Bridges noticed during this Trip of Pardon that there were far
fewer Yahgan in Yahgashaga than his predecessors had reported, and
he learned from the Yahgan that during "the period of isolation" (Lucas Bridges) an epidemic of some civilized disease had swept through
the population. It may have been measles, pneumonia, influenza; it
may or may not have been brought by sealers. Conceivably, the murdered missionaries had left unintentional revenge behind. The year after the Trip of Pardon another epidemic further reduced the
population. Among the dead this time was the man with the most ex-
tensive and prolonged association with whites of any Yahgan, beginning with the trip to England in 1828. Jemmy Button died in the 1864
epidemic.

The establishment of the mission (and the settlement) took place in
stages while the Keppel Island shuttles continued. In 1869 Thomas
Bridges was summoned back to England for his ordination, and Stirling spent that winter alone in Ushuaia without harm or harassment.
Stirling was lonely, and he admits that a tear came into his eye when
the *Allen Gardiner* returned in the spring. While in England on a fund-
raising tour for the mission society, Thomas met Mary Varder of Harberton, South Devon, fell in love, and after a whirlwind courtship
married her. The brave woman agreed to share his life in Fuegia. As a
first step, she accompanied him to the Falklands, where a year later she

gave birth to a daughter, Mary. Then on October 17, 1871, after a miserable forty-five-day slog against the wind, the *Allen Gardiner* anchored in Bahía Ushuaia. They would be the first white people to settle permanently in Fuegia. In 1874, Mary gave birth to "the first white citizen of Ushuaia," Thomas Despard Bridges. On December 31, 1874, Lucas Bridges was born in Ushuaia. Soon afterward another interesting female figure, Joanna Varder, arrived from England to help her sister manage the family. *Yekadahby* was the Yahgan word for "aunt on the mother's side," or literally, "little mother." A farmer in Devon, *Yekadahby* was, according to Lucas, an "authority on . . . butter, junket, cheese, jam, and strawberries and cream; and an expert at rearing chickens, ducks, and geese," all things that had never been done here before. I wish the Varder women had written memoirs of life in Fuegia.

Thomas Bridges, who with Mary and *Yekadahby* raised five children in Fuegia, took a census of the Yahgan in 1884, finding 273 men, 314 women, and 413 children. Another measles epidemic pounded the Yahgan for three months, and when it had run its course 397 Yahgan survived in the entire archipelago, according to Thomas's 1886 census. That same year, he quit the mission, accepted Argentine citizenship (Argentina officially founded Ushuaia in 1884) and a grant of land of his choice as a gesture of gratitude by that nation. Bridges chose that fine land he'd inspected during the Trip of Pardon on the shore of Tierra del Fuego near Gable Island. Estancia Harberton became a place of refuge for the Yahgan, who settled on the grounds. We visited the neat, sad little cemetery where they are buried. Thomas Bridges employed and protected them; he traveled by open boat tending to the rest of the scattered flock, settling disputes when he could, bringing medicine, but he knew that his work was cultural hospice. Individuals lived on, but the Yahgan way of life was already extinct. Thomas died on July 15, 1898, but thankfully his son, who grew up in Fuegia, lived to write *Uttermost Part of the Earth*.

❧

We had had enough of Wulaia by the time the rains came. We took a quick look inside the villa, the door unlocked, and found more tanning paraphernalia, mattresses and refuse left behind by fishermen or cattlemen camping in the house. In an upper-story room with fancy molding and twelve-foot ceilings, we found a high stack of cured hides splayed out as flat and stiff as plywood sheets; even the tails stuck straight out. On that note, we dinghied back to *Pelagic* in a quiet, melancholy mood.

Our trip was near its end now. Tomorrow we'd use the beautiful, sylvan Murray Narrows to reach the Beagle Channel, before heading east to Puerto Williams in order to clear Chilean customs. And the following day we would backtrack west again to Ushuaia, where we would leave *Pelagic* and the ocean wilderness behind.

After a long dinner-table silence, Kate said, "It was the tails that got me, sticking straight out like that."

20

"The Wet
and Cold Life"

At the dock in Ushuaia, our gear was packed up, and the customs man had come and gone. Boat cabins always look bereft at the end of a trip when you've cleaned them up, and it's time to step ashore. David, Dick, and Jonathan had already done so, heading up the hill with the first load. Tim and I lingered, accepting the offer of a last cuppa, prolonging our association with *Pelagic* and her people. Stepping onto the dock is often a final severing. (Unready to detach from the environment, I spent a week in and around Ushuaia, visited the Bridges estancia at Harberton, hiked to the head of the Martial Glacier above the city, but that was different. That was land travel.) Kate and Hamish had business ashore, calls to make, and the time had come to say good-bye. That's what we were doing, saying good-bye, promising to stay in touch, when there came a knocking on the doghouse roof.

"Hello, *Pelagic*. It is Jarli."

"Jarli!" shouted Hamish and Kate in unison. When he reached the foot of the companionway, they gave him a delighted hug. Jarli had returned from a watery grave.

Slender, fit, blue-eyed, shy, handsome, not a day over twenty, Jarli looked like a Viking, just as Kate had said. Guys who looked just like him sailed with Bjarni Herjolfsson in 985, the first white men ever to lay eyes on the North American continent.

Introductions done, we waited for Jarli to tell the story, but he didn't. He leaned against the ladder, happy to be here, apparently, grinning but silent.

"So. Jarli. Back from the dead," Hamish prompted. "We thought you were a goner."

"Yah. I am sorry for that. For your trouble."

"So tell us the story," said Hamish.

He shrugged, bowed his head after tossing a shock of blond hair from his eyes. "We flipped," he said, indicating with his flat hand a broaching sailboat. He might have been referring to a fender bender on the way home from the video store. They flipped, aw, bummer. Off to Antarctica "to see the seals and birds," they flipped in the middle of the Drake Passage aboard a twenty-six-foot plastic boat meant for day sailing and weekend cruising in bays. The weather had been fair for a few days out, big waves, but not bad ones. Then "storm, storm, storm." They lost the jib over the side. His English wasn't entirely clear, but it seemed they'd had problems with the outboard motor (which was mounted on a recreational-gauge aluminum stern bracket, Hamish had said). The only way to get it to start was to remove the spark plugs and heat them in the oven, but removing and installing the plugs required removing the engine cover, exposing it to the seas. It soon died of hypothermia, hot plugs or cold. On other sailboats at sea that would be a problem because without a working engine there would be no way to charge the batteries. You'd lose all your electronics, running lights, radio, GPS, radar. That wasn't a problem for Jarli because he didn't have any of those things. He had a handheld radio, but boarding seas drowned it two days out. "Rough, rough." The worst loss, he said, was the cabin heater, but I missed what happened to it, a boarding sea, I suppose.

Apparently the little boat had slipped beam-on to the wave. "So fast. It happened so fast." All accounts by small-boat sailors broached down by breakers agree on that, the instantaneousness of it. Too quickly to do a thing. Jarli wasn't too sure, but he thought she rolled 360 degrees. He had been in the cockpit attached to the boat by his safety-harness tether when she went, and his crewman, Dave, had been below trying to sleep. By some hydrodynamic miracle, she did not sink when the hatch boards were washed away, and water flooded below. But more astoundingly, the mast was still standing when the boat came back to even keel. How did this flimsy deck-stepped aluminum stick survive a rollover? If it had gone by the board, Jarli and Dave would probably not have survived, drifting helplessly eastward in the empty Southern Ocean. Both motor and bracket had gone to the bottom, but an outboard motor couldn't have gotten them home—only sail. Jarli mimed their frantic bailing, two feet of water in the cabin, with a bucket and a pasta pot. They bailed her out, the weather moderated (it needn't have been too severe to overwhelm Jarli's boat), and with that blessed salvation of a standing mast, they sailed back to Ushuaia in a week. She was anchored somewhere else, east, in order to save on harbor fees.

And what about Dave, Hamish asked, he'd never been to sea before, right?

"No, no, never on a sailboat ever before. At first he couldn't steer straight, but he learns. It is all a matter of attitude. Dave, he has a good attitude. What is it? Positive. A positive attitude."

But, Hamish reckoned, that was probably Dave's last boat trip.

"Oh, no, Dave likes the wet and cold life."

"But you're not going back, are you?" Kate said.

Jarli didn't think so, no. He and Dave had discussed it, but— He broke off, looked around at us, and cast his eyes down on the floorboards. "I am ashamed a little. The Drake, the ocean rejected us. I am ashamed for that. It would not do now to go south. North we must go. . . Maybe Brazil. To the jungle."

We, too, had to go north. We repeated our good-byes and bon voyages to *Pelagic* and Jarli, and climbed topside for the last time. Cold, soaking mist hung in the air. We climbed the rusty ladder rungs onto the puddled concrete pier, turned and waved to Kate and Hamish, who had come topside to see us off. They waved, and then ducked back into the warmth below.

As we walked toward the land, two things seemed clear. If I had been Dave's age (hell, even older) kicking around the higher latitudes looking for adventure, and some Viking invited me to cross the Drake to Antarctica in a twenty-six-foot Clorox bottle in order to see the seals and birds—I'd have accepted. Especially if, like Dave, I didn't know the pointy end from the square end. After all, it's just a matter of attitude, the wet and cold life.

I put it to Tim, a stable fellow: Would he have gone with Jarli?

He didn't answer for several steps, remembering twenty. "Sure," he said.

The other thing was related to the first. The "wet and cold life" and the "seals and birds" seemed emblems of the present relationship between humans and Cape Horn. The Yahgan are gone, and the great ships have passed into history, sea stories of man against nature from a time gone by. But the rest of it, the islands and channels down to the stalwart rock, remains. Humans have established isolated beachheads on the fringes of the Beagle, but south of Navarino nothing much has changed since Drake's day, except through erosion. Armand, that intense Chilean ready to fight to the death for Cape Horn, may have been wrong about his nation's attitude. Chile means to protect its *fin del mundo* treasures. One hears about overfishing in the archipelago, but there is no talk of "dual use" or rationalizations for the compatibility between oil derricks and caribou migration. The highly stressed environment is fragile, but for now at least, it seems free of external stress from profiteers. And the only reason to come here now is to observe the seals and birds, or as Pigafetta wrote, explaining why he sailed with Magellan, to experience "the great and terrible things of the Ocean Sea." In that sense, not much has changed between Pigafetta's time and Jarli's.

It began to snow.

Acknowledgments

I owe thanks to many people for their various and valuable advice and assistance. They are, in no special order: Sergio Robinson, R. Natalie P. Goodall, Ernesto Piana, Mario Guerra, Christian Cid Monroy, Maurice van de Maele, Oscar Pablo Zanola, Thomas Goodall, CADIC, Nick Lansing, Wade Leftwich, David Feit, Raymond Aker, Lucy Cross, the New York Yacht Club and William Watson, Sarah Shankman, Michael Carr, Vlad Murnikov, Roy Mullender, Ross MacPhee, John Thackray, Fred Hallett, Kathy Green, Nathan Boylan, Annabella Bushra, Julia Röhl, Hank Buchanan, John Rousmaniere, Erica Goode, Liz Maguire, Megan Hustad, Rick Pracher, Rich Lane, Major John, Skip Novak, Betsy Haggerty, Lydia Wills, Steven Schwartz, Melanie Schwartz, Nick McKinney, Norman Brouwer, Steve Jaffee, Mary Hogan, Robert Hogan, and especially Eugenia Leftwich. Then of course there are my shipmates aboard *Pelagic*, Dick Drinkrow, David Langhorne, Tim Millhiser, Jonathan Russo, Kate Ford, and Captain Hamish Laird.

Bibliography

Allen, Oliver E. *The Windjammers*. Alexandria, Va.: Time-Life Books, 1987.

Anderson, Romola. *The Sailing Ship*. New York: W. W. Norton, 1863.

Andrews, Kenneth R. *Drake's Voyages*. New York: Charles Scribner, 1967.

Attiwill, Ken. *Windjammer*. New York: Doubleday, Doran & Co., 1931.

Barker, James P. *The Log of a Limejuicer*. New York: Macmillan Co., 1936.

Bestic, Captain A. A. *Kicking Canvas*. London: Evans Brothers, Limited, 1957.

Boorstin, Daniel J. *The Discoverers*. New York: Random House, 1983.

Borrero, Luis Alberto and McEwan, Colin. "The Peopling of Patagonia," *Patagonia*. Princeton: Princeton University Press, 1977.

Braudel, Fernand. *A History of Civilizations*. New York: Penguin Books, 1993.

Bridges, Lucas E. *Uttermost Part of the Earth*. London: Hodder & Stoughton, 1951.

Bridges, Rev. Thomas. *Yamana-English Dictionary*. Buenos Aires: Zagier & Urruty, reprint 1987.

Brown, Dewer. *Alow and Aloft*. New York: Putnam, 1954.

Brown, Janet. *Voyaging*. Princeton: Princeton University Press, 1995.

Brown, Lloyd A. *The Story of Maps*. New York: Dover Publications, 1949.

Carr, Michael. *Weather Simplified*. Camden ME: International Marine, a Division of the McGraw-Hill Companies, 1999.

Chapelle, Howard I. *American Sailing Craft*. New York: Bonanza Books, 1976.

Clark, Gerry. *Tortorore Voyages*. New Zealand: Kerikeri, 1988.

Clements, Rex. *A Gypsy of the Horn*. London: Heath Cranton Ltd, 1924.

Colane, Francisco. *Cape Horn and Other Stories from the End of the World*. Pittsburgh: Latin American Literature Review Press, 1991.

Committee of the Patagonian Missionary Society. *A Brief Statement of the Rise and Progress of the Patagonian Mission*. Bristol: 1860.

Conrad, Joseph. *A Personal Record* and *The Mirror of the Sea*. London: Penguin Group, 1998.

———. *The Portable Conrad*. New York: Penguin, 1975.

Conway, Sir Martin. *Aconcagua & Tierra del Fuego*. London: Cassell & Company, 1922.

Corbett, Julian S. *Drake and the Tudor Navy*, Vol. 1. London: Longmans, Green & Co., 1912.

Corn, Charles. *The Scents of Eden*. New York: Kodansha Amer., Inc., 1999.

Course, Captain A.G. *The Wheel's Kick and the Wind's Song*. London: David & Charles, 1950.

Cummins, John. *Francis Drake*. New York: St. Martin's Press, 1995.

Cutler, Carl C. *Greyhounds of the Sea*. Annapolis: Naval Institute Press, 1960.

Dana, Richard Henry, Jr. *Two Years Before the Mast*. Harvard Classics Editions. New York: P. Collier & Son, 1909.

Darlington, Philip J. Jr. *The Biogeography of the Southern End of the World*. New York: McGraw-Hill, 1965.

Darwin, Charles. *Voyage of the Beagle*. London: Penguin Group, 1989.

_____. *Beagle Diary*. Keynes, R. D., ed. Cambridge: Cambridge University Press, 1988.

Deacon, George. *The Antarctic Circumpolar Ocean*. Cambridge: Cambridge University Press, 1985.

Diamond, Jared. *Guns, Germs, and Steel*. New York: W. W. Norton & Co., 1998.

Drake, Francis. *The World Encompassed*, Facsimile Editions. Cleveland: World Publishing Co., 1966.

Dunmore, John. *Pacific Explorers*. Annapolis: Naval Institute Press, 1985.

Fagan, Brian. *Floods, Famines, and Emperors*. New York: Basic Books, 1999.

FitzRoy, Robert. *A Narrative of the Voyage of H.M.S. Beagle*. Including diary and letters of Charles Darwin, notes from Midshipman Philip King, and Lt. Bartholomew Sulivan selected by David Stanbury. London: The Folio Society, 1977.

Faldmark, K.R. "Routes: Alternative Migration Corridors for Early Man in North America." *American Antiquity*, 44(1) 55–59, 1979.

Flemming, Fergus. *Barrow's Boys*. New York: Grove Press, 1998.

Goetzman, William H. *Exploration and Empire*. New York: Alfred A. Knopf, 1966.

_____. *New Lands, New Men*. New York: Viking, 1986.

Goodall, Rae Natalie Prosser. *Tierra del Fuego*. Buenos Aires: Ediciones Shanamaiim, 1970.

Gurney, Alan. *Below the Convergence*. New York: W.W. Norton, 2000.

_____. *The Race to the White Continent*. New York: W.W. Norton, 1997.

Hale, J.R. *Renaissance Exploration.* New York: W.W. Norton, 1968.

Hough, Richard. *The Blind Horn's Hate.* New York: W.W. Norton, 1971.

Hurst, Alex A. *The Medley of Mast and Sail.* Annapolis: Naval Institute Press, 1981.

Jones, William H.S. *The Cape Horn Breed.* New York: Criterion Books, 1956.

Kent, Rockwell. *Voyaging.* New York: Grosset & Dunlop, 1924.

Keynes, Richard Darwin. *Fossils, Finches and Fuegians.* Oxford: Oxford University Press, 2003.

King, H.G.R. *The Antarctic.* London: Blandford Press, 1969.

King, J.C., and Turner, J. *Antarctic Meteorology and Climatology.* Cambridge: Cambridge University Press, 1997.

Landes, David S. *The Wealth and Poverty of Nations.* New York: W.W. Norton, 1999.

Learmont, Captain James S. *Master in Sail.* London: Percival Marshall, 1950.

Lothrop, Samuel Kirkland. *The Indians of Tierra del Fuego.* Ushuaia: Zagier & Urruty, 1928.

Lubbock, Basil. *Round the Horn Before the Mast.* New York: E. P. Dutton & Co., 1902.

Marks, Richard Lee. *Three Men of the Beagle.* New York: Knopf, 1991.

McCulloch, Robert, Clapperton, Chalmers M., and Rabassa, Jorge. "The Glacial and Post-Glacial Environmental History of Fuego-Patagonia." *Patagonia.* Princeton: Princeton University Press, 1997.

Moorhead, Alan. *Darwin and the Beagle.* New York: Harper & Row, 1969.

Morison, Samuel Eliot. *Discovery of America: The Southern Voyages.* Boston: Houghton Mifflin, 1974.

National Imagery and Mapping Agency. *Sailing Directions, East and West Coast of South America,* 1997.

Newby, Eric. *The Last Grain Race.* New York: Penguin Group, 1984.

Parfit, Michael. *South Light.* New York: Macmillan Co., 1985.

Parry, J.H. *The Age of Reconnaissance.* New York: Mentor Book, 1963.

_____. *The Discovery of the Sea.* Berkeley: University of California Press, 1981.

Pena, Martin R., and Rumboll, Maurice. *Birds of Southern South America and Antarctica.* London: HarperCollins, 1998.

Pigafetta, Antonio. *Magellan's Voyage.* New York: Dover Publications, Inc., 1969.

Ralling, Christopher, ed. *The Voyage of Charles Darwin.* Autobiographical Writings. New York: Mayflower Books, 1979.

Randier, Jean. *Men and Ships Around Cape Horn.* New York: David McKay Company, Inc., 1966.

Riesenberg, Felix. *Cape Horn.* Woodbridge, Ct.: Ox Bow Press, 1995.

Roberts, Gail. *Atlas of Discovery,* with maps by Geographical Project. New York: Gallery Books, 1989.

Roche, T.W.E. *The Golden Hind.* New York: Praeger Publications, 1973.

Ross, James. *A Voyage of Discovery and Research in the Southern and Antarctic Regions during the Years 1839–1843.* London: David and Charles Reprints, 1969.

Roth, Hal. *Two Against Cape Horn.* New York: W.W. Norton, 1978.

Rousmaniere, John. *The Annapolis Book of Seamanship.* New York: Simon & Schuster, 1989.

Rydell, Raymond A. *Cape Horn to the Pacific.* Berkeley: University of California Press, 1952.

Sale, Kirkpatrick. *The Conquest of Paradise.* New York: Plume, 1990.

Schouten, Willem C. *The Relation of a Wonderfull Voiage by Wm Cornelison Schouten,* Facsimile Editions. Cleveland: World Publishing Co., 1966.

Shaw, David W. *Flying Cloud.* New York: William Morrow, 2000.

Silverberg, Robert. *The Longest Voyage.* Athens: Ohio University Press, 1972.

Slocum, Captain Joshua. *Sailing Alone Around the World.* Cape Cod: The Peninsula Press, 1995.

Snow, Parker. *A Two Years' Cruise off Tierra del Fuego, the Falkland Islands, Patagonia, and in the River Plate: A Narrative of Life in the Southern Seas.* London: Longman, Brown, Green, Longmans & Roberts, 1857.

Spiers, George. *The Wavertree: An Ocean Wanderer.* New York: South Street Seaport, 1969.

Stanton, William. *The Great United States Exploring Expedition.* Berkeley: University of California Press, 1975.

Tilman, H.W. *The Eight Sailing/Mountain-Exploration Books.* London: Diadem Books, 1987.

Tomkins, Warwick M. *To Fifty South.* New York: W.W. Norton & Co., 1938.

Tschiffely, A.F. *This Way Southward.* New York: W.W. Norton, 1940.

Turner, Frederick. *Beyond Geography.* New York: Viking, 1980.

Walter, Richard. *Anson's Voyage Round the World.* Boston: Charles E. Lauriat Co., 1928.

Van Dorn, William. *Oceanography and Seamanship.* New York: Dodd, Mead & Co., 1974.

Weddell, James. *A Voyage Towards the South Pole Performed in the Years 1822–24*. London: Longman, Hurst, Rees, Orme, Brown, and Green of Paternoster-Row, 1925.

Whipple, A.B.C. *The Challenge*. New York: Morrow, 1987.

Wilford, John Noble. *The Mapmakers*. New York: Vintage, 1981.

Williams, Francis Leigh. *Matthew Fontaine Maury*. New Brunswick, N.J.: Rutgers University Press, 1963.

Williams, Glyn. *The Prize of All the Oceans*. New York: Viking, 1999.

Wilmore, Ray C. *Square Rigger Round the Horn*. Camden: International Marine Publishing Co., 1972.

Withey, Lynne. *Voyages of Discovery*. Berkeley: University of California Press, 1989.

Vairo, Carlos Pedro. *The Yamana Canoe*. Ushuaia: Zagier & Urrity, 1995.

Villiers, Alan. *Cruise of the Conrad*. London: Hodder & Stoughton, Limited, 1937.

_____. *Falmouth For Orders*. New York: Charles Scribner's Sons, 1972.

_____. *The War With Cape Horn*. New York: Charles Scribner's Sons, 1971.

_____. *The Way of a Ship*. New York: Charles Scribner's Sons, 1970.

Index

About the Author

Dallas Murphy is the author of several novels, including *Lush Life* and *Apparent Wind*, and the plays *The Terrorists* and *The Explorers*. His column on piloting and boating safety appears in *Offshore* magazine. Murphy, who lives in New York City, races one-designs (J-24s) on Long Island Sound and sails offshore, preferably to wild places, whenever possible.